New Public Management

New Public Management: Current Trends and Future Prospects represents a critical evaluation of the nature and impact of new public management, reflecting the latest thinking in the field. The text offers a comprehensive analysis of the topic by leading authorities from around the world, from both theoretical and practical viewpoints. The authors examine the subject from six distinct approaches: in context, in action, in an international comparative context, in research, in evaluation and, finally, by looking at its future prospects. In order to provide the reader with the best possible mix of views, policy issues and management issues have been finely balanced.

This timely and constructive overview of new public management is an essential addition to the bookshelves of anybody teaching, studying or practising public management today. The book offers important lessons for public management across the world and provides an invaluable insight into the subject for those studying social policy, political science, public services management and public administration.

Kate McLaughlin is Lecturer in Public Management and Local Governance at the School of Public Policy, University of Birmingham. She is Co-Director of the Public Services MBA Programme and editor of the journal *Local Governance*. **Stephen P. Osborne** is Professor in Public Management and Director of the Research Degrees Programme at Aston Business School, Aston University. He is editor of the journal *Public Management Review* and series editor of Routledge Studies in the Management of Voluntary and Non-Profit Organizations. **Ewan Ferlie** is Professor of Public Services Management at Imperial College Management School, University of London. He is the co-author of many articles and several key texts on new public management, including *The New Public Management in Action* (Oxford University Press, 1996).

New Public Management

Current trends and
future prospects

Edited by Kate McLaughlin,
Stephen P. Osborne and
Ewan Ferlie

Routledge
Taylor & Francis Group

LONDON AND NEW YORK

First published 2002
by Routledge
2 Park Square, Milton Park, Abingdon, Oxon, OX14 4RN

Simultaneously published in the USA and Canada
by Routledge
270 Madison Avenue, New York, NY 10016

Reprinted 2003, 2005, 2006, 2008

Routledge is an imprint of the Taylor & Francis Group

Typeset in Baskerville and Gill Sans by
Prepress Projects Ltd, Perth, Scotland
Printed and bound in Great Britain by
MPG Books Ltd, Bodmin, Cornwall

British Library Cataloguing in Publication Data
A catalogue record for this book is available from the British Library

Library of Congress Cataloging in Publication Data
A catalogue record for this book is available from the Library of
Congress

ISBN 0–415–24362–9 (hbk)
ISBN 0–415–24363–7 (pbk)

ISBN 978–0–415–24362–9 (hbk)
ISBN 978–0–415–24363–6 (pbk)

In fond and loving memory of Tom McLaughlin

Contents

Contributors

Michael Barzelay is in the Interdisciplinary Institute of Management at the LSE, London, UK.

Sandford Borins is at the University of Toronto, Canada.

George Boyne is at Cardiff Business School, University of Wales, UK.

Jane Broadbent is at Royal Holloway College, London, UK.

Peter Carroll is at the University of Wollongong, Australia.

Anthony B.L. Cheung is in the Department of Public Administration at the City University of Hong Kong, Hong Kong SAR.

Charlotte Dargie is at the Judge Institute of Management, University of Cambridge, UK.

Sandra Dawson is at the Judge Institute of Management, University of Cambridge, UK.

Ewan Ferlie is at Imperial College Management School, London, UK.

Louise Fitzgerald is at De Montfort University, UK.

Norman Flynn is in the Public Services Management Unit at the LSE, London, UK.

Jenny Harrow is at South Bank University, UK.

Chris Huxham is at Strathclyde Business School, Strathclyde University, UK.

Kempe Ronald Hope Sr is at the University of Botswana, Botswana.

Richard Laughlin is at Kings College, London, UK.

Willy McCourt is in the Institute for Development Policy and Management at the University of Manchester, UK.

Kate McLaughlin is in the School of Public Policy at the University of Birmingham, UK.

Annabelle Mark is at Middlesex University, London, UK.

Steve Martin is at Cardiff Business School, University of Wales, UK.

Janet Newman is in the School of Public Policy at the University of Birmingham, UK.

Stephen P. Osborne is at Aston Business School, Aston University, UK.

Christopher Pollitt is in the Department of Public Administration at Erasmus University, Rotterdam, the Netherlands.

Isabella Proeller is at the University of St Gallen, Switzerland.

Kuno Schedler is at the University of St Gallen, Switzerland.

Peter Steane is at Macquarie University, Australia.

Marilyn Taylor is at the University of Brighton, UK.

Acknowledgements

The genesis of this book was in an ESRC (Economic and Social Research Council) seminar series which examined the development and critique of the New Public Management paradigm. Many of the chapters are developments of presentations at these seminars. Our thanks are expressed to the ESRC for its support. The chapter by Sandra Dawson and Charlotte Dargie is a development of a paper of the same name which appeared in *Public Management Review* (previously *Public Management*) (1, 4): 459–482. The chapter by Christopher Pollitt is a development of a paper entitled 'Is the emperor in his underwear?', which appeared in *Public Management Review* (previously *Public Management*) (2, 2): 181–200. The chapter by Stephen P. Osborne and Kate McLaughlin is an abridged revision of the introductory essay of *Critical Perspectives in Public Management* (Volume 1) to be published by Routledge in 2002.

Finally, our thanks go to Francesca Lumkin and all her colleagues at Routledge for their support of this project.

Current trends and future prospects of public management

A guide

Kate McLaughlin and Stephen P. Osborne

The UK has played a pivotal role in the development of the New Public Management (NPM) paradigm – and can arguably claim to have been its 'birthplace'. Indeed, the seminal paper which coined the term the NPM was the product of the UK experience (Hood 1991) – though the work in the US by Osborne and Gaebler (1992) was also important.

However, the impact of the NPM has spread far beyond this narrow focus and it has become one of the dominant paradigms for public management across the world, and in particular in North America, Australasia and the Pacific Rim (Flynn and Strehl 1995; Boston *et al.* 1996; Kettl 2000; Pollitt and Bouckaert 2000; McCourt and Minogue 2001; Osborne 2002). Both the World Bank and the OECD (Organization for Economic Co-operation and Development) are also now keen advocates of NPM reforms across the world (for example, OECD 1995).

Given the centrality, both of the NPM to the management of public services across the world and of the UK experience to its development, now is a good time to evaluate the nature and impact of the NPM in the UK and internationally. This is particularly so given current reforms across the world, such as the 'modernising government' agenda that the current Labour government is committed to in the UK and the programme of government reform embarked upon by the George Bush administration in the US. These developments raise the question of whether the NPM was a specific trend related to a time-specific period, such as the Conservative administration of 1979–97 in the UK, or whether it is likely to continue and/or be modified as a developing paradigm of public management.

This evaluation is the intention of this book. It is unique in that it brings together papers which review the *conceptual development* of the NPM paradigm, provide evidence of its *empirical reality*, place it in *international context* and give consideration of *research approaches* to its further analysis.

The first part of this book sets the context for the NPM debate as a whole and explores conceptual issues. Osborne and McLaughlin place the NPM in historical context, both in the UK and internationally. They argue that the NPM should not be seen as an approach linked to the marketization of public services alone. They argue that it is more fundamentally concerned with the shift from the unitary government provision and management of public services to the concepts of *the plural state* and the governance of public services, rather than their management. Barzelay then takes this discussion further by placing the NPM within theoretical developments in the fields of public administration and political science. Sandra Dawson and Charlotte Dargie provide a rather more empirical analysis of the spread and impact of the NPM in the UK, using evidence from the health service. Flynn addresses the important task of providing a typology of approaches under the umbrella of the NPM. He emphasizes the importance of national context for the development of the NPM variants across the world. Finally in Part I, Janet Newman takes the specific context of the *modernization agenda* of the current Labour government in the UK and the extent to which its discourse is congruent, or otherwise, with that of the NPM. This has import for other such modernization exercises across the world.

Part II explores some issues and debates about the NPM in more detail. Broadbent and Laughlin explore the hegemony of the language of *accounting logic* within the NPM and link this to the tenets of classical management. They question its sustainable applicability to the management of complex public services. Marilyn Taylor asks whether the NPM can be seen as ameliorating, or contributing to, social exclusion in the UK. She concludes that there is a need for the NPM to focus far more in the future on relationships, rather than on discrete units of service, if it is to address social exclusion in any fundamental manner. Steve Martin reviews the development of the Best Value regime in the UK and asks whether it reinforces the NPM or not. He argues that there are several paradoxes implicit in the Best Value approach which could test, and possibly pull apart, the NPM doctrine in the UK. Finally, Harrow considers the difficult balance among efficiency, equity and social justice within the NPM. She argues that these are not necessarily mutually exclusive concepts, but that their coexistence requires a more proactive approach from public managers to these issues.

Part III widens the discussion of the NPM to an international and comparative context, with important regional studies from Schedler and Proeller (mainland Europe), Borins (North America), Carroll and Steane (Australia), Hope (the African continent), McCourt (the developing world) and Cheung (East Asia). Concluding this section Christopher Pollitt provides a vital comparative evaluation of the claims and impact of the NPM.

Part IV considers the research tools which will aid the future analysis and evaluation of the NPM. Chris Huxham draws upon her extensive experience of action research to ask some key questions about its applicability to studies of the NPM. Ferlie and Mark and Boyne then consider the contributions of quantitative and qualitative research to such studies. The book concludes with a reflective chapter by Ewan Ferlie and Lorna Fitzgerald, which considers the sustainability of the NPM paradigm in the twenty-first century.

Taken together, these chapters constitute an essential reflection upon the nature of the NPM in contemporary public management and public administration. Its authors are neither advocates nor fundamentally opposed to the NPM paradigm. They eschew such normative positions. This book is intended to make a significant contribution to the ongoing debate about the contribution of the NPM to public management and to public services.

References

Boston, J., Martin, J., Pallot, J. and Walsh, P. (1996) *Public Management: the New Zealand Model* (Oxford University Press, Auckland).

Flynn, N. and Strehl, F. (eds) (1995) *Public Sector Management in Europe* (Prentice Hall, London).

Hood, C. (1991) 'A public management for all seasons?' *Public Administration* (69, 1) pp. 3–19.

Kettl, D. (2000) *The Global Public Management Revolution* (Brookings Institution Press, Washington, DC).

McCourt, W. and Minogue, M. (eds) (2001) *The Internationalization of Public Management: Reinventing the Third World State* (Edward Elgar, Cheltenham).

OECD (1995) *Governance in Transition* (PUMA/OECD, Paris).

Osborne, D. and Gaebler, T. (1992) *Reinventing Government* (Addison Wesley, Reading MA).

Osborne, S. (ed.) (2002) *Critical Perspectives in Public Management*, 5 vols (Routledge, London) (in press).

Pollitt, C. and Bouckaert, G. (2000) *Public Management Reform: a Comparative Analysis* (Oxford University Press, Oxford).

Part I

The New Public Management in context

Chapter 1

The New Public Management in context

Stephen P. Osborne and Kate McLaughlin

Introduction

Debate over the nature and import of the New Public Management (NPM) is as intense today as it has been over the last decade. This book is concerned with exploring this debate. This introduction will provide the context for the chapters which follow and frame some key questions to consider in this debate. The first section will situate the NPM within the historical development of public administration and management in the UK, and the second section will broaden this context to a global one. The concluding section will highlight some key questions to consider in evaluating the impact of the NPM.

Public management in the UK: a four-stage model

The nature of public services, and of research and theory about them, has changed dramatically over the last 100 years. Drawing upon the experience of the UK, it is possible to distinguish four distinctive stages of development, starting from the late nineteenth century onwards. Other nations will present with variations upon this model, but it is a useful classification, nonetheless.

The late nineteenth century, as Thatcher never tired of reminding us in the UK, was the period of *the minimal state*. This is the first stage of the development of public management. Government provision was seen, at best, as *a necessary evil*. The majority of public services were located in the charitable sector, or through private provision (Owen 1965). Indeed, in the US, such a model was elevated almost to the status of a social principle, as de Tocqueville (1971) noted at the time (see also Salamon 1987; Moulton and Anheier 2000). However, *the minimal state* or *the state as a necessary evil* is not the same thing as no state whatsoever. It was in these early days of public provision that the basic principles of public administration were laid out. Wilson (1887) famously distinguished between the constitutional structure of government and the administration of its roles.

The second stage of public management, commencing in the early twentieth century, is best characterized as that of *unequal partnership* between government and the charitable and private sectors. In part, this was a function of a larger ideological shift, from the traditional conservatism of the nineteenth century and towards social reformism and the Fabianism of the new century (Prochaska 1989). This shift contained three elements:

- First, a recasting of social and economic problems away from a focus on individual blame and towards a recognition of them as societal issues which concerned everyone (for example, the shift from the 'child savers' of the late nineteenth century, who saved individual children from maltreatment by their parents, towards child care legislation which established common standards for the care of all children).
- Second, the recognition that the state did have a legitimate role in providing at least some public services, such as sanitation.
- Third, that where the state did not provide public services then it needed to enter into a partnership with the charitable and private sectors for their provision – though this partnership was to be very much an unequal partnership, with the state as the senior partner.

This model of partnership in the provision of public services has sometimes been characterized as *the extending ladder* where the state provided a basic minimum of essential provision and the other two sectors extended beyond this (Kamerman and Kahn 1976). In doing so, the charitable sector in particular was held to bring some essential characteristics to public services – not least its flexibility and potential for innovation (Webb and Webb 1911).

The third stage is that of *the welfare state*, which in the UK extended from 1945 to the 1980s. Underpinning this model was the belief that charitable and private provision had failed because of the fragmentation and duplication of service provision, and because of their inefficient and ineffective management (Beveridge 1948). Consequently, the government was to meet all the needs of its citizens *'from the cradle to the grave'* (Beveridge 1942). These services would be managed by a professional cadre of public services in a professional and objective manner. In the UK, at least, this was certainly the high point of the hegemony of public administration upon the provision of public services.

The final stage, to date, is that of *the plural state*. From the late 1970s onwards, the Conservative Party in the UK began to propound a critique of the welfare state which articulated a number of emergent dissatisfactions with it. The welfare state had always focused upon the provision of a minimum standard of service to all citizens. This was very much a product of the rationing mentality of the post-Second World War era that it had evolved within. By the late twentieth century, however, the perceived needs of citizens had moved on, away from a concern with a basic level of service for all and towards services designed to meet individual needs. Moreover, service users increasingly demanded a greater say in the design and delivery of their public services, as well as a desire for greater choice. Finally, Thatcherism posited a critique of the 'professional cadres' who had long provided public services. Now it was these public officials who were inefficient and ineffective, and who were more concerned with their own needs than those of their service users, encapsulated by Thatcher in terms of the greedy and overbearing public sector trade unions which put the needs of their members above those of the local community (Mischra 1984).

The response of Thatcher to these perceived problems was the privatization and marketization of public services (Ascher 1987). In the economic sector, the role of the state was almost entirely eradicated (Farnham and Horton 1996). In the social and community sectors, the vision of the 'enabling state' was promoted, where the state, at the central and local levels, planned and (at least partly) financed public services but where provision was located within the 'independent sector' – comprising both the voluntary and community sectors and the for-profit sector (Rao 1991).

The focus of the 1979–97 Conservative government in the UK was very much upon market disciplines as the solution to the ills of the public sector, a position most forcefully articulated by the Adam Smith Institute. In this model, marketization was held to promote the efficient and effective provision of public services, while promoting responsiveness to individual need and user choice in service provision (Pirie 1988). Not all critics held to this version of the plural state, however. Increasingly, critiques have emerged stating that it was concerned more with economy and cost cutting than with effective service provision and that it assumed the superiority of the private sector and private sector management techniques above those of the public sector and public administration (Metcalfe 1989).

This debate became most focused in the 1990s as this approach became characterized as the NPM. This latter approach to public management was founded upon a trenchant critique of bureaucracy as the organizing principle within public administration (Dunleavy 1991), a concern with the ability of public administration to secure the economic, efficient and effective provision of public services (Hughes 1997), and a concern for the excesses of professional power within public services and the consequent disempowerment of service users (Falconer and Ross 1999).

Although there has been some debate over the precise nature of the NPM (Dunleavy and Hood 1994; Flynn: Chapter 4, this volume), the classic formulation of it (Hood 1991) holds that it comprised seven doctrines:

- a focus on *hands-on* and *entrepreneurial management*, as opposed to the traditional bureaucratic focus of the public administrator (Clarke and Newman 1993);
- explicit *standards* and *measures of performance* (Osborne *et al.* 1995);
- an emphasis on *output controls* (Boyne 1999);
- the importance of the *disaggregation* and *decentralization* of public services (Pollitt *et al.* 1998);
- a shift to the promotion of *competition* in the provision of public services (Walsh 1995);
- a stress on *private sector styles of management* and their superiority (Wilcox and Harrow 1992); and
- the promotion of *discipline* and *parsimony in resource allocation* (Metcalfe and Richards 1990).

To this formulation can reasonably be added an eighth doctrine – that of the separation of political decision-making from the direct management of public services (Stewart 1966).

However, it is argued here that this view both of public management and of the NPM is to pose too narrow a model of the NPM. To stay with our typology of the stages of public management in the UK, the NPM is very much part of the fourth stage, of the plural state. However, this did not end with the market-based model of Thatcher. From 1997 onwards, the 'New Labour' government has taken the development of the plural state a stage further. This has been away from a narrow focus on the marketization of public services and towards an emphasis upon *community governance* (Clarke and Stewart 1998). Here the public sector is no longer defined solely in relation to the presence, or otherwise, of the government as a planner or service provider. Rather the planning, management and provision of public services is seen as something to be negotiated between a number of actors, including government, the voluntary and community sectors and the private sector. In this model, the key task of government becomes the management of these complex networks of public service provision (Rhodes 1996; Kickert *et al.* 1997). Consequently, then, the debate about NPM has been broadened from the earlier narrow concern with marketization to one which focuses upon governance as the pre-eminent task of public management.

Public management in the international context

So far, the discussion of public management, public administration and the NPM has been focused solely upon the UK experience, as a microcosm of the international debate. It is important now to broaden this debate to the international level – as Part III of this book does. Here, the dichotomy between public administration and the NPM is even more sharply drawn, as are the battle lines. Around the world, public management has undergone tremendous changes over the past two decades. The twin traditions of public administration, incrementalism and administration, have been challenged by the more managerialist models of NPM.

At first these were discrete challenges in particular fields, such as 'management by objectives' within the personnel field and 'zero-based budgeting' within the financial field. Since the mid–late 1980s, however, these discrete challenges have been superseded by a more holistic model of managerialism which has pervaded all aspects of public organizations – and which has been identified earlier as the NPM. This term now enjoys international recognition to signify a pattern of reform of public management *per se*, as well as the associated growth of the plural state (Pollitt and Bouckaert 2000).

It is significant to note also that this holistic model of managerialism has itself been subject to refinement and incremental change in light of experience with its workability. In the US, for example, early NPM reforms were concerned with the replacement of public services by private ones (Savas 1987) and with creating an entrepreneurial and user-oriented culture within public organizations, much influenced by the *organizational excellence* approach of Peters and Waterman (1982). Latterly, the focus has shifted to *reinventing government* within the context of a plural state, as envisaged by Osborne and Gaebler (1992). Similarly, in mainland Europe, the focus has shifted from the *output control* of the Tilburg model (Schrijvers 1993) to the management of complex networks in *public governance* (Klijn and Teisman 2000). The NPM is thus not a static phenomenon but an evolving one.

Its proponents have argued that the NPM has brought benefits of cost efficiency and service effectiveness to public and non-profit management, and that it has helped to address fundamental weaknesses in the management of such organizations, and in the systems of accountability and control in public services (Lane 1999). It has not been welcomed uncritically, however. A great deal of subsequent writing on public management has been concerned either with the normative superiority, or otherwise, of the NPM as a model of public service management over 'old-style' public administration or with its status as a new paradigm of academic research and theory (for example, Lynn 1998; Gow and Dufour 2000; Dawson and Dargie: Chapter 3, this volume).

A range of critiques have suggested that, among other things, it has simply been a passing fad, it has undermined the accountability of public services to their communities and it has failed to deliver the promised efficiency and effectiveness of public services (Lynn 1998; Pollitt 2000). A debate has also raged both to the extent that it is a globally convergent or a more nationally specific (and Anglo-American) phenomenon (Kickert 1997) and to whether its apparent prevalence is due to its universal applicability or its adoption and promulgation by such international bodies as the World Bank and IMF as a universal panacea for both public service and civil society failures across the world (McCourt: Chapter 14, this volume).

Flynn (Chapter 4, this volume) has suggested that a wide range of internal and external drivers have to be taken into account in explaining the present ascendancy of the NPM globally. It has also been suggested that there are dangers associated with 'viewing the New Public Management as a coherent and unified set of ideas and practices' (Newman: Chapter 5, this volume) when research on the implementation of NPM reforms illustrates rather diversity and a 'complex body of ideas and practices' (Lowndes 1997). Moon and Welch (2000), among others, have attempted to develop a framework which can map and evaluate this diversity.

In summary, critics have questioned the extent to which there is a single model of the NPM which can be deployed as a tool for comparative analysis let alone global reform prescriptions. They also query the extent to which it has sufficient conceptual coherence to provide an alternative to public administration as either a theoretical construct for academic research or an approach to the management of public services.

Notwithstanding these debates, the NPM does still stand as, at worst, one of the two dominating paradigms of public management across the world at the turn of the new millennium. Whether the NPM is a direct competitor for public administration, as a new, convergent, paradigm of public management (Gow and Dufour 2000), or it is instead a development within the continuing, and nationally divergent, paradigm of public administration (Lynn 1998) is a debate which will continue, and to which this book contributes.

In reading this collection, readers may wish to focus on the following points when evaluating the impact of the NPM upon public management:

- The extent to which public management is a nationally specific or a genuinely globally convergent phenomenon.
- The way in which public management research articulates the methodological problems which are derived from its eclectic roots (not least in political science, policy studies and economics), applied focus and multiple levels of analysis.
- The extent to which the NPM does provide a coherent paradigm for academic research and enquiry and challenges the previous public administration paradigm.
- Consequently, whether the NPM and public administration are compatible or incompatible models of public management, and whether sustained criticism of the NPM implies a retreat back to the traditional model of public administration and the superiority of bureaucracy.
- Whether emerging developments around the world – such as *community governance* and *modernization* in the UK, *public governance* on mainland Europe and the *look east* model in the Pacific Asia region simply offer variants on the NPM or a challenge to its core values.
- Whether the unique nature of accountability within the public and third sectors renders inappropriate the generic management solutions advocated by many advocates of the NPM.

Acknowledgement

This chapter is an abridged and adapted version of S. Osborne and K. McLaughlin 'From public administration to public governance: public management in the twenty first century'. In S. Osborne (ed.) *Critical Perspectives in Public Management,* Vol. 1 (Routledge, London) (in press).

References

Ascher, K. (1987) *The Politics of Privatisation* (Macmillan, London).

Beveridge, W. (1942) *Social Insurance and Allied Services* (HMSO, London).

Beveridge, W. (1948) *Voluntary Action* (Allen and Unwin, London).

Boyne, G. (1999) Processes, performance and Best Value in local government. *Local Government Studies* (25,3) pp. 1–15.

Clarke, M. and Newman, J. (1993) The right to manage: a second managerial revolution? *Cultural Studies* (7,3) pp. 427–441.

Clarke, M. and Stewart, J. (1998) *Community Governance, Community Leadership and the New Labour Government* (YPS, York).

Dawson, S. and Dargie, C. (1999) New public management: an assessment and evaluation with special reference to UK health. *Public Management* (1,4) pp. 459–482.

Dunleavy, P. (1991) *Democracy Bureaucracy and Public Choice* (Harvester Wheatsheaf, New York).

Dunleavy, P. and Hood, C. (1994) From old public administration to new public management. *Public Money and Management*, July–September.

Falconer, P.K. and Ross, K. (1999) The citizen and public service provision: lessons from the UK experience. *International Review of Administrative Sciences* (65,5).

Farnham, D. and Horton, S. (1996) The political economy of public sector change. In D. Farnham and S. Horton (eds) *Managing the New Public Services* (Macmillan, London) pp. 3–24.

Gow, J. and Dufour, C. (2000) Is the new public management a paradigm? Does it matter? *International Review of Administrative Sciences* (66,4) pp. 573–598.

Hood, C. (1991) A new public management for all seasons? *Public Administration* (69,1) pp. 3–19.

Hughes, O. (1997) *Public Management and Administration* (Macmillan, Basingstoke).

Kamerman, S. and Kahn, A. (1976) *Social Services in the United States* (Temple University Press, Philadelphia).

Kickert, W. (1997) Public governance in the Netherlands: an alternative to Anglo-American managerialism. *Public Administration* (75) pp. 731–752.

Kickert, W., Klijn, H.-E. and Koppenjan, J. (eds) (1997) *Managing Complex Networks* (Sage, London).

Klijn, H.-E. and Teisman, G. (2000) Governing public–private partnerships: analysing and managing the processes and institutional characteristics of public–private partnerships. In S. Osborne (ed.) *Public–Private Partnerships. Theory and Practice in International Perspective* (Routledge, London) pp. 84–102.

Lane, J.-E. (1999) Contractualism in the public sector: some theoretical considerations. *Public Management* (1,2) pp. 179–194.

Lowndes, V. (1997) We are learning to accommodate mess: four propositions about managing change in local government. *Public Policy and Administration* (12,2).

Lynn, L. (1998) The New Public Management as an international phenomenon: a sceptical viewpoint. In L. Jones and K. Schedler (eds) *International Perspectives on the New Public Management* (JAI Press, Greenwich, CT).

Metcalfe, L. (1989) Accountable public management: UK concepts and experience. In A. Kakabadse, P. Brovetto and R. Holzen (eds) *Management Development in the Public Sector* (Avebury Press, Aldershot).

Metcalfe, L. and Richards, S. (1990) *Improving Public Service Management* (Sage, London).

Mischra, R. (1984) *The Welfare State in Crisis* (Wheatsheaf, Brighton).

Moon, M. and Welch, E. (2000) Managerial adaptation through the market in the public sector: theoretical framework and four models. *International Review of Public Administration* (5,2) pp. 129–142.

Moulton, L. and Anheier, H. (2000) Public–private partnerships in the United States: historical patterns and current trends. In S. Osborne (ed.) *Public–Private Partnerships. Theory and Practice in International Perspective* (Routledge, London) pp. 105–119.

Osborne, D. and Gaebler, D. (1992) *Reinventing Government* (Addison-Wesley, New York).

Osborne, S., Bovaird, T., Martin, J., Tricker, M. and Waterston, P. (1995) Performance management and accountability in complex public programmes. *Financial Accountability and Management* (11,1) pp. 1–18.

Owen, D. (1965) *English Philanthropy 1660–1960* (Belknapp Press, MA).

Peters, T. and Waterman, R. (1982) *In Search of Excellence* (Harper and Row, New York).

Pirie, M. (1988) *Privatization* (Wildwood House, Aldershot).

Pollitt, C. (2000) Is the emperor in his underwear? An analysis of the impacts of public management reform. *Public Management* (2,2) pp. 181–200.

Pollitt, C. and Bouckaert, G. (2000) *Public Management Reform: a Comparative Analysis* (Oxford University Press, Oxford).

Pollitt, C., Birchell, J. and Putnam, K. (1998) *Decentralising Public Service Management* (Macmillan, London).

Prochaska, P. (1989) *The Voluntary Impulse* (Faber, London).

Rao, N. (1991) *From Providing to Enabling* (Joseph Rowntree Foundation, York).

Rhodes, R. (1996) The new governance: governing without government. *Political Studies* (44,4) pp. 652–667.

Salamon, L. (1987) Of market failure, voluntary failure and third party government. Toward a theory of government – non-profit relations in the modern welfare state. *Journal of Voluntary Action Research* pp. 29–49.

Savas, E. (1987) *Alternatives for Delivering Public Services* (Westview Press, Boulder, CO).

Schrijvers, A. (1993) Management of a larger town. *Public Administration* pp. 595–603.

Stewart, J. (1996) A dogma of our times: separating policy making from implementation. *Public Money and Management*, July–September.

de Tocqueville, A. (1971) *Democracy in America* (Oxford University Press, London).

Walsh, K. (1995) *Public Services and Market Mechanisms: Competition, Contracting and the New Public Management* (Macmillan, London).

Webb, S. and Webb, B. (1911) *Prevention of Destitution* (Longman, London).

Willcox, L. and Harrow, J. (eds) (1992) *Rediscovering Public Services Management* (McGraw Hill, London).

Wilson, W. (1887) The study of administration. *Political Science Quarterly* pp. 481–506.

Chapter 2

Origins of the New Public Management

An international view from public administration/political science

Michael Barzelay

The New Public Management (NPM) began life as a conceptual device invented for purposes of structuring scholarly discussion of contemporary changes in the organization and management of executive government. The actual term was coined by political scientists working in the field of public administration in the UK and Australia (Hood 1991; Hood and Jackson 1991). These scholars conceived NPM as a point of view about organizational design in the public sector. This point of view was analysed as a serious argument and influential package of recycled doctrines about organization and management. In the decade after entering the literature, NPM acquired a wider range of meanings. For instance, some scholars have asserted that NPM is the application of new institutional economics to public management. Departing from the idea that NPM is a point of view about aspects of public management, many scholars have used this term in referring to a pattern of policy choices. This variation in usage means NPM is more a recognizable term than a fully established concept.

Scholars designing research projects or formulating arguments about NPM face choices about how to describe and analyse recent developments in public management. In deciding how to proceed, scholars are obliged to consider how NPM has been conceptualized since its inception. The reason for following this scholarly norm is to facilitate argumentation and knowledge development. Fulfilling this obligation is troublesome at the moment, since an adequate account of NPM's intellectual history is lacking. To mitigate this problem, the present chapter analyses NPM's early career within public administration/political science, from which the concept emerged onto the academic scene.

NPM: born as a Siamese twin

The most cited original reference on NPM is Hood (1991); however, an equally important work covering much of the same ground – and more – is Hood and Jackson's (hereafter H&J) *Administrative Argument* (1991). H&J conceived NPM as both an *administrative argument* and as an accepted *administrative philosophy*. These two concepts were fraternal rather than identical twins, as one inherited its personality from the theory of practical argumentation, while the other's genes came from empirically oriented political science (Barzelay 2000a). Pressing the biological metaphor further, the concepts of administrative argument and administrative philosophy were Siamese twins, incorporating the same concepts of *doctrines* and *organization design*. Both conceptions of NPM are apparent in writings on this subject by other scholars.

Figure 2.1 provides a simplified diagram of H&J's conceptual framework. In this map, the major concepts are represented as 'nodes', and relationships among these concepts are represented as 'links.' The concept of *administrative argument-ation* is introduced as the covering term for *administrative argument* and *administrative philosophy*. In what follows, I describe these two concepts in detail and discuss how NPM is an instance of both. In subsequent sections, I analyse other significant early works on NPM in relation to H&J.

NPM as an administrative argument

Administrative arguments are 'nested systems' (Simon 1969) of ideas concerned with organizational design. According to H&J, any administrative argument can be disaggregated into a set of subarguments. Whereas each administrative argument is typically concerned with a broad spectrum of organization design issues, each subargument is concerned with a single issue of organization design. This aspect of H&J's conception of administrative argument can be stated formally, as follows:

$$AA = \{aa_1, aa_2, aa_3, \ldots, aa_n\} \qquad (2.1)$$

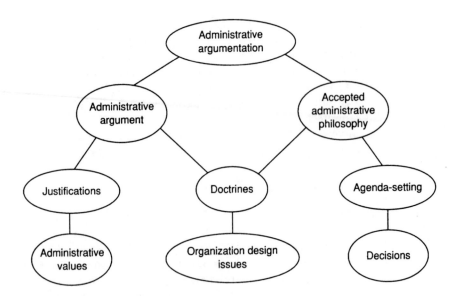

Figure 2.1 Administrative argumentation: a conceptual map

where *AA* refers to any given administrative argument and $\{aa_1, aa_2, aa_3, \dots, aa_n\}$ refers to *AA*'s subarguments. H&J went on to describe the structure of any given subargument, aa_i. The elements of this level of administrative argument were identified as administrative doctrines and justifications. A *doctrine* is a view of how a single organization design issue should be resolved, whereas a *justification* is a rationale for that view.

To a substantial degree, H&J's discussion tracks Stephen Toulmin's widely known approach outlined in *The Uses of Argument* (1958). As Toulmin's contribution to argumentation theory is well known within an intellectual community wider than public administration, it is useful to translate H&J's discussion into its terms.[1] A schematic representation of Toulmin's (1958) conception of an argument is as follows:

$$C = A \, (\bullet) \tag{2.2}$$

where *C* refers to an argument's claim and *A* $(\bullet)$ refers to the basis of the claim (Barzelay 2000a). The term A refers to the intellectual operation known as *argumentation*. A synonym for this operation is *practical inference* (Walton 1992). Under this operation, the reasonableness of *C* is inferred from various considerations.[2] These considerations are symbolized by the term $(\bullet)$. General considerations are called *warrants*, and the circumstances are called *grounds*. Thus,

$$C = A \, (W, G) \tag{2.2'}$$

where *W* refers to warrants and *G* refers to grounds.

H&J's discussion of administrative subarguments, aa_i, can be formalized in these same terms. Let us say that any given aa_i displays the structure, $C = A \, (\bullet)$ introduced as Equation 2.2. Without a doubt, the concept of administrative *doctrines* in H&J corresponds to *claims* within Toulmin's frame of reference. In translating H&J into Toulmin's framework, the term *C* in Equation 2.2 may be specified as d_i. The term *d* refers to *doctrine*, while *i* refers to the particular issue of organizational design with which a given *d* is concerned. Substituting d_i for *C* in Equation 2.2 yields the following representation of a unit of administrative argumentation, aa_i:

$$d_i = A \, (\bullet) \tag{2.3}$$

Translating H&J's concept of *justification* into Toulmin's frame of reference requires some interpretation, however. This concept may refer either to *considerations* $(\bullet)$, or to the relationship between $(\bullet)$ and their corresponding doctrine, d_i. Within Toulmin's framework, the relationship between *considerations* and *doctrines* is mediated by the intellectual operation of practical inference, symbolized in Equation 2.3 by A. In what follows, let us assume that *justification* in H&J refers to *considerations* $(\bullet)$, in Toulmin's frame of reference.

In analysing these *considerations*, H&J identified three affinity groups or clusters of *administrative values*. These clusters are sigma-type (σ) values, theta-type (θ) values and lambda-type (λ) values. The sigma cluster gives priority to the efficient performance of tasks, the theta cluster gives priority to honesty and fairness and the lambda cluster gives priority to robustness and adaptability of systems.[3] The concept of *administrative values* in H&J's analysis is closely related to *warrants* within Toulmin's framework. To express the idea that *doctrines* are backed by at least one cluster of *administrative values*, Equation 2.3's model of any given aa$_i$ can be restated as follows:

$$d_i = A\,(\sigma, \theta, \lambda) \tag{2.3$'$}$$

where σ, θ, λ represent the three clusters of administrative values identified by H&J.

We are finally in a position to understand what H&J meant by saying that NPM is an instance of an administrative argument. NPM is a point of view about organization design in government composed of subarguments, aa_1, aa_2, aa_3, ... , aa_n, whose doctrinal claims, d_1, d_2, d_3, ... , d_n, flow ultimately from administrative values. As an administrative argument, AA, NPM can be grasped by analysing this set of subarguments. H&J's analysis of these subarguments focused on their elements, specifically their *claims* and *warrants* in Toulmin's terms. In focusing on *claims*, H&J proposed a list of NPM *doctrines* (see Table 2.1). In focusing on *warrants*, NPM was described as a set of claims resting largely on sigma-type *administrative values*. In sum, NPM was described within the frame of reference of *administrative argument* in two complementary ways. Highlighting the left side of Equation 2.3$'$, NPM was portrayed as a set of doctrinal teachings about organization design in government. Highlighting the right side of Equation 2.3$'$, NPM was depicted as an administrative argument based on familiar, if debatable, administrative values.

Table 2.1 Doctrines of New Public Management

Use independent public bureaucracy
Use private/independent organization
Use differentiated ranks/one boss/delegation
Separate 'policy' and 'admin' specialism
Decide by discretion
Multi-source supply/between organizations
Multi-source supply/within organizations
Prefer admin/managerial skills
Contract out/for the field
Promote on merit/bosses' judgement
Prefer paid work/variable/pay by outcome
Limit tenure/by recall/hirer fires
Have a pluriform structure
Control through business methods
Control by output measures

Source: Hood and Jackson (1991: 33–4).

This model of administrative arguments allowed H&J to make three key points about NPM, directed mainly to colleagues in academic public administration in the UK and Australia, many of whom at the time dismissed ascendant approaches to public management in their countries. First, they characterized NPM as a *point of view* about organizational design in government. As a point of view, NPM was described neither as a theory of administration nor as an *ad hoc* collection of thoughts about public management. Second, and relatedly, H&J (and especially Hood 1991) argued that NPM was not utterly lacking in substance, since sigma-type values are plausible warrants for administrative doctrines. Third, H&J pointed out that a reasonable person might reject NPM on the grounds that theta-type values of honesty and fairness, for instance, should be given priority over the sigma-type values of efficient task performance.[4] In this way, the authors sought to enlarge the space for critical discussion (Walton 1992) of the NPM.

NPM as an administrative philosophy

As mentioned earlier, H&J characterized NPM not only as an administrative argument, but also as an accepted administrative philosophy concerning organization design in government that became accepted in the 1980s. Both concepts refer to a set of doctrinal arguments, although the concept of administrative philosophy suggests that these arguments share similar types of justifications.[5] According to H&J, administrative philosophies that enjoy acceptance at one time are typically rejected or forgotten at another. Analytically an accepted administrative philosophy (*AP*) at a given place p and time t can be written as a set of j doctrines:

$$AP_{p,t} = \{d_1 + \dots + d_j\} \tag{2.4}$$

The discussion of accepted administrative philosophies in H&J is part of a framework intended to explain the governmental agenda, and ultimately authoritative decisions, in a given place and time. In this sense, the concept of accepted administrative philosophy is a tool of political and historical analysis. H&J suggested that the governmental agenda is attributable to the climate of opinion about organization design, which they explained by drawing upon theories of persuasion codified in the literature on rhetoric. These theories were used to explain the acceptance of administrative doctrines in a given place and time. Using this framework H&J described the acceptance of NPM as an event which established a climate of opinion in favour of its various doctrines. The implication was that explanations of change in the organizational design of government should include a satisfying analysis of the process of doctrinal change – such as acceptance of NPM in the 1980s.

NPM as the odd couple

Although it did not use the term NPM, Aucoin (1990) is also considered a seminal work in the literature on this subject. This discussion was similar to H&J in contending that changes in accepted ideas help to account for administrative reform in the UK, Australia and New Zealand in the 1980s. However, Aucoin's analysis of this administrative philosophy differed from H&J's in significant ways. He argued that NPM is based on two fields of discourse or *paradigms*, known as public choice and managerialism. Public choice is a contemporary field of discourse about government with wider concerns than management, whereas managerialism is a field of discourse initially meant to apply to organizations in the private sector.[6]

Insofar as Aucoin was describing the role of ideas in administrative reform in the 1980s, his discussion of NPM corresponds to the right-hand side of Figure 2.1. However, Aucoin's analysis of these ideas was similar to H&J's discussion of NPM as an administrative argument. Under this interpretation, NPM refers to argumentation structured along the following lines:

$$T = A \ (PC, MAN) \tag{2.5}$$

where T refers to general or theoretical claims about how government should be organized and managed, PC refers to the *public choice paradigm*, and where MAN refers to *managerialism paradigm*.

Aucoin sought to describe the relationship between T on the left-hand side of Equation 2.5 and PC and MAN on the right-hand side. In doing so, Aucoin translated PC and MAN into a common frame of reference drawn from the professional–academic literature on organization structure. The terminology he used included the concepts of *centralization* and *decentralization*. In translating each discourse into the language of organizational structure, Aucoin inferred that the prevailing administrative philosophy incorporated arguments for centralization, originating in the public choice paradigm, along with arguments for decentralization, originating in managerialism. Aucoin then underscored his observation that the doctrinal claims constituting the prevailing administrative philosophy pointed in opposite directions, a situation he described as 'paradoxical.'[7]

Both Aucoin (1990) and Hood (1991) were widely seen as making the same broad points about contemporary changes in the organization and management of executive government in such countries as the UK, Australia and New Zealand: first, that a change in accepted administrative doctrines occurred during the 1980s; second, that these changes were integral to international public management trends; and, third, that the arguments behind these ideas should be analysed and assessed. However, as we have now seen, the details of their discussions differed. Aucoin's discussion was tied more closely to the fashionable discourses of public choice and managerialism, and he translated these ideas into a more conventional frame of reference about organization design. More substantively, Aucoin's view that the prevailing doctrines of administrative reform pointed in opposing directions was markedly different from H&J's assessment that NPM is a coherent, if skewed, administrative argument.[8]

NPM as new institutional economics

In 1991, Jonathan Boston, John Martin, June Pallot and Pat Walsh published *Restructuring the State: New Zealand's Bureaucratic Revolution*. The book included Boston's influential chapter on the 'theoretical underpinnings' of the New Zealand reforms (Boston 1991). This particular discussion was part of an argument intended to explain policy choices, related to public management, made by the New Zealand government in the 1980s. These choices were shaped by policy proposals offered by the Treasury. In accounting for the Treasury's proposals, Boston discussed the policy development process. The author's description of the process focused on argumentation about doctrines and policies. In describing this aspect of the policy development process, Boston played down organizational dynamics and highlighted the reasoning involved. The description of how the Treasury staff reasoned about public management illuminated three key components of the New Institutional Economics (NIE): public choice theory, transactions–cost economics and the economic theory of agency. These ideas – which were common currency for the Treasury's staff of trained economists – greatly influenced the department's proposals and ultimately the New Zealand government's policy choices.

Boston's discussion of that experience has greatly influenced scholarly and professional claims about NPM. Some take Boston to have said that NIE is the intellectual foundation for NPM (Aucoin 1995; Kettl 1997). What was put forward by a political scientist as an explanation for New Zealand's policy choices thereby became a much grander and more ambiguous claim. Grander, in the sense that NPM denoted an *international trend* (Aucoin 1990; Hood 1991), whereas Boston referred to recent history in one country. Ambiguous, in the sense that *intellectual foundations* suggests, without fully claiming, that NIE is the only serious way to argue about public management.

Boston's discussion relates to H&J's model of NPM as an administrative philosophy, situated on the right of Figure 2.1, because he sought to account for governmental policy decisions. The way he rendered this account, however, reflected the concept of administrative argument. Boston analysed the Treasury's doctrinal arguments in a similar manner as Aucoin analysed prevailing ideas about administrative reform in a wider range of cases. Specifically, he described how claims about public management were drawn from contemporary fields of discourse, rather than from a reservoir of catalogued doctrines and justifications, as in H&J. Boston outlined the reasoning behind doctrinal claims, such as 'purchasing and provision functions should be separated organizationally.' The considerations backing this claim were drawn from NIE, especially public choice theory and principal–agent theory. By way of illustration, this particular unit of argument can be modelled as follows:

$$d_s = A \ (NIE \ [T_{PC}, T_{PA}]) \tag{2.6}$$

where d_s refers to the doctrine of structuring government so that purchasing and providing functions are separated, NIE refers to New Institutional Economics, T_{PC} refers to public choice theory and T_{PA} refers to principal–agent theory.[9]

Boston also outlined the Treasury's reasoning about other issues of organizational design, including how relationships between ministers and top officials should be structured. The set of doctrinal claims about organizational design issues accepted by the Treasury can be referred to as this organization's theory, T, of public management. A general model of the Treasury's reasoning at the level of doctrine is, then, as follows:

$$T = A \; (NIE \; [T_{PC}, TCE, T_{PA}]) \tag{2.7}$$

where NIE refers to transactions cost economics, TCE, as well as to the other streams previously mentioned.

Boston also indicated how the Treasury moved from doctrinal claims to policy proposals. One of its proposals was to reorganize the machinery of government, so that chief executives would oversee either policy-making or operational functions, but not both. This reasoning involved a diagnosis that the economic efficiency of New Zealand's core public sector in the mid-1980s was limited by the formal organizational structure. Symbolically, this unit of argument was structured as follows:

$$D_{p,t} = A \; (S_{p,t}, T) \tag{2.8}$$

where $D_{p,t}$ refers to a diagnosis for New Zealand (p, for place) in the mid-1980s (t, for time), $S_{p,t}$ refers to a survey of New Zealand's administrative situation, and T refers to the Treasury's doctrine of public management. The Treasury's diagnosis became the basis of policy proposals involving the reorganization of government. Formally,

$$P_{p,t} = A \; (D_{p,t}) \tag{2.9}$$

Given the diagnosis, the implication was that reorganization was called for.

Thus, Boston described the multi-staged argumentation through which the Treasury arrived at policy proposals. He indicated how the Treasury staff's educational background in economics led them to draw practical inferences about plausible public management doctrines – such as 'separate purchasing from provision' – from the warrants embedded in NIE discourses. Boston described not only the Treasury's doctrinal argumentation, but also its *policy* argumentation. This phase of argumentation – what Herbert Simon (1945/1976: 38) called *administrative analysis* – took New Zealand's *administrative situation* into account in arriving at a *diagnosis*. The Treasury's diagnosis rested on the interaction between information about this situation and the doctrines of public management settled upon during an earlier round of argumentation, represented by Equation 2.7. The Treasury intended to eliminate the constraints identified in the course of its diagnostic argumentation. This department moved forward from its diagnosis to conclusions about what steps to take. Acting as a policy entrepreneur, the Treasury put forward specific proposals and supporting arguments to ministers. From this standpoint, what was significant about the Treasury's reasoning was not so much the presence of NIE on the right-hand side of Equation 2.7, but rather the multi-staged flow of reasoning moving from warrants embedded in this field of discourse through diagnostic argumentation (Equation 2.8) and on to argumentation about what steps to take in the circumstances (Equation 2.9). The interpretation that NIE constitutes the intellectual foundations of NPM, as can be seen, is due to shining the spotlight on the right-hand side of one unit of argument within a larger, situationally specific discussion.

NPM across the pond and down under

Written by two non-academics in the United States, *Reinventing Government* (Osborne and Gaebler 1992) became a best-seller in 1992. This work played a major role in the process by which NPM doctrines came to influence agenda-setting in the US Federal government during the first Clinton Administration (Kettl 1995). Its doctrines were expressed as slogans, such as 'steer, don't row.' Several of the slogans were meant to apply to broader questions of government than organization design as defined by H&J. Accordingly, this book broadened the subject of NPM to include fundamental changes in public service delivery, such as using tax-financed voucher schemes to fund education.

Research and argument based on a single experience

The year 1992 also saw publication in the US of *Breaking Through Bureaucracy: A New Vision for Managing in Government* (Barzelay 1992), which grew out of the Ford Foundation/Harvard University Program on Innovations in State and Local Government. The research site for this study was Minnesota state government in the period 1983–90. This work wove together two different types of discussion. One was a narrative account of organizational change in three staff agencies of the executive branch, primarily the Department of Administration and the Department of Employee Relations. The other discussion was the formulation of an administrative argument, mainly on the subject of the organizational strategy in staff agencies.

The first of these discussions corresponds to the right-hand side of Figure 2.1. Like H&J, this discussion stressed the mechanism of belief-formation (Hedström and Swedberg 1998) as an explanation for changes in the organization design of government. This similarity was evident in the author's detailed treatment of how the initiators of an 8-year-long 'organizational intervention' formulated their initial doctrinal views, as well as of how they sought to persuade others – including middle managers, executive colleagues and legislators – to accept changes in institutional rules and routines. Barzelay (1992) was, however, different from H&J in three main respects. One, the book was based on the study of a 'natural case', rather than on the analysis of an abstract or stylized case. In this sense it was more similar to Boston (1991). Two, Barzelay was not only concerned with agenda-setting, but also with the reworking of organizational routines and cultures in the implementation phase of the policy-making process (Kingdon 1984). In terms of Figure 2.1, Barzelay thus introduced an additional node for *implementation* or *organizational change*, situated in the lower right corner. The links between this new node and agenda-setting were described in terms of organizational interventions from positions of executive authority. Three, *Breaking Through Bureaucracy* explained change in Minnesota using narrative methods (Kiser 1986; Abbott 1992) linked to an implicit theory, whereas H&J applied a theoretically based framework to explain selected facts arising in their stylized case. Barzelay thus introduced the genre (Czarniawska 1999) of an extended narrative about a particular experience into the NPM literature.[10]

As indicated earlier, the second major discussion in Barzelay (1992) was an administrative argument. Barzelay's administrative argument was presented as a body of principles and supporting arguments about the organizational strategies of administrative functions and staff agencies. An illustrative principle was 'separate service from control.' This principle was much like a doctrine in H&J's sense: it framed and resolved an issue about organization design in government, and it was presented as a doctrinal teaching.[11] In *Breaking Through Bureaucracy*, the doctrines' justifications made scant reference to the professional–academic literature on management and government. Instead, the justificatory argumentation was mainly taken from the book's own narrative treatment of the Minnesota experience.[12] An attempt was made, as in H&J, to reveal the common essence of the proposed doctrinal arguments. Barzelay compared the justificatory arguments that were prevalent in Minnesota's staff agencies in the early 1990s with justificatory arguments that had been commonplace in the Minnesota state government before the 8-year-long executive intervention. On this basis, a comparison was developed of the *bureaucratic* and *post-bureaucratic paradigms*. The latter is one specification of NPM, conceived as an administrative argument.

Political analysis about Australia

The spate of works published in 1992 included Colin Campbell and John Halligan's study of executive leadership and public management policy-making in Australia during the eight years of Labor rule in Australia (1982–90). This work, *Political Leadership in an Age of Constraint* (1992), emerged from the political science wing of the public administration field. As such, its principal task was to describe and explain governmental decisions and their effects on both public bureaucracies and public policy. Decisions in this context included public management policies, especially in the areas of expenditure planning and financial management. Such decisions included use of a ministerial Expenditure Review Committee as part of the expenditure planning process, and the initiation of a Financial Management Improvement Program as part of financial management.

The significance of Campbell and Halligan's book derives from the fact it was an in-depth descriptive/explanatory study of public management policy change in Australia. The authors' case evidence related to changes in the two key dimensions of public management policy: institutional rules *and* organizational routines. Their method of explanation was to provide a narrative account. The major explanatory constructs implicitly employed by Campbell and Halligan came from literature on public policy-making (mainly to account for major decisions changing institutional rules), on one hand, and from literature on the conduct of organizational interventions from positions of executive authority (mainly to explain changes in routines), on the other.

Campbell and Halligan's book can usefully be contrasted with H&J in several respects. First, the authors' conceptual scheme was centred on the right side of Figure 2.1, as amended in the course of this chapter. In other words, their study was centrally concerned with the nodes of agenda-setting, decision-making and implementation as well as the links among them. Second, each of these nodes was analysed in detail as part of explaining the events making up the Australia case. Third, they gave accounts of 'opportunity emergence' (Kingdon 1984), or moments when the potential for policy or organizational change was significant. For instance, the budgetary effects of macro-economic policy reversals in the early 1980s were analysed in terms of how they helped to create an opportunity to change institutional rules and organizational routines in financial management. Fourth, and relatedly, Campbell and Halligan discussed how specific actors within the government capitalized on these opportunities. For instance, the authors explained how Malcolm Holmes, a career official in the Finance Department, collaborated with this central agency's top officials and minister in devising and operating the Financial Management Improvement Program. In sum, Campbell and Halligan provided a very different theory and method for studying NPM from H&J. A much broader conception of the policy-making process was applied. Policy decisions were seen to flow from much more than an accepted body of doctrinal beliefs.

NPM's awkward adolescence

In 1994, Hood published a book, *Explaining Economic Policy Reversals*, which included a chapter on NPM. Its principal task was to account for a dramatic shift in the style of organizing public services from Progressive Public Administration (PPA) to NPM. Hood's account of this shift was meant to be coherent, with explanations given for economic policy reversals presented in other chapters of the same volume. Each chapter critically analysed a fixed menu of explanations in the context of a single domain of economic policy. The chapter of interest here examined, with a critical eye, several contrasting explanations of the shift from the PPA style to that of NPM.

Hood (1994) was different from H&J in several significant respects. First, it focused on the right side of Figure 2.1. Indeed, the idea that NPM is an administrative argument was not mentioned. Second, NPM referred to a pattern of policy and practice described as a *style of organizing public services* and not to an administrative philosophy. The concept of style tended to blur the distinction between policy and practice, on the one hand, and administrative philosophy, on the other. Third, the 1994 book chapter introduced the concept of PPA – also conceived as a style of organizing public services – in order to *describe* a '*policy reversal*' (emphasis added). All told, Figure 2.1, based on Hood and Jackson (1991), is ill-equipped to describe the conceptual structure of Hood (1994).[13]

NPM scholarship comes of age

Peter Aucoin's *New Public Management: Canada in Comparative Perspective* appeared in 1995. This work contained a number of discussions, including an administrative argument. This argument was complex and included the formulation of a doctrinal argument on public management policy; an evaluation of public management policies in the UK, Australia, New Zealand and Canada; and an argument in favour of choosing and implementing selected policy alternatives in Canada. Aucoin's extended administrative argument thus encompassed both doctrinal and policy levels of argumentation. Aucoin's administrative argumentation is shown on the left side of Figure 2.1.

An ambitious argument about NPM

Aucoin's administrative argument was concerned with the preconditions of responsible and good government, defined as politically responsible and capable of formulating and implementing substantively valuable public policies. Aucoin's argument can be roughly divided in three: first, there is an argument in favour of having a career civil service. This argument was made by drawing lessons from history. Second, Aucoin argues that the question of how to structure and manage the relationship between the career civil service and ministers should be approached as if solving a principal–agent problem. The proposed solution was for ministers to write explicit contracts containing specific output goals. This argument was made by applying principal–agent theory to the circumstances of government. The third argument concerns the internal management of government agencies. Drawing on Brodtrick's (1991) concept of *well-performing organizations*, Aucoin argued in favour of an emphasis on people, participatory leadership, innovative work styles and strong client orientation. This argument was made by applying fashionable doctrines of management to public bureaucracies.

In developing and defending his doctrinal claims about public management, Aucoin brought three loosely coupled universes of discourses – normative public administration theory, new institutional economics and management thought – into close contact. The structure of Aucoin's doctrinal argumentation can be stated as:

$$T = A \, (PPG, NIE, MAN) \tag{2.10}$$

where T refers to doctrinal claims about public management, PPG refers to a public philosophy of governance, NIE refers to new institutional economics and MAN refers to management thought.

Aucoin's doctrinal argumentation is usefully compared with Boston's description of the Treasury's doctrinal argumentation in the 1980s. One evident difference is that Aucoin discusses lessons from history in translating ideals of good and responsible government into a granular, institutionally oriented PPG. The Treasury's PPG, by contrast, was tied in with NIE. A second difference is that Aucoin considered doctrinal arguments drawn from (a limited range of) management thought in addition to economic theory. A third difference is that Aucoin was more selective than the New Zealand Treasury in drawing on NIE. Specifically, Aucoin rejected public choice theory and worked out some of his doctrinal arguments on the basis of principal–agent theory.

Although the overall structure of Aucoin's administrative argument, labelled NPM, was clear, the details of his reasoning were often obscure. An illustrative example is Aucoin's argument that relations between politicians and the civil service should be structured through the use of explicit contracts. Aucoin told the reader that his argument was backed by principal–agent theory. Analysis of his argument reveals, however, that *explicit contracts* in Aucoin's framework is a radically different concept than *contracts* in principal–agent theory (Barzelay 2000a). In principal–agent theory, rational principals design contracts that provide efficient *incentives* to agents. In Aucoin's framework, however, the role of explicit contracts is to establish shared aspirations between ministers and civil servants, to specify a standard for evaluating the performance of government organizations and to reduce the perceived need to monitor the public service's actions in detail. The conceptual distance between NIE on the right side of Equation (2.10) and T on the left side is unbridgeable without additional argumentation, specifying the intellectual operation, A.[14]

Learning from experience

A book edited by Johan P. Olsen and B. Guy Peters, *Lessons from Experience: Experimental Learning in Administrative Reforms in Eight Democracies* was published in 1996. While the reach of this collective effort arguably exceeded its grasp, the chapter on the United Kingdom by Christopher Hood was both ambitious and highly successful. This chapter sought to explain such policy events in the UK as initiation of the Next Steps initiative. Unlike H&J, Hood (1996) examined the natural case of the UK during the 1980s rather than an abstract case styled on the UK, Australia and New Zealand. His method was to provide a narrative account of historically and analytically significant events within this natural case.

Hood's narrative account was the product of a particular sort of 'dialogue between ideas and evidence' (Ragin 1987). These ideas, developed in the first part of the chapter, were centred on the concept of 'political learning'. This concept referred to a type of process involving the social mechanism of belief-formation. The operation of this mechanism involved incumbent ministers drawing inferences about how to govern based on their own experience in office. The range of experience included their losing power in prior elections. In applying this theory to the UK case, Hood revealed the significance, for agenda-setting and decision-making in the Thatcher years, of events that occurred during the Conservative government of Edward Heath in the 1970s. Hood also adduced evidence showing that the Next Steps Initiative was linked to the Thatcher government's industrial privatization policy via the mechanism of political learning. In this way, Hood, in effect, claimed that Next Steps was a 'policy spillover effect' (Walker 1977) of privatization, at least in part. The larger significance of this chapter lay in showing the benefits of a particular style of case-oriented research, which involved narrative explanations of significant policy events, guided by an explicit theory in which the social mechanism of belief-formation is prominently featured.

A second study published in 1996 was Allen Schick's 'The Spirit of Reform', a study commissioned jointly by New Zealand's Treasury and State Services Commission. The first part of this study was a narrative report discussing how New Zealand's bureaucratic revolution took place. The majority of the chapters, however, presented an administrative argument. The subject of this argument was mainly New Zealand's public management policies, as implemented. These policies covered a wide array of areas, including expenditure planning and financial management, and civil service and labour relations. The author's main task was to evaluate the institutional rules and organizational routines in these areas, viewed as a system. Among many other points, Schick bestowed praise on a government-wide strategic planning process adopted in the 1990s as a corrective for limitations of public management policies implemented in the 1980s, and he also criticized New Zealand's rules and routines of expenditure planning and financial management for lacking a proper cost accounting system. Thus, unlike, Boston (1991), Schick was presenting his own administrative argument for purposes of elevating policy discussion about public management in New Zealand, rather than describing the Treasury's argument for purposes of explaining policy choices.[15]

In evaluating New Zealand's public management policies, Schick surveyed the administrative situation, which he implicitly considered in light of doctrinal arguments about public management policy. Accordingly, an element of his argumentation was as follows:

$$E_{p,t} = A \ (S_{p,t}, T) \tag{2.11}$$

where $E_{p,t}$ refers to the evaluation of public management policies in New Zealand (p) in the mid-1990s (t), $S_{p,t}$ refers to his survey of the administrative situation and T refers to his theory or doctrinal argument about public management policy.

An example of $E_{p,t}$ is Schick's criticism of the output orientation of New Zealand's budgeting practices. $S_{p,t}$ in this case refers to information about how decision-making in New Zealand's public service was influenced by structures and processes operating at the time. How Schick specified T is implicit in his report. The considerations mentioned include ideas about the purpose of government, the empirical regularity of a time delay between policy actions and outcomes, and doctrinal arguments about management. On this basis, Schick's doctrinal argumentation can be formalized as follows:

$$T = A \ (PPG, K_G, MAN \ [SM, MAN]) \tag{2.12}$$

where PPG refers to Schick's public philosophy of governance in which public management is part of solving complex social problems, K_G refers to knowledge of governmental processes such as policy implementation, and MAN refers to doctrinal arguments about management applicable to public as well as private organizations. Schick's ideas about management are associated with strategic management, SM, and management accounting and control, MAC. Thus, Schick's argument can be analysed as having a two-staged structure, including a doctrinal argument about public management policy and an evaluative argument about New Zealand's public management policies in the mid-1990s.

In another, if related, discussion, Schick criticized some aspects of prevalent doctrinal argumentation in New Zealand, which he called the *contractualist model*. One doctrine he criticized was that ministers are *purchasers* of outputs provided by government departments within their portfolios.[16] Schick argued that this doctrinal claim was unsound, unless qualified by the statement that ministers also possess an *ownership interest* in these organizations. Schick argued that influential policy-makers had failed to appreciate ministers' ownership interest in departments, which may have contributed to the evident lack of effort to develop proper cost accounting systems. In discussing the Treasury's argumentation, which Boston (1991) had described analytically, Schick took aim precisely at the contractualist model as a whole, which was assessed unfavourably against an alternative managerialist model.

Outlining Schick's argumentation makes it easier to see why he reached a different evaluation of NPM from Aucoin. Schick's argument was based on a different, and more detailed, survey, $S_{p,t}$, and a different theory or doctrinal argument about public management policy. In Schick's doctrinal argument, MAN was specified as SM and MAC rather than as four determinants of well-performing organizations; empirical knowledge of the governmental process (K_G) was introduced to take the lag structure of policy implementation into account; and PPG was specified as a *functional* view of good government, rather than an institutionalist view setting forth institutional requisites for good and responsible government. This comparative analysis of argumentation suggests that opportunities for both controversy and dialogue about NPM are plentiful.

Concluding remarks

The NPM has been approached in multiple ways by specialists in political science/public administration. H&J (1991) considered NPM as a point of view about organizational design in the public sector, which they specified as an *administrative argument* (described as a set of doctrines and an approach based on sigma-type administrative values) and as an agenda-setting climate of opinion, referred to as an accepted *administrative philosophy*. The notion that NPM is a point of view about organization design in the public sector has been advanced by other scholars. From his Canadian vantage point, Aucoin (1995) has pursued the idea that NPM is a doctrinal argument about organization design that draws on the NIE, codified views about how to achieve well-performing organizations, and conceptions of good and responsible government. Barzelay's (1992) post-bureaucratic paradigm, written in a US context, was a doctrinal argument about rules and routines for operating central administrative agencies. Schick's (1996) study applied his own plausible doctrines of public management policy to information about government-wide rules and routines for steering, motivating and controlling public organizations in New Zealand. The resulting evaluative judgments led Schick to challenge the Treasury's widely publicized doctrinal arguments, which he labelled the *contractualist model*. Instead, he proposed a mode of argumentation called the *managerialist model*. Thus, the political science/public administration field has taken forward the idea that NPM is an administrative argument. This idea has broadened into an ongoing professional and policy discussion, mainly about organization design in government.

The notion that NPM is an administrative philosophy has grown into a substantial empirical research effort intended to explain change in the organization design of government. This development was fully evident in Campbell and Halligan's (1992) study of initiatives pursued by the Australian Labor Party in the 1980s. Barzelay (1992) provided a narrative explanation of changes in organizational routines across Minnesota's staff agencies. An effort to explain organizational policy choices was manifest in Hood's (1994) discussion of the shift from Progressive Public Administration to NPM conceived as styles of organizing public services. A different, more stimulating effort was Hood's (1996) analytic narrative explaining specific policy choices in the UK case, including the Next Steps initiative.

In conclusion, the early formulation of NPM as an idea-dominated trend in organizational aspects of government has given rise to two types of scholarly discussions that befit a field of public policy research: argumentation over doctrinal and policy issues, on one hand, and explanatory analysis of policy choices and organizational change in complex governmental systems, on the other. These two types of discussions are increasingly recognizable as such in scholarly works. The stage is now set for more productive discussion of the doctrinal and policy issues and for the use of more sophisticated approaches to explaining policy choices and organizational change in government.

Notes

1 For a summary presentation and critique of Toulmin (1958), see Gaskins (1992). For a diagrammatic method of analysing arguments, also following Toulmin, see Dunn (1994).

2 Equation (2.2) is not a functional equation, since claims are not logically *derived* from warrants; claims are instead *drawn* from warrants via 'informal logic' (Walton 1992).

3 The conceptual relationship between administrative values and justifications appears styled on the Platonic metaphor that conceives ideals as the essence of ideas (Lakoff and Johnson 1999: 368).

4 This point is elaborated in Hood (1991).

5 In some parts of their text, H&J employ the term 'administrative philosophy' to mean an administrative argument that is backed by a relatively coherent set of justifications. I prefer to limit the meaning of 'administrative philosophy' to ideas making up the climate of opinion that influences what H&J refer to as the agenda of government (as represented by the right side of Figure 2.1). To avoid confusion, I would propose using the term 'coherent administrative argument' instead of 'administrative philosophy' when referring to an administrative argument backed up by a relatively coherent set of justifications. I thank Christian Leth Nielsen for pointing out the need to clarify this point.

6 Under Aucoin's analysis, neither field of discourse was centred on scholarly works. However, Aucoin mentioned an affinity between the public choice paradigm and Niskanen's (1971) thesis about budget-maximizing bureaucrats. Managerialism was identified in Peters and Waterman's (1982) best-seller, *In Search of Excellence*.

7 It is worth noting that Aucoin did not refer to the classic work on organization structure written by his compatriot Henry Mintzberg (1983). Accordingly, Aucoin's discussion of organization structure omitted such useful distinctions as horizontal vs. vertical decentralization and parallel vs. selective decentralization. Aucoin also avoided mention of such 'configurations' as the divisional structure. If he had done so, the coincidence of centralizing and decentralizing changes in organization structure might have seemed less paradoxical, since the divisional structure centralizes decisions about goals and resources and decentralizes decisions about how to achieve the goals.

8 Whereas H&J were mainly addressing public administrationists urging them to take NPM seriously, Aucoin, I think, was mainly addressing practitioners having difficulty making sense of their experience with administrative reform in the 1980s.

9 Bringing Aucoin (1990) back into our discussion might be helpful at this stage. First, the concept of 'public choice' in Aucoin, where it is a paradigm, is not the same as in Boston, where it is a field of academic discourse. Second, Aucoin does not analyse his identified paradigms in the same way as Boston analyses the Treasury's doctrinal arguments. Aucoin translates the diverse paradigms into a common language of organization structure; Boston describes NIE's three fields of discourse and suggests how the Treasury drew inferences about organization design in government from them. Third, Aucoin aimed to identify common elements of three experiences, whereas Boston was solely concerned with the New Zealand experience.

10 Some of the same experiences were discussed by Osborne and Gaebler (1992), but the genre they employed was the vignette (often referred to critically as 'anecdotes') rather than the extended narrative.

11 The main difference in this case is that the scope of the claim (Barzelay 2000a) was limited to administrative functions and staff agencies.

12 Barzelay (2000b), Chapter 5, discusses how references could – and arguably, should – have been made to professional–academic literatures on government and management.

13 A main point of similarity between H&J and Hood (1994) is that both analysed a stylized rather than a 'natural' case. A secondary point of similarity is that NPM mainly referred to organization design across all policy and programme areas in the public sector.

14 An attempt to bridge the gap is presented in Barzelay (2000a).

15 Boston and his collaborators did present their own administrative arguments within some chapters of their 1991 volume.
16 This doctrinal claim is a specification of the left-hand side term in Equation (2.11).

References

Abbott, Andrew (1992) 'What Do Cases Do? Some Notes on Activity in Sociological Analysis'. In *What is a Case? Exploring the Foundations of Social Inquiry*, eds Charles C. Ragin and Howard S. Becker. Cambridge: Cambridge University Press.

Aucoin, Peter (1990) 'Administrative Reform in Public Management: Paradigms, Principles, Paradoxes and Pendulums', *Governance*, 3: 115–137.

Aucoin, Peter (1995) *The New Public Management: Canada in Comparative Perspective*. Montreal: IRPP.

Barzelay, Michael (1992) *Breaking Through Bureaucracy: a New Vision for Managing in Government*. Berkeley: University of California Press.

Barzelay, Michael (2000a) 'How to Argue about the New Public Management', *International Public Management Journal*, 2: 183–216.

Barzelay, Michael (2000b) *The New Public Management: Improving Research and Policy Dialogue*. Berkeley: University of California Press.

Boston, Jonathan (1991) 'The Theoretical Underpinnings of Public Sector Restructuring in New Zealand'. In *Reshaping the State: New Zealand's Bureaucratic Revolution*, by Jonathan Boston, *et al.* Auckland, New Zealand: Oxford University Press.

Boston, Jonathan, John Martin, June Pallot, and Pat Walsh (1991) *Reshaping the State: New Zealand's Bureaucratic Revolution*. Auckland, New Zealand: Oxford University Press.

Brodtrick, Otto (1991) 'A Second Look at the Well-Performing Organization'. In *The Well-Performing Government Organization*, eds James C. McDavid and Brian Marson. Toronto: Institute of Public Administration of Canada.

Campbell, Colin, and John Halligan (1992) *Political Leadership in an Age of Constraint*. Pittsburgh, PA: University of Pittsburgh Press.

Czarniawska, Barbara (1999) *Writing Management: Organization Theory as a Literary Genre*. Oxford: Oxford University Press.

Dunn, William (1994) *Public Policy Analysis*, 2nd edn. Englewood Cliffs, NJ: Prentice-Hall.

Gaskins, Richard (1992) *Burdens of Proof and Modern Discourse*. New Haven, CT: Yale University Press.

Hedström, Peter, and Richard Swedberg (1998) 'Social Mechanisms: An Introductory Essay'. In *Social Mechanisms: An Analytical Approach to Social Theory*. Cambridge: Cambridge University Press.

Hood, Christopher (1991) 'A Public Management for All Seasons?' *Public Administration*, 69: 3–19.

Hood, Christopher (1994) *Explaining Economic Policy Reversals*. Buckingham: Open University Press.

Hood, Christopher (1996) 'United Kingdom: From Second Chance to Near-Miss Learning'. In *Lessons from Experience. Experimental Learning in Administrative Reforms in Eight Democracies*, eds Johan P. Olsen and B. Guy Peters. Oslo: Scandinavian University Press.

Hood, Christopher, and Michael Jackson (1991) *Administrative Argument*. Aldershot: Dartmouth.

Kettl, Donald F. (1997) 'The Global Revolution in Public Management: Driving Themes, Missing Links', *Journal of Policy Analysis and Management*, 16: 446–462.

Kingdon, John (1984) *Agendas, Alternatives, and Public Policies*. Boston, MA: Little Brown.

Kiser, Edgar (1986) 'The Revival of Narrative in Historical Sociology: What Rational Choice Theory Can Contribute', *Politics and Society*, 24: 249–271.

Lakoff, George, and Mark Johnson (1999) *Philosophy in the Flesh*. New York: Basic Books.

Niskanen, William (1971) *Bureaucracy and Representative Government*. Chicago: Aldine.

Olsen, Johan P., and B. Guy Peters, eds (1996) *Lessons from Experience. Experimental Learning in Administrative Reforms in Eight Democracies*. Oslo: Scandinavian University Press.

Osborne, David, and Ted Gaebler (1992) *Reinventing Government: How the Entrepreneurial Spirit is Transforming the Public Sector from Schoolhouse to Statehouse, City Hall to the Pentagon*. Reading, MA: Addison-Wesley.

Peters, Thomas, and Robert Waterman (1982) *In Search of Excellence*. New York: Warner Books.

Ragin, Charles (1987) *The Comparative Method*. Berkeley: University of California Press.

Schick, Allen (1996) *The Spirit of Reform: Managing the New Zealand State Sector in a Time of Change.* Wellington: State Services Commission and the Treasury.

Simon, Herbert A. (1945/1976) *Administrative Behavior*, 3rd edn. New York: Free Press.

Simon, Herbert A. (1969) 'The Architecture of Complexity'. In *Sciences of the Artificial*. Cambridge, MA: MIT Press.

Toulmin, Stephen (1958) *The Uses of Argument*. Cambridge: Cambridge University Press.

Walker, Jack (1977) 'Setting the Agenda in the US Senate', *British Journal of Political Science*, 7: 423–445.

Walton, Douglas (1992) *Plausible Argument in Everyday Conversation*. Albany, NY: SUNY Press.

Chapter 3

New Public Management

A discussion with special reference to UK health

Sandra Dawson and Charlotte Dargie

Introduction[1]

The term New Public Management (NPM) is used internationally in academic, governmental and organizational discussions, but it is rarely defined. In this chapter it is defined in three ways. First, as a movement; that is a set of beliefs or ideology from which actions followed in anticipation of particular consequences. It emerged in the 1980s among politicians and their advisers in countries where governments, at national, regional or local level, had strong traditions of directly organizing, providing and managing publicly funded, public services. Second, as a subject for study and commentary by academics. Third, as a set of practices that can be observed in recent public sector reform. This chapter assesses New Public Management after two decades which have seen its expansion and diversification in each of these three guises. Our aim is to reflect on the developments in NPM in terms of what it means for commentators on, and practitioners in, public services.

The health sector in the UK is the main vehicle for discussion. It has arguably undergone some of the most extensive NPM reform in the UK. This chapter explores the evidence for some of the assumed relationships between ideology, actions and consequences in NPM as they are found or not found in UK health services. It examines themes, issues and dilemmas that are revealed and asks what NPM means today, and whether its continuation and development relate in any way to its ability to deliver its promises in terms of cost containment, quality improvement and public support. Finally, we address the consequences of NPM for those working in public sector organizations.

NPM as a movement

The core of the ideology which can be discerned as influential in the development of public sector reform programmes in the 1980s and 1990s is that public sector provision was inefficient and often ineffective; that it led neither to cost containment nor to quality improvement; that it opened the way to undue influence for employees (whether they were protected by virtue of their membership of professional associations or of mass trade unions); and that, if unchecked, it would see unacceptable growth in tax bills, an increasingly dissatisfied electorate and declining standards of public service. On the basis of these beliefs a trio of goals, cost containment, public support and performance improvement, emerged as central drivers for reform. The resolution of tensions inherent in the espoused pursuit of diverse goals was little discussed.

With the problems so defined, politicians and their advisors turned to the private sector for advice on how to effect change. The ideology extended to a belief that the public and the private sectors did not have to be organized and managed in fundamentally different ways. Indeed that it would be better for the public services if they could be organized and managed as much like the private sector as possible. Similar movements were found in different corners of the globe, including New Zealand, Australia, the UK and Sweden, which, as McKevitt (1998) observes, are all countries that had a strong tradition of a large state-controlled public sector. Even in countries, such as the USA, where there was much less central provision of public goods, a movement spearheaded by Osborne and Gaebler (1992) advocated that government needed reinventing, in the sense of being made more entrepreneurial in order to secure more, better and for less. There was some imitation between countries, but much of the thinking emerged contemporaneously.

The focus of the NPM movement was on creating institutional and organizational contexts which as much as possible were to mirror what were seen as critical aspects of private sector modes of organizing and managing. This resulted in several questions: Could such critical aspects be identified? Could they be defined? Could they be transplanted; and if transplanted, with what effect?

With hindsight one of the most critical aspects was the construction of market mechanisms so that contracts rather than hierarchies became the dominant means of control. A key feature was the creation of 'quasi-markets' wherein new organizations were created and a split imposed between those (still public organizations) which were to commission or purchase public services and those (sometimes public and sometimes private organizations) which were to be contracted to provide the services. Other aspects followed, including the introduction of what were seen to be more 'business-like' management practices in human resource management (appraisal, performance management and seeking to recruit senior managers from the private sector) and a requirement to account, and to pay, for capital utilization (for example, NHS trusts and health authorities were required to make a return of 6 per cent per annum on capital employed).

The word quasi-market is important, because although market mechanisms were introduced in order to control the provision of services, in most cases the created market could only operate within two major constraints which are rarely, if at all, found in the private sector. The first constraint on the market was that the available funds in the market were determined on an annual basis by government decree. Thus even the most successful supplier could not increase the size of the total market. Any increase in funds flowing into one market segment was at the expense of funds flowing into other segments. Individual players could, however, at least technically, increase their market share at the expense of other players within an overall fixed budget. The second constraint on the market was that the activities in which the created organizations could engage were carefully circumscribed by statute. For example, although NHS trusts were created as providers of health care, they could not sell their services to private individuals. Similarly, under local management of schools (LMS) regulations, schools could not decide to diversify into, for example, mainstream educational publishing and seek to develop other lucrative businesses, nor could an entrepreneurial predator come along and bid to buy an NHS trust or LMS school.

Coincidentally, with trying to create a market between organizations, strong moves were taken to make the final customer of services, the 'ordinary citizen', aware of, and energized by, their rights to high-quality service. In the UK we had the spawning of various charters, for patients, for citizens, for rail passengers (Cabinet Office 1991). Although often not directly paying fees for service, citizens are paying for services through taxation, and they are the consumers. Citizens' rights were emphasized to counterbalance the providers who had traditionally been the sole arbiters of what were good and acceptable standards of service provision.

Within these various strands of belief and action represented in the NPM, we can discern some assumed relationships among ideology, actions and consequences.

First, traditionally organized and managed public services do not effectively control costs, so let us have as large an element of competition between providers as is feasible, hence the quasi-markets. Providers that are more expensive, are not eliminating waste, are not controlling costs, will secure fewer contracts than those which are. In this way the efficient, cost-controlling organizations will flourish, and their inefficient, wasteful counterparts will fail.

Second, traditionally organized and managed public services do not effectively improve quality, so let us have as large an element of competition between providers as is feasible, hence the quasi-markets. Those providers that are more effective in improving quality, better at innovating to secure better practices, will secure more contracts than those that are not.

Third, traditionally organized and managed public services do not effectively meet the standards of service expected by ordinary citizens, so let us give individuals a charter of rights to standards of service which they can legitimately expect. Those organizations that become known as being better at meeting their client's needs will flourish at the expense of those that do not. A set of public service organizations that meets citizen expectations will secure public support for the organizations and (helpfully for the politicians) for the governments that create them.

Fourth, traditionally organized and managed public services have given too much power and influence to special interest groups representing nationally organized workforces, on whom service provision depends; so let us try to reduce the power of public sector trade unions, and the professional associations of doctors, teachers, etc. The threat of decreasing rewards coupled with legislative restrictions on industrial action, the appeal to ethical codes and even the threat of large-scale privatization will secure changes in this aspect.

Thus NPM ideology (and legislation) begot new public organizations with their own (more or less independent) boards who were enjoined to employ new public managers, who were exhorted to be like their private sector counterparts.

Reflecting on the NPM movement in the UK in 2001, we can see that there has been no counter-revolution to the institutionalization of NPM in the first term of office for government of Blair's Labour Party. There is an acceptance of 'good practice' as defined by the government, along with previously contentious policies, such as private funding of public institutions and services, an entrepreneurial spirit in the public sector, performance measures across public services and strong central intervention for 'failing' institutions. There has been no large-scale opposition to the idea that improving the management of public services, as NPM seeks to, is the highest priority of government. The government's management of the health service,[2] schools[3] and even the privatized railways has been the most heavily scrutinized in this parliament. It is interesting that attention has been focused during the foot and mouth crisis on the government's management of the crisis rather than speculation about its cause and long-term impact.

In Blair's first term of office the four assumptions provide dominant themes in new and extended practices. First, competition between providers is focused around competition for centrally allocated funds. In the area of health the government is making increasing use of targeting money towards central initiatives, allocated on a competitive basis across providing organizations (Department of Health 2000a). Second, improvements in the quality of public services is to be achieved by competition between providers in the form of league tables and the publication of comparative performance data (Department of Health 1999). Third, the government's focus on users and citizens has been to create more organizations and to include user or citizen representatives in decision-making roles. The NHS Plan (Department of Health 2000b) established new local patient representatives to draw attention to issues such as dirty hospital wards, and there are to be patient representatives on many of the national decision-making bodies. The government has downplayed the use of charters themselves, promoting access to patients and users of public services through the Internet (NHS Direct: http://www.nhsdirect.nhs.uk/). Finally, the concern with curbing the power of professional groups and trade unions has continued, with attacks on self-regulation, the introduction of performance assessment and increased external inspection and audit of large professions such as the medical profession[4] and teachers.[5]

Academic commentary on New Public Management

Turning from the world of policy-makers and practitioners to the world of scholars and commentators on public service provision, we should immediately note that NPM as a movement was not in the main the outcome of prior theorizing. Academic communities which have studied public services neither predicted nor encouraged the shape of the reforms.[6] In contrast, the UK governments in the 1980s, led by Margaret Thatcher, were arguably influenced by economic perspectives on public services such as those of Niskanen (1971), and others, and through the influence of think tanks such as the Institute for Economic Affairs. However, once what became called NPM attracted attention, it quickly became the subject of much discussion and analysis.

Christopher Hood's 1991 article 'A public management for all seasons?' remains the most widely cited exposition of the concept of NPM. Hood examined the origins, rise and acceptance of NPM as well as its critics. He describes it as a doctrine, or at least as a label for a set of administrative doctrines which he and others identified as 'new'. Academic discourse of NPM was by the early 1990s distinct from earlier discussion in public administration with its focus on institutions, politics and value systems. In terms of theory, in addition to what Rhodes defines as 'causal statements' about political institutions, traditional public administration involved the analysis of political and administrative values (Gray and Jenkins 1995; Rhodes 1995). In contrast, NPM referred to private sector management practices, including performance incentives, and to markets. It drew on two competing conceptual frameworks. One, akin to managerialism, or 'neo-Taylorism' (Pollitt 1990), supported the introduction of private sector practices, which included attempts to manage professionals, introduce performance measures and incentive reward systems. The other, with its emphasis on markets, derived from variants of public choice, rational choice and 'new institutional economics' (Downs 1967; Niskanen 1971; Alchian and Demsetz 1972; Williamson 1975; Arrow 1984), and led to an emphasis on decentralization and competition that is at odds with the centralizing tendencies of the other.

A somewhat crude representation of the developments in NPM as an academic discussion is a brief analysis of the Bath Information Data Systems (BIDS) bibliographical database over the period in question. The words New Public Management did not appear in titles, keywords or journal abstracts throughout the 1980s. They were first noted in 1993. The figures show a steady increase in NPM as key words in social science: 1993 – 2; 1994 – 5; 1995 – 12; 1996 – 16; 1997 – 22; 1998 – 30; 1999 – 21; 2000 – 26.[7]

As practice developed and, coincidentally, discussion continued, so commentators began to note that what had looked like a unified reform movement was in fact revealed to be highly differentiated phenomena, in which there were national and sectoral differences. Furthermore, the reforms themselves were the subject of disagreement about their efficacy as commentators began to point out circumstances in which the promised consequences of NPM were not being achieved. The points on diversification are discussed first.

In the early 1990s there was an emerging consensus about the meaning of NPM as defined by Hood and others (such as Aucoin 1990; Pollitt 1990). Subsequently more diversity was revealed. For example, Dunleavy and Hood (1994) present four alternative NPM 'models': 'gridlock'; 'public bureaucracy state'; 'headless chicken'; and 'minimal purchasing state'. They are derived from a two-by-two matrix, with the density of rules in the system as one axis, and the degree of distinction between public and private sectors in personnel, structures and business methods as the second axis. Dunleavy and Hood suggest that there are not one but several movements within NPM which will drive the future.

Ferlie *et al.* (1996) also describe four NPM models in terms of 'The Efficiency Drive'; 'Downsizing and Decentralization'; 'In Search of Excellence'; and 'Public Service Orientation'. Their models are discrete, and are an attempt to interpret different types of NPM rather than predict general trends. Their definition of NPM is broad, including as it does the 'public service orientation' model, which, in promoting a special form of management for the distinctive public sector environment, is at odds with the early concepts of NPM that embraced assumed generic private sector management practices.

Rhodes (1997) relates NPM to a broader context, interpreting the movement as part of a shift from government to governance in the UK administrative system. Rhodes's interpretation makes sense of NPM within the context of the study of public administration and the machinery of government. He also considers the consequences of change, with the development of networks in government and 'hollowing out the state' explaining the shift to governance. He suggests there has been fundamental reform in British government within which NPM played a part. He describes a state that has lost functions through privatization, globalization, European Union institutions and alternative systems of delivering public services. In such a context Rhodes surmises that new operating mechanisms need to be found, and his attention is drawn to networks. Managing in these new, not unproblematic systems involves facilitating, accommodating and bargaining, as well as planning, regulation and competition. What Rhodes describes as the 'governance narrative' became a key theme under the ESRC's (Economic and Social research Council) Whitehall programme into British central government, under Rhodes's directorship (2000).

If we look outside the UK, we find alternative thinking on NPM, reflecting different political, cultural and organizational contexts. So, for example, NPM might be characterized as reinventing government or entrepreneurship in the United States; as citizenship, decentralization and deregulation in a European, predominantly Nordic model; as contracting in New Zealand; and as cost and control measures in the UK. More models may be found for the context of the developing world (Polidano 1998). There is scope for comparative analysis of why different models have been emphasized in different contexts, what accounts for the ways in which NPM has manifested itself internationally and its consequences in terms of outcomes, for example in terms of cost, effectiveness and public support (see also the previous chapter in this book).

Such an analysis is beyond the scope this chapter, although a recent symposium on the subject of NPM in *Public Administration Review* allows parallels to be drawn between UK and US discussion of NPM. First, there is considerable consideration given to the consequences of reforms for the role of public managers. Behn (1998) advocates the vital part public managers can play in overcoming the organizational, analytical, executive, legislative, political and judicial failures in the American system of governance, if they are able to exercise leadership. Terry (1998) critically appraises the role of public entrepreneurs in neo-managerialism and cautions that public entrepreneurs in neo-managerialist mode may pose a threat to democratic governance.

Second, discussion explores the link between political context and institutional arrangements. Kaboolian (1998) states 'these authors agree that the role of public managers and systems of public administration are endogenous to specific political systems'. This represents a shift from advocating the transplantation of ideas across different contexts, namely from the private to the public sector, to a reassertion of the approach of public administration scholars that, however desirable are efficient mechanisms for improving performance, public organizations need to be 'grounded in theories, assumptions, and understandings of reality that advance knowledge of, and give direction toward, attaining such [an inclusive, democratic] polity' (Kelly 1998).

Third, we are reminded of the differences in the appropriate unit of analysis for discussion, between the public manager, on the one hand, and politics and institutional arrangements on the other (Kaboolian 1998). In terms of contemporary UK literature, Ferlie *et al.* (1996) adopt the former and focus on the person and the role, and both Rhodes (1997) and Dunleavy and Hood (1994) adopt the latter and focus on the political context. Finally, there is recognition of different academic communities being involved in discussions. The US symposium had an explicit remit to bring together thinking from what it described as its 'public policy' and 'traditional public administration' communities (Terry 1998).

One important emergent issue in academic discussion about the NPM is that of public service values and ethics. Some academic commentators have argued that the traditional public service values, like probity, impartiality, fairness and equality, on which public administration was based, have been eroded. In the UK, the establishment of The Committee on Standards in Public Life in 1994[8] is an example of a government intervention made to deal with widespread public concern about the erosion of public service values. Similarly, the publication of codes of governance for publicly funded organizations was indicative of this concern. Actually measuring a decline in values would be extremely difficult, although surveys of public servants can ask questions about their perception of change. Other discussion has focused on particular cases of financial impropriety or allegations of the 'politicization' of public servants.

Discussion on NPM has grown to reflect the consequences of more explicit measures of control on processes that have been established as part of the shift from administration to management. Thus, commentators now discuss the increased levels of audit and regulation in central government (Power 1997; Hood *et al.* 1999); the increased activity of judicial review (Woodhouse 1995, 1998); the various new regulatory bodies that have been established such as the utility regulators; and the changing role of established bodies in the UK such as the Audit Commission and the National Audit Office.

In retrospect an interesting comparison can be discerned. In the 1980s, when support for public sector reform was gathering momentum among politicians and their public service advisors, gurus in private sector management were extolling the virtues of creating and sustaining a strong core of values to bind the best of employees to their employers in order to achieve improvements in performance that could not be achieved simply through financial incentives and contract conditions (Peters 1987; Kanter 1989). They maintained that management could achieve more and better results if there was a shared sense of mission built around common values and mutual trust. At the same time there were rumblings in the public sector that the move to NPM was eroding the values base which had hitherto bound public servants together in pursuit of values of equality, access, and so on. The public too began to question the values of public service. The emphasis on cost containment eroded public support as suspicion fuelled by media and special interest groups suggested that cost was the overriding criterion.

To summarize general shifts in the discussion of NPM over the last decade or so, we can note that whereas NPM was originally conceptually defined in terms of managerialism and rational choice subsequent debates included discussions of ethics, accountability, democracy, regulation and the intrinsic nature of the public sector. This shift in emphasis reasserted the relevance of what may be defined as traditional 'public' sector concepts and implicitly, if not explicitly, of public sector values. These developments in NPM would be interpreted as a documentation of its development and expansion into a more distinctly 'public' concept in the late 1990s. Academics who traditionally had the public sphere to themselves found it invaded by concepts of management. One can construe this as having posed a crude choice, either critique and reject the concepts of (new public) management for some alternative or adopt it as your own, seeking to mould, shape and adapt its understanding to the public sector context. Conceptual discussions of NPM in the late 1990s suggest that many commentators have taken the latter choice, not least, one may surmise, because to appear to stand against ways to improve efficiency and so on would be to assume the role of a Luddite and lose the ear of those whom they may be trying to influence.

It is in this context that we can interpret changes in the discipline of public administration which had been the traditional 'home' in social science for discussions on government institutions and processes. Gray and Jenkins (1995: 77–78) highlight the shift in thinking in public administration by contrasting standard texts from the 1970s, which focused on the administrative process, with the public management focus in the 1990s. They state: 'this simple exercise indicates how public management has, to a considerable extent, redefined the focus, language and theoretical basis of study of the public sector, drawing on literature and ideas often external to traditional public administration'. Gray and Jenkins (1995: 78–79) illustrate that public administration was expanding its horizons in the late 1960s and early 1970s with the inclusion of political scientists, organization theorists and other management specialists. There was more emphasis on policy analysis, and a less exclusive focus on institutions. They also characterize the period as one of confidence in administration, in terms of both academic discussion and in practice. In contrast, they see the mid-1970s as a period when confidence in administrative practice faltered in the UK (with economic decline and political change). It was in this context that there was a search for innovation, from which derived a new focus on management and the control of resources. This was associated with a lot of experimentation and change in practices in the 1980s.

However, it was not until the 1990s that we saw a rapid development of public management and NPM. It should not be forgotten that developments in practice drove change, and that change occurred in different states at the same time. From the perspective of an academic discussion, NPM was important in representing a shift in values that were the basis of traditional public administration. NPM thinking included ideas about the state, as well as about management. In addition to changing practice in financial management, agencies, contracting, performance measures and the introduction of markets and competition into the public sector, values changed with respect to two relevant themes: the role of professionals, and modes of accountability.

Gray and Jenkins (1995) point out that professionals lost influence or position in NPM practice because of changes in language, and because of the class of managers in public services that was superimposed on traditional structures. In terms of accountability, the terms responsibility and performance are defined individually in NPM, rather than notions of 'public' interest and accountability, a theme to which we will return.

Academic commentary on NPM has most recently focused on the international and comparative dimension; the observation of either converging or diverging trends in practice and theoretical developments that take account of the international or global picture of what is NPM (see Hood 1995; Ridley 1996; Kickert 1997; Lynn 1998). This chapter was originally presented at the Third International Research Symposium on Public Management. The theme of the Fourth Symposium was 'Public Management: a Globally Convergent or a Nationally Divergent Phenomenon?' Among other contributions to this debate about whether or not international phenomena make possible or refute the idea of a global 'NPM', a paper by Lynn (2000) explored the issue of globalization and administrative reform reflecting on the still varied disciplinary perspectives that contribute to this subject matter. Lynn argued for more data and more theory in order to explore the questions of convergence and divergence as well as further interdisciplinary work in formulating models of comparative institutional change.

Most recent commentary in the UK has focused on the introduction of the Blair government's philosophy, the 'third way', which after initial conceptual discussion has focused on the pragmatic 'what counts is what works'. A recent symposium in the journal *Public Administration* on New Labour and the modernization of public management focused on three themes: markets, bureaucracy and networks; a return to planning; and how to evaluate 'what works' (see Boyne 2001; Boyne *et al.* 2001; Jackson 2001; Kirkpatrick *et al.* 2001; Lane 2001; Newman 2001). It is often the case that it is only through retrospective analysis of governments that pragmatic politics is seen as part of a coherent reform strategy. However, in building on much of the past in its approach to public services, the Blair government is developing within a discourse which is familiar as NPM rather than a radical departure from it.

NPM in practice: the case of UK health

Focusing on the UK health sector as an example of developments in NPM means that this chapter can only present a partial picture; that is, of public management in a sphere wherein professionally trained providers occupy central positions, and where there is strong consensus that health is a vital public good. Other areas of public service are not professionally dominated, nor is there consensus on their place as a public good. That said, the UK health sector has been subject to some of the most wide-ranging and fundamental reforms involving organization and management in the public services throughout the 1980s and 1990s.

Our discussion in health takes place at the macro-level. We are interested in how the health sector can be used to illustrate some of the issues raised in our foregoing analysis of the development of NPM in the UK in the 1980s and 1990s. What does health reveal about how the NPM ideology is manifested in terms of action that takes place, and the nature of the consequences of that action, intended and unintended, for government, for performance, for international comparisons and for the organizations involved in providing services? Important aspects of the assumed links between ideology, actions and consequences in NPM can be questioned. Some of the questions we raise were asked at the earliest discussions of NPM. We also show how government and organizations have responded to the questions, how they have revealed new issues and how they have contributed to the expansion and diversification of NPM.

Does the market work to secure efficiency in the private sector?

Looking at some indices on comparative efficiency – remembering that an original driver for new management practice was a belief that private sector approaches may lead to improved efficiency in the public sector – two sets of comparison may be instructive. First, an examination of the comparative competitive position of the UK private sector compared with that of other nations. Second, to look at the comparative performance of the UK's health sector with other nations.

In 1998 the UK government published a White Paper on competitiveness, expressing concern about the UK's comparative position in international industrial competitiveness. 'Since the turn of the century the UK has been in relative economic decline. Our growth rate has been below the US and other leading European economies. Our productivity is 20–40 per cent behind these countries and the gap with France and Germany is not closing' (DTI 1998). The private sector alone is clearly not enough to secure relatively high performance.

Does a public health care system always under-perform a private system?

In contrast to the picture painted in the previous paragraph, Table 3.1 shows the relationship between the amount of health spending per capita and broad indicators of performance, in terms of life expectancy at birth and infant mortality rates. For the percentage of GDP (gross domestic product) a nation spends on health, the centrally funded and locally delivered UK national health service is revealed as relatively efficient in comparison with the US with its private free market. Anderson (1997) conducted an international comparison of costs, access and outcomes, and concluded that the US still spends more and fares worse on health indicators than most industrialized nations. Even with managed care, the rate of increase in health care spending in the US is still higher than the rate found in most other industrialized countries between 1990 and 1996, and yet health indicators are not noticeably better, and in some cases they are considerably worse. Of course national figures obscure a great deal of variation and inequality in all countries, but the variation in the US is greater than in the UK.

In comparison with the rest of the European Union (EU), the UK has a low-cost health system and yet sits mid-table in terms of performance. In the UK, 6.7 per cent of GDP is spent on health, compared with 10.6 per cent in Germany, 9.6 per cent in France and almost 8.6 per cent in the Netherlands. According to OECD data, the UK is placed fourteenth of twenty-nine OECD nations in terms of infant mortality, eleventh for male life expectancy and eighteenth for female life expectancy (1997).

Looking beyond average life expectancy, an overall assessment of health in the UK compared with European counterparts highlighted some positive and

Table 3.1 Relationship between health spending and performance

	Total expenditure on health	Infant mortality rate	Life expectancy at birth (years)	
	($ per capita)	(per 1,000 live births)	Females	Males
US	4178	7.2	79.4	73.6
UK	1607	5.9	79.7	74.6
Netherlands	2143	5.0	80.6	75.2
Germany	2769	4.8	80.3	74.1
France	2358	4.7	82.3	74.6

Source: OECD (2000).

some negative trends (World Health Organization 1997). UK performance was relatively good in terms of life expectancy, deaths from external causes (e.g. accidental and violent deaths and suicides) and car accidents, male cancer mortality and trends in adult smoking and nutrition patterns. Negative trends were often focused on women. UK women ranked fourth highest in years of life lost through death before sixty-five years, and life expectancy at that age was comparatively low for both sexes.

A European Union (1996) review of the state of health in the European Community remarked that while all health services are seeking to find ways to control costs, improve quality of care and lessen inequalities, they each have different institutional arrangements reflecting historical and political developments. Two basic patterns can be identified. Belgium, France, Germany, Luxembourg and the Netherlands have pluralist systems with public and private provision; the public organizations being financed mainly from compulsory health insurance. Denmark, Greece, Ireland, Italy, Portugal, Spain and the United Kingdom have national health services in which provision and financing are mainly within the public sector. Within each group there is great diversity in terms of structure, management, financing and ideology. Even so, and even taking the broadest view, it is difficult to relate performance on population health indicators to macro-institutional structures or operational management systems.

Finally, the World Health Organization, for its annual report in 2000, published an assessment of international health systems performance, ranking 191 countries according to aggregated measures covering both quality of the system or 'responsiveness' and equality or 'fairness' of financial contribution. The United Kingdom ranked eighteenth overall in the WHO rankings, with France and Italy at first and second respectively, Japan tenth, Germany twenty-fifth and the USA thirty-seventh (WHO 2000).

How are we able to determine and account for performance in health?

The excursion above into national health performance is important for two reasons. First, it confirms the difficulty of defining and measuring good performance. On what performance measures are health managers and policy-makers to concentrate? Are they going to focus on population indices of health? Or on inequalities between groups (as is highlighted in a White Paper, *Our Healthier Nation* (Department of Health 1998))? Or on the clinical outcomes of health interventions as experienced by individuals? Or on service/process indicators, such as waiting times or waiting lists, in respect of particular medical interventions? As well as multiple and conflicting measures of performance, whatever measures are given priority will lead to distortion as managers focus their behaviour on achieving specified performance indicators.

Second, the summary of differences between nations in terms of health indicators and institutional structures provides evidence that there are many more factors beyond operational institutional structures and managerial orientations that need to be taken into account if we are seeking to improve performance in this area of public service. Just as it can be argued, going back to the first comparison of private industry, that the UK's industrial performance is influenced by many factors, including the age of plant and machinery, fiscal arrangements, attitudes to risk, educational structures. So, the UK's health performance is influenced by many 'non-health' factors that are way beyond the influence of even the most senior policy-makers and managers who are 'in charge' of health. Some of these factors are shown in Figure 3.1, in respect to population health, and Figure 3.2, in respect to individual health. The figures remind us, as Ferlie and Pettigrew (1996) indicate, that one of the big challenges for managers in health care is to learn how to be effective in managing across

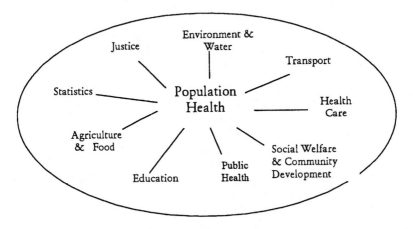

Figure 3.1 Non-health factors affecting population health

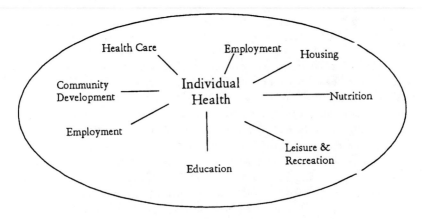

Figure 3.2 Non-health factors affecting individual health

boundaries and in networks since efforts to secure public goods require action across budgetary domains, professional disciplines and organizational structures.

To what extent can health be organized and managed just like other organizations?

Is health just another commodity? A collection of goods and services perhaps more complex than transport or electrical goods but fundamentally the same? Elsewhere, Dawson (1999) has argued that the special coincidence of five sources of complexity, illustrated in Figure 3.3, means that health systems are particularly difficult, complex and challenging to manage. Interaction between the five different worlds of industry, science and technology, professionals, the public and politicians creates unusual dynamics in supply, demand and political involvement. Each of the five worlds represents a highly complex set of players, relationships, power, influence, change and uncertainty; put them together and the resulting complexity is extraordinary. Elements of the health sector mean that there are similarities with other sectors, but the particular coincidence of the forces shown in Figure 3.3 create a particularly challenging managerial environment.

Who is accountable to whom, for what in health?

In the UK, we have a public health system funded largely out of taxation, organized as a regulated quasi-market, in which politicians are highly visible and managers and clinicians are managed within a framework of process and outcome performance measures. There are multiple accountabilities, such as spending public money, for delivering improved standards of public health, for effective diagnosis and treatment of ill-health, which create a web of regulatory,

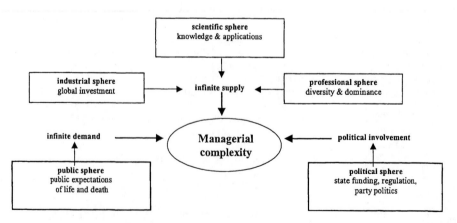

Figure 3.3 Sources of managerial complexity

Table 3.2 Accountabilities in UK health

Who is accountable/ to whom	For what	Levers for change
Parliament to Electorate	Public assessment of health provision Media presentation of health performance Personal experience Levels of taxation/co-payments	General elections
Government to Parliament	Health spend Public postbag Media presentation Public health performance measures Sickness service performance measures	Parliamentary votes/ debates and select committees
NHS executive to Ministers and government	Cost control/balanced budget Public assessment Media presentation Specified performance measures Anticipating/containing problems	Appointment Appraisal Instructions Guidance
Local Service provider boards (chairmen and executive non-executive directors) to Ministers NHS executive	Cost control/balanced budget Public assessment Media presentation Community Health Council assessment Anticipating/containing problems Managerial/professional relationships Clinical performance and governance	Appointment Instruction Guidance Performance targets
Local commissioning boards (chairmen and non-executive directors to Ministers NHS executive	Cost control/balanced budget Public assessment Media presentation Community Health Council assessment Anticipating/containing problems Managerial/professional relationships Clinical performance and governance Public Health indicators	Appointment Instructions Guidance Performance targets Gain/lose contracts for work
Local CEO and executive directors	Cost control/balanced budget Public assessment	Appointment Appraisal

Table 3.2 cont.

to	Media presentation	Performance-related
NHS executive, local chairman and non-executives	CHC (community watchdog) Anticipating/containing problems Managerial/professional relationships Clinical performance and governance Employment relations	pay Performance targets
Clinical directors to Local boards	Performance of clinical services cost control Employment relations	Appointment Appraisal Performance targets
Clinicians to Local boards Professional registration/ regulation bodies Patients Peers	Clinical performance Cost control Adherence to protocols	Appointment Appraisal Merit payments Clinical guideline/ protocols Reputation Gain/lose contracts for work

managerial, professional and political relationships. Table 3.2 illustrates some of the key accountabilities in UK health. It reveals a number of issues relating to NPM practice.

First, for all the talk there has been about emphasizing market rather than hierarchical mechanisms for achieving improved standards of health and health care in the UK, many of the levers available to effect change are top down. Second, the increasing role of the media in mediating relations between the government, professional groups and national and local managers in health and influencing priorities.

Third, there is a greater emphasis on developing protocols and guidelines to secure more uniformity of professional practice, thereby expanding the debate about performance in public management from the financial to include clinical performance. This has been coupled with pressure on the professional bodies to increase self-regulation and at the same time the establishment in April 1999 of a National Institute for Clinical Excellence to set guidelines (Department of Health 1997). These developments have not lessened the responsibilities of local managers. On the contrary, local managers are held accountable for clinical governance, just as they are held accountable for financial governance. So, there is an expansion and diversification of NPM mechanisms, tackling the more contested area of clinical performance and accountability, and forcing the powerful professional medical network to bring its own house to order.

Fourth, there are tensions between organizational layers. There is an indeterminacy about the relative roles of local quasi-autonomous boards that are required to take responsibility for delivering local services, a national executive which issues executive letters and monitors local performance, and a ministerial team that can create new duties and statutory responsibilities for any part of the public system. Many public services illustrate the tension between a desire to decentralize on the one hand and the desire to increase control measures on the other; tensions that stem from the dual economic and managerialist origins of UK NPM (Hood 1991). Health is a good example of a service that has never been truly devolved to local providers; thus there are complex links and tensions between centre and locality about who is responsible for what. For example, in the first of the Labour government's health White Papers (1997), managers were advised of their duty to 'engage in inter-agency partnership' and to be accountable for 'clinical governance'. Managerial processes are expected to deliver to an agenda that extends to the political and professional spheres.

What is the role of government in NPM?

An issue underlying debates about the proper role of government in public service provision is how to safeguard 'public goods'. These are the things that by rough consensus are seen to require acquisition by, and for, society. The definition of what is in this circle and what is outside it varies between countries. In the UK it includes literacy, health, public security. In the light of the disastrous handling of BSE the government set up the Food Standards Agency (*British Medical Journal* 1997, 1999). Public outcries about genetically modified food are adding to public pressure for 'safe food' to be seen as a public good and to be subject to more regulation. These responses are indicative of what we see to be an extension of the NPM (organizational forms established in an attempt to satisfy desires to control costs, increase quality, increase public support) rather than a reversal. There are few instances of government trying directly to intervene in order to resume operational control. However, government ensures that good comparative performance data are collected and made public, and that consistently bad performers are identified and given support to improve; if they fail to improve they are penalized, resulting in individuals losing their jobs and/or the work undertaken by the failing organization being given to another.

One explanation for continuing government intervention is that, although governments can devolve responsibility to locally managed, and sometimes self-governing, organizations such as NHS trusts or locally managed schools, when an organization fails its consumers, the public, it becomes a central government matter. When the Ridings School failed the government inspection it was left to central government to organize a 'hit squad' of replacement senior managers (OfSTED 1998). As noted above, one reason for the shift in responsibility may be our national media, who are quick to bring in the senior minister to answer questions (*The Guardian* 1999). If a minister is held directly to account on an issue by the media, it is likely he or she will want to take control over the solution.

The health service has other important characteristics. It is a *national* health service and was founded in a particular historical and political context in 1948. It is often linked symbolically with the government's 'stewardship' of other national institutions. The population's capacity for infinite demand for health care requires the government to set priorities, or ration certain provision, and to determine where public provision ends. The Conservative governments of the 1980s and early 1990s encouraged private sector health care, as well as introducing new charges for certain treatments, and an increase in over-the-counter pharmaceuticals. It is local health authorities who allocate resources as purchasers, but rationing by health authorities has led to disparities in treatment across the country, which has brought the debate back to the national level. The Labour government elected in 1997 is committed to delegating resource decisions to primary care organizations; at the same time, decisions on interventions which have significant resource implications, such as the availability of the drug Viagra, have recently been taken at the national, political level (Department of Health 1999). The new National Institute for Clinical Excellence is intended to deal with such issues on the basis of medical evidence but has already stated that it will work within central government resource constraints. Here we have more illustration of how the government is unable to do precisely what it promised in delegating resource decisions to those closest to the point of delivery, the general practitioner.

Reflecting on the role of central government, particularly in the light of the change in UK government in 1997, we find that when the public finds public services to be 'wanting' in good performance, governments deflect blame in two ways. One is to say that the blame lies with decisions made by a previous administration. The other is to say that the blame lies with local agents. For example, in a local Cambridge case, following publication of a highly critical report on the East Anglian Ambulance NHS Trust, the Secretary of State for Health said: 'I regard failings in an ambulance service as something that should never be allowed to happen.' 'The failings at East Anglian Ambulance Service have been primarily ones of management – not just recently but almost as soon as it was established.' (*Cambridge Town Crier*, 4 March 1999). It cannot, however, be forgotten that in public services it is central government that actually creates much of the context in which local managers work. It is the Secretary of State who appoints NHS trust chairpeople; yet in this ambulance service case, he was critical that there had been four chairmen and three chief executives in the first four years.

Investigating problems of poor performance in any organization always begs the question of whether the revealed problems are incompetence or systemic failure, or both. When it comes to public services, and given the political involvement described earlier, the choice is usually 'incompetence' or systemic failure if the timing is such that problems can be attributable to systems created by others. It is rarely attributed to systems created by those currently in power. Yet, as presently constituted in England, it is precisely the role of central government to exercise 'criteria power' over the NHS, and thus create the system that will secure desired performance.

Reflecting on the many changes that have taken place in the health sector over the last decades, the questions posed about who has the power to do what, and in particular the role of government central control, are extremely pertinent. A significant new NHS plan was published in July 2000 (Department of Health 2000b). The plan was accompanied by a substantial increase in funding for the NHS, which was announced following a winter of sustained pressure on the service including attacks from prominent Labour supporters. The plan was announced by Tony Blair, the Prime Minister, as a measure of his personal commitment. The Secretary of State for Health, Alan Milburn, is believed to have drafted significant portions of the document himself. The plan came at a time when the NHS was leaderless following the resignation of the chief executive, Sir Alan Langlands. The plan included the decision to combine the posts of NHS chief executive officer and Permanent Secretary at the Department of Health, thus drawing accountability for the NHS closer to central political control. Implementation of the plan is a top-down process. Networks, co-ordination, partnership are all features of the plan but the programmes of performance measurement and inspection, which allow 'earned autonomy' for high-performers but intervention from the centre for those who are under-performing, are significant.

Our earlier discussion of the assumed relationships within the NPM movement is relevant to the NHS Plan, which promotes targeted central funding of central initiatives such as cancer care and heart disease against local priority-setting according to local needs and promotes comparative performance assessment through an inspection system and a large number of performance indicators and targets that local organizations have to meet. It also raises the profile of users and citizens by increasing representation on national and local boards (such as the Patient Advocacy and Liaison Service (PALS)); and curbs the power of professionals by reducing demarcation between professional groups, introducing generic elements of professional training, and introduces regular, external appraisal for clinical staff.

Conclusion

What can be said about the extent to which the beliefs that gave rise to NPM appear to be current today? One can surmise that their currency will reflect the extent to which they have delivered desired cost containment, quality improvement and have received public support. Also, what is the extent to which changes in macro-level policy and institutional structure have resulted in a different approach to operational management in public sector organizations?

Looking at UK health, there was much talk about ending the internal market in health in the election campaign of 1997. The change in government brought about a change of language. The words of collaboration and partnership superseded the discourse of markets or contracts. However, the institutional structure created in the 1990s has been elaborated rather than eradicated. There are still quasi-autonomous organizations that determine the nature of local health care and which organize other semi-self-governing organizations to provide health services to given specifications. There is now more emphasis on the importance of setting standards, measuring performance against benchmarks and acting to eradicate persistent poor performers. This can be seen in many ways as the government acting to remedy the deficiencies of the market, not by abandoning it, but by creating new organizations and roles to take action to secure the 'public interest' in circumstances where this is not secured by well-informed consumers. Government's role in securing, but not directly managing, regulatory frameworks and chastising poor performers has become more pronounced. This in no way equates to a return to 'old public management', but it does perhaps indicate that there is a 'newer than new' approach in the making.

Over the last thirty years in the UK, we can discern at least three different emphases in public management and organization. We have moved from large, state-owned bureaucracies under hierarchical control to quasi-independent operational units, connected through contract and varying degrees of arm's length control, to networks of organizations which can operate with a fair degree of autonomy providing they meet specified performance targets. Persistent failure, however, invites state intervention. What we have witnessed in the late 1990s is a change of emphasis in mechanisms of control. Competition from alternative public providers or private contractors was seen as a mechanism to ensure performance in the late 1980s and early 1990s. In the late 1990s organizations are still controlled by contracts, whether or not they have become longer-term service agreements between a single purchaser and a single supplier, and it is failure to meet performance targets within these agreements that brings organizations back under the control of the centre.

Notes

1 This chapter is a second edition of a paper first presented at the Third International Public Management Research Symposium in 1999 and subsequently published in *Public Management* in 1999 (Dawson, S.J.N., Dargie, C. 1999 New Public Management: an assessment and evaluation with special reference to UK health. *Public Management* 1 (4): 459–48). There are additions to each of the main sections of the paper reflecting developments from 1999 to 2001.
2 *The Times*, 16 February 2001. Editorial: The doctors' doctor.
3 *The Guardian*, 23 November 1999. Private Manoeuvres.
4 http://www.ncaa.nhs.uk/
5 http://www.pmforschools.dfee.gov.uk/default1.htm
6 Alain Enthoven's paper urging consideration of the creation of an internal market for health in the UK was in this respect unusual (1985).
7 The BIDS database was analysed from 1981 to 1998 inclusive. The figures represent the number of items each year which include the words 'New Public Management'. It should be noted that abstracts and keywords have developed in BIDS over time. So, for example, Hood's 1991 *Public Administration* article is not picked up because 'New Public Management' does not appear in the title. Although 'New Public

Management' appears in Hood's abstract, some abstracts were not included in BIDS at that time.
8   http://www.public-standards.gov.uk/annreps/forewor.htm

References

Alchian, A.A. and Demsetz, H. (1972) Productive information and economic organization. *American Economic Review* 6(2): 777–95.

Anderson, G.F. (1997) In search of value: an international comparison of cost, access and outcomes. *Health Affairs* 16(6): 163–71.

Arrow, K.J. (1984) *Collected Papers of Kenneth J. Arrow* (several volumes) (Oxford: Blackwell).

Aucoin, P. (1990) Administrative reform in public management: paradigm, principles, paradoxes and pendulums. *Governance* 3: 115–57.

Banks, S. (1998) Codes of ethics and ethical conduct: a view from the caring professions. *Public Money and Management* 18(1): 27–30.

Behn, R.D. (1998) What right do public managers have to lead? *Public Administration Review* 58(3): 209–24.

Boyne, G. (2001) Planning, performance and public services. *Public Administration* 79(1): 73–88.

Boyne, G., Kirkpatrick, I. *et al.* (2001). Introduction to the symposium on New Labour and the modernization of public management. *Public Administration* 79(1): 1–4.

Cabinet Office (1991) *Citizen's Charter: raising the standard.* CM 1599 (London: The Stationery Office).

Dawson, S.J.N. (1999) Managing, organising and performing in health care: what do we know and how can we learn? In Mark, A.L. and Dopson, S. (eds) *Organisational Behaviour in Health Care* (Basingstoke: Macmillan): 7–24.

Department of Health (1997) *The New NHS. Modern. Dependable* (London: The Stationery Office).

Department of Health (1998) *Our Healthier Nation* (London: The Stationery Office).

Department of Health (1999) *The NHS Performance Assessment Framework* (London: The Stationery Office).

Department of Health (2000a) *The NHS Cancer Plan: a plan for investment, a plan for reform* (Leeds: The Department of Health).

Department of Health (2000b) *The NHS Cancer Plan: a plan for investment, a plan for reform* (London: The Stationery Office).

Department of Trade and Industry (1998) *Our Competitive Future: building the knowledge driven economy* (London: The Stationery Office).

Downs, A. (1967) *Inside Bureaucracy* (Boston: Little, Brown).

Dunleavy, P. and Hood, C. (1994) From old public administration to new public management. *Public Money and Management* 14(3): 9–16.

Enthoven, A. (1985) *Reflections on the Management of the National Health Service. An American looks at incentives to efficiency in health services management in the UK* (London: Nuffield Provisional Hospitals Trust).

European Commission (1996) *Report from the Commission on the State of Health in the European Community* (Luxembourg: Office for Official Publications of the European Communities).

Ferlie, E. and Pettigrew, A. (1996) Managing through networks: some issues and implications for the NHS. *British Journal of Management* 7(Special Issue): S81–S99.

Ferlie, E., Ashburner, L., Fitzgerald, L. and Pettigrew, A. (1996) *The New Public Management in Action* (Oxford: Oxford University Press).

Gray, A. and Jenkins, B. (1995) From public administration to public management: reassessing a revolution? *Public Administration* 73(1): 75–100.

The Guardian (1999) Borough of hate and hit squads (19 March 1999).

Hood, C. (1991) A public management for all seasons? *Public Administration* 69(1): 3–19.

Hood, C. (1995) Contemporary public management: a new global paradigm. *Public Policy and Administration* 10(2): 104–17.

Hood, C., James, O., Jones, G., Scott, C. and Travers, T. (1999) *Regulation Inside Government: waste-watchers, quality police and sleaze-busters* (Oxford: Oxford University Press).

Jackson, P.M. (2001) Public sector added value: can bureaucracy deliver? *Public Administration* 79(1): 5–28.

Kaboolian, L. (1998) The New Public Management: challenging the boundaries of the management vs. administration debate. *Public Administration Review* 58(3): 189–93.

Kanter, R.M. (1989) *When Giants Learn to Dance* (New York: Simon and Schuster).

Kelly, R.M. (1998) An inclusive democratic polity, representative bureaucracies, and the New Public Management. *Public Administration Review* 58(3): 201–8.

Kickert, W. (1997) Public Management in the United States and Europe. In W. Kickert. (ed.) *Public Management and Administrative Reform in Western Europe* (Cheltenham: Edward Elgar) 15–38.

Kirkpatrick, I., Kitchener M., *et al.* (2001) Out of sight, out of mind: assessing the impact of markets for children's residential care. *Public Administration* 79(1): 49–71.

Lane, J.-E. (2001) From long-term to short-term contracting. *Public Administration* 79(1): 29–47.

Lynn, L.E. (1998) The New Public Management: how to transform a theme into a legacy. *Public Administration Review* 58(3): 231–37.

Lynn, L.E. (2000) *Globalization and Administrative Reform: what is happening in theory?* (Rotterdam: IRSPM IV).

McKevitt, D. (1998) *Managing Core Public Services* (Oxford: Basil Blackwell).

Newman, J. (2001) What counts is what works? Constructing evaluations of market mechanisms. *Public Administration* 79(1): 89–103.

NHS Executive (1999) *Treatment for Impotence*. Health Service Circular HSC 1999/115 http://www.doh.gov.uk/hsc115.htm.

Niskanen, W. (1971) *Bureaucracy and Representative Government* (Chicago: Aldine-Atherton).

OECD (1997) *Health Data 97* (CD Rom database) (Paris: OECD).

OfSTED (1998) *The Ridings School: a report from the Office of Her Majesty's Chief Inspector of Schools*. http://www.ofsted.gov.uk/reports/107/107567.htm.

Osborne, D. and Gaebler, T. (1992) *Reinventing Government: how the entrepreneurial spirit is transforming the Public Sector* (Reading, MA: Addison Wesley).

Peters, T. (1987) *Thriving on Chaos* (London: Pan).

Polidano, C. (1998) Introduction: new public management, old hat? *Journal of International Development* 10(3): 373–5.

Pollitt, C. (1990) *Managerialism and the Public Services* (Oxford: Basil Blackwell).

Power, M. (1997) *The Audit Society: rituals of verification* (Oxford: Clarendon Press).

Rhodes, R.A.W. (ed.) (1995) British public administration: the state of the discipline. *Public Administration* 73(1) (Special issue).

Rhodes, R.A.W. (1997) *Understanding Governance* (Buckingham: Open University Press).

Rhodes, R.A.W. (2000) The Governance narrative: key findings from the ESRC's Whitehall Programme. *Public Administration* 78(2): 345–63.

Ridley, F. (1996) The New Public Management in Europe: comparative perspectives. *Public Policy and Administration* 11(1): 16–29.

Smith, R. (1998) Regulation of doctors and the Bristol inquiry. *British Medical Journal* 317: 1539–40.

Terry, L.D. (ed.) (1998a) 'Symposium: leadership, democracy and the New Public Management', *Public Administration Review* 58(3): 189–237.

Terry, L.D. (1998b) Administrative leadership, neo-managerialism, and the public management movement. *Public Administration Review* 58(3): 194–200.

The Times (1998) Backward Britain marked down by UN (9 September 1998).

Warden, J. (1997) UK food standards agency aims to rebuild trust in food. *British Medical Journal* 314: 1433.

Warden, J. (1999) UK plan for Food Standards Agency. *British Medical Journal* 318: 351.

Williamson, O. (1975) *Markets and Hierarchies: analysis and anti-trust implications* (New York: Free Press).

Woodhouse, D. (1995) Public administration and the courts: a clash of values? *Public Money and Management* 15(1): 53–9.

Woodhouse, D. (1998) The judiciary in the 1990s: guardian of the welfare state? *Policy and Politics* 26(4): 457–70.

World Health Organization (1997) *Highlights on Health in the United Kingdom* (Copenhagen: WHO).

World Health Organization (2000) *The World Health Report 2000: health systems: improving performance* (Geneva, WHO).

Chapter 4

Explaining the New Public Management

The importance of context

Norman Flynn

Ferlie *et al.* (1996) made a four-part classification of NPM approaches, based on four diagnoses of the problem by government. Their models were the efficiency drive; downsizing and decentralization; 'in search of excellence;' and 'public service orientation'. Peters (1996) also proposed a four-part taxonomy of models of governing, market, participative, flexible and deregulated, which was also related to different diagnoses of the problems seen by governments. Our work (Flynn and Strehl 1996) of the same year shied away from trying to classify the management changes in seven European countries because we were still trying to identify the changes, their causes and consequences. We did, however, find some big differences among apparently similar countries and sought some tentative explanations for those differences. Ferlie *et al.* acknowledged different 'national type' contexts as well as sectoral differences while Peters's analysis, although geographically wide-ranging, emphasizes the differences between sectors as the main determinant of the applicability of each model.

Much of the debate about convergence and difference has been concerned with sub-groups of the OECD countries, the English-speaking countries sometimes referred to as Anglo-Saxon or Anglo-American (Kickert etc.) and Japan used as the only non-Western example. A parallel debate has been carried on in the literature on public sector management and economic development. Kiggundu (1998) for example examines the context in which civil service reform in Africa has rarely been successful. Discussing the institutional capacity for good government in six poor countries, Hilderbrand and Grindle (1997) produced a typology of the economic, political and social conditions, which they call the 'action environment', and the 'public sector institutional context' or the existing arrangements within the state.

McCourt and Minogue (2001) takes an explicitly contingency approach to the explanation of differences between approaches to management. He posits a four-part classification of approaches to public management, one of which is emerging and labelled 'strategic management'. The other three are 'Public Administration', the 'Washington Model' named after the 'Washington consensus' and NPM.

This chapter examines the proposition that different contexts generate different discourses, including different diagnoses of the problems that governments are seeking solutions to. The diagnoses do not arise automatically from the 'objective' problems but are constructed within economic, political, institutional and cultural contexts. It also asks how the contexts shape the decisions that are made about what to do about the problems as defined. As with the diagnoses, it asks whether contexts have an influence on decisions which are not likely to be made on objective or 'technical' criteria. Some writers have argued that there has been a small set of decisions or solutions to the problems of managing the public sector and that these decisions are converging around a common set. Governments facing similar problems may arrive at similar solutions: after all, communication about what governments do is now easily available to policy makers and managers and there seems to be a convergence around a set of market-oriented ideas about what governments do and how they behave and should behave. There has also been a counter-argument that there persist differences among governments and what they do and how they do it. These differences are the result of contexts and are not simply the result of different stages of development towards a single, convergent ideal type. National conditions differ and therefore so do national practices. The arguments are not necessarily completely contradictory. At a very high level of generality, then all governments are similar: all (or almost all) are concerned with the efficiency with which their public servants work, the standards of public services, the deleterious effects of corruption on economic development. At a fine level of detail, differences will always persist. Researchers will always be able to find differences in budgeting processes or personnel practices or the degree to which competition is applied in service provision.

Both are correct and this chapter is not designed to contribute to either side of this perpetual dichotomy. It looks for explanations for the significant differences in how governments discuss their public sectors and behave towards them. It also asks whether there are elements of the context that make implementing change easier or harder. Its third ambition is to raise questions that might be useful in making international comparisons of public management and public management reform. There is a growing interest in comparisons and a growing number of territories used in the comparisons: Pollitt and Bouckaert (2000) include ten states in their study of public management reform. The purpose of comparative work varies. Our study tried to map the changes that were happening in management in seven European countries and tried to find patterns of difference and similarity. We tentatively offered some explanations for the differences in the constitutional and legal frameworks and in cultural attitudes to the state as constraints on management changes. Pollitt and Bouckaert link national politics to management arrangements and changes. Usually 'reforms' or significant changes in management arrangements are the 'dependent variable'. In this case what is to be explained is the diagnosis of the problems as expressed by governments and other agencies, the decisions made about what to do about them and the degree of difficulty experienced in implementation of the changes.

At a macro-level, the actions with which we are concerned include changing the portfolio of activities carried out by government and therefore the size of the public sector, measured either by the money spent or the numbers of people employed. The most evident of these is the privatization of state industries in manufacturing, public utilities, transport and telecommunications. These changes have been most apparent in Europe, although experience has been patchy: telecommunications has largely been privatized; railways are sometimes state owned, sometimes privately owned and sometimes in mixed ownership; many countries still have state-owned industries. Other states have privatized the railways, e.g. Japan, and many states have divested themselves of state-owned enterprises, especially if they have been through 'structural adjustment programmes' imposed by lenders. There has been little sign of privatization or a shift in the activities undertaken by the state in the United States or Canada.

At a micro-level, the changes with which we are concerned are the ways in which the remaining activities in the public sector are managed, including restructuring to create more accountable and manageable entities, the use of outsourcing, financial management and accounting, performance management, including customer service, and personnel management. In these areas there is a wide range of experience that has caused academics to doubt the notion of a single label of 'new'. The argument is that within general categories of 'reforming' or even 'NPM' there are differences between countries, in the three areas of discourse about problems and their solutions, decisions about what to do and in implementation. Differences in discourse may be less pronounced than differences in the other two areas, because there seems to be a fairly common 'meta-language' (Lynn 1998) that is used to describe, diagnose and prescribe management problems and solutions. The differences include:

- the degree to which sectors or services are in practice transferred from the public to the private sector;
- the degree to which markets are actually established, whether structures are decentralized in practice and the degree to which control is maintained in a small number of central institutions;
- whether financial planning and control really switches from control over inputs to control through outputs or outcomes;
- whether tiers of management are removed or merely re-labelled;
- whether the recruitment and promotion of staff is organized through a labour market or not;
- whether customer orientation is based on empowerment of service users, on the development of direct democracy, on market-research type consultation processes;
- whether performance management is carried out through devolved decision-making and an emphasis on results or through centralized controls;
- a variety of structural changes;
- different degrees of reliance on NGOs in service delivery.

As well as differences within each of these areas, there are also differences in the emphasis that is placed on the elements in different governments and subnational government organizations. In some there is more emphasis on structural questions, in others on the mechanisms of financial accounting and management and in others on a management model based on empowerment of the front-line implemented through 'cultural change' programmes.

This chapter tries to spread the net fairly wide in its attempt to catch or at least identify the independent variables in the contexts in which governments operate. Contexts are divided into external and internal. The definition of the external context extends slightly that of Hilderbrand and Grindle. It includes the macro- and micro-economic environment; political conditions; political positions adopted by parties; the immediate problems facing governments and the institutional context in which changes are proposed, including the prevailing managerial climate, national culture, the socio-technical systems in the sectors affected and the institutional capacity for change.

The purpose is not to define some formula for 'best practice'. The argument is that practice can be explained, to some extent, by reference to the context in which practices operate. It is also that the success of changes at the level of proposals and implementation is to an extent contingent. Certain practices are more likely to be successful than others, but that success is as likely to be contingent on the context as on the skill with which the practices are done. If these propositions are correct, then the choice of approaches to management should be informed by analysis of the contexts.

The argument is not that governments and others involved in the process currently follow the processes identified in the contextual model. The context affects the process but not necessarily at the level of a systematic analysis. Indeed, the process may well start with the choice of proposals, rather than an analysis of the problems to be solved. It has often been argued that proposals such as those implied in the 'Washington consensus' are a one-size-fits-all approach that pays little attention to the local context. The same can be true of locally developed solutions that may derive more from the demonstration effect of other governments' presentation of their successes in management reforms than from locally existing problems.

Macro-economic conditions

Hood (1996), using four indicators of economic performance and a 'high, medium and low' classification of management changes, concluded that the level of economic performance was not a sufficient predictor of the level of implementation of NPM in the 1980s. Given the degree of variation in the adoption of the 'new' management methods, many other variables need to be included in the explanation, such as the size of government, the degree of integration of government, and so on. Hood finds that no single variable provides a good explanation for all cases and calls for research that includes a contingency and a diffusion approach. This has two implications for explanation. First, that there is a set of practices that can diffuse through different governments. Second, that as long as the contingent factors can be identified and measured, including how they change, they will explain changes in management practices. It could, on the other hand, be that sufficient explanation requires an understanding of the interaction of the variables, rather than treating each as an independent cause.

Macro-economic conditions do not automatically generate policy responses from governments. If there is an inflation target, price increases may trigger an interest rate rise, but the decision to control inflation through interest rates is the result of a political choice about the priority given to inflation over other economic indicators as a goal of government economic policy. For more complex political decisions as a result of macro-economic change, the political choices are more complex. For example, if there is an unpredicted fiscal deficit arising from reduced tax revenues in a recession there are various possible political responses. At one extreme, such as in Denmark in the late 1990s, the government can decide to meet all its previous spending commitments and fund them through a combination of tax rate increases and borrowing. At the other it can introduce austerity measures, reduce entitlements to state support and try to reduce the size of the public sector. Both are feasible political choices. In either case, there could simultaneously be a decision to introduce public sector reforms. In the first extreme case, it might be politically expedient to try to increase efficiency and reduce running cost expenditure as a gesture to those businesses and taxpayers who are asked to pay higher tax in a time of reduced incomes. In the latter case, saving on running costs might be part of the package of trying to reduce expenditure. There are many variants between the two extreme cases.

Take the opposite case: a government, such as Japan's between 1998 and 2001, that tries to take counter-cyclical macro-economic measures to reflate the economy. Since measures to encourage private spending failed, the government decided to increase public spending, especially on capital projects as a stimulus to the economy. Clearly, a period of fiscal loosening was required, despite the very large accumulated deficit. What effect might this have on the strength of efforts to reform the public sector? Little effort because of the fiscal loosening? Large effort because of the continuing recession and poor economic performance? In the event, the mediation of the political process, the loss of the hegemony of the LDP (Liberal Democratic Party) and the unpopularity of elements of the civil service all proved to be more important than the simple economic facts in explaining the calls for drastic cuts in civil service numbers and improvements in efficiency. The continued growth of employee numbers at local authority level since the start of the recession in 1989 also needs to be explained by local political factors rather than macro-economic management by central government. The deficit itself is of political origin as the LDP kept promises made at central and local level on spending and projects while unable to face the political consequences of raising taxes.

Our first category, shifting the boundary between the private and public sectors and changing the size of the state, is not a solution to short-term cyclical problems. It might be seen as a long-term solution if it reduces governments' commitments to spend. Serious structural changes have never been achieved during the period of a cyclical downturn. If governments do decide to shift the boundary of the state for macro-economic reasons it is because they have a view about what is appropriate for governments to do and how much resource they should control.

The appeal to the inevitability of 'globalization' and its impact on national economies and governments is such a case. New Zealand, a leader in both structural and management changes, made its public sector reforms as part of a general liberalization of the economy. The government claimed that an increase in productivity in the public sector would make a direct contribution to national competitiveness through its impact on the tax level. Corporatization of state activities and privatization of those for which there was no overwhelming case for them to be in the public sector were a major plank of the self-imposed structural adjustment programme (see Kelsey 1995). The management changes within the public sector, including structural changes, introduction of markets, separating policy-making from service provision, and so on, were also part of the package (see Boston *et al.* 1996). However, not all governments faced with problems of national competitiveness have taken this course of action. For example the French government used the need to improve national competitiveness as the reason for a series of 'modernization' efforts in the late 1980s and early 1990s, contemporaneous with the New Zealand changes but different from them.

Management changes can have little effect on budget deficits, especially in the short run. Reducing the running costs of public services, as opposed to transferring responsibilities to the private sector or to individuals, makes little difference to overall public spending except in those states where the level of spending is small in the first place and where most of the budget is spent on the salary bill. The major expenditures of European states, on welfare and education programmes, are unaffected by running-cost–productivity improvement.

In summary, when we consider the effects of the macro-economic circumstances on public sector reforms, we have to distinguish between the short-term efforts to reduce deficits and the long-term efforts to change the scale of state activities. We also need to consider the political processes that translate a budget deficit into government actions to cure it, or to wait until economic circumstances reduce the deficit by increasing tax revenues and reducing welfare expenditures. Different governments make different political choices. Governments faced with different macro-economic environments may also reach similar conclusions, although for different reasons. The drive to reduce costs and increase efficiency was not confined to governments with budget deficits.

Micro-economic conditions

The micro-economic context also has an impact of what sort of changes are proposed and can be implemented. First, there is the question of the state of the supply side. If governments wish to increase outsourcing they have to have companies or third sector service providers to which to outsource. Efforts to generate competition for supply of goods and services where there is an established market, for example in building or engineering work, will be more successful than in those sectors where there is little supply, such as medical services in states where the government has an existing near monopoly control of hospitals, clinics and staff as is the case in most of Scandinavia. Examples of problems in generating suppliers include the attempts to generate private management of water supply services and fee collection where companies do not yet exist in this sector (see, for example, Batley and Larbi 1999).

The structure of the market also has an impact on the success of competition policy. Oligopolies in sectors such as large computer systems supply and weapons procurement reduce the cost advantages of outsourcing.

Second, there is the question of the labour market conditions facing governments that want to introduce more flexibility in their public sector labour markets. On the one hand, if there are few or no alternative job opportunities for displaced civil servants and other pubic sector workers, a programme of downsizing will meet with strong resistance. On the other hand, if there are labour shortages of skilled staff, a programme of liberalization of employment conditions will not improve the skill levels in the public sector. More generally, Hilderbrand and Grindle cite the overall level of development of labour skills as a constraint on the development of capacity for economic development.

The micro-economic environment is also dynamic. A market may be created if there is commitment to purchasing and if contracts are written and managed in such a way as to generate the supplying of materials to companies. On the other hand, mergers and acquisitions among supplying companies can turn competitive markets into oligopolies and cartels over time.

Political conditions

The organization of power relationships through political institutions also has an important impact on decisions and actions about the public sector. A commonly invoked condition for successful change in the public sector is the willingness of political leaderships to drive through radical changes. Governments with large parliamentary majorities, clarity about what they want to do and individual champions of change are said to be an important element in breaking down resistance and overcoming inertia. Governments that rely on coalition politics are more likely to compromise when making changes that affect the interests of coalition partners. Parties that rely on the support of people such as civil servants or professionals for their survival in government are also likely to be more timid about change. Examples include the Lubbers government in the Netherlands in the 1980s, which had a radical programme of reform but not a wide base of support in a system that requires the development of consensus before changes are made. Various attempts at decentralization of financial control in France have been countered by the powerful Ministry of Finance, whose power and influence was threatened by such developments. President Clinton's efforts to make radical reforms of the US health insurance system were defeated by an alliance of political opposition and the powerful insurance industry.

Attempts at civil service reform have also floundered on the rocks of political patronage and the capture of institutions by party factions. Reduction in the number of ministries and privatization of some functions in Japan was stopped because of the potential loss of power bases by important factions of the LDP. If political parties and their constituent factions are closely allied to specific institutions and their powers, it is more difficult to reform those institutions or to abolish or slim them. The Italian parliament has sufficient members of the academic profession to curtail managerial inroads into the universities.

Institutions or the professions that staff them may also have support from their own constituencies, other than through the political parties. If the medical professions are held in high esteem they can call upon public support in their resistance to unwanted managerial changes. The opposite may also be true. When teachers are held in low esteem, for example, education reforms are easier to implement than when they are cherished by other teachers and parents. The status of civil servants varies from country to country, from one extreme where they are poorly (and sometimes rarely) paid, to the other, such as in France or Singapore, where they are well paid and generally held in high esteem. Governments may manipulate public opinion by praising or vilifying public employees, but the process takes time. In some cases, popular support wanes because of the perceived performance of the institutions. The Ministry of Finance in Japan lost its high status gained from its perceived role in helping bring about fast growth when growth slowed and corruption scandals occurred.

Another protection against civil service reform is the constitutional position of the civil service in relation to the government. We found (Flynn and Strehl 1996) that where there were strong and detailed administrative and constitutional laws, governmental desires to bring about management changes were slower and had less chance of success than in states where ministerial actions could be implemented without legal and constitutional change.

The particular form that managerial change takes is also influenced by the relative power of particular ministries or commissions. When the Treasury is dominant (as in New Zealand in the early 1980s) reforms will have an accounting flavour. When personnel departments are important, emphasis is more likely to be on human resource policies and practices. It is interesting that it took over a decade of reforms in New Zealand before the personnel implications of the changes were confronted, regarding recruitment, retention and development of staff under the redesigned regime.

In some states trade unions are powerful and can have an influence on the form and implementation path of changes. Jamaica is one example.

These issues are about the nature and structure of national politics. They relate to some extent to what is called 'regime type', where types are defined as dictatorships, autocratic, democratic, and so on. However, it is not possible to read off the types of reforms directly from regime type. Even dictatorships rely on coalitions of forces to stay in power, and democracies have a variety of political processes. The general point is that the political structures and processes have an influence on the way that issues are raised and put on the reform agenda. They also mediate the processes by which solutions are found and policies are formulated and implemented. All change generates winners and losers, whether they are changes to the functions carried out by government, the size of the public sector, the way in which services are delivered or the management arrangements of individual departments and institutions. It would be unusual for there to be a complete separation between the people making the choices and implementing the changes and those affected by them. In some cases the people are indistinguishable, since they belong to the same families and went to the same schools. The upper reaches of the British, Japanese and French civil service all have close connections with the upper reaches of the legislatures and other branches of the state. This does not mean that change is impossible, but the nature and speed of the change will be affected by that political fact. Mutual obligations formed by the connections[1] will inform the diagnosis and influence the actions taken.

Where the connections are less close and there is clear demarcation between the parts of the state and between the state and the outside world, the political processes of change will be different but they will still take place.

Another important political condition is the degree to which people outside the country influence decision-making. In the extreme, a debtor country has to submit to structural adjustment, privatization, management measures as well as macro-economic policies in exchange for loans. There are also slightly more subtle pressures as small states operate to some degree as clients of the USA or ex-colonial powers, following policies that were formed outside the country in which they are being implemented. The mechanisms for this are technical assistance missions, the World Bank (and Inter-American Bank and Asian Development Bank), which import ready-made solutions such as down-sizing, outsourcing, privatisation, and so on, prior to diagnosis of the specific problems.

Political positions on the public sector

As well as the political structures and positions being important, the positions adopted by the parties about the public sector are also a crucial influence on the analysis, diagnosis and actions taken towards reforming the state. Obviously influential positions were those of what became known as the 'New Right', despite the fact that many of them were far from new. In brief these are:

- that markets were more efficient than any other method of allocation and what could be left to the market should be;
- that all motivations are selfish, so managers should not be allowed to make big decisions on budgets or services because they will only serve their own interests and not those of the people who they should serve;
- that workers' motivations are the same and they should therefore be tightly controlled;

- that self-reliance is better than other-reliance and therefore the state should do as little as possible.

The consequences of these positions for policy towards the public sector include privatization, cutting back state functions, dictatorial management and the search for mechanisms to bring managers under political control. For all the publicity that these basic positions received, they were adopted by very few countries and even in those where they were espoused or adopted, implementation programmes were limited to a few states.

Linked but not identical is the view that it is morally right for the public sector and its workers and managers to suffer hardship just as other sectors have suffered. Since industries are subject to intensified competition and are laying off staff, closing plants, restructuring, delayering and asking everyone to work harder and smarter, then public sector workers should do the same. If politicians have close connections with business, they will be subjected to this moral argument and many will agree with it. The result of the position is that the public institutions should be subject to periods of staff cutting, restructuring, business process re-engineering whatever the impact on productivity or quality.

There is also the doctrine of 'modernization', in which all the institutions, including businesses, democratic processes and the public sector, should contribute to some sort of national renewal and lead to greater national competitiveness in world markets. This position was taken by the ruling parties in New Zealand and France in the early 1980s, in Malaysia in the mid-1990s and in Britain at the end of the 1990s. The consequence of this position is that there should be technical change and improvements at the customer interface level of the organization.

A variant is the view that the civil service and public sector in general are blocks to national and economic development. They probably cannot be turned into 'engines of change' (or some other mechanical metaphor) and should therefore be reformed sufficiently to stop them putting a brake on development. Corruption and/or unnecessary controls and 'red tape', which are part of the process of generating bribes, slow down economic development and building and should be rooted out. A variant is the US 'big government' line in which anything that government does is detrimental to entrepreneurship and should therefore be stopped. If this is not possible, then the public sector should become more entrepreneurial. The 'reinventing' campaign in the US was essentially legitimizing discretion at low levels of the organization in opposition to the rule-based culture of 'big government'. It was about empowering the individual manager against the system, rather than trying to change the system.

An alternative is consensual politics and a corporatist approach. States with evenly balanced coalitions of a group of parties have to have consensus building processes or frequent changes of leadership and policy. The coalition building sometimes goes beyond parties and includes representatives of workers, business, churches and other sectors. The epitome of this approach is the Netherlands' 'consociational democracy' (Lijphart), which has also been identified in Malaysia (Jesudason (1996) coins 'syncretic state'), for example. In these conditions, radical change is unlikely, as no party is likely to produce a set of proposals outside the consensus. This is the case of reforms in both the Netherlands and Malaysia, which have consisted of changes in working practices, quality improvements, enhancement of the relationships between government and citizens, rather than radical programmes of privatization, restructuring or redefining the role of the state.[2] Consensus and corporatism concern political process but also have an influence on the positions likely to be adopted by the parties involved in the processes.

So far we have discussed the public positions of parties with regard to the public sector. Covert positions include individual, faction or party enhancement. When politics is organized mainly for personal gain, policies towards state institutions may also be designed to gain power and reward. For example, a privatization might be organized to benefit a faction, or it might be avoided if a faction gains more from the institution's position in the public sector.[3] Or a party may propose the creation of new institutions in opposition to those in which the party's position is weak. The distribution of powers and responsibilities among central and sub-national governments is often organized to maximise ruling party control. When this form of power and reward-seeking dominates politics, it is difficult to predict the implications for public sector structure and process reform which will depend on the relative positions of the players.

Immediate problems

Politics concentrates the mind on the short term. In democracies, elections are the time horizon within which decisions are made. In autocracies, public support is nurtured by visible events and displays. Policy is often made in response to immediate events, especially negative ones. Spectacular failures of the civil service or public authorities generate demands for change. The response of the authorities to the victims of the earthquake that struck Kobe, Japan, caused a huge drop in confidence in the government and the ruling party and set off a search for reforms. The economic crisis in Asia produced calls for structural reforms in the relationship between government and the private sector in many countries. The original reforms in New Zealand were triggered by a balance of payments crisis.

Other events can be less spectacular and of longer duration. Failures to produce adequate urban water supply, long delays in registration of births, prolonged theft of public funds, visible bribery beyond the norm, all put pressure on politicians to do something to improve the situation. Sometimes the pressure comes from citizens as individuals, sometimes as pressure groups and sometimes from businesses, either within or outside the government's networks. Very poor performance, or absolute failure, generates the necessity for some action. At a lower level failure may be less spectacular but still apparent. It becomes obvious when an education or health system is not working to the satisfaction of the service users. Consistent failure leads to legitimation problems for the government and/or the ruling party or parties.

Among immediate events we can also count fiscal crises: periods in which the revenues collected are insufficient to pay the bills. Although the causes may be cyclical, predictable and temporary or structural and permanent, the occasion of a deficit and consequent borrowings (or, in extreme, failure to pay salaries of state workers) triggers a policy response. If the fiscal crisis results in borrowing, then the urge for reform is reinforced.

Diagnoses

All the above conditions vary from country to country. When governments decide what to do about the public sector, they are influenced, at least, by all of these factors. The diagnosis of the problem to be solved emerges as a response to the interpretation of the short- and long-term problems and is mediated by the political process.

Various ideal-type diagnoses have emerged. Peters (1996) identifies four: the monopoly position of government agencies in some services; the impenetrability of hierarchy; the inflexibility of permanence; the rigidity of excessive internal regulation. We could add to these: the state sector is too big because it is doing things that it should not be doing; public services are so unresponsive and ineffective as to generate public dissatisfaction with government; the public institutions, although performing the right functions, are inefficient and could do more with less; the public sector is hindering economic development and growth.

Not all these diagnoses are mutually exclusive and may appear in various combinations.

The diagnoses do not arise automatically from some 'objective' conditions. They are interpretations both of what is wrong and of what might be done about it. Take Peters's first: the diagnosis that governments should not have monopolies. In some states the question of a state monopoly of prisons, for example, does not arise, whereas in others private sector companies run most of the prisons. In those countries where the state runs all the prisons, monopoly as a diagnosis of the problem with prisons would only arise if there were the political possibility of alternative forms of provision. Or take the second: the fact that hierarchy prevents participation of workers and citizens in the decisions made by the organization. If hierarchy is a cultural norm and has been established for acceptable reasons, the existence of the hierarchy would not arise as the diagnosis of a problem.

And so on through the list. The diagnoses of the problems arise from the context. The context shapes the diagnoses, the solutions proposed as well as the possibilities of implementation. The three elements are closely connected. Diagnosis, as we see in the Peters example, presupposes a type of solution: competition as a cure for monopoly; flat structures as a cure for hierarchy. Diagnosing the state as too big presupposes re-drawing the boundaries; inefficiency presupposes cutting budgets. In extreme, the cure may be in search of the problem. It has been said that lenders and consultants have pre-selected solutions to problems they have yet to find.

Similarly with reform proposals and implementation. Successful implementation of reforms requires either that the change goes with the flow of the context, or that the relevant element of context can itself be changed to allow the reform to occur. Sometimes the proposals and implementation plans are so far out of line with the context that it may be questioned whether they were ever serious in the first place and were not simply a rhetorical device to satisfy some important stakeholder.

There are three elements of context that also influence the managerial solutions chosen and the success of their implementation. The first is what might be called the management climate or ideology. This means the approaches to management that are current, known to politicians and others designing reforms and likely to be acceptable to workers. The second, which has an impact on the first, is certain aspects of national culture that have an influence on the organizational cultures of the public sector. If management arrangements contradict the prevailing culture they are less likely to succeed. Third, there is a socio-technical system that operates in the sector(s) concerned. As in business organizations, where management solutions that are appropriate in a nuclear power plant might not work in a hotel, so solutions that are appropriate in prisons might not work in tax collection departments.

The institutional context

The management climate or ideology

Management climate varies with geography, time and sector. It consists of what companies and other organizations do, what academics and consultants teach, advise and write about and how management is represented in the media through stories of success and failure and the creations of heroes and heroines and villains. Politicians concerned about their approach to management are faced with libraries full of books, consultants keen to be hired and a general climate about what is currently in favour. They have to make some choices.

Some of the choices have been clear for half a century or longer. The 'human relations' school versus the close supervision and piecework school is till a debate that is acted out in choices about quality processes, whether to have performance-related pay, how much autonomy professionals should be allowed, and so on. Looking around management changes in the public sector you can see examples of both solutions.

The centralization–decentralization debate has gone in cycles in management thought. What companies do about how much autonomy divisions or units they should have vis-à-vis head office depends both on the preferences of managers and on the context in which companies find themselves. Public sector changes have periods of centralization and decentralization. A famous example is that of the self-managing schools experiment in Victoria State, Australia, which spread to many other places. The experimental arrangements have now been reversed by the government in Victoria because of its impact on equality of opportunity for pupils.

A third continuing debate is about the choice between vertical integration and specialization. The advantages of developing a high level of skill in a particular activity are weighed against the advantage of being able to control the whole of the production process. At any time, examples of both solutions can be found in the private sector. Outsourcing is an example of specialization in what is sometimes called 'the core business', and private sector experience of this is evinced in support. Examples of vertical integration, such as the European holiday industry with its vertically integrating bookings, airlines and hotels, are ignored.

Approaches to quality also vary. There are two opposed positions: that quality is best achieved through detailed design and control; and that quality is achieved through empowerment and participation. Both are used in approaches to quality in the public sector, sometimes simultaneously.

A related issue is whether products and services should be standardized (Fordism) or individually designed for each customer, or at least having the appearance of being such (post-Fordism). Manufacturing technology offers certain choices of design and finish that allows customization: should services also be customized?[4]

Apart from these five fundamental choices, there are fashions that arise and are promoted from time to time. Business process re-engineering is one example of a management practice marketed and promoted by two authors, Hammer and Champney, as if it was a new, discrete management process. More recent is the fashion for 'strategic alliances',[5] which emphasizes cooperation over competition, as a source of success. The 'new economy' has also become fashionable, emphasizing use of the internet in service delivery, call centres and efficient anonymity as a source of customer satisfaction. Governments are busy smartening up their web pages and installing or contracting for call centres.

Politicians are exposed to these ideas and trends and filter them through their decision-making processes. The language of the fashionable ideas quickly appear in documents, frequently with genuflection to 'private sector practice' as if there was a single set of good practices in business.

National cultures

Hofstede (1980, 1991) and Hampden-Turner and Trompenaars (1993) analysed large samples of managers to see if there was a pattern of national cultural characteristics that had an impact on the way organizations are managed. Hofstede's sample showed four consistent dimensions: attitudes to authority; the relationship between the individual and the group; 'masculinity' and 'femininity'; attitudes to uncertainty. Hampden-Turner and Trompenaars identified seven dilemmas: universalism versus particularism; analysis versus integration; individualism versus communitarianism; inner-directed versus outer-directed orientation; time as sequence versus time as synchronization; achieved status versus ascribed status; equality versus hierarchy. The two lists overlap somewhat.

In both cases, clusters of characteristics were assigned to countries. If management processes or management changes go against the flow of these clusters of characteristics they are less likely to be successful than if they go with the cultural flow. Although no detailed studies have been made of the impact of national cultures on public sector management, it is possible to surmise the likely impact of culture on specific management reforms.

Authority and power distance and achieved status and acquired status

Some reforms have involved reducing hierarchies and making individuals responsible. Recruitment practices that open up labour markets replace promotion through seniority with appointment on merit and performance. The cultural limits on these changes are that the prevailing beliefs may be challenged. If staff are unwilling to accept authority from those for whom they have no respect or who do not have sufficient seniority then the old hierarchies will re-establish themselves. A related cultural feature is the willingness to accept responsibility for decisions. A hierarchy which passes memoranda up and down to spread responsibility is fundamentally challenged when authority and responsibility are forced on individuals.

The individual and the group and individualism and collectivism

One aspect of personal responsibility is linking pay and promotion to individual performance. Where the individuals subsume their individuality within a group identity, individual appraisals and individual performance pay schemes will become an empty ritual.[6]

Masculinity and femininity

These terms are shorthand for styles of working and managing. They cover dichotomies between competition and collaboration, caring values versus material success, and so on (Hofstede 1991: 79–108). They do not imply that all women have feminine characteristics or that all men have the opposite.

Management changes in the public sector have involved both changes from 'feminine' to 'masculine' and vice versa. Regimenting the caring professions is an example of the former. Promoting collaboration rather than competition might represent the latter. Crudely, one would expect changes of the former sort to be effective in places that have high 'masculinity index scores' and the latter to be more successful in those that have low masculinity scores.

Universalism and particularism

This index relates to the preference for applying rules universally to all cases and making individual choices for particular cases. Clearly changes that increase individual discretion will have problems in cultures wedded to the universal application of rules.

Analysis versus integration

This dimension concerns the tendency to break problems into their component parts or to see them as a whole and find a whole solution in the broad context. A tendency to move towards management through effectiveness and management of outcomes clearly requires integration rather than analysis. A tendency towards analysis will favour management by outputs and individual units and activities.

Inner-directed versus outer-directed orientation

Inner-directedness is defined as a preference for looking inwards in decision-making as opposed to taking signals from the environment. Obviously it will be easier to create and manage outward-looking organizations in cultures that are conducive to that way of working.

Equality versus hierarchy

Creating teams of equals, project groups with no formal leader, quality circles and other techniques of the 'human relations' school will be easier in societies that are comfortable working in a non-hierarchical way.

It is not the intention to produce national culture stereotypes: Hampden-Turner and Trompenaars take the trouble to avoid such a charge and even distinguish cultures in different states in the USA. What such a set of categories does, however, is highlight dimensions of underlying beliefs that management changes might encounter. The reforms can either be designed to comply with the prevailing culture or engage in a culture change programme to alter it. Such programmes are not trivial since they have to deal with deep-seated beliefs.

The socio-technical system

Ferlie *et al.* said that the sector in which management changes are implemented makes a difference to the success of the changes. As in the business sector, the variety of products, services, technologies and skills generate a variety of management approaches. Since the industrial revolution it has been obvious that production lines require/are based on the division of labour. Armies require hierarchy and obedience. Policing requires a degree of autonomy for the officer at the scene of a crime. Courts have to comply with laws and exercise their defined discretion. Tax collection requires equal treatment of taxpayers.

Often management changes are expected to be generalized across all public services and all sectors. The anomalies soon become apparent. A pathology laboratory worker famously responded to a 'customer care' initiative that she never saw more than a few dozen cells of any patient. Any changes need to take account of the nature of the service delivery system that is involved.

The main variables are: Is the service routine and rule-bound or does it require the operation of discretion in everyday decision-making? Does the task have work processes that come from the profession rather than the organization (medical, engineering etc.)? Does the technology determine the working arrangements? Are alternative technical delivery systems available? Is the work susceptible to uncontroversial performance measurement?

The answers to these questions will form a strong context in which decisions about increased decentralization, devolved decision-making and managerial discretion are made. They will also provide strong clues about how management control and accountability can best be organized. General principles of management, whether derived from the private or public sectors, do not provide specific answers about how services should be managed. In addition to the above contextual conditions, the content of the work is crucial.

Institutional capacity

A major constraint on management changes is the ability of the people to carry them out. Reforms that rely on new costing and accounting arrangements need accountants and book-keepers to carry them out. Performance management requires skills from middle managers. Skills can be developed by training or acquired by hiring people, but both processes take time and may lag behind the reforms, making implementation slow and unsuccessful in the early years.

Crucially, a decision to provide services by outsourcing needs not only a range of suppliers but also the ability to write and monitor contracts with those suppliers. Batley and Larbi (1999) identified the lack of skill in this area as a constraint on the development of private urban water supply management in their sample of poor countries. The difficulty of being a 'smart' purchaser has been identified as a constraint on the development of contracting-out and market solutions (see, for example, Walsh), especially when the services to be outsourced are complex and specialized.

Desired outcomes

The real purposes of management changes is perhaps the hardest item to disentangle from the language in use in official documents. The litany of 'flexible, customer-centred, responsive' and so on is always a publicly stated aim. The politics of management change varies according to the political configuration: reorganizations can be used to benefit different factions; some reforms are designed to change the balance of power between politicians and professionals.

The ultimate outcomes are to gain or regain political support, whether from the electorate or business, or other interests. The support may be gained by cutting costs (and possibly taxes, although this has rarely happened) or improving services. More radical changes, such as moving the state–private sector boundary, might well also be an ultimate objective, introducing more opportunities for business to operate in the areas previously occupied by the state.

In the real world of politics, the connections between desired outcomes, diagnosis and proposals may be stretched or tenuous. Proposals may arise directly from the political process and the objectives may remain covert.

Reform proposals normally arise from some specific event or problem. A scandal exposes weakness; a deterioration in service reaches the point of intolerance by the public; an economic crisis exposes a country to outside influences; a party sees electoral advantage in improving in public services. Whatever the event, the politicians and senior public servants, often advised or informed by colleagues in other countries, and other outside agents such as consultants, look for solutions to the problems. The desired solutions are at different levels, from changing the role and functions of the state to increasing efficiency and improving customer service. The outcomes from those solutions may also vary: they may be to gain electoral advantage for the ruling party; to wrest control over public services from professionals to politicians; to cut taxes; to improve economic growth.

Conclusions

The argument has been, first, that there are differences among countries and sectors in the way management change is approached. Although at a highly abstract level, governments use similar language to describe their reforms, in practice there are different priorities and different objectives.

The context in which management changes take place account in part for the differences in the proposals and the success of their implementation. The elements of the context are summarized in Figure 4.1. The importance of the elements varies among countries, and each country will have its own particular set of contextual elements. Explanation of a particular reform process and its implementation requires the identification of the relevant context.

Implementation of the solutions also takes place in a specific institutional context, defined here as having four parts: the management climate, the national culture as it impacts on organizational culture, the socio-technical systems in the sectors to be reformed and the institutional capacity for change.

The positive and negative elements of the context need to be identified if this analysis is to be used to improve the chance of successful management changes. Some negative elements will be easier to change than others. For example, if there is a strong national culture that reinforces hierarchy and is comfortable with large power differences and reluctant to individualize responsibility, then a reorganization that removes tiers of management and devolves responsibility will be difficult. Other approaches to performance improvement, such as a hierarchical system of measurement and a collective responsibility, would be easier to implement. Devolved management is much more likely to be successful in a cultural climate that emphasizes individualism, competition and the acceptance of individual responsibility.

The context is not only important for the likely success of implementation but also for the sorts of solutions that are proposed. Basic political positions

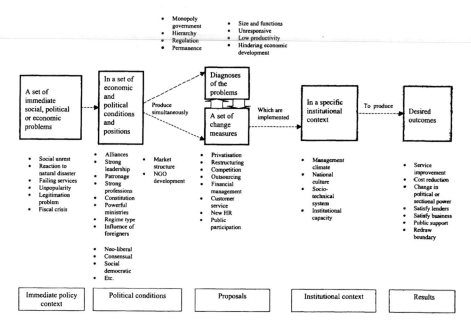

Figure 4.1 Public management changes in their contexts

about the role of the state and the market strongly colour the attitude to the big questions about state–private boundaries. Positions about motivation and attitudes to the workforce also colour the types of management arrangements that are put in place.

In addition to political positions or attitudes, there are underlying structural attributes of the political conditions, such as the degree of patronage, the relative strength of ministries and professions, that affect the process of managing and of managing changes.

All this might seem a heavy burden on people trying to bring about change. Inertia would seem to have the best chance of success. 'Path dependency' taken to extremes allows no options. That is not the purpose of the argument, rather that if we want to understand the processes involved in changing management in the public sector we need to take account of all the contexts. Practising politicians and managers know this, for their efforts are aided or thwarted by the contexts in which they work. The contexts help to explain not only the different management arrangements in place but also the different goals and problems in achieving them.

Notes

1 Where these connections are so strong that the boundary between the state and the society is invisible and there is a strong network of connections, the state might be referred to as a 'network state' (see Flynn 1999: Chapter 6).

2 Counter to the global trend, the Netherlands government has consolidated third sector pension schemes into a state sector, while other places are seeking non-state alternatives.
3 Japan's Postal Savings Bank is a case in point.
4 See 'Towards a Post-Fordist Welfare State?' for a discussion of this.
5 See, for example, Doz and Hamel (1998) and Child and Faulkner (1998).
6 There is evidence of this, e.g. among Chinese workers in Hong Kong.

References

Batley, R. and Larbi, G. (1999) The Role of Government in Adjusting Economies, Paper 41, University of Birmingham.

Boston, J., Martin, J., Pallot, J. and Walsh, P. (1996) Public Management, The New Zealand Model, Oxford, Oxford University Press.

Burrows, R. and Loader, B. (eds) (1994) Towards a Post-Fordist Welfare State? London, Routledge.

Child, J. and Faulkner, D. (1998) Strategies of Co-operation: managing alliances, networks and joint ventures, Oxford, Oxford University Press.

Doz, Y.L. and Hamel, G. (1998) Alliance Advantage: the art of creating value through partnering, Boston, Harvard Business School Press.

Ferlie, E., Pettigrew, A., Ashburner, L. and Fitzgerald, L. (1996) The New Public Management in Action, Oxford, Oxford University Press.

Flynn, N. (1999) Miracle to Meltdown in Asia: business, government and society, Oxford, Oxford University Press.

Flynn, N. and Strehl, F. (1996) Public Sector Management in Europe, London, Prentice-Hall.

Hampden-Turner, C. and Trompenaars, F. (1993) The Seven Cultures of Capitalism, New York, Doubleday.

Hilderbrand, M.E. and Grindle, M.S. (1997) Building Sustainable Capacity in the Public Sector. In Grindle, M.S. (ed.) Getting Good Government, Boston, Harvard Institute for International Development.

Hofstede, G. (1980) Culture's Consequences, Beverly Hills, Sage.

Hofstede, G. (1991) Cultures and Organizations, Maidenhead, McGraw Hill.

Hood, C. (1996) Exploring Variations in Public Management Reforms in the 1980s. In Bekke, H.A.G.M., Perry, J.L. and Toonen, T.A.J. (eds) Civil Service Systems in Comparative Perspective, Bloomington, University of Indiana Press.

Jesudason, J.V. (1996) Malaysia: the Syncretic State. In Rodan, G. (ed.) Political Oppositions in Industrialising Asia, London, Routledge.

Kelsey, J. (1995) Economic Fundamentalism, London, Pluto.

Kickert, W. (1995) Public governance in the Netherlands: an alternative to Anglo-American Managerialism, Administration and Society, 28 (1).

Kiggundu, M. (1998) Civil Service Reforms: limping into the twenty-first century. In Minogue, M., Polidano, C., Hulme, D. (eds) Beyond the New Public Management, London, Edward Elgar.

Lijphart (1985) Consociational Democracy, mimeo.

Lynn, L. (1998) The New Public Management: how to transform a theme into a legacy, Public Administration Review, 58 (3): 231–237.

McCourt, W. and Minogue, M. (eds) (2001) The Internationalisation of Public Management: reinventing the Third World State, Cheltenham, Edward Elgar.

Peters, B.G. (1996) The Future of Governing: four emerging models, Lawrence, KS, Kansas University Press.

Pollitt, C. and Bouckaert, G. (2000) Public Management Reform, Oxford, Oxford University Press.

Walsh, K. (1995) Public Services and Market Mechanisms: competition, contracting, and the New Public Management, Basingstoke, Macmillan.

Chapter 5

The New Public Management, modernization and institutional change

Disruptions, disjunctures and dilemmas

Janet Newman

Introduction

This chapter explores the interrelationship between the NPM and the modernization programme of the Labour government as it is being played out in the UK. There are significant points of continuity between the neo-liberal approach to public sector reform and that of 'New Labour', despite some differences of language and practice (see Hughes and Newman 1999; Newman 2000; Newman forthcoming). But the interface between NPM and modernization produces key tensions, which are played out in public service organizations as they seek to accommodate new definitions of role and purpose. This chapter traces themes and issues that highlight the tensions or points of disruption within modernization, the potential disjunctures between modernization and the NPM and the dilemmas for public managers which these produce.

To explore these tensions, the chapter focuses on the discourses of NPM and of modernization. A focus on discourses allows us to study shifts in language, practice and relations of power and the way in which these might be linked to tensions in the process of institutional change. Discourse analysis encompasses a wide range of theoretical orientations and methodological approaches (Grant *et al.* 1998). For the purposes of this chapter I view discourses as hierarchies of knowledge and expertise that legitimate the reordering of relationships within organizations, and between organizations and their various stakeholders. The discourses with which I am concerned are *contingent*: that is, they are formed within particular historical moments and are articulated through the relationships between organizations and their political and economic environments. The election of a Labour government produced a significant shift in public policy discourses, with the articulation of new discourses – joined-up government, social exclusion, evidence-based policy, Best Value, public involvement and a raft of others – interacting with the older discourses of managerialism, efficiency, quality and consumerism, which had become dominant during the Thatcher and Major administrations. A shift in discourse produces new logics of appropriate action, which are disseminated through policy networks, become embedded in government guidelines and legislation and are institutionalized through inspection and audit regimes. New discursive practices are adopted by organizations in order to establish or retain legitimacy in a changing policy climate. These in turn produce shifts in power and authority within organizations; different discourses are associated with different organizational regimes that constitute actors in particular ways, which preference particular forms of judgement ('decisional calculus') and which are based on particular forms of power and knowledge.

NPM as an unfinished project: organizational disjunctures and dilemmas

Old and new discourse will coexist uneasily during programmes of reform, leading to tensions as they are played out within organizations. The idea that there has been a wholesale shift from 'old' public administration, characterized by bureaucracy and hierarchy, to a 'new' public management characterized by efficiency, responsiveness and flexibility, has been challenged (Clarke and Newman 1997: Chapter 3; Lowndes 1997). Narratives of change structured around clear oppositions between past and present, or 'old and new', present an oversimplified view of change in at least two important respects. First, there may be differences between rhetoric and reality: that is, between what is described in official documents and what happens on the ground. This means that we can 'over-read' the extent and embeddedness of change, and underestimate important points of continuity with past regimes. Second, simple narratives of change that imply a general shift from the 'old' to the 'new' tend to tidy away some of the complexity and messiness of change. What is rather more interesting is to explore the way in which different elements of new and old are packaged and repackaged to produce organizational forms in which multiple regimes are overlaid on each other.

The 1980s and early 1990s, for example, are associated with the subordination of professional regimes to a new managerial regime which prioritized economic forms of judgement over other criteria of action. The growing pre-eminence of 'business' discourse in the public sector in the 1980s led to widespread programmes of restructuring into business units, with new logics of appropriate action based on business planning, performance management and devolved financial management. These were overlaid on older corporate and professional hierarchies, producing tensions between criteria of action based on securing the competitive position of the business unit and criteria based on the delivery of corporate or professional goals. The rise of NPM, then, led not to a complete closure around a new paradigm but to an unstable settlement between bureau-professional power and the new managerialism (Clarke and Newman 1997). Significant tensions operated between bureaucratic and consumerist models of accountability, between political centralization and managerial devolution, and between old, neo-Taylorist styles of management and the new managerial focus on culture, excellence and entrepreneurship (Newman 2000). Managers in the public domain did not have an unfettered 'right to manage', free from political interference, because of the nature of accountability and the political process itself (Lewis 1997). Many of the dilemmas that organizations had to work with stemmed from oscillations between different political imperatives, or from contradictory performance measures flowing from different government departments. Tensions also arose from the incomplete closure around the goals and values underpinning NPM. Many workers expressed discomfort at what they felt to be the erosion of public service and professional values. Others, however, welcomed the 'modernizing' thrust of change, viewing it as a source of innovation and a potential challenge to the paternalism, protectionism and parochialism that had characterized the 'old' public sector.

Disrupting the paradigm? NPM and modernization

The election of a Labour government in 1997 signalled a shift in the political terrain. Both the emerging policy agenda and the programme of institutional reform were underpinned by a *discourse of modernization*. Modernization was presented as a necessary process of updating services to match the expectations of modern consumers (who, for example, expect services to be organized around the convenience of those using them) and to meet the business requirements of the 'modern' world (for example enabling public services to draw on information technology (IT) advancements to deliver performance improvements). But modernization implied a deeper set of reforms in the relationship between the economy, state and civil society. It offered a particular conception of citizenship (empowered as active, and more participating, subjects); of work (as the source of opportunity for the 'socially excluded'); of community (non-antagonistic and homogeneous); and of a modern nation (setting out Britain's place in the changing global economy). It links a search for a distinctive political project – the elusive 'third way' – with a process of institutional reform.

There were many points of continuity between NPM and modernization. Ministerial speeches and policy documents about the public sector appeared to offer a modernized view of NPM that harnessed many of its rhetorics, narratives and strategies to Labour's political project. There was a continued focus on market mechanisms and public–private partnerships as key levers of reform. The public sector was still encouraged to look to the business world for models of good practice in a drive to inculcate entrepreneurial values and import dynamic styles of leadership. There was a continued drive to subordinate professional power bases – in health, education, probation, social work and elsewhere – to managerial forms of control. But despite significant areas of continuity, the discourse of '*modern* managerialism' suggests some subtle shifts. First, although the NPM was predominantly concerned with institutional reform (introducing competitive tendering, quasi-markets and purchaser–provider splits), modern managerialism was presented as a set of tools and techniques that could be captured to help achieve the policy outcomes on education, social exclusion and welfare reform at the heart of Labour's political agenda. Modern managerialism was presented as being about delivering long-term effectiveness rather than short-term efficiency. The reform of financial arrangements and the introduction of the 3-year comprehensive spending review introduced a longer planning cycle for public service organizations, linked to outcome-based goals and targets. Whereas NPM was focused on the benefits of competition, modern managerialism appeared to place more emphasis on collaboration in which the political goal of 'joined-up government' was to be matched by the managerial techniques of building partnerships and strategic alliances between agencies in the public, private and voluntary sectors. There was a stronger emphasis on capturing the support of public service staff to ensure long-term change, alongside a continued emphasis on performance. Labour has also emphasized the need for greater participation by citizens as well as by users in policy development and organizational decision-making.

These themes in the modernization agenda imply possible shifts in the logics of decision-making and in organizational and inter-organizational relations. In what follows I have labelled such shifts as 'emergent', in contrast with the 'dominant' organizational regime of NPM. The label 'emergent' does not imply some organic and evolutionary process by which one regime will be displaced by another. As I shall argue in the final section, fundamental shifts in relations of power are required for an emergent pattern to become realized.

Managers as partners in delivering policy outcomes

The character of New Labour's social policy agenda means that a modernized public sector is critical to the government's capacity to achieve its goals. The public sector becomes the agent through which the new policy agenda can be delivered rather than the main target of the reform programme itself. This suggests a shift away from 'organizational effectiveness' to 'policy effectiveness' as a criterion in strategic decision-making, and a stronger focus on the role of public managers in delivering policy outcomes. The White Paper *Modernising Government* (Cabinet Office 1999) contained a number of comments highlighting the limitations of past NPM type reforms. First, the focus on managerial reforms at the expense of policy issues is criticized. Second, the fragmenting effects of (earlier) managerial reforms are viewed as having negative consequences, in that organizations were judged according to their individual achievements rather than on their contribution to an overall 'strategic purpose'. Third, the opening up of sharper lines of separation between policy and management is viewed as limiting the input of managers to the policy process, and the White Paper calls for more 'inclusion' of front-line workers in the shaping of policy (Cabinet Office 1999: paras 4 and 5). This final theme is reflected in other key documents: for example the replacement of the Citizen's Charter programme with the Service First programme (Cabinet Office 1998) and the first report of the Social Exclusion Unit (1998). Policy-making, it was argued, needed to be more 'joined-up' and strategic, meaning that different policies that contribute to a particular issue should be made in a holistic way. This required managers to focus on integrating the delivery of related services by pooling budgets and other resources and by working in partnership across organizational boundaries.

This focus on networks and partnerships was not new. The previous

Conservative governments had introduced public–private partnerships as a means of bringing in new investment into the development of public sector infrastructure and, later, the management of public services. They had set up agencies (such as Training and Enterprise Councils and Urban Development Corporations) which brought together public and private sectors to tackle urban regeneration and economic development at a regional level. The 1980s and 1990s were also characterized by local collaborative developments around crime prevention, anti-drugs initiatives and community policing, and anti-poverty. The drive for partnership working, then, came from different directions. But a distinctive feature of Labour's approach has been the explicit focus on partnership as a way of governing. This focus is evident both in the strength of the partnership rhetoric and in the government's approach to the delivery of public policy, with an emphasis on extending public–private partnerships, on local coordination through a range of zonal initiatives, on better integration between health and social services, and on overcoming departmental barriers in central government. Policy documents repeatedly stressed the need for the integration of policy to address cross-cutting policy agendas, and talked of the need for culture change to overcome barriers to joint working.

In Jessop's terms this expansion was '... not meant to return Britain to a discredited corporatism ... but, rather, to address the real limitations of the market, state and mixed economy as means of dealing with various complex economic, political and social issues' (Jessop 2000: 11). While retaining elements of both market and hierarchy, Labour's emphasis on governing through partnership has been strongest in precisely those areas where it confronts complex policy agendas which previous attempts to solve have failed – in neighbourhood renewal, social exclusion, crime and community safety and other 'wicked issues'. In such areas Labour emphasized the need both for better horizontal integration (partnership working between public sector organizations, voluntary sector bodies and private sector companies) and stronger vertical integration (between central, local and community tiers of government, and between those involved in the shaping of policy and those affected by its delivery). This emphasis reflects concerns about the hierarchical, 'silo' relationships built into the UK system of government and calls for a more 'holistic' approach to governance (Table 5.1).

There are however important points of tension at the interface between 'dominant' and 'emergent' agendas limiting the extent to which new criteria of success and strategic decision-making can be realized. The first lies in the intractable politics of inter- and intra-organizational collaboration. Although the discourse of partnership signifies equality of power, shared values and the establishment of common agendas and goals, the organizational reality tends to be very different. Indeed the discourse itself serves to create an illusory unity that masks the need to engage with the dynamics of divergent inte conflicting goals. The focus on collaboration and inclusive processes direct attention away from proper analysis of the barriers created by ine of power and resources (Huxham 1996; Huxham and Vangen 1996).

Table 5.1 NPM and modernization: strategic decision making

New public management (dominant)	Modernization (emergent)
Organizational goals (survival and success of this organization)	Goals linked to the achievement of policy outcomes
Partnerships developed where these can contribute to the realization of organizational goals; organizational strategy not influenced by partners	Partnerships developed around super-ordinate policy goals
Accountable for organizational performance policy	Accountable for contribution to outcomes
Evaluated through performance indicators and league tables which indicate the performance of the individual organization	Evaluated through 'cross-cutting' performance measures

tension is formed at the point at which the requirement that different organizations continue to produce year-on-year efficiencies meets the requirement that they collaborate to deliver broad political outcomes. Although there have been some attempts to develop 'cross-cutting' performance indicators, the predominant focus of the external reviews of performance is on the efficiency of an organization in delivering whatever happens to be its core business (managing housing stocks, catching criminals or educating young people).

'Joined-up government', then, is likely to remain an aspiration rather than become an established feature of the modernization agenda. This does not however detract from its power as a discourse – a discourse which creates a new inflection for managerialism as a tool for delivering social outcomes through partnership and collaboration, and a welcome release from the narrow organizational focus of NPM. This is already producing important shifts in the languages and practices of public management and is likely to have implications for the reshaping of notions of leadership, strategy and organizational culture on which it draws.

Managers as partners in delivering performance improvements

Whereas NPM saw the market as the main lever for delivering performance improvements, Labour appears to offer a partnership with public sector managers in driving up performance, with privatization as a last resort for organizations unable to deliver.

However, two conflicting discourses are in play in the Labour government's programme of modernizing services. One is that of 'partnership', the other of 'principals and agents'. A partnership discourse is associated with the attempt by government to learn from and draw on developments arising within the public sector, to consult with its staff and include them in the development of policy, and to influence their actions through communication and persuasion rather than the exercise of direct control. A rather different, contractually based set of discourses runs alongside these, designed to ensure that local managers tighten control within organizations in order to ensure the delivery of central government goals and targets. This principal–agent form of relationship, in which local services are the agents mandated to deliver government policy but under conditions of tight monitoring and control, is strongly associated with Labour's attempt to ensure that key electoral pledges made when entering office (e.g. reducing hospital waiting lists, cutting class sizes) are delivered.

A partnership model is implied in the way in which Labour accommodated concerns arising from within public services and incorporated these into its modernization programme. These included the shift away from compulsory competitive tendering (CCT) in local government towards a Best-Value regime, the increasing focus on primary care in health, and the commitment to redress inequalities in the standards of health care offered in different regions. The 1997 White Paper on the NHS proposed an evolutionary model of change rather than major restructuring. Its language of 'going with the grain' of emerging patterns of change (DoH 1997: 5) implicitly acknowledges the staff of the NHS as an organizational and social force that needed to be accommodated in the reform programme. Poole (2000) suggests that Labour's language has been one of partnership and cooperation, with new pay and incentive packages for nurses and the promise of consultation and involvement the main carrot for the medical profession. Images of a new partnership between government and local government have been repeatedly used by Hilary Armstrong, the Minister responsible for Local Government, for example in the introduction of Best Value.

The initial assumptions of cooperation and partnership between government and public sector professionals were short lived. By July 1999 Blair was talking of the 'forces of conservatism', which he saw as blocking the progress of change, and of the 'scars on his back' produced by the unwillingness of the public sector to innovate (speech to The Venture Capitalists Association, July). Such representations mean that, despite the language of partnership, government has also drawn extensively on rather different models of change to ensure that 'agents' – organizations in the dispersed field of service delivery networks – deliver what the 'principal' – government – intends. A plethora of performance indicators, targets and standards have flowed from government, all reinforced by the growth of inspection and audit. Clarke et al. (2000) locate the growth of audit in the neo-liberal reforms of the 1980s, arguing that the new dispersed state form, in which provider organizations had enlarged autonomy for operational management, implied new issues of control for the centre. Labour's approach to modernizing public services such as education, health, social services and probation is based on strengthening this external oversight through functionally separate agencies such as the Audit Commission, OfSTED and the SSI (Social Services Inspectorate), all set up under previous administrations. It has also established a new Commission for Care Standards in each region to regulate social care in domiciliary and residential settings. The role of the Audit Commission has continued to expand, with new Housing and Best Value Inspectorates having been established under its aegis. A new body – Her Majesty's Inspector of Probation – has been introduced. The multiplication of inspection regimes has been accompanied by additional powers for Secretaries of State in education, social services and elsewhere to remove services from those bodies receiving poor inspection reports. The Commission for Health Improvement has power to intervene in the running of Primary Care Trusts alleged to be performing poorly. OfSTED inspections are backed up by powers for the Secretary of State to remove functions from LEAs (Local Education Authorities) or to close schools and reopen them under the Fresh Start initiative.

The development of audit and inspection is linked to a wider discourse of failure and the growth of threats and sanctions against organizations deemed to be performing poorly. The language of threat and coercion is now common:

> If you (local government) are unwilling or unable to work to the modern agenda, then the government will have to look to other partners to take on your role.
>
> (Blair 1998: 22)

> The choice is not a new NHS or the current NHS. It is the new NHS or no NHS
>
> (Dobson 1999: 18)

The division of local authorities, schools and other services into 'heroes' (or beacons for others to follow) or 'villains' ('failing' services) lays the foundation for the exercise of additional powers for Secretaries of State. Services deemed to be failing are required to produce action plans and demonstrate measurable improvements within a specific time period. Where these are not delivered, additional sanctions are available. For example, the 'fresh start' scheme for schools enabled secretaries of state to impose 'special measures' and ultimately to close 'failing' schools and reopen them under new leadership and with additional resources.[1] In the Health Service the language of partnership and 'going with the grain' gave way to more coercive strategies as the government became frustrated with the slow change. In March 2000 it was announced that Blair would take 'personal charge' of the government's efforts to improve the NHS by chairing a new cabinet committee to monitor NHS improvements in England after admitting failure to deliver election pledges. The extra resources were set against new measures to redress failure by withholding cash if performance targets were missed, and accompanied by the threat to replace managers by 'hit squads' of managers from successful units.[2] Blair spelled out a much harsher message for health service workers than that underpinning the earlier 'partnership' model, calling for a new realism on the part of health professionals and demanding that they 'strip out unnecessary demarcations,

Table 5.2 NPM and modernization: power and control

NPM: dominant mode of power and control	Modernization: emergent model of power and control
'Hands off' control through contracts and framework documents	'Hands on' control through tight performance regime
High levels of devolution to managers	Attempts to standardize practice across geographical differences
Competition used to drive up performance	Standards and targets used to drive up performance
Privatization where performance does not meet required standard	Privatization or direct intervention where performance does not meet required standard
Universal incentives and levers of control	Differentiated incentives and levers of control

introduce more flexible training and working practices' (Blair, reported in *The Guardian*, 23 March 2000: 23) (Table 5.2).

The process of auditing and inspection is underpinned by an assumption that subjects will regulate their own actions to deliver the desired results, with the 'perverse' consequence that they may prioritize performance in areas where results are likely to be measured, at the expense of other activities. Such considerations may lead organizations to focus their energies on the production of discourses of success – what Corvellec (1995) terms 'narratives of achievement' – to ensure survival in a competitive environment, at the possible expense of more realistic assessments of weaknesses and strengths.

The increasing imperative for agencies to meet centrally determined standards of performance is also likely to invoke the neo-Taylorist form of managerialism. At the same time strong leadership, which resonates with the 'excellence' discourse, is viewed as the key to success and a solution for 'failing' organizations (e.g. schools). The tension between these different agendas reflects some of the tensions within NPM. However the implications are different: a narrow focus on organizational performance linked to neo-Taylorist styles of management is likely to undermine attempts to address other parts of the modernization agenda, especially the theme of 'joined-up' government and enhanced user and citizen involvement in decision-making.

Managers as partners with the public

A further disjuncture between the NPM and the modernization agenda arises from the goal of engaging citizen and users in more active forms of decision-making. Public participation is central to the Labour government's programme of modernization. The White Paper 'Modernising Local Government' is tellingly subtitled 'In touch with the people', and requires local authorities to 'reconnect' with the communities they serve by giving local people a 'bigger say' in the way in which councils run services. The Best Value regime requires local authorities and other organizations to consult with users, local businesses and the wider community in setting service standards and planning performance improvements. Health authorities are required to consult the public on significant changes to health provision, and the creation of NHS primary care groups is intended to enhance public involvement in decision-making. Many of the mandatory plans introduced by the Labour government – for example on education, health improvement, policing – require consultation as part of the planning process. Evidence of consultation has been a requirement in bids for funding under many of the Labour government's programmes, while representatives of 'the public' have been included in the governance arrangements of Primary Care groups and other new institutions.

This emphasis on participation can be linked to a range of developments in public policy and management before the election of the Labour government in 1997, of which the most significant was undoubtedly the consumerist ethos of the 1980s. This was influenced by changes in public management (the importation of business techniques into the public sector), by government reforms (e.g. the Citizen's Charter of John Major's administration) and by the rise of user movements mediated by professional doctrines of 'user empowerment' in some services. Throughout the 1980s and 1990s the public were becoming involved in local decision-making forums and in the planning and commissioning of health and social care; tenants were involved in the running of housing associations and in new deliberative forums designed to enhance democratic decision-making. The new government built on and extended this agenda, both by encouraging an emphasis on participation and by incorporating it as a legislative requirement in many areas. In some policy documents the nature of the consultation is tightly prescribed (e.g. Best Value user satisfaction surveys) whereas in others there is ambiguity about what consultation means, leading to considerable variation in both the scale and depth of participation (Leach and Wingfield 1999).

Why has New Labour placed so much emphasis on public participation? A number of different themes can be traced in the discourse, including those of rebuilding trust between citizens and government, improving the policy process and enhancing the legitimacy of government and local government decisions. Public consultation on local authority service plans and performance is viewed as an important means of continuing the shift of power away from the providers and towards community charge payers and service users (DETR 1998a,b), whereas community participation is viewed as an essential element of neighbourhood renewal as well as a means of helping overcome social exclusion (Social Exclusion Unit 1998). Politically, participation is viewed as providing greater flexibility and sophistication than the blunt instrument of party voting (Mulgan 1994) and as a way of responding to issues of social differentiation and social exclusion (SEU 2000).

Public participation provides a plural and differentiated set of connections between state, service deliverers, users, citizens and other stakeholders. As such it appears to support the proposition that we are witnessing a shift from a 'hierarchy' to a 'network' form of governance. Public involvement is viewed as a means of building social capital and thus strengthening civil society. Democratic innovation is viewed as a means of responding to the fragmentation of authority and the problem of accountability in complex societies (Hirst 2000; Peters 2000). It suggests a broadening of focus by government beyond institutional concerns to encompass the involvement of 'civil society' in the process of governance (Table 5.3).

However, the emphasis on enhanced participation by the public raises significant challenges to the institutional practices of both the 'old' public service professional regime (based on bureaucratic power) and the institutions of the NPM (based on managerial power). Innovation in public participation and involvement has the capacity to open up new spaces which can be captured by user groups, voluntary organizations and community bodies seeking to claim a stronger role in decision-making. As a consequence, they have often elicited deep resistance on the part of many professionals, managers and local authority councillors, some of whom have rediscovered the tenets of liberalism in order to question the 'representativeness' of new voices. What is at stake is an uneasy configuration of political notions of representation, based on liberal democracy, and managerial concepts of ensuring representative sampling in the new

Table 5.3 NPM and modernization: relations with the public

NPM: Dominant logic of decision making	Modernization: emergent logic of decision making
Managers free to make decisions within the legislative and policy frameworks set by politicians	Managers the agents for delivering the wishes or aspirations of citizens or users
Organizations designed to deliver efficiency through structures linking common function or forms of professional expertise	Organizations designed around the concept of efficiency of use (e.g. ease of access, availability of services, integration of services to localities or client groups)
Strong organizational boundaries, weak networks	Open organizational boundaries, well-developed networks
Relations with consumers governed through limited feedback mechanisms (e.g. complaints procedures, market research)	Relations with consumers governed through their participation in service design and planning
Relations with the public governed through the (weakened) institutions of representative democracy	Relations with the public governed through participative or dialogic alongside representative democracy

technologies of participation. Neither of these models of representation deals adequately with the politics of diversity. The forms of public dialogue and community involvement which are emerging in public management typically rest on ungendered and unracialized conceptions of 'the public' and non-antagonistic images of 'community' (Hughes and Mooney 1998). The focus in the modernization agenda on enhancing participation and highlights the importance of viewing the 'public realm' as itself contested (Fraser 1997) and raises difficult political questions about the relationship between managerial action and political judgement. Such questions cannot be resolved at the level of the organization, however sophisticated the new technologies of participation which are developed.

Conclusion: towards a new organizational regime?

Different forms of explanation might be offered for the possible limits on the extent to which the new agenda may become embedded. One is technical: How far can organizations develop and deploy effective techniques of partnership working and public participation? The evidence is that some are well able to do so, but that innovation in these areas currently remains largely on the margins, rather than the mainstream, of public sector practice. This leads directly to the second limiting factor: the challenge which new forms of practice presents to traditional institutions and to the relations of power on which they are based. The issue here is not whether the techniques are available to pursue the new agenda, but whether there is a will to inscribe them into the way in which organizations are governed. The themes of innovation, integration and participation all challenge established power bases, and are likely to be the focus of organizational resistance.

A third concerns the interplay of tensions within the new agenda itself. The modernization agenda is likely to replicate some of the internal tensions of NPM, especially those between devolution and flexibility on the one hand (required to enable organizations to be innovative and entrepreneurial) and the requirements of central control to ensure standards and performance targets are delivered on the other. It may also open up new lines of tension. The focus on 'joined up government' and inter-organizational collaboration requires new styles of leadership which are not well represented within the public sector. The capacity for managers both to deliver business success for their particular organization and to collaborate around the more diffuse goals and outcomes involved in tackling 'cross-cutting issues' may be limited. The focus on achieving the long-term outcomes required by New Labour's policy agenda goes against the grain of delivering short-term efficiencies.

The new agenda offers many points of engagement – even excitement – for managers who felt themselves to be constrained by the goals of previous regimes. But it is already clear that in reorganizing services to tackle the wider agendas of health, social exclusion, family support and so on, the 'old' agendas of meeting short-term targets and efficiency savings cannot be ignored. It is also clear that entrepreneurialism and innovation needs to be set against a renewed focus on ethics and probity. New patterns of accountability for outcomes sit uneasily with organizationally focused inspection and audit regimes that retain a strong focus on more limited conceptions of accountability and that emphasize the need to limit risk-taking behaviour.

The rhetoric of change assumes that the earlier goals of NPM have been accomplished: that the public sector has been transformed around the goals of efficiency, and that competition and market mechanisms have broken the power of the public sector as a monopoly provider of services. But this is not the government's view. Its social goals – evident in policies on health, the environment, education, social exclusion and so on – sit rather uncomfortably alongside its economic goals which require an extension of the traditional NPM agenda combined with Labour's focus on standardization and performance improvement. More effective management is unlikely to resolve the tensions between economic and social goals. Few organizations can command the resources, even working in partnership, to address the real causes of ill-health or social exclusion, even if they could agree on what the causes were. Indeed, the managerial strategies required to deliver the continued strands of the NPM agenda (e.g. viewing labour as a flexible commodity) may actually exacerbate some of the social problems which New Labour is anxious to address.

The discourse of modernization is still emergent and unstable: it is the focus of continued social and political agency in the struggle to reshape a new settlement. The actual form of modernization is likely to be forged through the relative success or failure of different tiers and sphere of governance as they struggle to win institutional legitimacy (Cooper 1998). For example 'performance' is likely to be the focus of institutional conflict between different tiers of government, as the strong drive to centralize clashes with the rhetoric of local control, flexibility and innovation. The outcomes of the reform agenda will depend on the working through of such contradictions and the shaping of new alliances between established political formations with those seeking to shape a new political agenda. It also depends on the playing out of tensions between the social and economic goals of the Labour government.

This chapter has focused on the interaction between the discourses of modernization and of NPM. But it is important not to view discourse as part of a deterministic model of change. Discourses are given meaning within organizations, as actors learn new languages, acquire new knowledge and skills, and take on new roles and identities. That is, discourses are *constitutive*. But not all new discourses are 'successful'. People can learn to speak new languages, and deploy them in strategic forms of action, without internalizing the values or assumptions which they embody. Discourses can also be appropriated by those with 'alternative' agendas. The disjunctures, disruptions and dilemmas which this paper has discussed create the spaces in which the discourse of modernization may be reshaped and attached to counter discourses. For example, it may yet be possible for user, citizen or 'community' groups to appropriate the discourses of innovation, participation and accountability and to use them to challenge the managerial form in which they are currently embedded. But the political tensions within the modernization agenda are partially masked by the legacy of NPM and the organizational and management theories on which it draws. The discourses and practices of NPM apparently neutralize and displace the conflicts between different agendas (social, political, economic) and between the requirements of different stakeholders (government, citizens, users, 'communities'). A modern public service, then, is likely to be one in which a series of conflicts must be managed, contradictory imperatives balanced, and new and old agendas reconciled. Whether the models offered by the tools and technologies of NPM can enable public service organizations to fulfil these roles is another question.

Notes

1   The model of change here is based on the presumed power of heroic leadership: the capacity of individuals to transform organisations by motivating staff and putting in place new management systems.
2   Such 'super-heads', however, resigned in the first months of 2000 (*The Guardian*, 15 March 2000 4). These resignations, and the publicity surrounding them, raised concerns about the capacity of individuals to treat the symptoms of more structural problems in the education system by business recipes of organisational turnaround.

Bibliography

Blair, T. (1998) *Leading the Way: a new vision for local government*. London, Institute for Public Policy and Research.
Cabinet Office (1998) *Service First – the new charter programme*. London, The Stationery Office.
Cabinet Office (1999) *Modernising Government*. London, The Stationery Office.
Clarke, J. and Newman, J. (1997) *The Managerial State: power, politics and ideology in the remaking of social welfare*. London, Sage.
Clarke, J., Gewitz, S., Hughes, G. and Humphrey, J. (2000) 'Guarding the public interest? The rise of audit and inspection'. In Clarke, J., Gewitz, S. and McLaughlin, E., eds, *New Managerialism, New Welfare?* London, Sage.
Cooper, D. (1998) *Governing Out of Order: space, time and the politics of belonging*. Rivers Oram Press.
Corvellec, H. (1995) *Stories of Achievement: narrative features of organisational performance*. Malmo, Lund University Press.
Department of the Environment, Transport and the Regions (1998a) *Modern Local Government – in touch with the people*. London, The Stationery Office.
Department of the Environment, Transport and the Regions (1998b) *Enhancing Public Participation*. London, The Stationery Office.
Department of Health (1997) *The New NHS: modern – dependable*. Cm 3807. London, The Stationery Office.
Department of Health (1998) *Modernising Social Services: promoting independence, improving protection, raising standards*. Cm 4169. London, The Stationery Office.
Fraser, N. (1997) *Justice Interruptus: critical reflections on the 'postsocialist' condition*. London, Routledge.
Grant, D., Keenoy, T. and Oswick, C., eds (1998) *Discourse and Organisation*. London, Sage.
Hirst, P. (2000) 'Democracy and Governance'. In Pierre, J., ed., *Debating Governance*. Oxford, Oxford University Press.
Hughes, G. and Mooney, G. (1998) 'Community'. In Hughes, G., ed., *Imagining Welfare Futures*. London, Routledge.

Hughes, M. and Newman, J. (1999) 'From new public management to new labour: from "new to modern" '. Paper presented to the *Third International Symposium on Public Management*, University of Aston, March.

Huxham, C., ed. (1996) *Creating Collaborative Advantage*. London, Sage.

Huxham, C. and Vangen, S. (1996) 'Working together: key themes in the management of relationships between public and non profit organisations'. *International Journal of Public Sector Management*, 9, 5–17.

Jessop, B. (2000) 'Governance Failure'. In Stoker, G., ed., *The New Politics of British Urban Governance*. Basingstoke, Macmillan.

Leach, S. and Wingfield, M. (1999) 'Public participation and the democratic renewal agenda: prioritisation or marginalisation?' *Local Government Studies*, 25 (4), Winter.

Lewis, D. (1997) *Hidden Agendas: politics, law and disorder*. London, Hamish Hamilton.

Lowndes, V. (1997) 'We are learning to accommodate mess: four propositions about managing change in local government', *Public Policy and Administration*, 12 (2), Summer.

Mulgan, G. (1994) *Politics in an Anti-political Age*. Cambridge, Polity Press.

Newman, J. (2000) 'Beyond the new public management? Modernising public services'. In Clarke, J., Gewitz, S. and McLaughlin, E., eds, *New Managerialism, New Welfare?* London, Sage.

Newman, J. (forthcoming) 'Modernising governance: reshaping the public sphere', London, Sage

Peters, G. (2000) 'Comparative politics'. In Pierre, J., ed., *Debating Governance: authority, steering and democracy*. Oxford, Oxford University Press.

Poole, L. (2000) New Labour, Managerialism and the National Health Service. In Clarke, J., Gewitz, S. and McLaughlin, E., eds, *New Managerialism, New Welfare?* London, Sage.

School of Public Policy, University of Birmingham (1999) *Cross-cutting Issues in Public Policy and Public Service*. DETR.

Social Exclusion Unit (1998) *Bringing Britain Together: a national strategy for neighbourhood renewal*. Cm 4045. London, The Stationery Office.

Social Exclusion Unit (2000) *National Strategy for Neighbourhood Renewal: a framework for consultation*, London: Social Exclusion Unit.

Part II

The New Public Management in action

Chapter 6

Public service professionals and the New Public Management

Control of the professions in the public services

Jane Broadbent and Richard Laughlin

Introduction

At the beginning of the twentieth century the concern with efficiency promoted by the Progressive era led to a series of developments that have come to be known as 'classical management' techniques. These included attempts to promote the systematization of work using division of labour and standardization with a resulting justification of the role of management and control of working practices. Standardization provided the basis for control techniques such as operations management and, with the aid of accounting, standard costing (Miller and O'Leary 1987). Braverman's (1974) influential, but debated, critique of these management approaches cannot be dismissed lightly. The relevance of Braverman's analysis is that it highlights that the debate about the technical nature of the changes is just one thread of the complex tapestry that surrounds these issues. One of the elements that have been used to control labour is the technology of accounting, and this can be associated with classical management techniques that were developed in the context of attempts to control craft workers but whose contemporary relevance is in the control of professionals. The aim of this chapter is to seek to complement the literature that has looked at the relationship between professionals and managerialism in the broader sense (Exworthy and Halford 1999). To do this we focus on both the use of the technologies of accounting and what we call 'accounting logic' in the processes of management control.

The concern of this chapter is the public service sector in the UK where New Public Management (NPM) has sought to import 'private sector' techniques of management and accounting (Dunleavy and Hood 1994). This, despite a rhetorical appeal to the idea of implementing market-based controls, has included aspects of 'classical management'. Arguably, two key contextual issues affect the extent to which this move might be seen as appropriate or successful. First, many organizations in the public services are complex professional bureaucracies (Mintzberg 1983) characterized by the involvement of a number of professional groups. These groups have a history of relative autonomy over their working practices and often have a great deal of status which gives them power *vis à vis* other stakeholder groups. Second, arguably, the 'outputs' of these organizations (and in effect the professionals who work within them who are subject to these demands) are not easily standardized and measurable. The implications of these factors, we will argue, is that two important elements of the classical management techniques – a clear acceptance of the role of management to control activities and a possibility for standardization, – are missing in many parts of the public services.[1] This is particularly the case where professionals are involved in service delivery.

In order to explore the implications of this, we will first present a heuristic framework for analysis. The framework is derived from models of the ideal types of hierarchies, markets and clans developed by Ouchi (1979, 1980), which provides a way to reflect on the changing configuration of public service delivery. In this context we will seek to define what we mean by professions and to locate more closely the nature of the tasks over which control is sought. We will next use the Ouchi framework to reflect on the changes that NPM has brought before considering 'accounting logic' and the tension between this and the clan approach to control. Finally, we will explore the implications of the application of 'accounting logic' for professionals and the services they provide.

Contextual changes and a framework for analysis

The changes that have taken place over the last twenty years have come to be known as the NPM (see, for example, Hood 1991, 1995). Although the early rhetoric was to implement *market* approaches to increase efficiency, the changes were more complex and not always quite in keeping with the *laissez-faire* of the market.[2] The election of the New Labour government in 1997 brought some readjustment to the modes of organizing. The thrust of policy has been directed to both the building of public–private partnerships and the desire to ensure a defined set of outputs for the various services. The Labour government's strategy is based on the notion of 'modernizing government'. What is key is a view that it does not matter who produces the services, provided they are of an appropriate standard.

The framework of organizational controls developed by Ouchi (1979, 1980) provides a heuristic to allow some reflection on the changes of NPM. We use the framework, not with the intention that it should be seen as comprehensively descriptive, but to provide three 'ideal types', of market, hierarchy and clan, which characterize different approaches to control (see also Osborne 1997).

Ouchi followed Williamson's (1975) analysis of the mechanisms used for co-ordinating economic decisions. Williamson suggested, in turn, using the work of Coase (1937), that the issue of costs was important in deciding whether transactions should be coordinated through the medium of the market or through an organization. Individuals in situations of complexity and uncertainty are assumed to have bounded rationality and behave opportunistically, making contracts costly. The extent of the cost will depend on the level of the uncertainty and complexity surrounding the transactions and the possibility of using the skills and assets in the transactions in other situations. If complexity is high and there is no alternative use for the skills and assets, the transaction costs are likely to be high and an organization (or hierarchy) would form to minimize costs.

Ouchi, in exploring the problem of achieving cooperation between individuals with objectives which might not be the same (Ouchi 1979: 833), extended the categorization differentiating between markets, hierarchies and clans. Two elements define the most appropriate form of control; the extent of the knowledge of the transformation process and the ability to measure outputs.

- In a hierarchy, which can be associated with the traditional bureaucracy,[3] there is likely to be a focus on the *process*. The rules and regulations that characterize a bureaucracy are likely to relate more to the nature of the transformation process (although this does not suggest that there will be no concern with the nature of the outputs).
- In a market, the main focus must be on the *output* that is the subject of exchange. This means that for a market to work there must be sufficient information to facilitate exchange and for the norm of reciprocity to prevail. In essence this requires information about prices as well as a multiplicity of buyers and sellers. In a situation where there is good knowledge of the transformational process and the ability to define and price outputs is high, then there is opportunity for either market or hierarchical organization of the exchange process.
- Where there is neither an ability to measure outputs nor to specify behaviour through knowledge of the transaction process then Ouchi suggests the clan becomes a means to organize. A clan is seen to coordinate behaviour through ritual and shared norms and values. Arguably the profession is an example of clan control.

Ouchi and Williamson both recognized that the categorizations they offered were not necessarily neat ones. Ouchi, in particular, recognized that all elements of control would be found in all organizations and that the issue is one of the relative emphasis on the different elements.

What do we mean by a profession?

Like all heuristics, the Ouchi framework offers some elucidation and is in this respect helpful in focusing on the nature of the tasks involved and the implications of these; however, there are also elements that require more explanation. Associating clan control with professional control leaves some issues about what is meant by professionals unaddressed. This is a well-debated area with little resolution, but some well-defined and diverse positions[4] are clear. On one level, our adoption of the elements of the Ouchi framework means that our approach to the nature of professions is linked to a set of particular types of tasks. Thus, we are concerned with those who carry out activities that have outputs that are difficult to measure and processes that are difficult to define. In this sense we are accepting a 'task-based' definition of professionals as reflected in the work of Jamous and Peloille (1970), who differentiate the technical element of a task from that element which remains indeterminate. This approach has been criticized for a number of reasons. Who is to define what is indeterminate for example? Equally, the question has been asked whether all those groups that see themselves as professionals are the same – note the different status between lawyers and teachers for example. This has led some to argue that the whole notion of professionalism rests on the ability of a group to retain a monopoly over the area of competence that is attributed to them (Larson 1977). In this view then, the notion of professionalism is one that relates to the control of the knowledge and the access to that knowledge. In that respect certain groups may have differential power that allows them particular privilege. For example, Witz (1992) provides a thoughtful argument about the relationship of patriarchy and professionalism. Important as these arguments are, our concern is with the control of a particular type of task, and the fact that these are carried out by groups who seek to label themselves as 'professionals' is in some respects incidental. Our main analysis will therefore take what some might see as a somewhat unproblematic approach to the label professional. However, adopting this view alone would lose some of the richness that recognition of other approaches to the study of professionalism might produce. Thus, our argument recognizes that professions can be seen as providing a mode of controlling occupations (Johnson 1972), and that many of the groups over which control is being sought are ones that have been remarkably successful in retaining their autonomy (Freidson 1970a,b). This underlines the significance of the battle for control in these areas of activity and provides the impetus for looking more carefully at the control of these tasks. We also recognize (following Exworthy and Halford 1999) that professionals themselves are implicated in management processes – they act as managers in many situations. We recognize the irony that it is accountants, themselves a professional group, who are proponents of the technology of accounting that is used to control. However, our main focus remains on the nature of the technologies of control, rather than on who is doing the controlling.

Developments in management control

Early developments in management thought were associated with hierarchies. Whereas Coase and Williamson were seeking to find an analytical framework for understanding the formation of organizations, writers in management were seeking to provide a normative framework to guide management. In the early part of the twentieth century the techniques that have come to be known as 'classical management' emerged. Given these techniques were organizationally based it is unsurprising that they were associated with a hierarchical approach. The approaches were not necessarily new and novel developments, but their configuration and dissemination by certain key advocates was significant. Central among the theorists was F.W. Taylor, whose ideas on scientific management have been so influential, although the nature of that impact is often debated.

Taylor's (1947) insights were informed by his time spent working as a supervisor and were concerned with task management and control of the workforce. His approach was based on techniques for standardization of process. He sought to ensure that there was specialization by all concerned in the production process and this led to the split between conception and execution of tasks and hence the split of worker and manager. Braverman's argument that this was a degradation of work is based on the alienating tendencies of this approach for the workforce.

Although the detail of Braverman's argument has been well debated (Wood 1982), undoubtedly the key tenets of standardization and division of labour engendered provided a potential for management control. Equally, the belief in a manager's right to manage, enshrined in the notion of the split of conception and execution, has been influential. Miller and O'Leary (1987) provide a persuasive account of the linkage between scientific management and the use of standard costing techniques as a means by which to create the 'governable person'. In essence the accounting techniques of standard costing allowed the quantification of output and allowed management to peruse results from a distance. Thus managers did not need to apply direct supervision to control the workforce. These techniques are well used today and find a place on the syllabi of the professional examinations of all the UK accounting bodies. Thus the role of the accounting technology of standard costing provides a method of control for use where outputs can be specified and tasks broken into definable costable elements. More importantly, the fact that this mode of control is available provides an incentive to reconstitute tasks to enable the adoption of this type of control approach.

Our argument is that although the changes in the public services are ones that have claimed to move away from bureaucratic structures to those that are market driven, this is not the case. Instead, the changes introduced have similarities to those Tayloristic changes to control of the work processes that are described above and have been centrally concerned with control of task and process. At the same time there has been an attempt to define outputs and tie resourcing to the achievement of different output levels. Thus, the changes have introduced *both* tighter hierarchical and market controls, undermining professional or clan control.

Changes in the public services

Bureaucracies and clan control

As Ouchi argued, all organizations tend to have elements of all types of control, albeit with differing emphases. Public services, arguably, prior to the raft of changes called NPM, tended to adopt hierarchical bureaucratic structures. However, they did not necessarily accompany this by the tight task control provided by standardization and costing of outputs. Instead they relied upon a control based on rules of process for many, but not all, workers, and management control of professionals was not seen as appropriate. Hierarchical control was, thus, aligned with a clan control of the professionals. Mintzberg (1983) calls these organizations professional bureaucracies, and health and education are prime examples. Although the possibility of accounting and task control being used to implement tight management control was enabled by the bureaucratic structure, it was not operationalized prior to NPM.

Markets and control and the role of accounting

The justification for the adoption of NPM was often the argument that the bureaucracies were inefficient and self-serving. Hence, markets were promoted as an approach that would eliminate these elements through the competition that they incorporated. In a market there is a need to determine and price an output that can be traded, and the technology of accounting provides one way of calculating prices. Accounting also enables the predominant way of showing the efficiency of organizations by providing the calculation of financial profits. It was argued that the 'discipline' of the market and customer pressure would provide the lever for 'better' public services and the control emphasis moved from process to outputs. Thus control of organizations was to be through the provision, for the customer, of the services that they wanted and resources would follow customers.[5]

During the Conservative administration attempts were made to provide a purchaser–provider split in different ways in different services; purchasers were to be one type of customer. The implications of this for social policy have been discussed at length and without clear conclusion (see, for example, Cloke 1992; Manning and Page 1992; Broadbent 1998b). Our concern is with the implications for professional groups of the supposedly market-based approach to control that NPM brought. Accountability for the quality of the services provided by these groups was not previously formalized and had tended to operate through the application of professional norms and codes. In the context of the 'Ouchi' framework, this had provided clan control in the areas where neither the outputs could be clearly measured nor the process well defined. It was assumed that the market could, through its allocative mechanisms, provide an indirect discipline on these professional groups.

In the course of the implementation of a market or quasi-market approach (see Glennester 1991; Le Grand 1991), the use of the technology of accounting in the processes of control changed. Accounting technologies became implicated more actively in the construction of the resource flows as they were used to price the outputs and 'create' the ultimate visibility of the organization. In this context accounting therefore became a more important element of the control processes.

Neo-liberalism: bringing together task and market controls

We have argued elsewhere (Broadbent and Laughlin 1997b) that the reforms, far from being market based, are in fact neo-liberalist (Miller and Rose 1991) with a strong centralizing tendency. There seems to have been a delegation of responsibility to the local level, as for example in the case of schools where local management of schools has delegated budgetary control to the school level. However, this has been accompanied by a strong definition of the outputs that must be achieved. The market element of control is reflected through the focus on outputs. However, as the reforms have been implemented and the difficulties of achieving allocative efficiencies through the working of the market place have become apparent, the emphasis has turned more to task control over these outputs. There has developed, therefore, a strong element of process control through the use of inspection. Bodies such as the Office for Standards in Education (OfSTED) (in the case of schools) have been formed to look directly at the processes being used to undertake the task in question. Thus the tendency to centralize control is based on the implementation of both output and task controls that are implemented by external bodies, rather than on the rule governed structure of the bureaucracy. The changes reflect a distrust of professional autonomy (Broadbent and Laughlin 1997b). They bring together the technologies of accounting that can be used in both hierarchical and market approaches to give even tighter forms of control. We will argue that neo-liberalism achieves this tight control by using not just accounting but also an 'accounting logic'.

NPM, 'accounting logic', clans and control

'Accounting logic' (Laughlin 1992) is a wider concept than simply implementing the technologies of accounting. It is a general approach built on two assumptions:

1   That any activity needs to be evaluated in terms of some measurable outputs achieved and the value added in the course of any activity.
2   That is possible to undertake this evaluation in and through the financial resources actually used or received.

Thus, a central element of the mode of thinking is the view that it is possible to quantify outputs and outcomes and link them to *financial* inputs. Clearly 'accounting logic' fits the ethos of the quasi-market approach as it seeks to price the outputs and the technology of accounting provides the price that is essential for the allocative mechanism to work. 'Accounting logic' is also consistent with a hierarchical classical management approach to control, particularly to the extent that the standardization of tasks enables the calculation of the value added. 'Accounting logic' is, however, not appropriate in situations where clan control is seen as relevant, as the former is closely concerned with the quantification of outputs and clans are seen as appropriate in situations where this is not possible.

We see 'accounting logic' as pervasive and extensive; it imbues society and seems to be extending in the context of NPM. It is a mode of thought, which if operated in full, requires that relationships be reflected in measurable outputs related to financial inputs. The implication is that the structure of relationships could be changed to allow this type of quantification. It is similar to the notion of economic reason, the key difference being that 'accounting logic' can operationalize the underlying assumptions through the technologies of accounting (Broadbent 1998a).

'Accounting logic' is particularly powerful because of its potential societal impact. Expressed particularly through the technologies of accounting, it produces an aura of factual representation, promoting a general perception that it generates 'neutral, objective, independent and fair' information (Gallhofer and Haslam 1991: 495). It is a public language that creates visibilities and downplays as unimportant anything not made visible (Broadbent 1995, 1998a). The ascendancy of the 'accounting logic' is related to a societal rationalization process, which leads to a 'spread of countings and accountings.' (Meyer 1986: 347). This process itself also emphasizes notions of standardization and a search for common measurable yardsticks which aid that standardization process. It can also be seen as a manifestation of a Benthamite move from direct behaviour control to a more indirect form of constraint over people's behaviour (Gallhofer and Haslam 1994a,b).

'Accounting logic' and market-based controls promote, enable and are logically consistent with each other. The quantification of outputs and emphasis on finances can also be relevant in the context of hierarchical control. They are *essential* to operate a market-based approach to control in that there is a need to measure activity outputs and to attach prices to them to facilitate exchange. 'Accounting logic' is inconsistent with notions of clan control and professionals would see it as inapplicable in the context of the control of their professional work. This assumes a particular view of professional practice that may well not be appropriate to all, but may well be relevant to some, element of work that professionals do (Dietrich and Roberts 1995). The question that remains to be debated is the extent of that part of professional work for which 'accounting logic' is inappropriate.

As noted earlier, our argument does not deny that there might be elements of a monopoly of competence (Larson 1977) around the tasks that come under the control of certain professional groupings. It does not deny that professional groups will engage in attempts at closure around their area of activity (Witz 1992). Despite this we accept that there is also some level of tacit knowledge (Polanyi 1962, 1967; Nelson and Winter 1982) which is needed by professionals in order to carry out their tasks successfully. The work of Jamous and Peloille (1970), which differentiates between indetermination (I) and technicality (T), characterizes professions by the high ratio of indetermination to technicality (what they refer to as the I/T ratio) and highlights the notion in a rather different fashion. However, we would argue that the professionals see their I/T ratio as relatively high. It follows that the ability to define the nature of the transformation process is limited and that the definition of the outputs of the activity is also potentially problematic. In essence this should render these tasks as unsuitable for both market and hierarchical controls and more relevant to *clan* approaches to control. The lack of ability to define outputs and specify the process also makes the adoption of 'accounting logic' problematic.

If the approach to control relies on the logic of either controlling outputs or process then at least two logical solutions exist. One is to admit that the prerequisites for control approaches based on markets or hierarchies are inappropriate and that the clan control suggested by Ouchi's framework is the more relevant form. The other, characteristic of the neo-liberalist approach of NPM, is to systematize the tasks in question and standardize the outputs, i.e. to reinvent the tasks in such a way that they become appropriate for the application of such logic. The work of Gorz (1989) suggests this latter solution can be inappropriate. Gorz (1989) argues that economic rationality[6] was appropriate where activities had four characteristics: they created use values; existed for exchange as commodities; existed in the public sphere; and were produced in a measurable amount of time, at as high a level of productivity as possible. The caring professions fail, on the last of these criteria, to be suitable for the application of economic reason. Gorz argues that, alongside the provision of the service, is a gift relationship from the carer that cannot be encompassed by maximization of outputs. Indeed, he notes that the efficiency of carers might be in inverse proportion to their visible quantitative output (Gorz 1989: 143). This has particular implications for the public services. If there is a tacit element of the professional task then the systematization might well be as degrading as the application of scientific management to craft processes and we may lose skills that can enhance our social welfare.

Despite arguments against the appropriateness of applying economic reason or 'accounting logic', the possibilities provided by the adoption of such approaches are arguably attractive to management as they offer a powerful control device. It is a control device that has been applied to professionals in areas of the public services. The theoretical critique is reflected empirically. Our previous work has illustrated that teachers and GPs, for example, are sceptical about the ability of the control systems to encapsulate the entirety of their activities in the output indicators that are being used. If this is correct it follows that an approach based on output measurement is likely, at best, to measure only part of the activity of the group concerned. A possibility is that the attempt to define and control through output measures may, in fact, lead to change in the nature of the activity (Broadbent 1995). This may be because there has been a 'colonization' (Laughlin 1991) of the activity by the values imposed by the measurement system, for example where school teachers see that the achievement of particular examination grades is more important than any other element of school life.

As well as imposing measures of outputs, legislation has sought to define the professional activity itself. In this sense a 'classical management' approach has been adopted in the sense that tasks can be standardized and that managers have a right to determine what the professionals should do. For example, OfSTED in its inspection of schools provides a particular model of how schools should organize themselves and, arguably, favours particular approaches to teaching. Equally, the GP Contract[7] imposed a requirement to adopt health promotion within the primary medical care setting. The linkage between achieving certain outputs and doing so in a particular way is a move beyond market control and is more clearly related to control of the labour process.

The effects of the use of this approach to control are not neutral. The measurement of outputs along with the specification of process can impose an approach that individualizes accountability (Roberts 1996; Townley 1996; Broadbent *et al.* 1999), and this can have a demoralizing and alienating effect if the required individual targets are not achieved. For example, in the case of schools there is a clear link to individualization of the accountability processes (Broadbent *et al.* 1999). The individual grades of pupils are important to the success of the school; equally a teacher's individual performance in achieving both student grades and in their performance at inspection is linked to the whole school report that OfSTED undertakes. In both these cases individual performance is linked to the success or failure of the organization as a whole and this amplifies the impact of any failure. The danger of this individualizing tendency is that it can have the capacity to undermine social cohesion and organizational action (Broadbent *et al.* 1999: 342).

Another effect of standardization is that in defining the nature of the services required there is a sense in which professional discretion to provide for the individual client that which s/he is judged to need has been undermined.[8] In this way the balance of control of the professional has been moved away from a clan approach where the professional norms and values and regulations guided the behaviour of the professionals concerned. In some cases this may well be beneficial, and this is an issue that is being debated more carefully in the wake of the problems in the medical profession; for example, following the cases in Bristol where heart surgery on babies and children was later seen to be woefully inadequate. In some cases the imposition of a standard solution may be seen to undermine the personal relationship between client and professional.

Implications

Past legislation has sought to place a much greater emphasis on the measurement of outputs and outcomes and makes linkages between these and finances. Despite the rhetoric of a market approach to control, 'accounting logic' has provided the vehicle for a neo-liberalist approach. 'Accounting logic' emphasizes the evaluation of activities both in terms of measurable outputs and through the lens of financial resources. Implementing this type of logic is through a modelling of the processes and this demands their specification. In specifying these activities there is inevitably a process of standardization to enable the costing of these activities to take place. This has implications for professionals as it undermines the approaches to control to which they have been subject.

Professionals would undoubtedly argue a need for an ability to control their own spheres of activity. In that respect they have great discretion over their tasks and this has sometimes led to criticism. The control structures that have developed are ones that have made them accountable to each other for the adherence to professional standards and norms. They have argued that the definition of outputs is difficult and the process of professional judgement is not amenable to quantification or to detailed definition. In these circumstances the controls that develop are more akin to Ouchi's notion of clan control.

Since 'accounting logic' requires the expression of outputs and outcomes linked to *financial* inputs, it places emphasis on the notion of measurable outputs. The use of this approach has to define both process and outputs. Recent legislation has attempted to define outputs for various areas of professional work – examination results for teachers, health promotion activities for GPs. Alongside this are attempts to define the transformation process. The definition of the curriculum for teachers and the specification of prescribing for doctors indicate that the government is seeking to implement a more direct control over the activities of professionals. The conclusion is that they wish to exercise a more hierarchical control over the professionals involved that is based more closely on the task control of classical management. This may be driven by the ethos that 'accounting logic' provides. An alternative is that the desire to control the professionals is driving the application of 'accounting logic' in this particular situation. It is more likely that the two elements feed each other, reflexively.

The question remains whether the accountability that is being implemented via 'accounting logic' is appropriate. Professionals are very sceptical of the possibility that the output measures can actually capture the essence of their practice (Broadbent 1995). They see the specification of their activities as infeasible, because of the tacit nature of the knowledge base. Arguably, just as scientific management provided a means of developing task control in the manual labour force, so the present changes are seeking to make visible certain aspects of professional activity to provide a means of control.

The research we have undertaken with teachers and GPs suggests that these groups have made great efforts to limit the impact of the initiatives, which they see as damaging to their professional aims (for an overview see Broadbent and Laughlin 1998). This 'absorption' process, as we have called it, is problematic from many perspectives. One possibility is that the areas which are given visibility and which are controlled by the implementation of the NPM-driven changes might well undermine the other aspects of the tasks, which are at the same time rendered invisible. In this way the whole nature of the professional activities could be changed. Another possibility is that those who cannot justify their activities in financial terms may be disadvantaged in the bid for scarce resources. Elsewhere we have raised concerns about the 'individualizing' nature of the accountabilities that are being developed and the extent to which these might undermine communal action (Broadbent *et al.* 1999). We should also consider the effects of the changes on the possibility of retaining a trust relationship between the professionals and both their clients and society in general. There are implications of not trusting the professional. One GP commented '... the government might not trust us, but it will cost them dear not to.' He was referring not just to the demoralization he felt as a professional, but to the personal and societal time money and effort that he had to be exerted to meet the demands of government legislation.

In conclusion, we would argue that NPM, through the application of 'accounting logic', has provided the opportunity for the implementation of a neo-liberalist approach. This combines elements of task control characteristic of classical management alongside a market approach. Rather than provide some relaxation of the central control of the hierarchy, the thrust has been to reduce the autonomy of the professional. Hence 'accounting logic' provides a technology for implementing a control of professionals akin to the scientific management approach. The legislative activity following the election of the New Labour government has intensified these changes. Whether this intensification of control is good or bad needs to be debated. In this debate we could draw upon what is now known about the implementation of scientific management at the start of the twentieth century. The advisability of the current changes remains substantially un-debated, especially with regard to the potential effects on professional activity. In this respect we must be aware that the imposition of 'accounting logic' is not an imposition of a neutral technical control device, but has constitutive power through the visibilities it creates. Our plea is for some broader evaluation of the changes (Laughlin and Broadbent 1996; Broadbent and Laughlin 1997a). This should include consideration of the imposition of accountabilities that are meaningful to the professionals themselves as well as to those for whom they provide their services, both as individuals and as members of a wider society.

Notes

1 It should also be noted that the difficulty of defining outputs also makes a market difficult to operationalize.
2 We should be also be aware of the diversity of practices that comprise this approach (Olson *et al.* 1998). However, our argument is based on the acceptance of some general themes that characterize the ethos of the changes if not their actual detail.
3 See also Osborne (1997).
4 Witz (1992: Chapter 2) provides an overview.
5 It should be recognized that the notion of the customer as an independent entity is somewhat problematic as it was the government that provided the legislation that created the customer. Equally in many instances the state also created intermediate agencies in this respect, acting as a quasi-customer, e.g. OfSTED.
6 Which we have argued is closely aligned to 'accounting logic'.
7 Imposed on General Medical Practitioners to regulate their payment from the state for care of their patients. This linked payment to the achievement of various targets, such as the achievement of target levels of vaccinations and cervical screening.
8 This may well be appropriate and it should be recognized that we should not be taken to advocate a position of allowing professionals to do as they please. Clans have different forms of control, but are controlled nevertheless.

References

Braverman, H. (1974) *Labor and Monopoly Capital*, New York: Monthly Review Press.
Broadbent, J. (1995) 'The Values of Accounting and Education: Some Implications of the Creation of Visibilities and Invisibilities in Schools'. *Advances in Public Interest Accounting*, Vol. 6, pp. 69–89.

Broadbent, J. (1998a) 'The Gendered Nature of "Accounting Logic": Pointers to an Accounting that Encompasses Multiple Values'. *Critical Perspectives on Accounting*, Vol. 9, pp. 267–297.

Broadbent, J. (1998b) 'New Public Management and Issues of Policy: So Where Do We Go From Here?' In Guthrie, J., Humphrey, C. and Olsen, O. (eds) *Global Warning: International Financial Management Changes*, Oslo: Cappelen Akademisk Forlag, pp. 415–434.

Broadbent, J. and Laughlin, R. (1997a) 'Evaluating the "New Public Management" Reforms in the UK: A Constitutional Possibility?' *Public Administration*, Vol. 75, No. 3, pp. 487–507.

Broadbent, J. and Laughlin, R. (1997b) 'Contracts and Competition? A Reflection on the Nature and Effects of Recent Legislation on Modes of Control in Schools'. *Cambridge Journal of Economics* Vol. 21, No. 2, pp. 277–290.

Broadbent, J. and Laughlin, R. (1998) 'Resisting the "New Public Management": Absorption and Absorbing Groups in Schools and GP Practices in the UK'. *Accounting, Auditing and Accountability Journal*, Vol. 11, No. 4, pp. 403–435.

Broadbent, J., Jacobs, K. and Laughlin, R. (1999) 'Comparing Schools in the UK and New Zealand: Individualising and Socializing Accountabilities and Some Implications for Management Control'. *Management Accounting Research*, Vol. 10, pp. 339–361.

Coase, R.H. (1937) 'The Nature of the Firm', *Economica*, November, pp. 386–405.

Cloke, P. (ed.) (1992) *Policy and Change in Thatcher's Britain*, Oxford: Pergamon.

Dietrich, M. and Roberts, J. (1995) 'Economics and the Professions: the Limits of Free Markets', *Political Economy Working Papers, No.4*. PERC, University of Sheffield.

Dunleavy, P. and Hood, C.(1994) 'From Old Public Administration to New Public Management'. *Public Money and Management*, July–September, pp. 9–16.

Exworthy, M. and Halford, S. (1999) *Professionals and the New Managerialism in the Public Sector*, Buckingham: OU Press.

Friedson, E. (1970a) *Professional Dominance: the Social Structure of Medical Care*, New York: Atherton Press.

Friedson, E. (1970b) *Profession of Medicine: a Study of the Sociology of Applied Knowledge*, New York: Harper Row.

Gallhofer, S. and Haslam, J. (1991) 'The Aura of Accounting in the Context of a Crisis: Germany and the First World War'. *Accounting, Organizations and Society*, Vol. 16, no. 5/6, pp. 487–520.

Gallhofer, S. and Haslam, J. (1994a) 'Accounting and the Benthams: Accounting as Negation'. *Accounting, Business and Financial History*, Vol. 4, No. 2, pp. 239–274.

Gallhofer, S. and Haslam, J. (1994b) 'Accounting and the Benthams: or Accounting's Potentialities'. *Accounting, Business and Financial History*, Vol. 4, No. 3, pp. 431–460.

Glennerster, H. (1991) 'Quasi-markets for Education?' *The Economic Journal*, Vol. 101, pp. 1268–1276.

Gorz, A. (1989) *Critique of Economic Reason*, translated by Handyside, G. and Turner, C., London: Verso.

Hood, C. (1991) 'A Public Management for All Seasons?' *Public Administration*, pp. 3–19.

Hood, C. (1995) 'The "New Public Management in the 1980s": Variations on a Theme'. *Accounting, Organizations and Society*, Vol. 20, No. 3, pp. 93–109.

Jamous, H. and Peloille, B. (1970) 'Changes in the French University Hospital System'. In Jackson, J.A. (ed.) *Professions and Professionalization*, Cambridge: Cambridge University Press.

Johnson, T. (1972) *Professions and Power*, London: Macmillan.

Larson, M.S. (1977) *The Rise of Professionalism: a Sociological Analysis*, Berkeley: University of California Press.

Laughlin, R. (1991) 'Environmental Disturbances and Organisational Transitions and Transformations: Some Alternative Models'. *Organization Studies*, Vol. 12, No. 2, pp. 209–232.

Laughlin, R. (1992) 'Accounting Control and Controlling Accounting: The Battle for the Public Sector?' Inaugural Lecture, *Sheffield University Management School* Discussion Paper 92.29.

Laughlin, R. and Broadbent, J. (1996) 'Redesigning Fourth Generation Evaluation: An Evaluation Model for the Public Sector Reforms in the UK?' *Evaluation*, Vol. 2, No. 4, pp. 431–451.

Le Grand, J. (1991) 'Quasi-Markets and Social Policy'. *The Economic Journal*, Vol. 101, pp. 1256–1267.

Manning, N. and Page, R. (eds) (1992) *Social Policy Review*, Vol 4. London: Social Policy Association.

Meyer, J.W. (1986) 'Social Environments and Organizational Accounting'. *Accounting, Organizations and Society*, Vol. 11, No. 4, pp. 345–356.

Miller, P. and O'Leary, T. (1987) 'Accounting and the Construction of the Governable Person'. *Accounting Oganizations and Society*, Vol. 12, No. 3, pp. 235–265.

Miller, P. and Rose, N. (1991) 'Programming the Poor: Poverty Calculation and Expertise'. In Lehto, J. (ed.) *Deprivation, Social Welfare and Expertise*, Helsinki: National Agency for Welfare and Health Research, Report 7, pp. 117–140.

Mintzberg, H. (1983) *Structure in Fives: Designing Effective Organizations*, Englewood Cliffs, NJ: Prentice Hall.

Nelson, R.R. and Winter, S.G. (1982) *An Evolutionary Theory of Economic Change*, Boston: Harvard University Press.

Olson, O., Guthrie, J. and Humphrey, C. (1998) *Global Warning! Debating International Developments in New Public Financial Management,* Oslo: Cappelen Akademisk Forlag.

Osborne, S. (1997) 'Managing the Coordination of Social Services in the Mixed Economy of Welfare: Competition, Co-operation or Common Cause?' *British Journal of Management*, Vol. 8, pp. 317–328.

Ouchi, W. (1979) 'A Conceptual Framework for the Design of Organisational Control Mechanisms'. *Management Science*, Vol. 25, No. 9, pp. 95–112.

Ouchi, W.G. (1980) 'Markets, Bureaucracies and Clans'. *Administrative Science Quarterly*, Vol. 25, No. 1, pp. 129–141.

Polanyi, M. (1962) *Personal Knowledge: Towards a Post-critical Philosophy*, London: Harper and Row.

Polanyi, M. (1967) *The Tacit Dimension*, London: Routledge and Kegan Paul.

Roberts, J. (1996) 'From Discipline to Dialogue: Individualizing and Socializing Forms of Accountability'. In Munro, R. and Mouritsen, J. (eds) *Accountability: Power, Ethos and the Technologies of Managing*, London: International Thompson Press, pp. 40–61.

Taylor, F.W. (1947) *Scientific Management*, New York: Harper and Row.

Townley, B. (1996) 'Accounting in Detail: Accounting for Individual Performance'. *Critical Perspectives on Accounting*, Vol. 7, No. 5, pp. 565–584.

Williamson, O.E. (1975) *Market and Hierarchies: Analysis and Antitrust Implications*, New York: Free Press.

Witz, A. (1992) *Professions and Patriarchy*, London: Routledge.

Wood, S. (ed.) (1982) *The Degradation of Work?* London: Hutchinson.

Chapter 7

The New Public Management and social exclusion

Cause or response?

Marilyn Taylor

Over the last generation, this has become a more divided country. While most areas have benefited from rising living standards, the poorest neighbourhoods have tended to become more rundown, more prone to crime and more cut off from the labour market. The national picture conceals pockets of intense deprivation where the problems of unemployment and crime are acute and hopelessly tangled up with poor health, housing and education. They have become no-go areas for some and no-exit zones for others (Social Exclusion Unit 1998: 9).

The growing polarization of incomes and wealth within Britain has been well documented. Research has also demonstrated how low income is associated with certain groups in the population, including social housing estates (Joseph Rowntree Foundation 1995), producing a spiral of deprivation from which it is increasingly difficult to escape (Social Exclusion Unit 1998).

This phenomenon has become known as social exclusion. This is a concept which can be traced to mainland Europe (Room 1995). It contrasts with the concept of poverty that has dominated the UK social policy discourse until recent years, in that it draws attention to social, political and economic relationships rather than individual characteristics.

As a characteristic of individuals, poverty lent itself to blame and moral sanction, from the days of the Poor Law through to more recent debates about an 'underclass' (Murray 1984), morally divorced from the rest of society and responsible for its own predicament. It also lends itself to counting, measuring, classifying and processing. Social exclusion, on the other hand, is a relational concept, focusing not on the individual and their classification but on the relationship between individuals and the rest of society and the ways in which lack of income has acted as a barrier to participation in normal life. Insofar as it draws attention to the processes through which economic, political and social processes conspire to exclude whole groups in the population, the concept of social exclusion also draws attention to the positive social and political rights of citizenship.

'Want', along with idleness, disease and squalor, was one of the giants which the UK welfare state was supposed to conquer. But by the mid-1960s, its failure to achieve a significant redistribution of income was well established.

Nonetheless, debates about the existence and nature of poverty were still very much alive in the 1980s, when the Conservative government dismissed studies of 'relative' poverty as an attempt to massage up the poverty statistics, preferring to adhere to an absolute concept that reduced the problem to a minimum.

The election of a New Labour government in 1997, signalled a change of approach. The new government created a Social Exclusion Unit (SEU) at the centre of government early in its term of office and, in doing so, embraced a concept of poverty which recognized both its relational nature and its complexity. The resources and time that it committed to understanding and finding new approaches to tackling area-based exclusion were impressive. The publication of *Bringing Britain Together* by the Social Exclusion Unit in 1998 was followed by extensive consultations through eighteen Priority Action Teams, which brought a wide range of people from outside government into the policy-making process and took government officials out to many areas and projects. The resulting *National Strategy for Neighbourhood Renewal* (SEU 2000) was itself subject to extensive consultation with statutory and non-statutory organizations, and there is a clear commitment to continued learning and evaluation in its Action Plan (SEU 2001).

The National Strategy embodies a range of responses to exclusion, including measures to get people back to work, to revive economies and to revive communities. There is a strong emphasis on getting people back into the labour market, in keeping with this government's general approach to social exclusion (Levitas 1999). But a second key feature of the strategy is its emphasis on the need to improve the quality of services to excluded communities through improved and more user-responsive forms of management, and it is this which is the focus of this chapter. The chapter considers the impact of the New Public Management (NPM) of the 1980s on social exclusion. It then explores the new ideas about management in the National Strategy and assesses their potential to bring a new approach to bear. It agrees with other chapters in this volume that although the harsher edges of the NPM have softened the reworking of the concept under New Labour, there is still much continuity with earlier versions. It concludes by placing a managerial approach in the context of a wider vision that has the capacity to revolutionize public service cultures and ideas about service production.

New Public Management: the cause of social exclusion?

The main features of the NPM as introduced in the 1980s can be described as:

- the introduction of techniques of business management, with an emphasis on efficiency;
- a greater service and client orientedness;
- the introduction of market mechanisms and competition into public life.

It replaced the post-war settlement between bureaucratic and professional authority (Newman: Chapter 5) that was seen by the New Right as inefficient, dominated by providers and unresponsive to consumer needs and preferences.

But, as many scholars have argued, the adoption of business practices by the public sector was hampered by a conservative (small 'c') interpretation of good practice in business, which failed to take into account cutting-edge practice and new business thinking. As I have argued elsewhere, it was also hampered by the ability of many within government – local and national – to do 'what we've always done in a different wrapping' (Taylor 2000). As Pollitt and colleagues remarked in 1998: 'Enormous institutional resistance and inertia has transformed what government intended as revolution into more reform.'

In reality it was the professional part of the bureau-professional system that bore the brunt of the changes. As Newman points out (Chapter 5, this volume), professionals were themselves drawn into management at different levels – doctors turned into managers in the different parts of the NHS, the social worker reborn as care manager. But as service delivery was separated from planning and management, a new set of professions gained ascendancy in the public sector – the auditor, the accountant, the legal advisor, the contract manager (Perkin 1989). As professional decision-making was decentralized, the centre kept control through a new regime of regulation, performance management and quality control (Hambleton *et al.* 1997).

This led to what some have called an 'audit explosion' (Power 1994). The audit culture tended inevitably to focus on the most easily measurable aspects of a service – an approach which was ill-suited to capturing the relational focus of the social exclusion discourse. Performance management was introduced across the board, characterized by what Hambleton *et al.* (1997) refer to as 'tick and bash' indicators. The new regime was also marked by an increase in surveillance and the development of a blame culture (Thomas and Dunkerley 1999). These developments focused attention inwards towards systems, inputs and outputs rather than broader outcomes, turning means into ends. This in turn created its own time-consuming counterculture: 'An audit culture generates its own complex games of deception and counter-deception, which are now a common feature of working life' (Amman 1995).

In regeneration programmes, monitoring focused on outputs instead of the inputs that had characterized the bureau-professional systems. But these had to be agreed and defined in advance and favoured the easily measurable. Programmes were characterized by complex application, accounting and monitoring systems which were in danger of excluding all but the most well-resourced professionalized voluntary organizations from entering partnerships. One of the people cited in the *National Strategy for Neighbourhood Renewal* (SEU 2000: 26) argued that: 'Local government or government-funded bodies ... almost always end up with a hierarchical approach to community development that denies all opportunity for such initiatives to be owned by local people.'

The problems generated by this approach were also recognized in parts of government. For example, a report on cross-cutting working from the government's Performance and Innovation Unit (2000) stated that: 'systems of accountability (e.g. audit) and the way risk is handled can militate against innovative cross-cutting working.'

The PIU report went on to argue that financial accountability must be combined with policy accountability, if cross-cutting working is to deliver. In a public service, money should not be the only bottom line.

Wilkinson and Applebee (1999: 35) agree that: 'The pressure and volume of the waves of public sector reforms have placed great emphasis on top-down change, short-term outputs, external audit and "competitive" behaviours.'

But they also draw attention to the more positive aspects of the reforms: 'The development of market mechanisms has been an important spur to change. They challenged poor performance and in its more simplistic forms made it visible. ... Certainly there was a need for some of the changes with better accountability for the stewardship of public resources and a much clearer focus on results.'

Better regulated and more accountable services would surely benefit the most excluded in society.

However, there were a number of factors, other than the preoccupation with audit and measurement, which complicated this simple route to effectiveness. The first was the financial and political environment within which NPM was introduced. The policies of the 1980s were characterized by public expenditure cuts and the erosion of local authority powers. In areas that are highly dependent on public services, NPM cannot be assessed in isolation from the pressure on public expenditure and the low morale caused by these policies. Public expenditure cuts and the rationing they brought with them, the drive for efficiency savings and the general erosion of morale in the public sector bore particularly heavily on areas where people could not opt out into the private sector. The emphasis on value for money in service contracts also encouraged 'cream-skimming' (Le Grand 1992), whereby service providers would go for the clients who were likely to be relatively cheap to serve and produce the most favourable results.

The second complication was that the operation of the market itself intensified social exclusion. Statistics showed a widening gap between rich and poor as industrial restructuring took its toll and the introduction of market principles and consumer choice into welfare accelerated this gap. The introduction of choice and the 'right to buy' to the housing market soon concentrated those with no choice in the least desirable housing. The absence of a market in social housing estates combined with increasing environmental decay and rising crime to drive away shops, businesses and financial services and to encourage post-code discrimination. Run-down estates were not in a position to attract good doctors. Parental choice meant that schools in run-down areas languished at the bottom of school league tables or excluded children in order to improve their performance. Care in the Community policies, while laudable in principle, usually meant moving more vulnerable people into areas already struggling to survive, without the resources to support them. The evidence suggested that the benefits of economically driven special initiatives to turn around areas in decline were bypassing the poorest part of the population altogether. Where wealth was created, it was not trickling down.

A third problem for the NPM was that with the rise of the welfare market, a comprehensive approach to the problems of excluded areas was increasingly difficult to achieve. The emphasis on consumer responsiveness, while in itself welcome, tended to obscure the need for political accountability for broad strategies and patterns of provision (Pollitt *et al.* 1998). In these circumstances, competition and contracting out risked creating an increasingly fragmented institutional environment as a range of non-statutory providers and quangos began to operate alongside the local authority at neighbourhood level. Performance indicators and service-specific standards reinforced the departmental divisions which had already been strong in a bureau-professional system. Budget pressures created rivalries between departments. The departmental mould of decision-making and standard setting failed to match lived experience and the spiral of exclusion which affected people on low incomes concentrated in particular areas could not be tackled in a coherent way.

A fourth problem area was illustrated by the ambivalent response of non-statutory providers themselves to the new opportunities created by the transfer of service delivery away from the state. Against the background of state welfare, voluntary organizations had developed a complementary role, which they felt played to their strengths as organizations which were supposed to be more flexible, closer to consumers and more able to reach out to the excluded than the state. Many felt that acting as agents of state purchasers would prejudice these distinctive characteristics – a view forcibly expressed by the National Council for Voluntary Organisations at the time (Gutch 1992). If this happened, their role in reaching those needs not met by the state, and in providing the complementary services that prevented crisis, would be crowded out.

A sector that had largely been funded through grant-aid and with few strings attached was nervous about the implications of a 'contract culture'. Thus, while some welcomed the increased role for the voluntary and community sectors that welfare markets introduced, there were fears that purchasing agencies within government would dictate whom provider agencies could and could not serve and would also demand conformity to public sector management approaches. The stricter requirements of the NPM could also restrict opportunities for excluded communities to be involved in managing and volunteering in the voluntary sector because of the 'risks' involved (Russell and Scott 1998).

It is hard to say as yet whether these fears were justified. The evidence towards the end of the 1990s was mixed (Taylor 1997; Hems and Passey 1998). Efficiency was a worthy aim of the NPM – inefficient and poorly managed services are in no-one's interests – and there were many in the voluntary sector who welcomed the drive for improved management within the sector. Larger organizations or those who were major suppliers in an area could actually wield a lot of power in negotiations, and there were authorities who explicitly reserved funds for preventive and non-mainstream activities. An emphasis on consumerism meant that advocacy services were positively encouraged in some areas (Unwin and Westland 1996). Some volunteers – especially those who made a longer-term commitment – felt that they were able to make a more significant contribution as their organizations assumed a more central role in welfare (Russell and Scott 1998).

But there was also evidence that the sustainability and diversity of the voluntary sector contribution might be at risk as its organizations were expected to deliver more for less. Despite the new opportunities, medium-sized organiz- ations in particular were at risk of being squeezed (Hems and Passey 1998) and found themselves living in an increasingly uncertain world (Russell *et al.* 1995). In addition, the move from grant to contract funding left many smaller organizations starved of the core funds on which development, negotiating for contract funds and effective involvement in partnership depend. The survival of the voluntary sector *per se* is not the concern of this chapter, except insofar as it offers the diversity that a comprehensive welfare system needs if it is to be responsive to the needs of a diverse population. Of more concern is the fact that early studies of contracting argued that while voluntary organizations were finding their feet in the contracts market, users were not benefiting (Deakin 1996). Some argued that, as those organizations who were most successful in the contracts market learned the ropes, they would be co-opted into the ways of operating and cultures of public authorities, leaving others – who remained closer to their users and to excluded groups in society – out in the cold (Knight 1993).

The environment within which the NPM was introduced was, in summary, one of increasing public expenditure constraint and one where divisions between rich and poor were increasing. In some ways, the NPM reinforced exclusion. The public service cultures which the NPM had been brought in to attack remained remarkably resistant to change and were in some ways reinforced by the rapid growth of an audit culture. Meanwhile, voluntary organizations felt that too strong an adherence to market and contract principles put their distinctive contribution to meeting the needs of excluded populations at risk and, as later governments were to acknowledge, the fragmentation of the market prevented any concerted attack on exclusion.

Transition: softening the edges?

The Conservative administrations of the 1990s offered the opportunity to address some of these issues. Its emphasis on partnership sought to bring the fragments together again and to address issues of exclusion in a more targeted, joined-up way. The first City Challenge and then the Single Regeneration Budget Challenge Fund, which brought together over twenty separate government programmes, offered an integrated approach to tackling regeneration and placed an emphasis on community involvement. But their competitive nature still stereotyped excluded areas, requiring them to parade their disadvantage in a parody of the market in order to get money. It also raised expectations in areas and communities which were not then funded. The availability of large amounts of money to some areas and not to others led to resentment from outside and competitiveness within, putting integration at risk. The rules of the partnership game were often dominated by public and private partners, and economically driven communities remained on the margins.

Nonetheless, there were some gains. The emphasis on user involvement did provide the opportunity for disabled people, parents and tenants to take increasing control over their services, especially during the latter years of the Conservative administration. The burdens faced by carers attracted growing attention and they were seen as a constituency that government needed to support. The climate of user empowerment also provided opportunities for joint working between users (or carers) and professionals – for example, in estate management boards, where responsibility for housing management was shared, in joint planning process in health and social care and in schools.

The New Labour analysis

Harrow (Chapter 9, this volume) notes that the major concern of the NPM was with efficiency, economy and effectiveness, not equity. It was not designed to tackle social exclusion, except insofar as management improvements 'trickled down' to the least-favoured consumers. But with the arrival of New Labour, addressing social exclusion became a priority. A Social Exclusion Unit (SEU) was set up at the heart of government and given the time and resources, as we have seen, to develop policy in full consultation with communities and other stakeholders.

Managerial reform remained a priority with the new government, not least because, in the words of the SEU (2001:19): 'the poorest communities have received the poorest services'. Thus, in 1999 a senior minister gave a commitment to: 'bringing all public services up to the level of the best and delivering what users want in an efficient and effective way' (Mo Mowlam, launching the Executive Agencies 1999 report).

Addressing the problems of fragmentation and competition – from Whitehall down – was a priority in the search for a new approach. Three main service themes stood out in the Social Exclusion Unit's initial work on a national strategy for neighbourhood renewal (Social Exclusion Unit 2000). These were:

- joined-up action;
- re-engineering mainstream programmes;
- maximizing community involvement.

Joined-up action

Central to the SEU's argument was the observation that social exclusion is 'a joined-up problem' that 'has never been dealt with in a joined-up way'. In this, the SEU was in tune with a number of critics, who saw the fragmentation and functional divisions within government as a major source of failure in tackling social exclusion, especially in dealing with the 'wicked issues' of community safety, poor health, joblessness and underachievement (Hambleton *et al.* 1997; Leat *et al.* 1999; Stewart 1999; Wilkinson and Applebee 1999). Such divisions wasted time, knowledge and resources. Indeed, as Diana Leat argued: 'The waste of information and knowledge in public sector organizations would be a public scandal if it were money.'

While partnership was by no means a new idea, the evidence of a succession of initiatives over the past thirty years was that public service cultures remained implacably resistant to change in many areas (2000a). Performance incentives, standards and careers were based firmly in departmental 'silos'. Budgets remained vertical and functional (Leat 2000; Performance and Innovation Unit 2000), and even where there was some joining up (e.g. through special initiatives), they quickly unravelled again once the bid was won, or were corralled by the most powerful partners (Wilkinson and Applebee 1999).

Re-engineering mainstream programmes

The SEU argued that special initiatives could not deliver the changes that neighbourhood renewal required. Even the money available for government's New Deal for Communities, which far outstrips per area earlier programmes like City Challenge and the SRB, was a drop in the ocean compared with the mainstream funding that was spent in run-down neighbourhoods. Despite this, the SEU argued, the quality of public services in most social housing estates, especially those in peripheral areas, was markedly inferior to that elsewhere. To address social exclusion, the quality of services in these areas would need to be raised to the level which other more empowered consumers would expect. This would mean spending mainstream budgets differently – in a way that more effectively met the needs of those who needed the services.

Maximizing community involvement

Joined-up thinking and action had to include local communities as well as the range of service providers. In his foreword to the *National Strategy for Neighbourhood Renewal* consultation document (SEU 2000: 5), the Prime Minister insisted that: 'Unless the community is fully engaged in shaping and delivering regeneration, even the best plans on paper will fail to deliver in practice.'

The relentless message from the top has therefore been that communities must be at the heart of this and other programmes. Increasingly, regeneration partnerships have been asked to demonstrate community involvement in the development of programmes in order to gain funding. At the same time, Rounds 5 and 6 of the Single Regeneration Budget Challenge Fund incorporated capacity building into their objectives. Community involvement, with the possibility of community leadership, was also built into both the New Deal for Communities and the Sure Start programme – a cross-departmental programme for children under four and their families. Of the latter programme, the Chancellor of the Exchequer said that:

> Instead of the state – local or national – running these programmes, these can be run by volunteers, charities, and community organizations. Indeed, we should be prepared to pass over the responsibility for services in these geographical areas to the voluntary partnership.
>
> (Brown 2000)

In order to make this possible, both programmes introduced longer lead-in times, and made funding available for the development of bids. Although areas selected for these programmes had to submit bids and then delivery plans, competition between areas was abandoned. Outputs did not have to be set at the outset for the whole programme, but could be defined and refined at different stages within the ten years. The word on the ground has been that 'there is permission to do things differently', and there have also been centrally funded opportunities for activists from different areas to meet and share experience and knowledge.

NPM mark II: a response?

At the beginning of 2001, the above principles were crystallized in the government's *Action Plan for Neighbourhood Renewal*, which was to be implemented by a new Neighbourhood Renewal Unit, situated in the Department of the Environment, Transport and the Regions. The Plan set out a range of new policies, funding and targets to tackle problems such as unemployment, crime and poor services.

These were to be driven by two key 'drivers of change' at the local level. The first was to be the Local Strategic Partnership (LSP):

> a single body that brings together at local level the different parts of the public sector as well as private, voluntary and community sectors so that different initiatives and services support rather than contradict each other.
>
> (SEU 2001:10)

The LSP was to oversee the strategy for neighbourhood renewal, identifying priority neighbourhoods and setting targets for change. It would be able to draw down additional funding from a Neighbourhood Renewal Fund, subject to accreditation but by central government offices in the regions. The Action Plan also established funds to support community involvement in LSPs. LSPs were also expected to contribute to the wider community strategies that local authorities are now charged to produce. In this way, government hoped to integrate the proliferation of partnerships which had resulted from the sheer pace and extent of policy change and which were now threatening to create new kinds of fragmentation at the local level. There was a real danger that territorialism over service empires would give way to territorialism over partnerships.

The second 'driver' at the local level was to be neighbourhood management. The concept of neighbourhood management aims to bring together the whole range of services at local level. This would involve 'devolving power down to a single person or neighbourhood institution and might involve making service level agreements, running local services or managing a devolved budget' (SEU 2001). Even though money might be available to kick-start and support such initiatives, the major emphasis would be on changing the way in which mainstream budgets were spent, seeking to make spending in the area more transparent and accountable and to find ways of spending this money more effectively. Implementation would be secured through devolved commissioning of services and through agreements with participating agencies. However, the responsibility for developing an agreed plan and targets in the Action Plan appeared to lie with the LSP. It would be up these bodies to decide how much power would be devolved to neighbourhood level in practice.

The report of the Social Exclusion Unit's Priority Action Team 4, which focused on neighbourhood management, provides more detail about the initial thinking on neighbourhood management. This report envisages a range of delivery mechanisms, including tenant management organizations and community development trusts but also housing associations and local authorities. It also envisages a neighbourhood board with residents fully involved. This is picked up in the Prime Minister's foreword to the National Strategy, which argues that effective local leadership means 'developing ways of putting deprived communities in the driving seat'. But little attention is paid to how this would be developed and constituted – the main emphasis in that report is on the 'someone in charge' and the 'tools for the job'. As an idea, it is still under development – government proposes to fund a number of 'pathfinder' projects to take it forward.

Previous special initiatives and joint working arrangements have left behind them some foundations on which to build (Taylor 2000). These include a range of area coordination initiatives in different local authorities across the country, and more specific strategies to join up both money and accountability. They also include imaginative attempts in Birmingham to apply cross-boundary performance targets where the Director of Education is required, for example, to achieve a target of increased birthweights. In one London Borough, a condition for participation in bids for Single Regeneration Budget funds was to be that participating agencies should show what funds they were committing to the local strategy and open up their own budgets to scrutiny. Savings made through working together would then be reinvested. These examples have, however, been the exception rather than the rule and have only covered some services.

Nonetheless, it is possible to see how the NPM mark II is shaping up from the Action Plan (SEU 2001). This creates a wide range of targets which services are expected to meet in order to tackle unemployment, crime, ill health, underachievement and a poor physical environment, and identifies a range of 'key ideas' which will help to address those targets. It illustrates these with reference to what it considers to be 'good practice' across the country.

The Action Plan recognizes the problems of excessive bureaucracy and seeks a culture change, but the culture is still managerial, with targets at the forefront, and charter marks and service agreements seen as important vehicles for change. In the debates about the strategy, too, there has been a strong emphasis on delivery, best practice, knowledge management and performance. However, in those debates, this managerialist language has rubbed up against concepts of learning and development, while a strong emphasis is placed on the knowledge of residents as well as professionals. This reflects a much wider phenomenon described by Healey (1997).

As Fischer argues, there is a pervasive struggle in the terrain of governance at the present time between pluralistic democratic tendencies, which seek to acknowledge a wider range of stakeholders, forms of knowledge and value bases, and techno-corporate ones, which seek to keep control over the management of our societies, using the tools of technical analysis and management, or the knowledge and interests of key corporate interests.

Much will depend on how this tension is resolved, what kinds of cultures are promoted, the incentive structures that are used to drive cultural change at all levels of government, and how far the willingness to try and get the process right, which characterized the consultation stage, follows through into implementation.

Will the rhetoric from the top about risk and flexibility and 'communities at the heart of change' survive the journey through layers of accountability and implementation? I have argued elsewhere that good intentions are too often thwarted 'back at the ranch' by those who design the impossible forms, the hoops to jump through and who have ultimate control over the way the 'rules of the game' are interpreted (Taylor 2000). The intention to allow more flexibility to authorities which meet their outcome targets is welcome, but experience of the past suggests that managerialist imperatives and the demands of accountability and audit can too easily override such intentions.

The experience of other New Labour programmes on this is mixed. Even in the New Deal for Communities, the all-important decisions about how to benchmark and how to measure performance have tended to come from the top. Time pressures alone are likely to mean that centrally defined targets will inevitably take precedence over those which come up from communities. And it remains to be seen how the tensions between public accountability and flexibility in the spending of public money will be resolved. It remains to be seen, too, how far the new ways of working which should characterize the New Deal will flow back into mainstream practice.

The wider vision

Neighbourhood management is only one answer to the problem of neighbourhood renewal. Research suggests (Taylor 2000) that it needs to be seen as part of a wider picture. Parts of this picture are visible in the National Strategy, which embraces ideas about leadership and joint working, community knowledge, learning and development and social enterprise. But what is the potential for these other elements to drive rather than follow the managerialist agenda?

The crucial elements of a wider vision are:

- community governance;
- co-production;
- co-evolution.

Community governance: new approaches to decision-making

The *National Strategy for Neighbourhood Renewal* includes many recommendations for reforming the management of services. But proposals to address social exclusion must not only consider how services are provided but also how they are planned and governed. The National Strategy's focus is on the kind of leadership that is needed at local authority level – its major proposal is for the local strategic partnerships referred to above. But there is little as yet on governance at the neighbourhood level in either the National Strategy Action Plan or the earlier PAT4 report on neighbourhood management.

There has been some experimentation on the ground. Communities are involved in a growing number of cross-cutting partnerships. Local authorities in many areas are also developing neighbourhood forums and other methods of deliberative democracy to give communities a greater say in services and strategies for their areas. It is comparatively rare for such forums to have formal powers over services – the emphasis is on influence rather than formal authority – but the evidence is that they do build networks, bringing key players face to face with each other, and they do force local services to give an account at neighbourhood level even if there are no formal sanctions (Taylor 2000a).

However, there is considerable variation in the way partnerships are being implemented – across the country and even within authorities. Commitment sometimes goes only skin deep, with agencies sending along junior staff to partnership meetings or failing to communicate the joined-up message back through their own organization. Staff from one part of an authority often know little about partnerships led from other departments. Councillors find it difficult to give up control. The evidence suggests that, even where partnerships are constituted in ways which should give community control, local authorities as accountable bodies often have the power of interpreting the rules as well as superior resources and information, which means that community members remain relatively marginal.

The fresh impetus given to the issue of community involvement in new policies, such as the New Deal for Communities, Sure Start and the *National Strategy for Neighbourhood Renewal* means that considerable thought is now being given to the way in which the governing bodies of these initiatives should be constituted. If they are to be effective and to reflect the interests of whole communities and their partners, any number of difficult questions are raised – which deserve a paper all to themselves. These include questions about the legitimacy and accountability of such partnerships and their relationship to the local democratic system, about how partners are represented and are accountable to their constituencies. They include questions about power: about who determines the rules of the game and how the multiple accountabilities of partnership are negotiated. There is also the challenge of how those who are socially excluded within disadvantaged areas can be given a voice. Government tends to talk about 'the community' – in each of these neighbourhoods, there are many diverse communities and finding a way of representing their different interests is a difficult task.

Other chapters in this book have argued that partnership is a comfortable word but one which masks major tensions – tensions which have rarely been acknowledged in the past and to which there is no easy solution. It is in the new partnership arenas that those tensions are being addressed: between public accountability, risk and innovation; between leadership and participation; between the need to establish common ground and the acknowledgement of conflict and diversity. However, the governance structures that are being developed tend to be embedded in tried and tested models. There is a need for more fundamental institutional innovation. While there is a great deal of change going on at present – with the Modernising Local Government Agenda and the growth of partnership – there is little evidence of genuine new thinking about the links between the democratic system and governance. This leaves many councillors adrift and on the defensive. Without new thinking, local strategic partnerships run the risk of repeating the failed experiments of past co-ordination strategies – just another partnership where success depends on the willingness of a few key individuals to embrace a new vision.

Whatever happens at local level, tackling exclusion will require a joined-up centre – at local, regional and central level. Part of the job of government at regional and national level will be to put in place the resources and infrastructure that will drive and support local action. At each level, neighbourhood strategies will need to be tied into wider economic strategies. But, a key challenge will be to join up Whitehall.

Local initiatives have in the past foundered on competition or simple lack of coordination between ministries and departments. Can central government deliver on the joined-up agenda? This is likely to be the ultimate test for new strategies. Otherwise, joined-up working is likely to dissipate back into the chimneys or silos from whence it came, with joined-up outcome indicators unpacked back into departmental priorities dictated from above.

Co-production: changing the way services are produced

The managerial solution is a response to the question: How can existing services work better together? It aims to make existing services function more effectively and produce a better outcome for the consumer. It also aims to involve communities in the work of the professionals. But definitions of what is needed still tend to start from the top, even though communities are consulted on the way. More opportunities are also provided for residents to have their say as consumers, through surveys and panels. But the power of interpreting those voices lies at the centre.

If social exclusion is to be addressed, the likelihood is that it will need to reframe the debate from one about re-engineering existing services to a new set of ideas about the production of services. This is the approach that is advanced by community-based regeneration organizations – and particularly the Development Trusts movement. They ask not how existing services can work better but how these services should be produced. They see residents not only as consumers, nor even only as citizens, but as co-producers, aiming to transform the production of local services through community assets and enterprises which produce local jobs and income streams.

Advocates of this way of thinking argue that both jobs and wealth in an excluded area circulate outside the area. Wealth leaks out of the area to paid professionals who live elsewhere or to businesses and financial services outside the areas. People in excluded areas are more dependent than most on public services, whatever their quality, and cannot opt out. They have low expectations. But an increasing number of examples of resident-run services show how local people, given the skills and confidence, can make a major contribution to developing local social capital, and also bring assets under resident control. Mutual organizations, like LETS (Local Exchange and Trading System) or Credit Unions, and community-based Development Trusts have often reintroduced services withdrawn by public and private providers as well as providing jobs and thereby circulating wealth locally (Leadbeater and Christie 1999). The 'exit strategies' from some City Challenge and now SRB programmes have left behind endowments and new community-based structures with assets of their own, which not only create economic opportunities but give community partners much more to bargain with at the partnership table.

This approach to neighbourhood renewal would see the priority of the new neighbourhood strategy as employing local people in local services managed by local people. Advocates of this approach would see neighbourhood renewal as developing from the bottom-up, with community-led mutually owned organizations acting as a hub for joined-up working.

To encourage these developments across the country will require investment and institutional innovation. The National Strategy does see the potential for social entrepreneurs to act as drivers for change. But too often these can appear as charismatic individuals with a talent for making things happen and selling themselves and their ideas. Leadership is important, but unless these talents are spread and social enterprise seen as a collective endeavour, change will not be sustainable.

Co-evolution: changing the way we work

A growing number of critics argue that new governance structures and even new organizations will not be enough to turn around social exclusion. It is cultures that will have to change. A new approach to the production of public services will not only include the co-production option discussed above but also wholesale revolutions in public sector cultures. This is the approach taken by those who advocate whole systems approaches to change (Pratt *et al.* 1999; Stewart 1999; Wilkinson and Applebee 1999).

Thus, Pratt *et al.* (1999) argue for a move from co-ordination and collaboration to co-evolution, based on new systems of knowledge production and learning. They argue that: 'If we do what we always did, we'll get what we always got.'

Cooperation and coordination – where participating organizations maintain their boundaries and separate identities – may, they argue, be the most appropriate strategies for known and predictable goals, but co-evolution is more appropriate where:

- The environment is uncertain.
- There is agreement about broad aims but not about precise objectives.
- Problems are complex and multi-faceted.
- Strategies to resolve problems are unknown.

Tackling social exclusion clearly fits this template. As Pratt *et al.* (1999) argue, where goals are difficult to predict, partners need to be bound in more closely and risk needs to be shared. Fundamentally new ways of working are also advanced by the other authors cited above. Leat *et al.* (1999) for example, contrast the 'strong' tools – which tend to be associated with the NPM – of regulation, pooled budget incentives, inspection and sanctions – with the weak tools of persuasion, information, learning systems, building networks, setting or borrowing examples, evaluating and changing cultures: 'Strong tools are useful for short sprints. But weak tools...are the long distance runners.'

Wilkinson and Applebee (1999) argue that knowledge rather than money is the currency of the twenty-first century and new approaches need to focus on the production and circulation of knowledge and learning, crucially recognizing the value of 'tacit' as well as professional knowledge (Leadbeater 1999). Government strategies these days tend to highlight the need to identify and share 'best practice'. But the concept of best practice itself can be contested. Like its close cousin, Best Value, a lot depends on who is defining 'best', the context within which that practice developed and how it is transferred:

> Policy makers seize on an initiative or approach that seems to work and that fits in with their assumptions at that time (e.g. in terms of cost, partnerships, joined up solutions, etc.) and promote it across the board.
>
> (Paton 1998)

There is unlikely to be a blueprint. New ways of working will mean borrowing the language of the 'learning organization' from the best of the private sector and developing new learning systems across organizations and between them and the community. This language has begun to filter into the SEU documentation (SEU 2001: 58–9). How far will local authorities and others who lead local strategic partnerships be prepared to go down this route?

Healey (1997: 241) argues that the current 'rules of the game' privilege rationalist processes and scientific ways of knowing, reinforcing the dominance of highly resourced, managerial and technical forms of knowledge. Tacit knowledge in contrast is neglected, if not rejected out of hand. Research also suggests that conflict and argument are avoided – which tends to reinforce existing power relationships rather than challenging them (Hastings *et al.* 1996).

If partnership working is to engage with tensions and diversity, Healey echoes Leat *et al.*'s view that 'hard' procedures will need to be embedded in 'soft' processes which encourage mutual listening and learning, understanding and relationship building in order to build social, political and intellectual capital. The 'harder processes' need to grow out of the knowledge produced in this way, rather than pre-empting it. However, politicians tend to be impatient with process. The development of the National Strategy demonstrated a willingness to take the time to learn. This needs to be continued through into implementation if learning is to inform future progress and we are to learn what produces successful outcomes.

What this requires

This chapter has discussed managerial approaches to social exclusion, with a particular emphasis on neighbourhood renewal. It has argued that managerial approaches need to be combined with new approaches to governance and the production of public services if socially excluded people are to be involved as consumers, citizens and co-producers. It has also argued that management has to be conceived in terms of processes rather than procedures through a process of co-evolution. But this is still not quite the whole story. Two more things are needed.

One is people who can work in new ways. New ways of working, whichever of the above headings they fall under, will require new skills and new capacity, a point clearly recognized by a recent report from the government's Performance and Innovation Unit (PIU 2000). Much is said and written about capacity building in the community; less attention has been paid to date to the need for new skills within the public sector, such as mediation, brokerage, networking, knowledge production, conflict resolution. Fundamental cultural change needs to be driven from above. Sanctions, incentives, professional and career opportunities, and standards will need to support joined-up action rather than reinforce departmental and professional boundaries. Risk-averse cultures need to be confronted at all levels of government and new ways found of handling risk. For this reason, capacity building needs to reach beyond the frontline or even the middle manager. It is the auditors and accountants who have been the *éminences grises* behind the NPM mark I, and if systems are to change fundamentally then they too have to change.

It is important that risk is not pushed down the system. Change, uncertainty and conflict can foster defensiveness and resistance. Bureaucracies are set up, after all, to minimize uncertainty and the NPM itself is centrally concerned with monitoring and control. If support is not available for those who need to change within the system as well as for communities themselves, too much will depend on the existence of champions at local and central level. Champions move on or burn out. Unless innovation and connections are spread throughout institutions, practice will all too easily revert to the traditional and safe. The National Strategy will not work if is about pockets of excellence. It will only work if it institutionalises innovation and change.

The other pre-requisite for new approaches to inclusion, is the wider policy environment within which they take place. Habermas has argued that many of the programmes that are presented by governments to tackle endemic structural inequalities are presented in one of two ways. The first is to present them as something confined to marginal groups; the second as problems that can be solved by better management. This form of presentation is required so that the legitimacy of the system is not endangered and offers a symbolic solution. These have been the solutions presented in the past. But European research on partnerships has suggested that the more problems are structural in nature, the less likely it is that partnerships will of themselves provide solutions (Geddes 1998). David Page (2000), too, has commented that so long as investment in public services continues to deteriorate, neighbourhood renewal programmes will be swimming against the tide. Many of those involved in government's new programmes to tackle social exclusion can see windows of opportunity, new allies and cracks in the old ways of doing things – all of which can be exploited. But unless fundamental political action is taken to address structural inequalities, these areas may end up, however imaginatively, managing their own exclusion.

Conclusions

Social exclusion is a relational concept. It requires approaches to public management which address relationships rather than individuals as units to be processed by a system or even courted by a market. Managerial approaches in the past that have prioritized measurement, primarily of individuals, and operated on rationalist assumptions can only go some of the way towards addressing exclusion. This chapter has argued that they need to be placed in the context of wider approaches that embed individual achievement and outputs – the training places, the educational achievements, the successful service episodes – in a wider context, which also addresses systems of governance, of production and of organizational and institutional learning.

As such it is likely that the 'one template fits all' approach of 'best practice' and 'performance indicators' will be of limited value. Good ideas will always be useful, but they will have to be mediated through different local relationships and circumstances and they are only likely to work if the underlying principles are fully understood as the result of a more intensive process of learning and change – one moreover which can work with uncertainty and complexity (see, for example, Haynes 1999; Taylor 2000). If this is to happen the training and career structures of those in public services, whether as officers or councillors will have to change fundamentally. Other chapters in this volume have argued that, while the harsher edges of the NPM have been softened by the New Labour reworking of the concept, there is still much continuity between the two manifestations. The concept of an enabling council has been around for some considerable time, but if cultures have changed at all, it is arguable that they have simply exchanged one form of control for another.

Hardy (cited in Leat 2000) argues that, with all its limitations, joint planning in health and social services 'led to mutual organizational learning, clarification of differences, an upward spiral of trust and growing consensus about aims, principles and priorities'. I do not wish to argue against an emphasis on producing better outcomes for people in excluded areas. Monitoring is important, just as identifying and sharing effective practice is important. But ultimately what will determine the success of the strategy will not be stick-on solutions or carrots and sticks. It will be the success of the learning and development strategies discussed on pp. 58 and 59 of the Action Plan (SEU 2001) and the extent to which they equip the widest possible range of public servants and residents to adapt what is going on elsewhere to their own situation and come up with their own solutions – to learn to problem solve in an imaginative and effective way.

Acknowledgement

Thanks to Jenny Harrow for comments on the original draft.

Note

This chapter was written before the 2001 general election, and it was not possible to take account of any restructuring that might occur under a new government.

Bibliography

Amman, R. (1995) Article in *The Times Higher Education Supplement*, 1 September.

Atkinson, R. (2000) 'Narratives of policy: the construction of urban problems and urban policy in the official discourse of British government 1968–98', *Critical Social Policy*, 20 (2) pp. 211–232.

Dahrendorf, R. (1995) 'Can we combine economic opportunity with civil society and political liberty?' *The Responsive Community*, 5 (3).

Deakin, N. (1996) 'What does contracting do to users?' In Billis, D. and Harris, M. (eds) *Voluntary Agencies: challenges of organisation and management*, Basingstoke: Macmillan.

Geddes, M. (1998) 'Local Partnership: a successful strategy for local cohesion?' European Foundation for the Improvement of Living and Working Conditions.

Gutch, R. (1992) *Contracting: lessons from the United States*, London: NCVO.

Hambleton, R., Hoggett, P. and Razzaque, K. (1997) *Freedom Within Boundaries: developing effective approaches to decentralisation*, London: Local Government Management Board.

Hastings, A., McArthur, A. and McGregor, A. (1996) *Less than Equal: community organisations and estate regeneration partnerships*, Bristol: The Policy Press.

Haynes, P. (1999) *Complex Policy Planning: the Government strategic management of the social care market*, Aldershot: Ashgate.

Healey, P. (1997) *Collaborative Planning: shaping places in fragmented societies*, Basingstoke: Macmillan.

Hems, L. and Passey, A. (1998) *The Voluntary Sector Almanac*, London: National Council for Voluntary Organisations.

Joseph Rowntree Foundation (1995) *Income and Wealth: Report of the JRF Inquiry Group*, York: Joseph Rowntree Foundation.

Knight, B. (1993) *Voluntary Action*, London: The Home Office.

Leadbeater, C. (1999) *Living on Thin Air*, London: Viking.

Leadbeater, C. and Christie, I. (1999) *To Our Mutual Advantage*, London: Demos.

Leadbeater, C. and Goss, S. (1998) *Civic Entrepreneurship*, London: Demos and the Public Management Foundation.

Leat, D. (2000) Holistic Budgets, Demos unpublished.

Leat, D., Seltzer, K. and Stoker, G. (1999) *Governing in the Round: strategies for holistic government*, London: Demos.

Le Grand, J. (1992) *Paying For or Providing Welfare, Studies in Decentralisation and Quasi-Markets*, no. 16, Bristol: School for Advanced Urban Studies.

Levitas, R. (1999) *The Inclusive Society? Social Exclusion and New Labour*, London: Macmillan.

Murray, C. (1990) *The Emerging British Underclass*, London: Institute of Economic Affairs Health and Welfare Unit.

Page, D. (2000) *Communities in the Balance: the reality of social exclusion on housing estates*, York: York Publishing Services.

Paton, R. (1998) 'The "managerial state" as an environment for social enterprises', paper presented at the Centre for Voluntary Organisations, London School of Economics, September.

Performance and Innovation Unit (2000) *Wiring It Up: Whitehall's management of cross-cutting services*, London: The Stationery Office.

Perkin, H. (1989) *The Rise of Professional Society*, London: Routledge.

Pollitt, C., Birchall, J. and Putnam, K. (1998) *Decentralising Public Service Management*, Basingstoke: Macmillan.

Power, M. (1994) *The Audit Explosion*, London: Demos.

Pratt, J., Gordon, P. and Plamping, D. (1999) *Working Whole Systems*, London: King's Fund.

Robinson, D., Dunn, K. and Ballintyne, S. (1998) *Social Enterprise Zones: building innovation into regeneration*, York: Joseph Rowntree Foundation.

Room, G. (1995) 'Poverty in Europe: competing paradigms of analysis', *Policy and Politics*, 23 (2) pp. 103–113.

Russell, J. and Scott, D. (1998) *Very Active Citizens? The impact of the contract culture on volunteers*, University of Manchester: Department of Social Policy and Social Work.

Russell, J., Scott, D. and Wilding, P. (1995) *Mixed Fortunes: the funding of the voluntary sector*, Manchester: University of Manchester.

Social Exclusion Unit (1998) *Bringing Britain Together: a national strategy for neighbourhood renewal*, Cm 4045, London: The Stationery Office.

Social Exclusion Unit (2000) *National Strategy for Neighbourhood Renewal: a framework for consultation*, London: Social Exclusion Unit.

Social Exclusion Unit (2001) *Action Plan for Neighbourhood Renewal*.

Stewart, M. (1999) 'Local action to counter exclusion', report to the Local Government Research Unit, DETR.

Taylor, M. (1997) *The Best of Both Worlds: the voluntary sector and local government*, York: Joseph Rowntree Foundation.

Taylor, M. (2000) *Top Down Meets Bottom Up: neighbourhood management*, York: Joseph Rowntree Foundation.

Thomas, R. and Dunkerley, D. (1999) 'Janus and the bureaucrats: middle management in the public sector', *Public Policy and Administration*, 14 (1) pp. 28–41.

Unwin, J. and Westland, P. (1996) *Trends, Myths and Realities: funding policies and the local voluntary sector*, London: Association of Charitable Foundations/Charities Aid Foundation.

Wilkinson, D. and Applebee, E. (1999) *Implementing Holistic Government: joined up action on the ground*, Bristol: The Policy Press.

Chapter 8

Best Value

New Public Management or new direction?

Steve Martin

Introduction

This chapter examines the extent to which the concept of 'Best Value' as it is being developed within the UK public sector can be seen as the NPM 'in action'. It suggests that in some senses the new regime appears to be the high-water mark of the NPM. However, it is likely to test to destruction a number of the underlying assumptions of the NPM framework and in the process to demonstrate the need for a more sophisticated analysis of the role of local public services and approaches to their regulation. In particular the apparent paradoxes of the Best Value regime need to be understood in the context of conflicting interests and agendas of central and local government, business, organized labour and service users and the internal tensions within the British Labour Party between the 'modernizers' and other factions.

The New Public Management

Both the NPM and Best Value are slippery concepts susceptible to a multitude of overlapping and, in the case of Best Value, apparently contradictory interpretations. According to some accounts (notably successive OECD studies – 1990, 1993, 1995, 1997) the NPM constitutes a unified, consistent and coherent set of 'business like' or neo-managerial practices. Promoted by fiscal crises and the resulting search for 'cost-effectiveness' or 'value for money', the NPM is seen as having increasingly dominated public governance and public service delivery in most Western democracies. There has, we are told, been a shift from tight *ex ante* control of inputs by the senior management. The centre has apparently become increasingly concerned with 'steering and strategic control', and responsibility for service delivery has been devolved to front-line staff operating within a system of 'continuously monitored management by objectives with accountability for results' (OECD 1994: 54).

This account has of course been contested by a number of commentators. Polidano *et al.* (1998: 21) have concluded that there really is 'no such thing as a single model of New Public Management reform'. Kickert (1997, 1999) has argued that there is an Anglo-American bias in many descriptions of the NPM which glosses over the very different types, different rates and different trajectories of change in different countries, services, sectors and sub-national jurisdictions, and empirical studies by Naschold (1996) and Flynn and Strehl (1996) seem to bear this out. Naschold (1996: 2) reports that 'Contrary to the official view taken by the OECD ... there is no evidence of a linear homogenous trend in public service development'. Flynn and Strehl (1996: 4) note that: 'There are many variables which affect how reforms are designed and implemented', highlighting in particular 'the constitutional arrangements in place, political opinions at national and subnational level, public attitudes towards the state and its employees, and the skills and knowledge of public sector managers'.

Nevertheless, the NPM has continued to provide what Pollitt (1995: 133) describes as 'a kind of shopping basket for those who wish to modernize the public sectors of Western industrial societies' and has typically be seen as consisting of a cocktail of:

- cost cutting, capping budgets and seeking greater transparency in resource allocation;
- the disaggregating of traditional bureaucratic organizations into separate agencies;
- the decentralization of management authority within public agencies;
- a clearer separation of purchaser and providers roles;
- the introduction of market and quasi-market mechanisms;
- the introduction of performance targets, performance indicators and output objectives;
- increased flexibility of pay and conditions, the break-up of national pay scales and conditions and the growth of 'performance related pay' linked to improvements in service outcomes;
- increasing emphasis on the quality of services, setting standards for quality and responding to customer's priorities (see Hood 1991; Pollitt 1993, 1995; Dunleavy and Hood 1994).

The Best Value regime

The phrase Best Value is closely associated with private sector management techniques such as 'value planning', 'value engineering' and 'value analysis', and concepts of 'customer value'. The version of Best Value being developed in the UK also has strong links to the rise of performance measurement, performance review, stakeholder involvement and corporate strategic management. The use of the phrase Best Value in the public sector seems to date from 1989 when it was applied to US navy procurement and intended to encourage purchasers to take more account of non-cost-based criteria. 'Best Value principles' have since been adopted in other areas of US defence procurement (Alderman 1993), in the appraisal of procurement and capital investment schemes in a number of public services in Australia (Bovaird and Halachmi 1998) and in regional (though not local) government in New Zealand

(McKinlay 1998). The phrase has however only come to the fore in the UK since the 1997 general election.

Although initially billed simply as a replacement for compulsory competitive tendering (CCT) (see Doyle 1996), Best Value rapidly gained a much wider importance. The minister responsible for local and regional government in England has repeatedly claimed that 'At its heart Best Value seeks to reshape the relationship between government and the electorate' and the regime has emerged as the centrepiece of central government's attempts to promote 'a radical refocusing of councils' traditional roles' (Cm 4104 1998: 5). It was extended well beyond local government to fire, police, social services and non-clinical support in the National Health Service and is now seen as underpinning the present UK government's entire approach to public services management (see House of Commons 1998: 94 and 96; Cm 4310).

The key features of the regime in England were set out in consultation and white papers (DETR 1998 and Cm 4104), the Best Value legislation (HMSO 1999) and the statutory guidance (DETR 1999a). Analogous provisions were introduced in Wales and Scotland (Boyne *et al.* 1999; Midwinter and McGarvey 1999; Sheffield and Bowman 1999). The regime builds upon, but also seeks to move beyond, previous local government reforms (Martin 2000). As the Audit Commission's guide to preparing for 'Best Value' put it, the new regime 'runs wider and deeper' than previous regulations (Audit Commission 1998). Unlike the CCT legislation which it replaced, Best Value applies to all local authority activities. Moreover, whereas CCT revolved around episodic improvements linked to the renewal of time-limited contracts, the Best Value regime imposes on authorities a legal duty to 'secure *continuous* improvement in the way functions are exercised' (HMSO 1999, clause 3.1, emphasis added).

Best Value also goes well beyond previous attempts to strengthen the role of service users. Councils now have a legal duty to consult not just with users but also with local taxpayers and any other groups who have 'an interest in any area within which the authority carries out functions' (HMSO 1999: clause 3.2). Authorities must seek views not only about past performance but also about future targets and priorities which have to be published in annual 'Best Value performance plans' agreed by the full council and distributed widely to the public (Cm 4104: para 7.31).

All councils are also being set new performance targets and, under the Best Value regime, have to seek to reach the standards currently attained by the top quartile of authorities by the year 2005 as well as achieving annual efficiency savings of two per cent. Services are therefore monitored through new performance indicators and audit and inspection routines (Audit Commission 1999a,b) and secretaries of state have extensive new powers to intervene where services are 'failing' (DETR 1999b).

As with CCT, competition is seen as 'an essential management tool' (Cm 4104, para 7.27) and services can not be delivered directly by authorities 'if other more efficient and effective means are available' (DETR 1998: 20). However, under Best Value local authorities are also expected to create, nurture and manage markets in order to promote a 'mixed economy of provision' by creating 'the conditions under which there is likely to be greater interest from the private and voluntary sectors in working with local government to deliver quality services' (Cm 4014: clause 7.30).

On the face of it then, the Best Value regime appears to delve deep into the NPM 'shopping basket'. It emphasizes at least four of the key features of the NPM highlighted by Pollitt, namely cost cutting, market mechanisms, performance management/management by objectives, and raising the quality of services. This is only part of the story for, as a number of commentators (including Newman Chapter 5, this volume) have observed, the discourse of 'modernization' adopted by New Labour is a paradoxical one. On the one hand there is a strong emphasis on the market, national minimum standards, league tables and performance monitoring. On the other there is encouragement of local responsiveness, collaboration and innovation. The tensions which this creates are not easily resolved and the picture is undoubtedly complicated by the way in which ministerial pronouncements are carefully crafted to avoid startling the inhabitants of 'middle England' while also deflecting opposition from within the party. However, this is not a simple case of New Labour cloaking itself in the New Right's approach to local authorities. The present government's attitude to public services is distinguishable from that of its predecessors in a number of important respects.

His closest aides claim that Prime Minister Blair is 'passionately committed' to improving the quality of public services, believing this to be vital both to his party's electoral prospects and to the nation's economic success. Thus while the progenitors of the Best Value regime, all committed 'modernizers' with roots in local government, have been uncompromising about the need for rapid service improvement (see Filkin *et al.* 1999), the current Prime Minister is said not to assume that private contractors are necessarily more efficient and effective than in-house teams. As a key member of his policy unit put it recently: 'We are genuinely agnostic about who delivers services'. New Labour has adopted what appears to be a much more open, inclusive and experimental approach to policy formulation than other recent administrations. Past attempts to enforce detailed regulations of the kind associated with CCT are seen as having failed. In their place there has been a concerted attempt to win 'bottom up' support for service improvement and to encourage a more constructive relationship between central and local government. Ministers moved quickly to sign the symbolically important European Charter on Local Self Government and establish the 'central–local partnership' as a forum for discussions between ministers and local authority leaders (Briscoe 1997). The 'social partners' (businesses and unions) plus national representatives of local government were closely involved in shaping the new regime and individual authorities were actively encouraged to pilot Best Value principles in advance of the legislation (Martin and Sanderson 1999). The language of threats and punishments to which local authorities became so accustomed under the Conservatives is now accompanied by the promise of rewards for councils that do 'deliver' substantial improvements. Local authority leaders have been warned: 'If you are unwilling or unable to work to the modern agenda then the government will have to look to other partners to take on your role' (IPPR 1998). However, according to his advisers, Blair also 'believes very strongly in incentives for individuals and groups'.

A third important difference is the increasing recognition of the need for a sophisticated approach to regulating local services that takes account of the wide variations in local authority performance. Although senior figures in the Audit Commission have talked privately for some years about 'leading authorities', 'laggards' and 'the mediocre authorities in the middle', the Best Value inspection regime makes these kinds of distinctions explicit for the first time, recognizing four categories of authorities – 'Beacons', 'Striving', 'Coasting' and 'Failing' (Audit Commission 2000). This in turn paves the way for a very different type of relationship between central and local government. 'Failing authorities' will be subject to swift intervention. Those that are 'coasting' or 'striving' to improve will be subject to much closer monitoring and inspection than ever before. The 'Beacons' will receive 'lighter touch inspection' together with additional freedoms and perhaps fund raising powers. This of course poses awkward questions about the adequacy of current performance measures and the ability of inspectors and auditors to distinguish between 'excellent' and 'failing' authorities. However, the regime seems designed to fragment the local government community with the old conflicts between central and local government becoming less relevant as new battle lines are drawn between the 'modernizers' and 'Old Labour'. As one senior Labour local authority leader put it recently: 'I don't really give a toss if Hackney goes down the pan. But we're not having them drag us down with them'.

Perhaps most significantly of all, the present government has shown increasing signs of an awareness of the need to enhance the capacity of local authorities to improve services (Martin 1999). The moribund Local Government Management Board has been replaced by an Improvement and Development Agency for local government (IDeA), which offers consultancy support to individual authorities and oversees two major capacity building initiatives apparently modelled on the support offered to small and medium-sized enterprises by the Department of Trade and Industry and its attempts to encourage 'technology transfer' between companies. The 'Local Government Improvement Project' seeks to encourage improvement 'from within' through a process of peer review (LGA 1999). The Beacon Council Scheme is designed to disseminate 'good practice' by encouraging authorities that are judged to be performing well to share their expertise with others (DETR 1999c). The DETR also established its own in-house team (the Local Government Modernisation Group) of former senior local government managers to support authorities in responding to 'modernization agenda'. It is too early to judge their effectiveness or that of their successors. However, together with the more participative approach to policy formulation these initiatives are indicative of a search for what Rhodes (1997) has called a 'new operating code' and of the blurring of the traditional roles of central and local government (Martin 2000). The former no longer sees itself simply as writing and policing national regulations but is now playing a more pro-active role in implementing change. Local government meanwhile is no longer simply required to conform to regulations 'handed down' from Westminster and Whitehall but is being asked to play a greater role in developing and piloting the new regime and in implementing it 'imaginatively in the spirit in which it has been designed' (DETR 1999d: para 10).

Local implementation

In this context the pattern of local implementation is therefore crucial. Much will of course depend on the stance taken by inspectors and external auditors neither of whom had, at the time of writing, 'begun to bite'. However, some indications of the ways in which authorities may respond to the Best Value regime can be deduced from the pilot programmes that preceded the legislation (Martin et al. 2001). Detailed evaluation of the English pilot programme reveals four broad approaches to implementation that we have labelled 'service', 'market', 'corporate' and 'community' – see Table 8.1.

Many of the pilot reviews have been focused on functionally organized services delivered through traditional, hierarchical, departmental structures and processes. In these cases what constitutes 'Best Value' was defined in terms of professional standards and norms and service-based performance indicators. Best Value reviews were driven by those who might be seen as having the greatest interest in minimizing disruption to existing approaches to service delivery (the chairs of service committees, service managers and front-line staff). Entirely new approaches to service delivery and broader strategic issues did not loom large. Comparisons were usually made with 'similar' authorities. Consultation often focused primarily on the needs of users (as opposed to taxpayers), and there was often little fundamental questioning of service from the perspective of non-users. Competition did not feature strongly and externalization was frequently seen as a 'last resort' to address of chronic under-performance or gross inefficiency.

A second group of pilot initiatives focused on market testing and/or the creation of new service delivery partnerships. They were typically been driven by a desire to reduce spending or attract new capital investment (for example in school buildings, leisure centres, catering services, residential homes and public sector housing). Best Value has been defined largely in terms of measures of cost and efficiency and determined through market testing and benchmarking. Users' views were not a key driver for change. Front-line staff and service managers played only a minor role and elected members sometimes found the conclusions reached by review teams unpalatable.

A third group of pilots attempted to develop 'whole authority' approaches to implementing Best Value principles by developing corporate review programmes linked explicitly to their strategic objectives. Most developed corporate Best Value methodologies or 'toolkits' and performance management systems, sometimes based on the Business Excellence Model (see James and Field 1999).

Table 8.1 Typology of approaches to Best Value

	In-house service focus	Market focus	Issue focus	Community focus
Principal aims	Produce	Procure	Ensure appropriate provision	Engage with communities
Emphasis	Compare (standards)	Compete (VCT)	Collaborate	Consult
Means	Incremental improvement in traditional welfare state	Contracting out and joint ventures	Corporate re-engineering and cultural change	Empowering communities
Structures	Strong departments and service committees	Commissioner/provider split, public–private partnerships	Corporate management team and political executive	Neighbourhood offices, area forums
Value defined in terms of	Professional standards and service-based PIs	Costs	Corporate and community priorities	Community needs and aspirations
Predominant mode of regulation	Hierarchy	Market	Provider networks	Community based networks
Approach to partnership	Minimal	Public–private	Strategic partnerships	Community and service delivery partnerships
Champions	Service managers, committee chairs, front-line staff	Central government, business	Corporate managers executive elected members	Community groups, neighbourhood managers, ward councillors

Source: Adapted from Martin (2000).

Reviews were often led by senior officers or executive elected members with no direct links to the service(s) being scrutinized. Reviews teams usually included external advisers. There was a strong emphasis on the need to ensure more effective joint working across internal departments and with external agencies and this approach therefore lent itself to 'cross-cutting reviews' focused on issues such as community safety, regeneration and public health.

A fourth group of pilot initiatives focused on the needs and priorities of specific communities of place, identity or interest. The size of the target areas, the nature of the client groups and the number of services reviewed varied. However, the unifying theme was the attempt to reconfigure or 'join up' services so that they responded to community needs. Review processes therefore typically spanned a number of departments. Review teams usually included senior corporate officers, service managers and representatives of other agencies. There was often a strong link to community planning processes and, in a small number of cases, local people have begun, albeit in relatively modest ways, to 'co-produce' services.

The strengths, weaknesses, likely champions and opponents of each of these four emphases are explored in detail elsewhere (Geddes and Martin 2000). In brief, as the DETR acknowledged, a service-based approach is likely to be the 'most straightforward' (DETR 1998: para 4.7). However, it seems unlikely that such an approach will meet the demand for more joined-up government. Similarly, it is not clear that externalizing services will necessarily produce 'citizen-centred' services. Moreover, both the Best Value pilots, and the separate programme of Best Value partnerships networks set up specifically to demonstrate the benefits of public–private partnerships, have encountered major difficulties in getting the private sector interested in new forms of contracting.

A corporate approach focused on 'cross-cutting' themes may enable authorities to 'join-up services' and to address key strategic issues. It also reflects a managerialist approach that clearly resonates with the wider 'modernizing agenda' and may be compatible with the introduction of new political executives – another key element of current local government reforms. However, the pilots that have attempted to implement this approach have found that reviews have often proved to be complex and time-consuming and many authorities fear that 'cross-cutting' reviews will not produce tangible improvements in services within the timescales that ministers appear to be working to.

Like a corporate approach to Best Value, focusing on the needs of particular communities also challenges the traditional professional/producer-driven approach but emphasizes collective as opposed to individual customers' interests. It may prove to be an effective means of implementing Best Value in authorities that already have decentralized structures (area committees, neighbourhood forums, etc.). However, it is widely regarded as being both politically risky and potentially expensive. It also appears to fly in the face of the regulatory infrastructure being established by central government, implying as it does the need for a more facilitative approach based on self-regulating and self-governing associations and networks (Hoggett and Thompson 1998).

Conclusions

The Best Value regime being introduced in the UK does not therefore herald
the arrival of a new, hegemonic 'outcomes-focused paradigm'. Nor however is it
simply 'more of the same'. There is no 'blueprint' for achieving Best Value. But
there is a common set of core issues that all authorities are finding that they
have to confront as they seek to implement the new regime. In contrast to the
change strategy pursued by recent Conservative governments, which appeared
to relish public battles with local government, trades unions and the key
professional associations, New Labour is intent on playing down potential
differences between 'stakeholders'. It has therefore sought to win acceptance of
the 'necessity', or at least the inevitability, of change and has sought to build up
local capacity for continuous improvement from within local government itself.
The result is a somewhat ambiguous framework which allows a plurality of
approaches and consists of an intriguing interplay of 'governing structures'
including hierarchical, market based and collaborative approaches to managing
service delivery. However, this brings with it new tensions and makes more
explicit a number of classic policy dilemmas including the apparently conflicting
imperatives of cost reduction and service improvement, increased competition
and greater collaboration, short-term gains and sustainable, long-term
improvement.

Far from sweeping away previous reforms, the Best Value regime seeks to
build upon them – expanding the role of the market, making local authorities
more accountable to tax payers and service users and encouraging a more
performance-oriented culture. In some senses it can therefore be seen as the
high-water mark of the NPM. Indeed, because of the unprecedented demands
it makes of managers, markets, contractors, inspectors, auditors and service
users/citizens, Best Value threatens to test to destruction many of the key tenets
of NPM. It has already begun to demonstrate the inadequacy of many supply
markets. It is presenting new challenges to those businesses that became
accustomed in the 1990s to securing large local government contracts simply by
reducing staff numbers, pay and conditions. It is ruthlessly exposing the limits
of most local authority's performance management systems and is throwing
into question the adequacy of council consultation strategies that have hitherto
been considered to be 'state of the art'. It is also posing some tricky questions
for inspectors and auditors who are charged with making new kinds of judgement
about service standards and authorities' capacity to improve. Crucially, it is
testing to the limit the willingness of service users and citizens to engage in
meaningful ways with local service providers.

In so doing the Best Value regime may enable us to begin to move beyond the
NPM, based as it is on the now dated 'old private sector management' of the
1970s and early 1980s and to leaven these approaches with more recent private
sector thinking based on a more sophisticated understanding of the respective
strengths and roles of state and the market. The implementation of Best Value
in UK local government and other domains is therefore likely to offer new

opportunities, not simply to test out the limitations of the NPM framework as a means of transforming and reinventing public services.

It may also encourage us to pay much more attention to the politics of local service delivery since the regime can only really be understood as part of a wider, carefully orchestrated, and hitherto surprisingly successful, campaign to establish a consensus in support of 'modernization'. This in turn needs to be seen against the backdrop of the internal politics of the Labour party and the complex nature of central–local relations under New Labour. Conservative ministers were dealing with a local government community dominated by opposition parties. They therefore adopted, and indeed appeared to relish, a highly confrontational approach. By contrast, the 'modernizers' in New Labour, although they share many of their predecessors' doubts about the ability of local councils to deliver effective services, face a situation in which many of the authorities which they see as being in most urgent need of reform are under the control of their party colleagues. They have not as yet been willing to risk outright conflict with other factions of the party over local government reform (which is not seen as a key priority) and have therefore had to proceed rather cautiously, pursuing by stealth policies that remain unpalatable to many party activists and trades unions. How long their patience will hold and the rather fragile local–central partnership can be maintained is not yet clear. Having declared themselves to be 'tight on outcomes but loose on the means of achieving them', ministers will no doubt feel obliged to intervene in at least some 'failing' authorities. The real shock to the system will come if they decide that services are improving too slowly and more radical measures than the Best Value regime are required (including for example the removal of key functions such as education and social services from local authority control).

Ultimately, the combined forces of globalization and advances in information and communications technologies may well sweep existing patterns of service delivery to one side. Notions of what constitutes 'Best Value' are likely to be transformed as developments in information and communications technology open up new opportunities for e-government and the electronic delivery of some local services which allow much more immediate and differentiated forms of interaction between citizens/users and public service providers. New policy initiatives, including local Public Service Agreements and local strategic partnerships, may perhaps come to be seen as the key determinants of local service standards. For the time being though the Best Value regime offers a fascinating framework within which to explore some of the most important conceptual and policy questions relating to the improvement and regulation of public services and will continue to repay careful study.

References

Alderman, K.C. (1993) 'Performance measurement: management for best value' *Armed Forces Comptroller* 38 (3) pp. 1–13.

Audit Commission (1998) *Better by Far: preparing for best value* (Audit Commission: London).

Audit Commission (1999a) *Performance Indicators for 2000/2001*. A joint consultation document produced by the DETR and the Audit Commission on Best value and local authority performance indicators (Audit Commission: London).

Audit Commission (1999b) *Principles of Inspection* (Audit Commission: London).

Audit Commission (2000) *Seeing is Believing: how the Audit Commission will carry out best value inspection in England.* (Audit Commission: London).

Bovaird, A.G. and Halachmi, A. (1998) 'Citizens, community organisations, the private sector and other stakeholders in performance assessment for best value'. In Neely, A.D. and Waggoner, D.B. (eds) *Performance Measurement – theory and practice* (Judge Institute of Management Studies: Cambridge).

Boyne, G., Gould-Williams, J., Law, J. and Walker, R. (1999) 'Best Value in Welsh Local Government: progress and prospects', *Local Government Studies* 25 (2) pp. 68–86.

Briscoe, B. (1997) 'The new local government agenda', *Public Money and Management* 17 (4) pp. 4–6.

Cm 4104 (1998) *Modern Local Government: in touch with the people* (Stationery Office: London).

Cm 4310 (1999) *Modernising Government* (Stationery Office: London).

DETR (1998) *Modernising Local Government: improving local services through Best Value* (DETR: London).

DETR (1999a) *Implementing Best Value: statutory guidance* (DETR: London).

DETR (1999b) *Protocol on Intervention Powers* (DETR: London).

DETR (1999c) *The Beacon Council Scheme: prospectus* (DETR: London).

DETR (1999d) *Preparing for Best Value: initial guidance* (DETR: London).

Doyle, P. (1996) 'An alternative to CCT', *Municipal Journal* 28, June, p. 18.

Dunleavy, P. and Hood, C. (1994) 'From old public administration to new public management', *Public Money and Management* 14 (3) pp. 9–16.

Fikin, G., Bassam, S., Corrigan, P., Stokes, G. and Tizard, J. (1999) *Starting to Modernise: the change agenda for local government* (Joseph Rowntree Foundation: York).

Flynn, N. and Strehl, F. (1996) *Public Sector Management in Europe* (Prentice Hall: London).

Geddes, M.N. and Martin, S.J. (2000) 'The policy and politics of Best Value: currents, cross-current and undercurrents in the new regime', *Policy and Politics* 28 (3) pp. 377–394.

HMSO (1999) *Local Government Act 1999* (HMSO: London).

Hoggett, P. and Thompson, S. (1998) 'The delivery of welfare: the associationist vision'. In Carter, J. (ed.) *Postmodernity and the Fragmentation of Welfare* (Routledge: London).

Hood, C. (1991) 'A public management for all seasons', *Public Administration* 69 (1) pp. 3–9.

House of Commons (1998) *Implementation of the Best Value Framework,* House of Commons Environment, Transport and Regional Affairs Sub-committee, minutes of evidence (Stationery Office: London).

IPPR (1998) *Leading the Way: a new vision for local government* (IPPR: London).

James, D.B. and Field, J.J. (1999) 'A whole authority approach to testing and developing Best Value', *Local Government Studies* 25 (2) pp. 119–140.

Kickert, W. (1997) 'Public governance in the Netherlands: an alternative to Anglo-American "managerialism" ', *Public Administration* 75 (4) pp. 731–752.

Kickert, W. (1999) 'Public governance in Europe: an international and historical perspective'. Paper presented to the ESRC Seminar Recent developments in the New Public Management, Aston University, November.

LGA (1999) *Improving from Within: Local Government Improvement Project – final report and recommendations* (Local Government Association: London).

McKinlay, P. (1998) 'Local government reform: what was ordered and what has been delivered?' Unpublished paper.

Martin, S.J. (1999) 'Learning to modernise: creating the capacity to improve public services', *Public Policy and Administration* 14 (3) pp. 54–66.

Martin, S.J. (2000) 'Implementing Best Value: local public services in transition', *Public Administration* 78 (1) pp. 209–227.

Martin, S.J. and Sanderson, I. (2001) 'Evaluating public policy experiments: measuring outcomes, monitoring processes or managing pilots?', *Evaluation* 5 (3) pp. 245–258.

Martin, S.J., Davis, H., Bovaird, A.G., Downe, J., Geddes, M., Hartley, J.F., Lewis, M., Sanderson, I. and Sapwell, P. (2001) *Improving Local Public Services: final evaluation of the Best Value pilot programme* (Stationery Office: London).

Midwinter, A. and McGarvey, N. (1999) 'Developing Best Value in Scotland: concepts and contradictions', *Local Government Studies* 25 (2) pp. 87–101.

Naschold, F. (1996) *New Frontiers in Public Sector Management: trends and issues in state and local government in Europe* (W. de Gruyter: Berlin).

OECD (1990) *Public Management Developments: survey* (OECD: Paris).

OECD (1993) *Public Management Developments: survey* (OECD: Paris).

OECD (1994) *Performance Management in Government: Performance Measurement and Results-Oriented Management*. Public Management Occasional Papers, No. 3 (OECD: Paris).

OECD (1995) *Governance in Transition: public management reforms in OECD countries* (OECD: Paris).

OECD (1997) *In Search of Results: Performance Management Practices* (OECD: Paris).

Polidano, C., Hulme, D. and Minogue, M. (1998) 'Conclusion'. In Minogue, M. *et al.* (eds) *Beyond the New Public Management: changing ideas and practices in governance* (Edward Elgar: Cheltenham) (quoted in Newman, J. 1999).

Pollitt, C. (1993) *Mangerialism and the Public Services* (Basil Blackwell: Oxford).

Pollitt, C. (1995) 'Justification by works or by faith?', *Evaluation* 1 (2) pp. 133–154.

Rhodes, R.A.W. (1997) 'From marketisation to diplomacy: it's the mix that matters', *Public Policy and Administration* 12 (2) pp. 31–50.

Sheffield, J. and Bowman, M. (1999) 'An emergent audit agenda: comparative lessons drawn from Best Value development in Local Government in Scotland compared with England', *Public Policy and Administration* 14 (3) pp. 67–89.

Chapter 9

New Public Management and social justice

Just efficiency or equity as well?

Jenny Harrow

Introduction

Exploration of NPM to discern its stance on social justice offers contrasting perspectives. Social justice may be thought largely absent from NPM thinking. If and where its signs appear, these are rare occurrences, like a comet's passing, intriguing but transitory. Alternatively, social justice may be felt capable of delivery only where public provision is demonstrably efficient and users' voices heard. Thus, social justice is a star in the NPM firmament, set to shine more brightly as NPM tenets take increased hold. This chapter explores the extent to which social justice and equity concerns and outcomes are present or absent in NPM thinking and practice. It is underpinned by the assumption that the social justice record of NPM deserves scrutiny.

The chapter commences with a consideration of what is understood here by NPM, and how notions of social justice and equity may be defined. It continues by consideration of the cases which may be made for the polar opposite perceptions of NPM in relation to the promotion and achievement of social justice. First, that NPM's efficiency preoccupation and combined characteristics preclude an equity focus; leaving wider social justice concerns beyond its remit. Second, that NPM's characteristics include and may even secure improved equity in public provision, making it a key factor in reaching social justice goals. For both these cases, examples are drawn predominantly from health, and to a lesser extent from prison and local government (especially urban) services, and these mainly in UK contexts. The chapter goes on to reflect on the balance of the arguments made, and declares as 'non-proven' the charge that NPM has been eliminating social justice objectives in public policy. It suggests that equity 'guardians' in NPM contexts are more likely to found in shifting coalitions, as public services simultaneously or variously fragment and are 'joined up', rather than in a single coherent group, such as elected representatives or public service professionals. It examines some theoretical and service contextual implications for juxtaposing equity and efficiency as NPM goals. Finally, it highlights a need for increased knowledge concerning new public managers' working values, and the place of social justice and equity concerns within those values.

New Public Management: a cluster of institutional characteristics or a set of public values?

Earlier chapters have critiqued and presented interpretations of the nature of NPM, highlighting NPM most prominently as a collection of government-led activities displaying recognizable characteristics including controlled delegation, increased emphasis on user orientation and the measurement of performance, most commonly by 'business' style measures. Barberis (1998: 453) sees NPM, in Britain as '… associated with a number of specific (institutional) initiatives'. At the same time, these sets of primarily institution-based characteristics may also be grouped together, to constitute NPM as 'a global public service reform movement' (Thompson 2000: 198).

NPM may be seen also as rooted in public choice theory, which emphasizes the self-interested behaviour of public bureaucrats, and in agency theory, where conflict of interest between agent and principal in task performance is a given. Persistent monitoring of the former by the latter is vital. (see Thompson 2000: 202–203.) A minimalist interpretation of NPM is that '… in effect there is no management at all. Instead, there is highly instrumental role playing by the assembly line workers of performance-oriented government, who at best are engaged in continuous quality improvement; in effect, a 'shrunken view of public management' (Lynn 2000: 116.). Where managerial roles are retained, those which give primacy to general management skills over professional expertise and seek to control '… open ended features of professional practice, in order to conform with broader corporate goals and resource constraints' (Flynn 1999: 35; see also Kitchener *et al.* 2000, for exploration of issues of the supervision of professional work under NPM).

This chapter tries to take a mid-point – which is not intended to be a 'third way' – view of NPM, by taking it as a reform movement for changing ways of thinking about delivery of 'public services' in their broadest sense, most likely to be characterized by structural change and formal outcome assessments, and underpinned by a series of values which are themselves ambiguous, sometimes aligned and sometimes conflicting. These are predominantly values which laud public services' efficiency and effectiveness. In the search for effectiveness, however, the values – and the outcomes – of equity – are not excluded. What then is understood in this chapter by 'social justice' and 'equity'?

Defining 'social justice' and 'equity'

Understandings of 'social justice' and 'equity', as both concepts interact with the provision or denial of public services, are complex. Many discussions are 'grounded in a distributive paradigm' (Allison 2000: 2, citing Young 1990), often accompanied by assessments of institutional arrangement and conditions that explain particular distributions of wealth, status and power. Allison argues that 'as doers and actors we seek to promote many values of social justice in addition to fairness in the distribution of goods', including 'participating in forming and running' and 'receiving recognition for such participation' (Allison 2000: 2).

Thus, 'social justice ... concerns the degree to which societal institutions promote the conditions necessary for the realisation of these values' (Allison 2000: 2). 'Injustice' is defined by 'the extent to which the pursuit of such values are inhibited by the oppressive institutional constraints and barriers that inhibit self-determination and growth (Allison 2000: 2). Prominent among the conditions of constraint is the experience of 'marginalization', the extent to which groups of people are 'expelled from useful participation in social life' (Young 1990: 55). (See Chapter 7 for exploration of social exclusion and inclusion concepts and policy development.)

Other commentators make 'fairness' the dominant plank in any consideration of the justice concept. Centrally, Rawls's (1971) theory of justice is developed to take account of societal pluralism. Rawls asks: 'how is it possible that there may exist over time a stable and just society of free and equal citizens, profoundly divided by reasonable though incompatible religious, moral and philosophical doctrines?' (Rawls 1993). His solution (discussed at length by Jones 1995) is a form of political liberalism, where people endorse a 'freestanding' view of justice, aside from their individual beliefs. Thus 'fair' social arrangements are those evolved to suit prevailing social conditions.

A further defence of a plural theory of justice is found in Miller (1999), where three component principles, the 'practical' rather than the abstract principles that guide beliefs, are identified (Miller 1999: 24). These are the principles of desert, need and equality. Matravers (2000: 710), reviewing Miller's work, highlights the distinction made by people between 'genuine need and mere preferences' and focuses on the notion of 'desert' as the distinctive contribution of this study. 'Justice as equality' is a strong theme in much literature, but often lacking in specificity. Pereira (1993: 45), for example, finds it 'disheartening' that international debates on equity in health often disregard specification of equity objectives. Pereira's own account of equity interpretations shows the range of approaches available, including equity as health maximization in the community (a distribution issue) and equity as choice (invoking issues of need and preference). Culyer (1991, discussed by Saltman 1997: 445), identifying four forms of health equity, does offer specificity, with the opportunity of application elsewhere. These equal access to services, equal treatment received for the same condition or situation, treatment based on the need for care and equal health status or outcome. Against these four forms of equity, a service's performance may thus be assessed – for the 'exceptions' as well as the 'rules'.

For the purposes of this chapter, 'social justice' is taken as the achievement of widest possible social outcome in relation to 'fairness' and 'need', whereas 'equity' is seen as its 'lead' component, that necessary if not wholly sufficient element in social justice which can be identified, measured, challenged and promoted.

To any formulaic view of social justice should be added the equally problematic element of intuitive responses to justice. Albeit from a research design perspective, Altheide and Johnson (1997: 173) identify the importance of 'the sense of justice' rather than the requirement to recognize 'an absolute standard'.

They see social justice as 'an emotional commitment to a standard, expectation and value of fairness, rightness and orderliness' (Altheide and Johnson 1997: 173). They further see 'a sense of justice' as '... acquired, tested and realized when it is absent in everyday situations ... when all is said and done, it is routine interaction that produces and sustains major problems involving social justice' (Altheide and Johnson 1997: 173). This additional view of social justice, giving some sense of a social justice climate, in which public managers, public servants, service users and citizens interact, also seems apposite in any consideration of NPM and its social justice credentials. An examination of those credentials, taking the two polar positions discussed above, now follows.

New Public Management: precluding equity?

For those contending that primacy of efficiency values in NPM negates social justice concerns, or that NPM's preoccupation with efficiency precludes an equity focus, four views may be articulated:

1   that NPM was never intended to incorporate equity and social justice concerns;
2   that although NPM was not set up to exclude equity issues, its practice has been to create a catalogue of inequities;
3   that the NPM ideology and practice is too brash with its business-orientation, creating a feeling of unease that social justice cannot be delivered;
4   that NPM cannot be expected to incorporate equity and social justice values, since these are ceasing to be core public values.

NPM was never intended in to incorporate equity and social justice concerns

For some, that 'efficiency wipes out equity' is lived experience. Williamson (1995), for example, asserts the damage wrought by UK NHS marketization. His question 'Does so much concern to save money have an impact on our ability to provide compassionate, supportive and loving care for all?' is answered in his paper's title 'Love is not a marketable commodity: new public management in the British NHS'. Seedhouse's (1994) striking phrase 'Fortress NHS' is used by Williamson to assert how efficiency and egalitarian principles conflict in health provision. He concludes that 'the discrimination, alienation and dehumanisation, which reflect NPM values, are representatives of ... a "hate culture" ' (Seedhouse 1994: 984). With such a perspective, the delivery of existing or new equalities would be seen as aberrant.

A less strident version of this argument suggests that NPM's 'pleasing the customer' is not equity-directed – unless, in a managerial nightmare scenario, all customers arrive together. 'Pleasing the customer' may create distortions, as choices of other customers (absent or less vocal) go unheard. Paradoxically, such responsiveness makes for less long-term accountability to citizens generally.

The entrepreneurial NPM manager – villain or saviour – personalizes this dilemma. Commentators defining public entrepreneurship show that competitiveness and risk-taking must be present (see, for example, Boyett 1996), attributes which do not necessarily align well with a preference for equity.

NPM was not set up to exclude equity issues, but its practice has been to create a catalogue of inequities

This approach argues that NPM outcomes show it wanting, although the suggestion that social justice 'slipped out' of the NPM package seems less reprehensible than deliberate exclusion. Altered relations with named, contactable public officials subject to response times may have enhanced public feelings of the opportunity for fairer treatment than before, so increasing equity expectations. It is difficult to judge whether such developments are marginal or central gains. Disdain of seemingly shop window 'initiatives' such as the 'named nurse' for hospital patients may not always be deserved. These are, after all, some of the 'routine interactions' which may define social justice.

That market mechanisms widen inequalities is a given for some commentators, for example in relation to 'GP fundholding', in the UK. This appeared to produce the classic British public policy *faux pas* – 'queue jumping' – through selected practices holding budgets and buying defined services from hospitals (Iliffe 1995: 39). Subsequent abolition of the fundholding system made much of these inequities (Goddard and Mannion 1998), although a 'residue of competition (is) being retained, in opportunities to shift finances away from poorly performing providers' (Davies and Mannion 1999: 56).

NPM outcomes as damaging equity also show in other arenas. The fragmentation of governmental institutions and incentivization that characterize NPM have implications, for example for gender equality. Margetts (1996: 130) asks: 'Will the changes in public management result in alternative structures more conducive to women's inclusion or will they erode the advances in sex equality policies made in the last fifteen years?' She considers that as state institutions fragment, opportunities for centrally directed initiatives towards attaining sex equality diminish. Organization shrinkage and restructuring may be the most critical, as reflected by one interviewee: '… it is almost inevitable that you are going to end up with slimmer organizations with more men in them' (Margetts 1996: 140). Incentivization also produces inequalities between staff. Hunter (1995), for example, catalogues sometimes 'vicious animosities' arising between 'goodies' (doctors and nurses) and 'baddies' (managers and clerical staff).

NPM ideology and practice is too brash with its business orientation, creating a feeling that social justice cannot be delivered

The misery of academic commentators in the late 1980s and early 1990s, faced with unmodified overexuberant introduction of private sector management practices into public service domains is a matter of record (see for example Willcocks and Harrow 1992). Some such commentaries now seem outdated, as boundaries between 'public', 'private' and 'voluntary' sectors blur. More sophisticated variants of managerial practice models are developing and an evolutionary approach to NPM is recognized (see for example Hannigan 1998). Even so, Box (1999), examining the implications of the intensity of pro-business strategies for public services in an American context, exemplifies the existence of unease: '... despite the considerable success of market-like reforms in increasing the efficiency of governmental bureaucracies, there remains a sense that something is wrong. For people who are concerned about the quality of public service and attention to issues of social injustice, fairness in governmental action, environmental protection and so on, something about running government like a business does not feel right ...' (Box 1999: 19).

The constellation of developments Box describes – the 'reinventing' approach – is presented as a way of tackling public alienation from government and urban problems. However, theoretical analysis in the US of the 'reinventing' literature has also produced the 'refounding' literature, advancing an alternative paradigm, the 'New Public Administration'. Russell and Waste (1998) give a thorough exposition of both theoretical positions. They note the internal inconsistencies of 'reinventing'; for example, that greater short-term efficiency in hiring may compromise the search for merit, thereby reducing long-term efficiency. They also trace the development of 'refounding' thinking, with its roots in 'demand for greater social equity', and a 'governance' model of public provision. Their examination of the latter suggests that it is not and could not be concerned with notions of 'cost'. Overall, however academic disbelief that equity has any place in NPM scenarios because of its business roots may also follow from the academic community's being largely left behind in the early theoretical and practical developments which constituted NPM, leaving them to commentary rather than creativity or discovery roles.

At practitioner levels, the pace of NPM development, culturally and linguistically, may be such that some managers miss the signposts, suggesting that the pro-equity value has a remaining significance in public policy. One city manager's 'voice', responding to practitioner debate in the International City Management Association concerning 'reform of the reforms', for example, deftly buries equity amidst the rest of the 'Es'. Here, he refers to the need for managers 'covering the entire Es skills set: excellence, effectiveness, equity, eclecticism and entrepreneurialism ...' (Schluckebier 1999).

NPM cannot be expected to incorporate equity and social justice values

The possibility that NPM might represent a passing fad was raised by Hood (1991), and may yet be a source of comfort to those who would still prefer to wake and find it gone. However, it may also be that it is the presumptions supporting equity which are now outmoded. If NPM is seen as citizen responsive, to the extent that it reflects society's values, then an erosion of equity values is explained in terms of an altered shift in preference among citizens generally towards competitive behaviour and individualist responsibility.

There is much evidence that individualist thinking is replacing collectivist thinking, where social justice proponents have been traditionally strong, in relation to decision making regarding resource allocation in public services. In the UK, living with inequities arising from inter-organizational competition as a result of these strategies appears the price to pay for being given the chance to 'outbid' others. Thus, Brooksbank *et al.* (1999) explore the arguments of 'unfair advantage' among UK development agencies' competitive bidding for foreign direct investment, with the Scottish and Welsh agencies 'reluctance to accept that the English RDAs would get an equal slice of the development cake'.

The displacement of equity values in societies generally is discussed by Lindbladh *et al.* (1998). Their starting point is the Swedish government's signature to the World Health Organization-defined target of health equity as a priority yet marked lack of measures to reduce well-documented health inequalities. In Sweden, '... inequality has lost ground as an issue in the public debate during the last two decades ... and the egalitarian view has become out of date' (Lindbladh *et al.* 1998: 1022). From this, Linbladh and colleagues (1998: 1023) infer that where health equity programmes exist, they are expressions of efficiency, maximizing public health: '... on the assumption that you get more health per dollar by aiming at the health of the poor'. Saltman (1997: 443) also considers that since the 1990s 'the political willingness to prioritize equity, or ... to prioritize the concept of social justice within which equity in health is a component, is at best uncertain'. Further, changes in what Van Oorschot (2000: 33) describes as 'conditionality of solidarity among the public', with altered perceptions towards service rationing, may also be redefining equity as a conditional notion, dependent upon reciprocity and 'deservingness' (Van Oorschot 2000: 34). This raises Miller's (1999) approach of social justice as incorporating the notion of 'desert'.

Voters' preferences may be leading those of professionals and public servants. In government-funded research in the Netherlands, panels of 'patients', 'public', 'health professionals' and 'health insurers' and 'civil servants' analysed health care options against budgetary constraints, identifying priorities. Stronks *et al.* (1997) reported that 'the main difference between these groups seems to be the extent to which they took the principle of equal access into consideration'. Unlike professionals and civil servants, the 'public' panels most frequently emphasized the importance of individual responsibility. In the UK, experimentation with 'citizen juries' for local decision-making, or for national policy level sounding boards (such as the Cabinet Office's 'People's Panel', see Martin and Boaz 2000), must offer the same uncertain outcomes.

Thus far, the 'case against' NPM having social justice or equity intentions – even pretensions – is mounting. The lack of priority awarded to equity objectives in successive NPM-based changes and ways of operating in the UK (for example the widespread use of market testing in the civil service and compulsory competitive testing of some services delivery in local government) is a matter of record. At best, it could be argued that equity considerations never rated prominence because of uncertainty – or reinterpretation – of what this meant, unless or except where it was interpreted by relevant professionals. By contrast, the notion of 'efficiency' seems to have a free-standing popular understanding and constituency of support. This is notwithstanding that technical efficiency gains may be made, often at the expense of allocative efficiency, when another favoured policy mantra, that of services 'targeting', either to those most in need and/or those able to show the results from services received, comes in to play.

NPM: including equity?

Nevertheless, the 'case against' is not entirely secure. Despite the strength of some of the convictions discussed above, it may also be argued that NPM and social justice concerns are not necessarily, or not even, in opposing camps. Efficiency may be seen as the vital prerequisite for equitable provision. A major critique of an 'inefficient' public service may be that known need cannot then be met, let alone unmet. Arguments here range from the possibility that NPM, now 'over the worst shocks', can afford to relax a little to those which see social justice best ensured by individualism or the inbuilt audit of organizations to assess their continuing capability against criteria which include or infer social justice goals. The following propositions may be made:

1   that even though NPM had relegated social justice questions down governmental agendas, it is now, by virtue of efficiency and effectiveness gains, able to incorporate even better equity goals;
2   that NPM, being pre-dated by extensive inequities (often resulting from service professionals' preferential decision making favouring some users), cannot be blamed for inequity *per se*, and offers opportunities to improve this situation by virtue of attempts to control those professionals' decisions;
3   that NPM incorporates emphasis on social justice values since its emphasis on service openness and accountability gives a renewed focus on 'what is going on and why';
4   that NPM characteristic of using competition for funding initiatives helps ensure a fairer societal distribution and encourages recipient organizations to review their own efficiency and effectiveness.

NPM is now able to incorporate equity goals

This appears faint praise, with NPM proponents recovering memories about equity in public services. Yet it has some credence with observations that NPM stridency is diminishing and equity concerns are re-appearing, albeit still in market contexts. For example, Locock and Dopson (1999: 45, citing Whitehead *et al.* 1997), examining changing relations between 'centre' and 'field' in the UK NHS, note that 'there is international evidence that other countries are beginning to rethink their market reforms. Further, they see an emphasis 'now on co-operation rather than competition, with renewed interest in issues of equity and national priority setting' (Locock and Dopson 1999). Such developments may reflect the age of NPM strategies, as they move from youth into maturity, leading to 'Middle-Aged Public Management', where a certain mellowing has occurred. Thus the UK government's 1996 Health White Paper appeared to give a mellowing example, with broad objectives including 'a responsive service, sensitive to differing needs 'and identification of 'non contentious improvements in the quality of care' (Harrison and New 1997: 210).

Support for this perspective comes from the extent to which an incoming Labour government in the UK in the mid-1990s, far from reversing public services reforms, retained them and moved forward incrementally rather than radically. Harrow (1996: 128) observed that value-for-money considerations in public services were unlikely to fall away from any governmental agenda, 'even if the related measures of 'quality' are about to become different'; and so it has generally proved.

At the same time, the idea of NPM 'loosening up' and giving equity an increased (if belated) profile needs to be scrutinized in outcome as well as input and policy intention terms. Accepting that compulsory competitive tendering in local government had no equity agenda at all, its successor, the Best Value regime, now seems also to be far less of a sea change than it promised. 'Competition' as the driving force of local innovation and improvement is retained. The lauded requirement for 'consultation with the local community' (an implied but unpredictable potential source of evidence of social justice concerns) does itself have cost implications. For Keenan (2000: 49) 'the irony could be that with scarce resources directed towards Best Value, front line users could end up with either a poorer service provision or possibly a higher quality service provision with reduction in service coverage'.

NPM cannot be blamed for inequity per se

The theme of professionals exercising power leading to inequity by virtue of recipients' position (race, class, gender, age) is familiar in the sociology of professions literature. NPM cannot therefore be blamed for ushering these inequalities in, and indeed can be praised for efforts to control those same professionals. Possibly only NPM style disciplines can redirect professionals' decisions, which may or may not include those concerning user inequity.

Smaje's (1998) work on equity and the ethnic patterning of GP services in Britain instances situations where such professionals' power appears retained. This explores evidence of higher levels of GP consultation, higher incidence of prescribing, lower use of outpatient services and fewer home visits following GP consultations among minority ethnic groups than in the white majority population. For Smaje (1998: 128) 'it is possible that high levels of prescription are a reflection of poor communication, inappropriate prescription and hence poorer quality care'. Although Smaje's work is not at all as an NPM apologist, it evidences a case for controlling or at least knowing more about professionals' behaviour and decisions.

The reality of NPM regimes affecting professionals' work may however contrast with the rhetoric. Thus, Kitchener *et al.* (2000), studying the supervision of professional work in social services departments, demonstrate the 'resilience' of 'custodial' (in this context, non-NPM style) mode of supervision and resistance to bureaucratic forms. However, it may provide a limited antidote to romanticized accounts of public services and professionals' roles pre-NPM. In the UK NHS, for example, NPM thinking did not invent cost strictures as a ruse to scale down hitherto fairly distributed services, nor were financial crises anything new (see for example the Guillebaud Committee 1956). Further, the extent to which the NHS's formation redressed glaring health care inequalities and inequities has been challenged. Powell's (1992) closely argued evaluation of the geographical provision of health care before the NHS challenges conventional wisdom of dire pre-war inequalities with which the NHS had to grapple. Powell is no apologist for the inadequacies of this health care 'system' (medical staff shortages, poor accommodation, lack of coordination and neglect of the chronic sick). However, he finds the gross inequity argument 'less than convincing'; the result partly of 'a mass of comparisons without the data sources, faulty arguments and selective and linear quotations, with little reference back to primary sources' (Powell 1992: 78–79). Arguments of NPM's 'dismantling' of major achievements, in NHS terms, therefore may need to be treated with similar caution.

NPM incorporates emphasis on social justice values, ensures a fairer societal distribution and encourages recipient organizations to review their own efficiency and effectiveness

Propositions 3 and 4 together give the strongest base yet for securing a measure of agreement that NPM can offer 'equity as well'. The focus on consumer choice, causing demands for increased consumer knowledge, appears to lead to a major increase in the amount of information publicly available, enhanced further by public services use of websites. Widening information availability and sources has the potential for highlighting and addressing existing inequities and for tracking over time the degree to which disparity of provision or outcomes of service have changed. On its own, such information makes no policy change, but its very availability enhances the chances of change, for an informed citizenry acts together.

The notion of competition as driving service improvement can also be seen as equitable, where 'the best' demonstrates 'what can be done', so ensuring that higher standards for all are then achieved – and if not questions are asked. This is illustrated, by some (now retrospective) analyses on GP fundholding. Cowton and Drake (1999: 36) report one lead partner in a practice reflecting on its impact on colleagues: '... people are annoyed when I get better services for my patients, but it bloody well makes them pull their finger out and do a bit ...'.

Nor are such instances a function of NPM in Western states only. Polidano and Hulme (1999: 127) cite examples of Indian NGOs demanding access to information about decisions by district administrators, with some 'extraordinary successes in making local administrative actions transparent'. In states where the names of government scheme beneficiaries are read out, the villagers are enraged that they have been listed for grants never received, and they are demanding that those who have taken the grants (administrators and local elites) are punished. Polidano and Hulme (1999) note that the routine assumption of official records' secrecy is no longer open to local bureaucrats in those states. Although transparency cannot on its own deliver equity – and may only make suspected inequity that much more known – it is a critical element in equity achievement. Using performance measures and targets not only for efficiency gains but to counter corruption is also examined; for example, Tanzania's creation of a national revenue service. Thus, although NPM critics in Western countries have argued that business-style reforms may encourage corruption and undermine previously well-understood ethical practice frameworks, Polidano and Hulme (1999: 123) comment that in developing countries '... they are being used to counter corruption'.

The all-pervasive approach of NPM has meant that some public services delivered 'behind closed doors' – where equity issues will be least prominent – are now scrutinized increasingly. Two contrasting examples from the UK, where NPM regimes may seen, incrementally, to have improved and not detracted from equity in provision, may be cited: community care and prison services. Both have a degree of invisibility in public service terms, for different reasons . In community care, debates about equity and efficiency, or lack of both, have run side by side. Davies's (1997) work reviewing developments implies some degree of improvement, albeit limited, in both areas of concern: 'Equity and efficiency in community care: from muddle to model, and model ...?' This work presents the findings of research among users, caregivers and care managers in a cohort of new users recruited in 1984/5 and 1995. Survey research took place in twelve areas, from the then 103 local authorities in England and Wales. Highlighting 'idiosyncratic' allocations of care support, prior to the changes, Davies discusses questions of consistency of allocations between like users, hitherto seen as an area of weakness. While noting that consistency is 'not synonymous with efficiency and equity' (Davies 1997: 339), his research shows improvement in this area since the mid-1980s, reflecting 'the new flexibility and support to caregivers' that reforms enabled. Where equity issues are need-associated, Davies, using 'before' and 'after' studies, notes that 'post reform patterns suggest that a reduced share of resources was consumed by low need recipients' with a 'redistribution towards those of higher' interests and conflicted in twenty-one per cent of cases. Questions of balance, concerning relative fairness among 'competing' users were thus raised. Despite these problems, Davies is positive: 'notwithstanding the mistakes and distortions, it is not too late to correct most of them' (Davies 1997: 353).

The prison service provides a further intriguing demonstration of the extent to which apparent technical and efficiency-led changes seem to have structured managerial opportunities at senior levels in prisons so that quality and equity concerns may be addressed. Equity in prison service terms includes focus on comparable treatment as between prisoners' experiences, in relation to designated prisons (for example, if in a 'training' prison), and managerial and policy makers' awareness of comparable outputs from prisons and outcomes of their work. NPM in the UK prison service – aside from agencization debates – has shifted emphasis onto the need to have and to use comparative management information. By devolving down to the institution level it is looking for service delivery, and accountability for that delivery. Comparative costs analyses may have begun as insensitive decision-making tools but are capable of, and are, being refined. The experience of benchmarking is also placing a lever in managerial hands in relation to staff (Prison Officers' Association) demands and expectations; notably in relation to past working practices.

The Prison Service's development of Key Performance Indicators provides a balance of information concerning prison as a 'holding place' (for example, number of escapes, mandatory drug tests) and as an 'experience' for prisoners (association time/time unlocked, degree of productive activity). With a recent (1998) top-level reorganization, a further development of a second level of key performance targets, against which institutions will be measured, is taking place. In parallel is the development of individual 'audit' assessments of prisons (looking at development of activity based costing), the role of which is to advise the governor – again a further lever of opportunity for change. Devolution within the service thus sheds light on local responsibility to deliver across a range of targets, and gives increased prominence to service failures. The logic of 'people doing what they are best at' also supports the case for NHS responsibility for prison health services, but operationally this will prove complex. NPM is therefore leading to increased openness about what is happening and why in individual institutions. This is an engine for improvement in both equity and efficiency terms. Critically, it isolates and challenges what at best might be called 'whimsical management' in closed institutions, where this has led to persistent inequities for prisoners (Harrow 1999).

Yet both these arguments – about renewed openness and the inexorable pressures for betterment that competition may provide – contain extensive flaws. The very development of an informed community of citizens may increase or exacerbate the contrasts as well as commonalities of interests; leading to the expression of rival preferences. The increasing prominence of stakeholder theory indicates imbalances between stakeholders in public management settings. (see, for example, Winstanley et al. 1995; Thomas and Palfrey 1996). Thus, the drawing-in of parents as formal stakeholders in the management of schools, which may be seen as directly equity-inspired, has been assessed as a 'façade of parental stakeholding' (Farrell and Jones 2000). Initiatives to draw in excluded communities 'or groups' through 'consultation processes' may fail. Thus Martin and Boaz assess that despite major effort in the 'Better Government for Older People' pilots, 'it has proved very difficult to persuade the most excluded older people to participate'; whilst in BV pilots, groups at the 'greatest risk of exclusion' were 'the most inclined to favour passive approaches to consultation'. (Martin and Boaz 2000: 51). Finally, Taylor (2000: 253) is emphatic that 'the market has taught us about both the strengths and weaknesses of consumer power', where, for example, exclusion of some housing estates and their poor quality services 'can be seen as the direct result of the choices that others have exercised'.

Together, these concerns about the extent to which openness and competitive behaviour within NPM have supported rather than stifled equity in provision emphasize the need to return to a comprehensive review of accountability within public services. For Barberis (2000: 468) at central government level: '... NPM, while not the root cause of the disparity between the doctrine and the reality of accountability, has further exposed the accountability gap'. More generally, the growth of judicial review, the spread of quasi-judicial procedures in other areas of public management, such as land use, and the access to the European Court for plaintiffs against public decisions are significant trends, identified by Terry (2000: 6) in his review of 'Public Management 2010'. For the time being, these rule-bound approaches may be seen as a result of the NPM 'promises' – for involvement, choice, participation and improving services – as public expectations are heightened. They are also costly in resources terms.

Some reflections and conclusions

The definitional ambiguities flagged at the beginning of this chapter persist in encouraging uncertainty about the relative prominence of equity values in NPM provision. It has been variously suggested that social justice was the planned or unplanned first casualty of NPM change, or an intended or real beneficiary once efficiencies have been developed, or even as they develop. Although opponents of NPM-based change will doubt that its advocates are closet egalitarians, the incentive to be frugal with 'someone else's money' does not by itself impair equity-directed policies. Nor is being inefficient on purpose in the spurious name of equity likely to have many takers. Indeed it could be argued that where resources are capable of being 'saved', flexible responses to the sudden emergence of hitherto unmet or new need are the more feasible.

Since individual decisions about justice or injustice appear, in Rawls's terms to be a function of both rationality and reasonableness, it is also possible for NPM both to reduce and to increase social justice opportunities across different areas of provision and in different localities. This likelihood is increased given that 'public' provision may be made by fully public, quasi-public, non-governmental and private organizations.

That notions of equity and efficiency are not necessarily the polar opposites implied in this chapter's title, but rather closely intertwined, is however becoming clear. Critically for the 'efficiency first' proponents, for example, if alleged inequitable outcomes for users and staff are affecting morale so adversely in public services, as some commentators insist, then the primary (or sole) goal of efficiency may also be in jeopardy. This seems a consequence which the most aggressive anti-public-employee arguments seem not to have taken fully into account. A symbiotic rather than parasitic relationship between efficiency and equity in organizations across sectors is also demonstrated, as some sectors of the business community adopt equity goals for economic and social purposes (see for example Lawrence's 2000: 400, discussion on the 'mainstreaming' of and 'the business case' for equal opportunities work).

Such an intertwining suggests that equity opportunities may rise in some NPM services while falling or stalling in others. This may be illustrated by the use of a positional matrix which encourages a 'service specific' equity/efficiency balance analysis. An initial matrix might appear as in Figure 9.1.

Such a matrix may have some explanatory as well as descriptive value. Thus a service which 'scores' highly on equity considerations but poorly in efficiency terms may be so because of user groups' intervention rather than through extravagance or waste. Examples include the retention of a local school, hospital or fire station in the face of rising resource constraints but strong public feeling to avert closure. Intra-service comparisons might be enabled – for example, the contrasting or same-quadrant locations for those prisons managed within the public and the private sectors.

From this, a multiple matrix might develop which distinguished between a service's design, its implementation and its outcome, tracking the possibility of a 'promising' area of policy (that is 'high' on the equity and efficiency 'promises'), moving quadrants as the policy realities came home; or conversely one which promised little, but which delivered unexpected benefits. Over time, for example, the Best Value regime might be usefully examined, particularly given Boyne's (2000) work, showing how a large regulatory superstructure has been set up and concluding that regulation costs may outweigh the benefits.

Jorgensen (1999: 581) shows the wide universe of possible public values, including probity and honesty as well as justice, fairness, impartiality and equity. Who then protects these values, and in particular, who are the equity guardians in NPM contexts? Managers of public provision are obvious candidates. Yet what is known about public managers at a range of levels and their dispositions towards social justice and equity values? How, if at all, do those dispositions compare among managers who have a prior background in professional service domains, those with solely managerial careers and those with managerial experience in

'equity'		'efficiency'	
	High	Public service 'w'	Public service 'y'
		Public service 'x'	Public service 'z'
		Low	High

Figure 9.1 New public management: the efficiency/equity balance in service delivery

other sectors? Is the manager with business values or with older public administration values more or less disposed to insert equity considerations in his/her decision-making? Research matching evidence on managers revealed dispositions with their organizations' practices, policies and services outcomes, and in particular identifying their personal models of social justice and equity, would be welcome. This may be especially important, given the mosaic of service provision that is a result of NPM, so that those who are 'public managers' may be in a variety of public, voluntary and sometimes privately contracted endeavours, or coming together for cross-organizational initiatives which are themselves temporary.

Starting points might include the 'public practitioner model' of public manager, proposed by Box (1998, 1999). Here the managerial role is akin to 'helping', providing technical information and facilitating the process of dialogue and deliberation, which enables 'citizens to choose the directions they seek for public policy' (see Thomas 1999). Another would be a study of the results of managerial ethics education and training for public managers (see, for example, Louw 1998; De Soto et al. 1999). Given that 'public managers' themselves are hardly a unified grouping, service delivery professionals will also have varying guardianship roles, both in leading and in mediating decisions. As the Netherlands study showed: 'It is not clear that including all the different actors in the decision-making process of prioritisation of health services will lead to more equitable or broadly supported outcomes. ... It is quite remarkable that it is the medical profession that seemed most concerned about the common good and the distribution of services' (Stronks et al. 1997).

Again, such research might commence from managerial responses to the efficiency/equity matrix, both in terms of their personal (dispositional) locations and the locations of those services which they manage. From this, some possible 'titles' for the four quadrants may emerge, emulating Roberts's (2000: 220) 'organizational configurations' on a more narrow efficiency/effectiveness matrix. Here a 'generative' organizational configuration gains optimal efficiency and effectiveness (with no precise exemplars cited), whereas in a 'responsive configuration' the 'tension between efficiency and effectiveness is relieved by minimising attention to both dimensions' (Roberts 2000: 224).

A constitutional, particularly European, dimension may also affect the 'equity guardian' role, as 'Euro-global' regulation impacts on individual states (see, for example, Walby 1999). Vincent (1996: 59) has argued that regarding the (alleged) encouragement of risk-taking by public managers in public services in Europe 'constitutional rather than strictly managerial issues appear to prevail. ... Thus European public servants are more concerned about the chain of responsibility than the workings of the market and their application to public services'. European developments therefore may demonstrate how constitutional brakes can be applied to or encourage NPM activity, and the impact of this on equity.

One reading of NPM is that it contains an inherent expansionist logic for those who manage it. As and whether managers are empowered to manage, their emotional responses to equity debates become critical. Hence the argument that a research focus on managers' values is needed, if social justice achievement is to be assessed under NPM governmental regimes and systems. There is, however, continuing complexity inherent in assessing any and all NPM 'results'. This is demonstrated authoritatively in Pollitt and Bouckaert's (2000: 97–133) 'taxonomy of results' and their perception of public management reform results as seen 'through a glass, darkly'. If achieving social justice is seen in the 'most strategic sense of result', where systems have shifted towards 'a desired or ideal state' (Pollitt and Bouckaert 2000: 99), the NPM track record is uncertain and opaque. This may become increasingly evident if Newman and Clarke's (1997) perceptions of the managerialist state being unable to resolve a widening range of social problems are supported and new areas of inequity arise, among, for example, refugees, debt-laden students and 'older' workers unable to fund their retirement.

For the present, the case that NPM has excluded social justice goals has to remain 'non-proven'. This is particularly important if public managers themselves are not to be routinely and automatically blamed for sidelining equity concerns. The emphasis on public managers' values as the touchstone of the state of social justice achievements in public services is also important, given that some interpretations or roots of NPM, notably public choice theory, have seen those managers and their institutions as a major part of 'the problem' rather than the means for its 'solution'. Taylor (2000: 253) uses a cricketing analogy to describe the public sector as a whole as having been 'pushed onto the back foot by constant criticisms from the centre'. Yet from such defensive and desperate actions are major innings sometimes secured, shaky partnerships solidified and matches – or series – sometimes won.

Acknowledgement

The author is most grateful for the insights and suggestions, including possible matrix development, received from the anonymous reviewer of an earlier draft of this chapter.

Bibliography

Allison, M.T. (2000) Leisure, diversity and social justice, *Journal of Leisure Research*, 32, 1, 2–6.

Altheide, D.L. and Johnson, J.M. (1997) Ethnography and justice. In Miller, G. and Dingwall, R., eds, *Context and Method in Qualitative Research*, Sage, London.

Barberis, P. (1998) The new public management and a new accountability, *Public Administration*, 76, Autumn, 451–470.

Box, R.C. (1998) *Leading American Communities into the Twenty First Century*, Sage, Thousand Oaks, CA.

Box, R.C. (1999) Running government like a business: implications for public administration theory and practice, *American Review of Public Administration*, 29, 1, 19–43.

Boyett, I. (1996) The public sector entrepreneur – a definition, *International Journal of Public Sector Management* 9, 2, 36–51.

Boyne, G. (2000) External regulation and best value in local government, *Public Money and Management*, July–September, 7–12.

Brooksbank, D., Connolly, M. and Morgan, B. (1999) Competitive bidding and regional development in the UK, *Public Money and Management*, 19, 2, 7–12.

Cowton, C.J. and Drake, J.E. (1999) Went fundholding, going commissioning: some evidence-based reflections on the prospects for primary care groups, *Public Money and Management*, 19, 2, 33–38.

Culyer, A.J. (1997) Maximising the health of the whole community: the case for (The Rationing Debate), *British Medical Journal*, 1 March, 667–669.

Culyer, T. (1991) Reforming Health Services: frameworks for the Swedish Review. In Culyer, A.J. *et al.*, eds, *International Review of the Swedish Health Care System*, Occasional Paper no. 34, SNS, Stockholm; cited in Saltman, R. (1997).

Davies, B. (1997) Equity and efficiency in community care: from muddle to model and model to ...?, *Policy and Politics*, 25, 4, 337–359.

Davies, H.T.O. and Mannion, R. (1999) The rise of oversight and the decline of mutuality, *Public Money and Management*, 19, 2, 55–59.

De Soto, W., Opheim, C. and Tajalli, H. (1999) Apples and Oranges? Comparing the attitudes of public policy versus public administration students, *American Review of Public Administration*, 29, 1, 77–91.

Farrell, C.M. and Jones, J. (2000) Evaluating stakeholder participation in public services – parents and schools, *Policy and Politics*, 28, 2, 251–262.

Flynn, R. (1999) Managerialism, professionalism and quasi-markets. In Exworthy, M. and Halford, S., eds, *Professionals and the New Managerialism in the Public Sector*, Open University Press, Buckingham.

Goddard, M. and Mannion, R. (1998) From competition to co-operation: new economic relationships in the National Health Service, *Health Economics*, 7, 105–119.

Guillebaud Committee (1956) *Enquiry into the Cost of the National Health Service*, Cm 9663, HMSO, London.

Hannigan, B. (1998) Assessing the new public management: the case of the National Health Service, *Journal of Nursing Management*, 6, 307–312.

Harrison, A. and New, B. (1997) 'Health'. In Jackson, P. and Lavender, M., eds, *The Public Services Yearbook, 1997–98*, Pitman Publishing, London, 205–216.

Harrow, J. (1996) The Civil Service. In Jackson, P. and Lavender, M., eds, *Public Services Yearbook, 1998–6-7*, Pitman Publishing, London, 111–130.

Harrow, J. (1999) Personal communication with John Smith, Governor, HMP Manchester, UK.

Hood, C. (1991) A public management for all seasons, *Public Administration*, 69, 3–19.

Hunter, R. (1995) NHS changes: impact on staff, *Critical Public Health*, 6, 3, 51–55.

Iliffe, S. (1995) The retreat from equity: implications of the shift towards a primary care-led NHS, *Critical Public Health*, 6, 3, 36–51.

Jones, P. (1995) Review article: two conceptions of liberalism, two conceptions of justice, *British Journal of Political Science*, 25, 4, 515–551.

Jorgensen, T. (1999) The public sector in an in-between time: searching for new public values, *Public Administration*, 77, 3, 565–584.

Keenan, J. (2000) Just how new is Best Value? *Public Money and Management*, July–September, 45–49.

Kitchener, M., Kirkpatrick, I. and Whipp, R. (2000) Supervising professional work under new public management: evidence from an 'invisible trade', *British Journal of Management*, 11, 2, 213–226.

Lawrence, E. (2000) Equal opportunities officers and managing equality changes, *Personnel Review*, 29, 3, 381–401.

Lindbladh, E., Lyttkens, C.H., Hanson, B.S. and Ostergren, P.-O. (1998) Equity is out of fashion? An essay on autonomy and health policy in individualised society, *Social Science and Medicine*, 46, 8, 1017–1025.

Locock, L. and Dopson, S. (1999) The three in one and one in three: changing relations between centre and field in the NHS in the UK, *Public Management: an International Journal of Research and Theory*, 1, 1, 27–47.

Louw, R. (1998) The quest for ethical behaviour in the South African Public Service, *Teaching Public Administration* XVIII, 1, 65–75.

Lynn, L.E. Jr (2000) Introduction: in government, does management matter? In Brudney, J.L., O'Toole, L.J. Jr and Rainey, H.G., eds, *Advancing Public Management: new developments in theory, methods and practice*, Georgetown University Press, Washington, DC, 15–18.

Margetts, H. (1996) Public management change and sex equality within the state, *Parliamentary Affairs*, 49, 130–143.

Martin, S. and Boaz, A. (2000) Public participation and citizen-centred local government: lessons from the best value and better government for older people pilot programme, *Public Money and Management*, April–June, 47–53.

Matravers, M. (2000) Principles of Social Justice, *American Political Science Review*, 94, 3, 710–711.

Miller, D. (1999) *Principles of Social Justice*, Harvard University Press, Cambridge, MA.

Newman, J. and Clarke, J. (1997) *The Managerial State*, Sage, London.

Pereira, J. (1993) What does equity in health mean? *Journal of Social Policy*, 22, 1, 19–48.

Polidano, C. and Hulme, D. (1999) Public management reform in developing countries, *Public Management: an International Journal of Research and Theory*, 1, 1, 121–132.

Pollitt, C. and Bouckaert, G. (2000) *Public Management Reform: a comparative analysis*, Oxford University Press, Oxford.

Powell, M. (1992) A tale of two cities: a critical evaluation of the geographical provision of health care before the NHS, *Public Administration*, 70, 1, 68–80.

Rawls, J. (1971) *A Theory of Justice*, Oxford University Press, Oxford.

Rawls, J. (1993) *Political Liberalism*, Columbia University Press, New York.

Roberts, N.C. (2000) Organisational configurations: four approaches to public sector management. In Brudney, J.L., O'Toole, L.J. Jr and Rainey, H.G., eds, *Advancing Public Management: new developments in theory, methods and practice*, Georgetown University Press, Washington, DC, 217–234.

Russell, G.D. and Waste, R.J.(1998) The limits of reinventing government, *American Review of Public Administration*, 28, 4, 325–346.

Saltman, R.B. (1997) Equity and distributive justice in European health care reform, *International Journal of Health Services*, 27, 3, 443–453.

Schluckebier, J. (1999) Letters, *Public Management*, May, 3.

Secretary of State for Health (1998) *The New NHS: Modern, Dependable*, HMSO, London.

Seedhouse, D. (1994) *Fortress NHS: a Philosophical Review of the National Health Service*, John Wiley, Chichester.

Smaje, C. (1998) Equity and the ethnic patterning of GP services in Britain, *Social Policy and Administration*, 32, 2, 116–131.

Stronks, K., Stribjus, A.-M., Wendte, J.F. and Gunning-Schepers, L. (1997) Who should decide? Qualitative analysis of panel data from public, patients, health care professionals and insurers on priorities in healthcare, *British Medical Journal*, 315, 92–96.

Taylor, M. (2000) Maintaining community involvement in regeneration: what are the issues? *Local Economy*, 15, 3, 251–255.

Terry, F. (2000) Public management 2010, Editorial, *Public Money and Management*, January–March, 4–6.

Thomas, J.C. (1999) Bringing the public into public administration, *Public Administration Review*, 59, 1, 83–88.

Thomas, P. and Palfrey, C. (1996) Evaluation stakeholder-focused criteria, *Social Policy and Administration*, 30, 2, 125–142.

Thompson, J.R. (2000) Quasi markets and strategic change in public organisations. In Brudney, J.L., O'Toole, L.J., Jr and Rainey, H.G., eds, *Advancing Public Management: new developments in theory, methods and practice*, Georgetown University Press, Washington, DC, 197–216.

Van Oorschot, W. (2000) Who should get what and why? On deservingness criteria and the conditionality of solidarity among the public, *Policy and Politics*, 28, 1, 33–48.

Vincent, J. (1996) Managing risk in public services: an overview of the international literature, *International Journal of Public Sector Management* 9, 2, 57–64.

Whitehead, M., Gustafsson, R.A. and Diderichsen, F. (1997) Why is Sweden rethinking its NHS style reforms? *British Medical Journal*, 315, 935–939.

Walby, S. (1999) The new regulatory state: the social powers of the European Union, *The British Journal of Sociology*, 50, 1, 118–140.

Willcocks, L. and Harrow, J. (1992) *Rediscovering Public Services Management*, McGraw Hill, Maidenhead, UK.

Williamson, M.J. (1995) Love is not a marketable commodity: new public management in the British Health Service, *Journal of Advanced Nursing*, 21, 980–987.

Winstanley, D., Sorabji, D. and Dawson, S. (1995) When the pieces don't fit: a stakeholder power matrix to analyse public sector restructuring, *Public Money and Management*, April–June, 19–26.

Young, I. (1990) *Justice and the Politics of Difference*, Princeton University Press, Princeton, NJ.

Part III

The New Public Management in comparative context

Chapter 10

The New Public Management

A perspective from mainland Europe

Kuno Schedler and Isabella Proeller

Introduction

NPM has become a standard international model for public administration reform. The term NPM originally came from New Zealand, describing the reforms initiated there in the 1980s. Nowadays, NPM is used as a generic term for the movement of similar public management reforms spreading around the world. The distinct feature of all those reforms is the shift from input to output orientation (Schedler and Proeller 2000: 5). NPM reforms started out in Anglo-Saxon countries, like the UK, USA or New Zealand. In the meantime the name as well as the basic ideas of NPM are in discussion in most Western industrialized nations. Also, in continental Europe many municipalities claim to have launched NPM reforms.

It is no secret that there exists no such thing as one NPM reform model. NPM is a generic term, for some even a paradigm. Löffler (1997: 4) states:

> For analytical purposes, the NPM *paradigm* can be considered to the function of a meta-catalogue of principles to be valid for the public sector. *Administrative modernization* means the translation of those abstract principles into modernization programs, management models and law by political and administrative actors. *Modernization strategies* ... are the concretization of these still rather abstract policy objectives.

This article will take a closer look on NPM modernization in continental Europe. It will examine what kind of reform initiatives are designated 'NPM reforms', and what characterizes the different national modernization models. Thereby the analysis will focus on the developments on the local level. The article argues that NPM modernization strategies are shaped in reaction to perceived challenges. This understanding leads to the approach underlying this article and illustrated in Figure 10.1. On the one hand, NPM delivers a *supply-driven concept* of theories that led to a 'NPM tool-box'. On the other hand, local governments *demand* remedies against particular problems they are facing. The *supply* of instruments through NPM and the *demand* to counteract specific problems are matched by varying the priority of certain NPM elements within

Figure 10.1 Matching of 'practical local demand' and 'theoretical supply' determines reform agenda

the local reform agenda. NPM elements that are suitable to counteract current problems will be given greater emphasis.

After describing the determinants of this model more closely, several European local government reforms will be presented and examined according to this supply–demand matching approach. In this chapter the findings of the country reform analysis will be presented. The chapter concludes with an outlook on the future of European local government reform.

A 'supply-driven theory' to explain national differences of reform

In many countries NPM started out by learning from such examples as New Zealand or the UK. Even though each country developed its own administrative reform concept in accordance with national peculiarities, the terminology used in pioneer examples was exported internationally. The homogeneous terminology misleadingly suggests a comparable implementation of the model. Before proceeding to local modernization models in detail, the main elements and instruments which are offered by NPM theory are presented.

Elements of New Public Management

The literature on NPM or its national models and their elements and instruments is vast (Hood 1991; Osborne and Gaebler 1993; Schedler and Proeller 2000). At this point, the objective is to identify a common body of element categories and to provide a list of NPM elements.

A general scheme of element categories of NPM reform elements is shown in Table 10.1. Since some common ground had to be found on which to base the different local reform practices, it is evident that the categories must be open enough to cover different national features. The objective was to find generic categories in which the particular national elements could be bundled. The generic categories identified are shown in Table 10.1.

Table 10.1 Generic element categories of NPM

Category	Characteristics/objectives	Examples
Organizational restructuring	Delegation of responsibility Reduction of hierarchy Political and managerial roles	City managers Holding structure
Management instruments	Output orientation Entrepreneurship Efficiency	Performance agreements Products Performance-related pay
Budgetary reforms	Closer to private sector financial instruments	Cost accounting Balance sheet P + L statements
Participation	Involvement of the citizen	Neighbourhood councils E-democracy
Customer orientation Quality management	Gain legitimacy in service delivery Re-engineering	One-stop shops Service level agreements E-government
Marketization Privatization	Reduction of public sector Efficiency gains through competition	Contracting out PPP

P + L, profit and loss; PPP, public–private partnerships.

Local NPM modernization concepts: supply-driven theory and demand-driven practical use

In all countries NPM reforms were initiated in reaction to current political challenges. The objectives that were pursued with the reforms varied significantly throughout European local governments. Sometimes NPM was introduced to save money, sometimes to fight the loss of legitimacy of public administration and on other occasions to deal with dissatisfaction of their public managers and politicians or the opacity of the bureaucracy. How can a single reform concept encounter this broad range of challenges? (Figure 10.2).

The hypothesis in this chapter is that the particular tool set a government chooses for its reform model is defined by the political circumstances it faces. For example, a city that faces financial distress will use NPM elements that will counteract this problem. Such elements would probably be privatization elements, contract management and competition, rather than participation or democratization.

Mastronardi (1998: 49) compared NPM to a 'quarry': reformers can choose from a range of elements that they consider suitable to fight current challenges. NPM offers a variety of instruments of which some, but rarely all, are implemented and used in the different local administrative modernization concepts. In effect, it is very common that claims to have implemented NPM

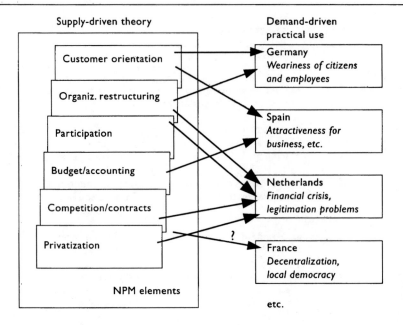

Figure 10.2 NPM as supply-driven theory and its demand-driven practical use

have a strong bias towards certain (single) elements and do not guarantee that the basic principles of NPM are put into practice. Mastronardi (1998: 59) therefore rightly points out that the metaphor is not to be mistaken in the sense that any element implemented for itself already is NPM, but that a minimum set of elements has to be combined. Otherwise the basic mechanisms and principles NPM is based on will not be put into action. It is not the objective of this chapter to identify the minimum set of elements. But it is important to evaluate the local reform efforts in accordance with these findings.

In addition, Naschold (1995: 12) showed in his analysis that municipalities have multiple possibilities to react to challenges. The same challenge does not automatically lead to a similar arrangement of toolsets in the local NPM concept. For example, financial crisis is sometimes answered with traditional cutback strategies as well as administrative modernization. Probably the same is true for modernization concepts which are based on the NPM paradigm. Dissatisfaction with public administration might be answered with radical marketization (examples for this are the USA or the UK) or purely internal organizational restructuring.

In the following chapter NPM reforms in different countries are presented. Subsequently the country studies are analysed regarding two dimensions: the challenges that led to NPM reforms and the NPM elements primarily used within the specific reform programmes. Owing to limited space, it will not be possible to describe the respective country's reform in-depth. For an overview, however, this short description will be sufficient.

Selected countries' reforms

The reform examples presented in this chapter only give an overview of NPM reforms going on in the different countries. The country studies are presented in chronological order. They are based primarily on literature available in English.

The Netherlands

The Netherlands are divided in about 650 municipalities varying in size from about 750,000 inhabitants in Amsterdam to a few hundred in small municipalities (OECD 1997: 335). Because of this difference in size, the array of tasks assigned and provided by local authorities varies between municipalities (van Ruller 1996: 161). The municipalities are relatively free in shaping the organization of their public administration. Consequently, organizational structures and reforms are not identical in the whole country. Local particularities and variations are the rule.

Nevertheless, a general trend of NPM reform and the mainly used NPM elements in most local reforms can be identified. Despite the organizational freedom, the predominant elements of reforms were the same in most municipalities. For this reason, it can be said that prominent examples of the reforms in the Netherlands, such as the city of Delft, are exemplary rather than an exception.

The breeding grounds for local administrative reforms were the municipalities themselves. Even though the central government did not initiate the reforms, it has fostered them. The supportive attitude of the central government probably had a major impact on the dissemination of the reforms and explains why the reform model does not vary significantly throughout the country.

Regarding NPM reforms in Europe, Dutch local governments are considered as early movers. At the beginning of the 1980s the Netherlands had to face economic recession, which led to a fiscal stringency in public budgets. It became more and more obvious that the administrative organization suffered from opacity, lack of productivity and hierarchy. Politics proved to have insufficient control over the bureaucratic process, when choices had to be made to cut back expenditures (Hendriks and Tops 2000: 7).

The actual reforms of the 1980s – which became internationally known as the Tilburg Model – focused mainly on rearranging responsibilities and introducing a decentralized 'holding structure'. The main characteristics were the concern division model and contract management (Kickert 1997: 23). The concern division, or holding structure, model means that the local authorities were organized in relatively independent divisions with their own managerial responsibility, and were set boundaries by the political leaders. The mayor and the council take this political leadership role at the local level. Along with this organizational structure contracts between the management and the executive agencies became the new steering instruments. The steering on output parameters became more and more important and led to the introduction of output budgeting, performance indicators, etc. References by Swiss and German reformers to the Tilburg model highlight these innovations.[1]

In comparison with other Western European countries – most of whom use contract management – the Netherlands showed strong commitment to change and had already managed to introduce cost accounting and lump sum budgets at all levels of government in 1985.

Reforms at all levels of government during the 1980s were aimed at efficiency gains and reconsideration of public expenditures (van Mierlo 1998: 335ff.). This goal was compatible with the challenge of fiscal stringency at that time. In the course of time the motivators as well as the goals of reform changed. The results of the 1990 and 1994 local elections showed that the electorate was discontented with or indifferent towards an increasingly self-centred administrative system (Hendriks and Tops 2000: 9f.). In 1990 the reform goals switched from a focus on internal organization of production to a focus on the external environment. The role of the citizen (versus the customer) was (re-)emphasized. The traditional Tilburg Model of the 1980s focused on measures within the administrative organization. The major issues of reform in the 1990s were the professionalization of the civil service, the strengthening of the client orientation and productivity of public organizations.

In the city of Tilburg – which stands as an example of many Dutch municipalities for the more recent reforms as well – the new focus on external stakeholders of the administration led to the definition of dimension which characterize the interaction between municipality and citizens. The formerly task-orientated divisions of local government were redefined according to this reorientation. Depending on the role of the citizen the following organizational dimensions were found: 'urban development' – citizen, 'neighbourhood management' – resident, 'service delivery' – consumer and customer (Hendriks and Tops 2000: 13). In Tilburg – but also in other municipalities – the definition of these dimensions led to a new organizational structure in which the old issue-based divisions were replaced by a new dimension-based structure. Even though this reorganization was a major change, it did not attract as much publicity as the reform elements of the 1980s.

France

France has a historical tradition of centralism and a strong elitist career civil service. The administration is built on a complex system of administrative law. Since 1982–86, there have been four levels of administration in France: the central state, the regions, the departments and the municipalities. There are about 36,000 municipalities, and their size varies from very few inhabitants to over two million in Paris (OECD 1997: 195). France used to be a unitary state, in which subnational governments had no regulatory power independent of the central state, let alone any legislative power. Over the last twenty years local autonomy has grown rapidly, especially because of the decentralization laws of 1982–86. The induced managerial reforms are regarded as having changed local public management considerably (Halgand 1998: 99). Given the deeply anchored centralist tradition in France, the decentralization movement now has been blocked and it seems that there has been a spreading centralism at the local level, especially around the local actors who have originally benefited from the shift of power (Halgand 2001).

Traditional concepts of public management have often received less attention in France than in other Western, especially Anglo-Saxon, countries. The same is true for NPM: compared with its European neighbours, modernization in the sense of NPM reform has hardly happened in France (Rouban 1998: 358). Nevertheless, there was modernization. France has developed its own distinctive thinking and rhetoric about administrative reform, based on a series of separate initiatives by different governments (Pollitt and Boukaert 2000: 227ff.). In effect, one area of reform mainly affected the local level. The general trend of reforms was decentralization and devolution of tasks and responsibilities to lower levels of administration and state. Besides the reform efforts of decentralization to lower levels of government, a comprehensive modernization policy concerning human resource policy, accountability, evaluation and citizen orientation was launched at the central state level (OECD 1992: 97; Rouban 1997: 147ff.).

The decisive step for local public management was taken through the 1982 Act of Decentralization. Local collectivities were created as autonomous authorities. Direct elections for regional councils were introduced and new legislation gave local collectivities significant new taxing and budget-making powers. The legislation after the Act of Decentralization gave full democratic legitimacy to local authorities, with elected councils and exclusive local competencies in areas like health, social welfare, education, sports, culture and urban policy (Rouban 1998: 366). A lack of local democracy and shortcomings of centralist governance in specific task areas motivated this modernization strategy.

The decentralization policy was not embedded in a NPM-like reform concept. It has succeeded without any NPM rhetoric or NPM concept lying beneath (Wollmann n.d.: 12). Thus, the basic idea of our analytical concept, the match of NPM theory supply and practical demand, did not take place in France. There is no empirical evidence why France, in particular, has not been engaging in NPM.

A consequence stemming from the decentralization process which might be considered as in line with NPM reforms on the local level was the promotion of managerialism and the transformation of elected officials into 'managers', who in turn were boosting the spread of delegated management principles (Halgand 1998: 78 and 90). Further introduction of NPM reforms and elements at the local level was solely initiated by the local authorities themselves. To our knowledge there are no comprehensive programmes in place. There was no incentive from the central state to foster NPM reforms at the local level, but there was the provision of more room to manoeuvre through decentralization policy. Therefore achievements towards NPM are highly dependent on local capacities and commitment.

A very popular instrument in French public administration in general is contract management. According to Rouban (1998: 370) this contract management must not be misunderstood as a first step towards NPM. At the local level the use of contracts has a long tradition in France. It is a heritage from the past, when local authorities had to provide services without having the organization and resources to do so on their own. Even though the contracts gained some managerial aspects recently, they are highly political instruments. Preferences for local providers, party influence and other political variables are still main features in the contractual provision of public services in France. Other authors, like Halgand (1998: 90), stress the increased use of private or semi-private bodies for the running of public services as a consequence of the managerial reforms that came along with decentralization. Thus, the decisions to provide a service through a public or private body have been progressively based on cost–benefit reasoning.

To sum up, it can be stated that NPM rhetoric is hardly encountered in French modernization programmes. Regarding the actual reform elements at the local level, it can be concluded that some elements and principles of NPM are found, but they seem not to be embedded in a comprehensive NPM reform strategy. Even though some modernization elements can be regarded as NPM orientated, and NPM principles tackle some of the problems that local authorities face, France seems to have followed its own distinctive reform concept.

Interestingly, a certain hesitation towards NPM seems to exist in all French-speaking regions in Europe. Besides France, the Walloon area of Belgium is rather reserved regarding NPM reforms, while the Flemish administration is rather progressive with respect to NPM implementation. Also, in Switzerland, a cleavage between reforms in the German and the French sectors can be seen. The French sector is relatively reluctant to introduce 'pure' NPM reforms. In particular, compared with the Swiss–German sector it is clear that the devotion to NPM principles is much more diluted in the French-speaking areas.

Germany

German public administration is often cited as a close example of Weberian bureaucracy (Löffler and Klages 1995: 374; Heady 1996: 206). Public administration is characterized by classical hierarchical structures; traditional principles of the civil service, such as lifelong employment privilege or tenure-related pay, are explicitly guaranteed by the German Constitution. The bureaucratic features are more strongly developed in the bigger administrations at the federal and state level than at the local level.

Germany has three administrative levels: federal, state and the local level. The local level falls into two levels: municipalities and counties consisting of the municipalities within the county territory (OECD 1997: 213).[2] Germany has fewer than 15,000 municipalities, two-fifths of which are situated in former East Germany. There exist different types of organizational structures for municipalities, determined by relevant state laws. Recently, a trend following the South German Mayor system has been noticed, in which the mayor is elected directly by the local electorate .

The principle of local self-administration provides considerable scope to regulate their own affairs. The municipal autonomy means that the municipalities have the right and actual ability to run all local affairs under their own jurisdiction. But the federal legal framework sets up clear restrictions on this freedom through the civil service law, the budgetary law and the procedural law, etc. Regarding the local responsibilities, a distinction is made between tasks which the municipalities and counties fulfil within their own remit and delegated tasks. The local authorities perform numerous delegated and mandatory tasks as directed at the federal and state levels. Opposed to self-government matters, local governments are not only subject to supervision about the legality of these tasks but are also given detailed instruction on how to execute them (OECD 1997: 218).

NPM reform started in the late 1980s and the early 1990s, rather late compared with other countries like the Netherlands or the UK. The main driving factor for the reform was the dissatisfaction of the city managers, politicians and other managing civil servants within the traditional bureaucratic management system of local authorities. Accordingly, the reform was mainly pushed forward by practitioners within local government. The KGSt, the association of municipalities for managerial reform, which acts like a consulting agency for local governments, took a decisive role regarding the development of the so-called 'New Steering' model. The New Steering model is the theoretical framework for public management reform in Germany (Jann 1997: 85; Naschold 1999: 45). Interestingly, the reform movement started and succeeded solely because of the efforts of the municipalities and counties. The federal government as well as the states hardly[3] offered any support or guidelines for the reforms. So far, NPM reforms are only initiated at the local level and to some extent at the state level. The federal administration is working on their own reform agenda and has hardly any influence on local government reforms.

Local government reform in Germany was triggered off by the widespread dissatisfaction of local government practitioners and politicians with the status quo, i.e. the shortcomings of the traditional bureaucratic system. The German administrative system, in general, suffers from over-bureaucratization. Financial pressure certainly helped to propel the rise of the New Steering model, even though it was not as strong a cause as in many other countries. With regard to the model developed in this chapter, it is interesting to note that NPM at the local government level was concerned with accountability, legitimacy, problems of democracy, but not with ideological or micro-economic efficiency arguments.

The main features of the New Steering model are based to a large extent on the experiences of the Dutch city of Tilburg (see the Netherlands). This so-called (old) 'Tilburg Model' was largely influenced by the private sector corporate management concept. The New Steering model was developed along the lines of the Tilburg model. Partly it 'copied' the Dutch concept into the German context. Over the years it has been adapted to the different German legal, political and cultural conditions (Reichard 1997: 64).

The New Steering model emphasizes the reform of internal organizational structures and steering systems. The main contents of the concept are the introduction of product descriptions, internal management contracts, decentralized responsibility for results and resources, product-based budgeting, cost accounting and controlling. Its preference for and focus on internal restructuring and 'hard facts' like organization, budgeting and the product approach characterizes German local government reform. In the meantime, more and more municipalities became involved in quality management aspects, personnel management issues and (still primarily) non-market instruments of competition, like internal benchmarking. The New Steering model, as a theoretical framework, has been extended in this sense.

Prominent examples of local NPM reform are the city of Passau and the city-state of Berlin. Passau started its administrative reform with the creation of a mission statement. The mission statement was developed by the citizens, the administration and the city councillors. The city administration was organized like a holding company. The departments became 'service companies'. They work with lump-sum budgets and can decide on the use of their resources. A cost-accounting system was introduced for the whole administration and the newly created 'service companies'. Monthly customer feedback systems provide the 'service companies' with information on the perception of citizens.

Berlin also launched a comprehensive reform programme. The main features of the Berlin reform are decentralized resource competencies, cost-accounting systems, quality and human resource management.

Local governments were the forerunners of NPM reform in Germany. The distinction of the German model is its focus on internal reform, even though in the past few years trends to more interaction with the environment, for example through PPP or citizen empowerment, are emerging.

Switzerland

Switzerland is perceived in European circles as a small independent but diverse country. Indeed, it has approximately seven million inhabitants, who live in four different linguistic regions. In spite of its small size it is divided into twenty-six cantons (more or less sovereign states) and 2,903 municipalities. Switzerland has a three-tier system, which includes a national level, a cantonal level and a local level. More than half of the local municipalities have fewer than 1,000 inhabitants. A further indication of this small culture is that the Swiss regard a city as having more than 10,000 inhabitants (in the UK, a city is expected to have at least 100,000 inhabitants, or a cathedral).

The unique feature of the Swiss politico-administrative system is direct democracy. Swiss democracy allows the right to instigate a referendum against a law that has been passed by parliament and the right to hand in an initiative that proposes a new law or legal article. At the local level, it is not uncommon to hold full assemblies, where decisions on the yearly budget, the level of taxation, as well as single-case spending on, for instance, a new roundabout or a new snowplough, are taken. Thus we are led to the most important precondition for reforms in Switzerland: comprehensive democratic compatibility. Not only is it indisputable that the visionary concept to be implemented is compatible with the existing democracy, but also the process of experimentation and implementation needs to follow democratic principles.

The early movers among Switzerland's local authorities have followed a general trend to implement public management reforms of the NPM type since 1993. As in Germany, the shining example for Swiss cities was the Dutch city of Tilburg, whose concern division model attracted attention because of its clear separation of political and managerial roles. In other words, the Swiss reformers were fascinated by the impression made by the Tilburg model that it was possible to formulate a non-arbitrary performance contract between a political body (City Council) and the Administration. At the same time, the early 1990s, the New Zealand approach to public management was studied by Swiss researchers, and in 1994, the two models were compared and combined for Swiss purposes. Ernst Buschor (1993), former professor for Public Management at St Gallen University and at the time of writing Minister of Education in the Canton of Zurich, named these reforms *Wirkungsorientierte Verwaltungsführung* (results-oriented public management).

In Switzerland, NPM is seen as a reaction to three major areas of deficiency: (1) input control and opacity on outputs and impacts; (2) inflexibility caused by a lack of market pressure; and (3) bureaucracy and political over-control of operative decisions.

The Swiss NPM movement started out at the cantonal level and spread to the municipalities. The federal level has also engaged partially in NPM reforms, but has hardly any influence on the reforms at the local level. As in Germany the driving actors are normally to be found within the public administration, where small, but strong, groups of administrative staff backed by single politicians lead the reform projects. The main reason for NPM reform was dissatisfaction with the old model. Financial pressure might have helped, but it does not explain why NPM was chosen for reform.

Ladner *et al.* (2000: 130) found that one-third of German-speaking Swiss municipalities claim to be undertaking reforms of the NPM type. Although a purely quantitative view will most certainly not be able to give insight into the real reform situation, it is nevertheless able to give indications in a cross-comparative perspective. Reforms in human resource management are most often undertaken in Swiss municipalities, whereas NPM-specific performance management instruments, such as surveys, performance contracts, lump-sum budgets or product definitions, have only a limited degree of implementation. It can be said, therefore, that many claims to have implemented NPM have a bias towards certain (single) elements and do not guarantee that the whole repertoire of NPM is used in practical reforms.

Nevertheless there are some municipalities that pursue comprehensive NPM reforms. Notably, municipalities in the Berne area, as well as the city of Berne, have launched various NPM projects. Contradictory to the earlier statement, in this region financial pressure probably was one of the main driving factors. In general, local NPM reform projects mainly focus on organizational restructuring through which competencies are delegated to the public administrators and strategic and operative roles become more distinctive. In more comprehensive initiatives tools like lump-sum budgets and performance contracts are introduced. Interestingly, marketization plays a rather unimportant role in Swiss local government reforms.

The unique characteristic of Swiss NPM reform especially on local and cantonal level is the interplay of political and administrative spheres. The parliaments or local assemblies are involved in the implementation process and engage actively in the discussion and further development of the model. As a result the NPM reforms in Switzerland really turn into reforms of the politico-administrative system. Decision instruments for parliaments or councils are adapted to the new steering philosophy. Thereby – in municipalities which adopted NPM – politicians have learned how to 'steer' public administration more expressively than before.

Spain

Spanish public administration reform has to be considered in the wider context of its historical development. The Spanish democratic state only came into existence in 1978 after the Franco era. In the meantime, Spain had been transformed from a highly centralized state into a democratic politically decentralized state. The decentralization was encouraged by the introduction of the three-tier system.[4] The whole state is divided into regions, or Autonomous Communities, and subdivided into provinces and municipalities, which together constitute the local level. The competencies delegated to each Autonomous Community vary substantially depending on individual arrangements between the region and the central state. This system accounts for the political situation that has to deal with separatist movements (Mendoza and Puig 1996: 175f.).

In general, over the last twenty years the reform movement mainly focused on the building of decentralized, democratic structures. The whole administrative organization at the regional level had to be created; the competencies between the levels had to be distributed. From today's perspective the decentralization efforts have been a success. The local level was basically left aside in the decentralization efforts between the central and regional level (Alba 1997: 183ff.; OECD 1997: 399).

In the 1980s the national government proclaimed the introduction of a NPM-like reform programme including organizational redesign, budgeting by objectives and human resource reorganization. Despite some efficiency gains in certain areas, the programme in general is largely considered to have failed (Parrado 1996: 275).

On the local level, municipalities almost traditionally have to deal with fiscal scarcity. The scope of services they have to provide varies according to their size. Despite the pressure of scarce resource there has not been a broad reform movement at the local level. Only single examples of NPM modernization are encountered.

An example of local reform is the use of city managers in Valencian local authorities. In this respect Valencia is the exception rather than an example. The reason why city manager models have not become very popular might be that the councillors – who elect the mayor – are appointed by the mayor to run different services. This politicization of top management positions within the public administration leads to the fact that the councillors oppose any movement towards more professional management, since it would stop the mutual influence between mayor and councillors. A city manager who has human and financial resource competencies and reports directly to the mayor is a threat to the councillors who are appointed to run services (Parrado 1996: 274). Another perspective on the dislike of more managerial control in public administration might be that the historical experience throughout the Franco era fostered systematic democratization – and therefore politicization – of public administration. Since an authoritarian system relies on a strong administration, as a precaution today public administration is 'controlled' through weakening by political appointees and democratic legitimatization which favours elected politicians over managers.

Another example for local NPM reform is the city of Barcelona, which recently launched efforts to evaluate service delivery through accomplishment indicators. Since 1994, all municipalities present a balance sheet, an operation statement and a statement of initial and actual budget. Generally accepted accounting principles were introduced.

The main reforms at the local level where initiated by the central state. In 1995 a one-stop-shop policy was launched. The competencies between the levels of government are not always very clear and procedures require the involvement of different agencies. In the one-stop shops the citizens can take care of their entire administrative request, regardless of the destination department and the level of government. The one-stop shops are set up in municipalities and citizens can use them to address applications to the state or regional administrations. Almost 1,000 municipalities and ten regions have participated in this program up to now. The one-stop shop for citizens is an experiment and is not yet as developed as the one-stop shops for businesses described in the next paragraph.

Based on similar reasoning – involvement of many agencies and government levels, complex procedures – one-stop shops for business start-ups were set up. Similar to the Italian approach, the project aims to give people interested in creating and developing small and medium-sized enterprises a single reference place to obtain information and carry out specific administrative procedures. The one-stop shop for business also works in cooperation with the three levels of government plus the chambers of commerce. To date, six business one-stop shops have been opened throughout the country (OECD 2000: 3).

Findings

The short country studies allow a general – although simplified – overview of NPM reform taking place in continental Europe. Even though they only highlight certain characteristics of reform models, they give a rough insight into the motivators for NPM reform and international similarities of reforms. It is not the purpose of this chapter to give detailed comparisons between single concepts or municipalities.

According to the hypothesis formulated at the beginning of the chapter, the relationship between challenges that led to NPM reform and reactions thereupon will now be analysed. Figure 10.3 shows the main relationships as a result of the county studies. Only the main demand factors for reform have been taken into account. This procedure is a simplification of the original evaluation and does not show secondary relations, as it was necessary to keep the figure clear and understandable.

The reform examples in the preceding section showed that there exists a wide range of motivators – or demand variables according to our model – for reform. In Figure 10.3 the different driving factors were aggregated to demand variables. The demand categories used in this figure are defined as:

- *Financial distress*
  Reforms were initiated because the public sector was facing budget deficits.

Practical demand	Organizational restructuring	Management instrument	Budgetary reforms	Participation	Customer orientation	Marketization	Non-IPM reactions
Financial distress	NL, CH	CH	NL, ES			NL	
Dissatisfaction within public administration	CH, DE	CH, DE					
Over-bureaucratization	DE	DE			DE		
Displeasure of citizens					ES		
More/democracy participation				NL			FR
Competition to attract business			ES		ES		

Figure 10.3 Bias towards certain supply elements of NPM theory in local NPM reform concept in relation to practical demand

The motto at times of financial distress is to save money and to gain control over the budget again. The financial criteria of the Maastricht Treaty put some countries under similar restrictions.

- *Dissatisfaction within public administration*
  Reforms are also initiated because public administrators or politicians are tired of shortcomings in the traditional system. Impetus for reform comes from within the system, e.g. people who work with and know public administration.
- *Over-bureaucratization*
  Bureaucracy as describe by Weber is an idealist model. If mechanisms and instruments of this system are used *ad absurdum* we speak of over-bureaucratization. The famous US$400 hammer in US federal administration is one possible result.
- *Displeasure of citizens*
  Citizens as customers, users, tax-payers or legitimators of public administration are dissatisfied with public administration. The negative attitude towards public administration might aim at quality standards or institutional criticism in general, such as inefficiency of bureaucracy, public servants, etc.
- *More democracy/participation*
  The need for reform is based on the feeling that citizens lack democratic and individual influence. Citizens want to be more involved, the feeling of taking part in public life is an ideal.
- *Competition to attract business*
  Globalization, the European Market and other developments strengthen competition to attract businesses. The fact that public administration has influence on the attractiveness of the location (Schedler 1997: 195ff.) might make administrative reform a necessary means to attract business.

The first interesting insight is that just by looking it becomes obvious that the main areas of emphasis in the different reform concepts do vary. Second, municipalities who face similar challenges tend to use a similar set of NPM tools. Even though the same challenge might be answered by a different assembly of elements, some congruency is found. An example is that financial distress only led to the comprehensive use of marketization in the Netherlands, whereas in Spain neither marketization nor organizational restructuring is used. Third, national groups which have to fight similar challenges seem to correspond to cultural groups.

In general, it can be stated that NPM reforms in continental Europe are widespread and very diverse both between the different countries and between municipalities in the same country. The main characteristics of local NPM reform in continental Europe might be summarized as follows:

- A distinction has to be made between unitary, centralist states and federal states. In federal states, reform have started from below, e.g. at local or state level. This accounts for a wider variety of reform models in the same country. In centralist states, local reform has to be initiated by the central state. It seems that centralist continental European governments have not noticed the chances of NPM reform at the local level until the 1990s.

- Marketization plays a rather unimportant role in local NPM reforms in continental Europe. Even though some countries like the Netherlands implemented marketization instruments, it is not as popular as in reforms in Anglo-Saxon countries. An explanation might be that, except for the Netherlands, local government reforms in continental Europe did start until the early 1990s. By then, the ideological discussion on privatization had already lost a lot of attraction as a consequence of the fall of the Communist bloc. Although in the 1980s the reform debates mainly centred on neo-liberal arguments, this was not the case when most continental European countries started their efforts. The Netherlands, however, launched their modernization programmes much earlier in the 1980s.
- Challenges for public administration do change in time. Whereas efficiency, management and transparency were the main concerns of reform in the early 1990s, customer orientation, citizen involvement and e-government will be the challenges of the coming years. As the Netherland's example showed, the challenges faced by reform programmes are determined politically, in elections. The political agenda needs new topics even though the old ones might still be present-day problems. For example, most municipalities or countries face more public debt and expenditures than many years ago. But the electorate is tired of this subject. Therefore, modernization programmes will keep developing to meet the new challenges/political topics. In turn, this leads to a steady increase in NPM elements and instruments.

Prospects

NPM reform in continental Europe used to be inspired by the developments and early achievements of the Anglo-Saxon reforms. In the meantime, continental European municipalities developed their own NPM models and adapted them for their specific environment. The coming years will show a consolidation and wider implementation in those municipalities which already engage in NPM reforms. NPM will change from being a reform programme to become the normal administrative system.

Another question is whether countries and municipalities that have not already adopted the NPM will do so in the near future. Certainly, there will be single municipalities which will start NPM projects. More likely those examples will be found in countries in which other municipalities already experiment with NPM.

In countries where NPM has not really been a topic of discussion yet, we suspect that local reforms will mainly focus on e-government. The systematic use of IT for public service provision allows for new possibilities regarding customer orientation and internal reorganization. The reform measure will probably not be labelled NPM, but many elements and ideas of NPM will be transferred into the new concepts. First indicators for this development can be found in German-speaking areas.

NPM concepts and implementation will develop with regard to interfaces. Politicians, citizens, and employees are more and more involved in the evolution and consolidation process. Involvement of different stakeholders might foster the cultural change that is needed to make NPM the 'new steering philosophy' of public administration.

The coming years will also highlight the influence of the different legal systems in continental Europe and in the Anglo-Saxon system. Almost all countries presented in this chapter have a very complex and comprehensive system of public law. The challenge will be to find a reasonable level of public law regulations in the first place. In the international perspective the distinction of public and private law will show clear differences in the handling and use of contracting, employment rules and marketization instruments.

Notes

1 See the sections on Switzerland and Germany in this chapter.
2 There exist non-county municipalities, which generally are bigger cities that are independent of a county and thus unite the two local levels.
3 Some states offered experimental clauses in their legal framework, very few, like Saarland, engaged in accompanying measures.
4 During the Franco era there was only the central and local level.

References

Alba, C. (1997) Modernizing Spanish Public Administration: Old Inertias and New Challenges. In Kickert, W. (ed.) *Public Management and Administrative Reform in Western Europe*, Cheltenham, UK: Edward Elgar, pp. 177–195.

Buschor, E. (1993) *Wirkungsorientierte Verwaltungsführung, Wirtschaftliche Publikationen der Züricher Handelskammer*, Zurich: ZHK.

Farnham, D. *et al.* (eds) (1996) *New Public Managers in Europe: public servants in transition*, London: Macmillan.

Halgand, N. (1998) Centralism, Secrecy and Unaccountability: A Long Road to Reform in France. In Olson, O. *et al.* (eds) *Global Warning! Debating International Developments in New Public Financial Management*, Oslo: Cappelen Akademisk Forlag.

Halgand, N. (2001) Re: Paper, E-mail to Kuno Schedler on the 13 May 2001.

Heady, F. (1996) *Public Administration: a comparative perspective*, New York: Dekker.

Hendriks, F. and Tops, P. (2000) Winds of Change: New Public Management in Dutch Local Government, unpublished paper.

Hood, C. (1991) A Public Management for All Seasons? *Public Administration*, Vol. 69, pp. 3–19.

Jann, W. (1997) Public Management Reform in Germany: A Revolution without a Theory? In Kickert, W. (ed.) *Public Management and Administrative Reform in Western Europe*, Cheltenham, UK: Edward Elgar, pp. 81–100.

Kickert, W. (1997) Public Management in the United States and Europe. In Kickert, W. (ed.) *Public Management and Administrative Reform in Western Europe*, Cheltenham, UK: Edward Elgar, pp. 15–38

Ladner, A. *et al.* (2000) *Gemeindereformen zwischen Handlungsfähigkeit und Legitimation*, Berne: IPW/IOP, University of Berne.

Löffler, E. (1997) *The Modernization of the Public Sector in an International Comparative Perspective – Implementation Strategies in Germany, Great Britain and the United States*, Speyerer Forschungsberichte 174, Speyer: Forschungsinstitut für öffentliche Verwaltung.

Löffler, E. and Klages, H. (1995) Administrative Modernization in Germany – a Big Qualitative Jump in Small Steps, *International Review of Administrative Sciences*, Vol. 61, pp. 373–383.

Mastronardi, P. (1998) New Public Management im Kontext unserer Staatsordnung. In Schedler, K. and Mastronardi, P. (eds) *New Public Management in Staat und Recht*, Bern: Verlag Paul Haupt.

Mendoza, X. and Puig, P. (1996) The Public Administration System of Spain. In Brovetto, P. (ed.) *European Government: a guide through diversity*, Milan: EGEAS, pp. 177–202.

Naschold, F. (1995) *Ergebnissteuerung, Wettbewerb, Qualtiätspolitik. Entwicklungspfade des öffentlichen Sektors in Europa*, Berlin: Edition Sigma.

Naschold, F. (1999) Learning from the Pioneers: Modernizing Local Government. Part 1, *International Public Management Journal*, Vol. 2(1), pp. 25–51.

OECD (1992) *Public Management: Profiles*, Paris: OECD.

OECD (1997) *Managing across Levels of Government*, Paris: OECD.

OECD (2000) *Public Management Developments in Spain: Update*, Paris: OECD.

Osborne, S. and Gaebler, T. (1993) *Der innovative Staat: mit Unternehmergeist zur Verwaltung der Zukunft*, Wiesbaden: Gabler.

Parrado, S. (1996) Spain. In *New Public Managers in Europe: public servants in transition*, London: Macmillan, pp. 257–277.

Pollitt, C. and Boukaert, G. (2000) *Public Management Reform: a comparative analysis*, New York: Oxford University Press.

Reichard, C. (1997) Neues Steuerungsmodell: Local Reform in Germany. In Kickert, W. (ed.) *Public Management and Administrative Reform in Western Europe*, Cheltenham, UK: Edward Elgar, pp. 59–79

Rouban, L. (1997) The Administrative Modernisation Policy in France. In Kickert, W. (ed.) *Public Management and Administrative Reform in Western Europe*, Cheltenham, UK: Edward Elgar, pp. 141–156

Rouban, L. (1998) France: a Different Approach to Reform. In *Innovation in Public Management: Perspectives from East and West Europe*, Cheltenham, UK: Edward Elgar, pp. 356–382

Schedler, K. (1997) *Öffentliche Institutionen als Standortfaktoren für die Schweiz*. In Schmid, H. and Slembeck, T. (eds) *Finanz- und Wirtschaftspolitik in Theorie und Praxis*: Festschrift zum 60. Geburtstag von Alfred Meier, Bern, Stuttgart, Wien: Paul Haupt, pp. 195–222

Schedler, K. and Proeller, I. (2000) *New Public Management*, Berne: Paul Haupt.

van Mierlo, H. (1998) Public Management in the Netherlands. In *Innovation in Public Management: perspectives from East and West Europe*, Cheltenham, UK: Edward Elgar, pp. 313–351.

van Ruller, H. (1996) The Public Administration System of the Netherlands. In Brovetto, P. (ed.) *European Gonernment: a guide through diversity*, Milan: EGEAS, pp. 159–175.

Verheijen, T. and Coombes, D. (eds) (1998) *Innovation in Public Management: perspectives from East and West Europe*, Cheltenham, UK: Edward Elgar.

Wollmann, H. (n.d.) Local Government Systems ('Path-dependent') Divergence or ('Globalizing') Convergence? The U.K., France and Germany as (Comparative) Cases in Point, Working paper, Humboldt-University, Berlin.

Chapter 11

New Public Management, North American style

Sandford Borins

In the last two decades, fundamental changes have been transforming societies all over the world. These changes include the development of a global economy, the end of the Cold War, and the rapid progress and widespread adoption of information technology. The public sector too is being transformed, leading to the emergence of what has been called the New Public Management. This chapter will outline the major characteristics of NPM and examine its influence in the US and Canada. The third major North American country, Mexico, will be discussed briefly. The presidential election cycles of the US and Mexico, as well as Canadian Prime Minister Jean Chretien's choice of an election date, have all coincided, with Mexico having held its national elections in July 2000 and both the US and Canada having held theirs four months later. This coincidence provides a common point of departure for speculation about the future of NPM initiatives in the three countries. The chapter will also make reference to New Zealand and the United Kingdom, the two countries widely regarded as the pioneers of NPM. The chapter begins with a definition of NPM. It then examines the pressures to transform the public sector, goes on to discuss the resulting changes, and concludes with a discussion of the prospects for future public sector reform.

A global paradigm

The Organization for Economic Cooperation and Development (OECD) observed in 1995 that 'a new paradigm for public management has emerged, aimed at fostering a performance-oriented culture in a less centralized public sector.' The report noted that implementation of the new paradigm was far from complete, and varied from country to country (OECD 1995: 8). At about the same time, the Commonwealth Association for Public Administration and Management (CAPAM), an organization for public administration practitioners and academics in the fifty-four countries of the British Commonwealth, held its inaugural conference. As rapporteur at that conference, I summarized a set of common themes in the experience of public sector reform in this diverse group of countries and outlined the major characteristics of NPM:

- providing high-quality services that citizens value;
- demanding, measuring, and rewarding improved organizational and individual performance;
- advocating managerial autonomy, particularly by reducing central agency controls;
- recognizing the importance of providing the human and technological resources managers need to meet their performance targets; and
- maintaining receptiveness to competition and open-mindedness about which public purposes should be performed by public servants as opposed to the private sector or non-governmental organizations (Borins 1995: 5–11).

Defined in this way, the NPM can be interpreted as an agreement between the public and their elected representatives on the one hand and the public service on the other. The public and politicians want high-quality public services and better performance by public sector organizations, what Vice President Al Gore called 'government that works better and costs less' (Gore 1993). To get it, they are willing to give public servants more managerial autonomy, as well as the human and technological resources (i.e. training and information technology) to meet their goals. In addition, the public and politicians are willing to reward strong performance, for example through performance pay. The last component of the NPM paradigm is a way of enforcing this agreement. If public servants do not improve performance, politicians and the public are willing to introduce competition within the public sector, or move activities to the private sector or NGOs.

This new agreement marks a significant shift from traditional practice. Under the old model, public servants were expected to give politicians unbiased policy advice and to implement the decisions taken by them. In return, they could expect to work in anonymity, with security of tenure. Although security of tenure explicitly referred to changes of government, it was implicitly taken to mean lifetime employment. In marked contrast, the new agreement is silent about lifetime employment. Indeed, the combined impact of budget cuts needed to restore fiscal balance and the growing application of information technology (IT) is expected to reduce the size of the public service until a new, lower equilibrium is reached.

The impetus for change

Three factors, operating together, have tended to drive the adoption of NPM. They are economic pressures, high-level political commitment to change and a set of ideas to shape change. The experiences of the UK and New Zealand are most similar here. Both faced strong economic pressure to change and both had deeply committed high-level champions of change with clear ideas. In the UK, Margaret Thatcher took office in 1979 with a firm resolve to reshape a sluggish British economy and a lethargic public service (Thatcher 1993: 41–9). For New Zealand, the turning point came in July 1984 with the election of the Labour

Party and the subsequent run on the New Zealand dollar. While the Labour Party that was elected in 1984 had traditionally been strongly interventionist, its leaders all came to the conclusion that interventionist economic policies had failed. Officials in the New Zealand Treasury proposed a radical solution, consisting of economic deregulation, privatization of many state-owned enterprises and public management reform (Osborne and Plastrik 1997: 75–83).

In both the UK and New Zealand political leaders embraced a set of ideas that would lead to major institutional change in the public sector. Their two main sources of inspiration were public choice theory and agency theory, both of which had been developed by economists. Public choice theory applies the assumption of self-interested rationality to both bureaucrats and politicians. Just as businesses seek to maximize profits, bureaucrats are assumed to maximize their departmental budgets, and politicians to maximize their chances of re-election. The theory predicts that bureaucrats will expand their empires and politicians will use the public purse to confer benefits on interest groups, with the consequence that the public sector will grow at the expense of the private sector, and that a host of regulations and subsidies will be put in place that will reduce economic growth (Boston *et al.* 1996: 17–18). Agency theory analyses social and political relationships as a series of negotiated contracts between principals and their agents. The nature of these contracts depends on both the information available to principals and agents and their bargaining skills. In the case of politicians (as principals) and public servants (as agents), it was felt that the public servants had exploited their informational advantage. Politicians in both the UK and New Zealand wanted to reshape their relationship with public servants in a way that would offset that advantage (Boston *et al.* 1996: 18–21).

In discussing the US and Canada, it is important to remember that, unlike the unitary governments of the UK and New Zealand, they are both federal states. At the US federal level, the performance of the public sector did not rank high on the agendas of Presidents Reagan or George Bush, both of whom concentrated on foreign policy issues. Both administrations distrusted the public service and occasionally indulged in the rhetoric of bureaucrat bashing, but neither had any comprehensive programme for public service reform. That issue was most recently raised by Bill Clinton and Al Gore in the 1992 election.

The main locus of public service reform and source of new ideas about public administration, up until 1992, was state and local government. Innovative practices were being recognized and information about them disseminated through professional networks and innovation awards. The most notable was the Ford Foundation's Innovations in State and Local Government programme, initiated in 1986. One of its objectives was to counteract criticism of government by publicizing examples of innovative and effective programmes. The awards programme struck a chord, receiving approximately 1500 applications every year. This wave of 'bottom-up' innovation identified by the programme was recognized and celebrated in Osborne and Gaebler's (1992) best-seller *Reinventing Government*.

Bill Clinton, who had established a reputation as an innovative and progressive governor, made 'reinventing government' one of the key themes of his 1992 campaign, promising to introduce at the federal level the sort of reforms Osborne and Gaebler had documented at the state and local levels. Shortly after taking office in 1993, Clinton assigned Vice President Al Gore the responsibility of producing a blueprint for administrative reform in the federal government. Gore assembled a large team of advisers, including David Osborne, and produced his report (Gore 1993) in September 1993. The report's title – 'Creating a Government that Works Better and Costs Less' – clearly summarized its findings. Gore and his advisers believed substantial efficiency gains could be achieved and customer service improved by cutting red tape, re-engineering and applying IT. The report promised to produce savings of $108 billion in five years and reduce the size of the civilian public sector workforce by twelve per cent, or 252,000 positions, over five years. Gore's team, known as the National Performance Review, was installed in the Office of the Vice President and proceeded to implement administrative reform.

Consider the three catalysts for change – economic pressure, ideas and high-level commitment – in an American context. Vice President Gore's involvement clearly represented a high-level commitment on the part of a key player. Still, high-level commitment was not as whole-hearted as it might have been.[1] Implementing the Gore Report required both executive orders, which are within the power of the President, and legislative change. Clinton introduced the required executive orders. He might have submitted all-encompassing government reform legislation early in his term. Instead, he placed a higher legislative priority on health care reform. Government reform legislation was introduced piece-meal, with the result that some reforms were accepted by Congress, while others were not.

The intellectual context for administrative reform in the US encompassed a wide variety of ideas and models, Osborne and Gaebler's *Reinventing Government* among them. In addition, many public sector innovators were applying ideas from the business world. These included service quality, total quality management and business process re-engineering. Unlike the models reformers in the UK and New Zealand derived from economic theory, these business-inspired ideas were not premised on distrust of the public sector. Vice President Gore employed a very different rhetoric when talking about the public service, always noting that the federal government had many intelligent, devoted and innovative public servants. Unfortunately they had been trapped in a faulty system suffering from, among other things, excessive central agency micro-management. Thus, the answer was to change the system to allow the innate creativity of public servants to emerge. Gore's approach can also be seen as a way of interpreting public sector reform from a Democratic, rather than Republican, perspective.

The third catalyst for change, economic pressure, was certainly present in the US. The federal government was running a substantial deficit of $300 billion when Clinton took office. The administration was committed to reducing the deficit, and public management reforms that would reduce cost were looked on favourably. That said, the economic pressure was less intense than in either the UK or New Zealand. There was no sense of crisis.

Consider Canada in terms of the three factors leading to public sector transformation. Ideas for public sector change most closely resembled those in the US. Canadian public servants were attempting to apply ideas from the business world and were also reading *Reinventing Government*. In 1990, the Institute of Public Administration of Canada launched a public management innovation award, open to all levels of government, which now receives approximately 100 applications every year. The themes of the applications – integration of services, application of information technology, organizational redesign, and empowerment of workers and citizens – are very similar to those of the Ford Foundation's Innovation Programme (Borins 2000). The hard-edged public choice and agency theories that motivated reform in the UK and New Zealand were not often heard in Canada.

Economic pressure for public administration reform was building slowly. The Mulroney government took office in 1984 with a large deficit that was a result of the recession of the early eighties. Although the Canadian economy grew rapidly in the mid- to late eighties, the federal deficit was not eliminated. When the economy went into recession in the early nineties, the federal deficit ballooned from over $30 billion in 1991 to over $40 billion in 1993 – approximately six per cent of GDP (gross domestic product). The fiscal situation in the provinces was similar. Though the Province of Ontario was experiencing booming growth in the late eighties, the Government of Ontario was increasing its expenditures so rapidly that it could achieve only small surpluses. As soon as the recession hit in 1991, it went to a deficit of over $10 billion.

The result of years of deficits was that the accumulated debt of the federal and provincial governments soared, equalling Canada's total GDP by 1995 (OECD 1999: 5). Initially global capital markets were quite willing to fund Canada's deficits and service its debt.[2] By the mid-nineties, however, the capital markets came to see Canada as a country that could not get its fiscal house in order, and the bond rating agencies downgraded both federal and provincial debt. The pressure on Canada's governments to eliminate their deficits and begin tackling their debt problems had become intense.

Prime Minister Brian Mulroney's tenure in office, from 1984 to 1993, coincides with the UK and New Zealand's period of major reforms. Mulroney, however, did not provide the same determined leadership. He came to office with a Thatcherite distrust of the bureaucracy, and immediately established a task force chaired by Deputy Prime Minister Erik Neilsen to review all federal government programmes. The task force's recommendations included privatization, devolution and many programme cuts. Ultimately, the recommendations were shelved. Mulroney was unwilling to champion public sector reform for a number of reasons. He gave other initiatives – the free trade agreement, the Goods and Services Tax and constitutional negotiations – higher priority. Although he was willing to confront interest groups on those issues, he was not willing to anger them on less important ones, like public service reform and the deficit. Finally, for most of his term in office there was neither external pressure from capital markets nor internal political pressure to tackle the deficit (Osborne and Plastrik 1997: 91–99, 320–325). Margaret Thatcher's assessment of Mulroney provides – from her perspective – an appropriate last word: 'As Leader of the Progressive Conservatives I thought he put too much stress on the adjective as opposed to the noun' (Thatcher 1993: 321).

Jean Chretien's Liberal Party resoundingly defeated the Conservatives in 1993 and was re-elected as a majority government in 1997 and 2000. The Chretien Government's public sector reform efforts have both differed from and resembled Mulroney's. The obvious difference is that faced with the pressure of the global capital markets, as well as public opinion that was at least receptive to eliminating the deficit, the Chretien government was willing to make the hard political decisions necessary to achieve that goal. The key player was Finance Minister Paul Martin, acting with Chretien's clear support (Greenspon and Wilson-Smith 1997). The main similarity to the Mulroney era is that the Chretien Government has not shown a great deal of interest in public administration reform *per se*. The responsibility for public administration reform has rested with the President of the Treasury Board and the ministers who have served in that position have all been of middling influence.

To summarize, in both the UK and New Zealand, all the stars were in alignment for dramatic change in the public service: strong economic pressure, committed politicians and a set of ideas implying radical solutions. In the US, the Clinton administration had a committed champion in Vice President Gore, a rather less radical set of ideas and moderate economic pressure. In Canada, the key driver was economic pressure, largely absent for the Mulroney government, but increasingly intense during Chretien's first mandate. Chretien and his cabinet ultimately became strongly committed to ending the deficit, but their commitment to public service reform was less far-reaching.

The nature of change

Given the convergence of multiple strong triggers for change in both the UK and New Zealand it is not surprising that they both launched comprehensive public sector reform programmes. Their programmes included privatization, structural reform separating operating agencies from policy ministries, financial management reform and initiatives to improve service quality (Boston *et al.* 1996; Osborne and Plastrik 1997; Pollitt and Bouckaert 2000).

The reinvention initiative of the US federal government has been much less dramatic than the reforms in the UK and New Zealand. There was no impetus for privatization, because the US has had relatively little public ownership since World War II. In addition, the responsibility for oversight of the bureaucracy is shared between the administration and Congress, and Congress has generally been unwilling to relinquish its power. For example, in 1995, Vice President Gore proposed the creation of performance-based organizations (PBOs) modelled on the operating agencies established in the UK and New Zealand agencies. The administration did not ask Congress, with its Republican majority, for blanket approval to create PBOs, but rather sought approval on an agency-by-agency basis (Roberts 1997). So far, one PBO, dealing with the administration of college student loans, has been approved.

The most interesting organizational initiative in the US federal government has been the creation of reinvention laboratories. In 1993, Vice President Gore called upon the departments to establish reinvention laboratories, or pilot projects for new ways of delivering service. If the projects were successful, the parent department would then adopt the new approach more widely. The ideas for many of the laboratories came from front-line workers or middle managers. Research on the several hundred reinvention laboratories that were established has shown that there have been both successes and failures (Thompson 2000). Some of the key success factors identified include top-level commitment to reform; a meaningful, clear vision, set of goals and action plan, all of which were understood throughout the organization; a sense of urgency; persistence in overcoming obstacles to change; performance measures and a willingness to learn from mistakes; recognition of successes; and institutionalization of continuous improvement (Jones and Thompson 1999: 47–106).

Thus, reinvention in the US has not involved root-and-branch organizational reform. Rather, it has focused on improving service, measuring and improving performance, reducing red tape and cost, and introducing information technology. In 1993, President Clinton directed all government departments to establish customer service standards and to measure their performance in meeting them. This was, in effect, a replication of the UK's Citizen's Charter. Over 4000 standards for 570 departments, agencies, organizations and programmes are now in place, and there is substantial evidence of ongoing improvements in performance. One particularly noteworthy achievement is that the Social Security Administration has been rated as the best among world-class providers of telephone service (Gore 1997). In 1993, Congress passed the Government Performance and Results Act, requiring all departments to establish performance indicators and measure their progress in meeting them. This act and the service standards directive represent political and societal interest in demanding and measuring the performance of the public service.

Although managerial autonomy was not enhanced by comprehensive organizational reforms, there have been some more limited reforms designed to achieve that end. Procurement reform legislation was enacted, reducing the cost of bulk purchases and acquisition time, particularly for computers. There has been substantial reduction in both the number of middle managers and the internal rules they enforced (Gore 1996: 12–17). The federal government reduced its workforce from 2.2 million in 1993 to 1.95 million in 1996. This reduction of staff by 250,000 met its target in three years, rather than five. Savings of $118 billion, $10 billion over target, were also achieved (Gore 1996: 1–4; Kettl 2000: 19–25). Given that the US is the most advanced nation in the world in the production and diffusion of information technology, it is not surprising that IT has become a major part of reinvention. Government departments are doing more of their communication with the public by means of the Internet, and an increasing number of public sector transactions are being handled electronically. As the Internet's capacity for electronic transactions expands, stand-alone electronic transactions systems will migrate to it.

Canada's public sector reform initiatives pose a more complicated case for assessment. Although many initiatives have been undertaken, only mixed results have been achieved. Consider the accomplishments first. Privatization began under the Mulroney government and continued under Chretien, including such major Crown corporations as Air Canada, Canadian National and Petro Canada. The federal government's Programme Review, undertaken in 1994 and 1995, was driven by the need to restore fiscal balance. Yet it also forced ministers and public servants to ask fundamental questions of government programmes, such as whether they were still useful, and, if so, whether they should be the responsibility of the federal government, provincial governments or the private sector. The programme review led to the abolition of some subsidies and the privatization of some activities such as airports and air navigation. In other instances, it was found that departments could fulfil their missions at greatly reduced cost through the application of IT. Two examples of the latter are Human Resources Development Canada's adoption of electronic kiosks for job searches and Industry Canada's creation of Strategis, a Web site that provides information for businesses. In addition to cutting costs by embracing IT, the federal government reduced its personnel by about twenty-five per cent. Thus it achieved a percentage reduction similar to the UK government, but much faster and twice the percentage reduction of the US federal government.

The application of IT has become as important a part of public sector reform in Canada as in the US. Canadian public sector organizations have made extensive use of such technologies as the Internet, electronic transactions and electronic kiosks. In some instances, they have developed new technologies. The ready availability under the Free Trade Agreement of technology developed in the US has speeded diffusion throughout the Canadian public sector.

Canada has not been a pioneer, however, in terms of the other components of public sector reform. For example, in 1989, the Mulroney Government launched an initiative called 'Public Service 2000.' Ten task forces of deputy ministers and senior civil servants were formed, and after two years' work, they made recommendations, many involving service improvement and the reduction of central agency controls. These recommendations met with substantial opposition from the federal Office of the Auditor General, members of Parliament, public-service unions and the media – a loosely organized community that Roberts referred to as the 'control lobby' (Roberts 1996). Their opposition might have been overcome with strong political support. During and after the period in which the Public Service 2000 task forces were doing their work, however, the politicians were focused almost exclusively on negotiations intended to amend the repatriated 1982 constitution sufficiently that Quebec would sign it.

The Chretien government committed itself to develop and publish service standards for major services by mid-1994 and to report performance a year later. Reports by the Auditor-General of Canada in 1996 and 2000 conclude that the government has been slow in implementing this commitment (Auditor General of Canada 1996, 2000). If we were to liken NPM to a buffet, we would conclude that the Canadian government has sampled everything, but not made a full meal of any dish (OECD 1999; Pollitt and Bouckaert 2000: 208–217).

The most distinctive organizational innovations in the Canadian public sector go under the rubric of alternative service delivery, which has been defined as a process of public sector restructuring that improves the delivery of services to clients by sharing governance functions with individuals, community groups, and other government entities (Ford and Zussman 1997: 6). Examples include Canadian Business Service Centres, involving both federal and provincial governments, and Navigation Canada, a non-profit corporation owned by the users and employees of the air navigation system. These partnerships reduce costly overlap and duplication, and perform activities that the federal government has devolved as a consequence of its Programme Review. These partnerships acknowledge the complexity of Canadian federalism by involving all stakeholders in the ongoing management of services or policy areas.

Though Canada has lacked in significant top-down public administration reform, it has had a wealth of bottom-up initiatives. These have been reported in the applications to the Institute of Public Administration of Canada's innovations awards. Indeed, provincial governments have had the strongest presence in these awards (Borins and Kocovski 1997). Similarly, Kettl (2000: 28) notes that pragmatic, results-oriented mayors such as Goldsmith in Indianapolis, White in Cleveland and Giuliani in New York have achieved notable successes in delivering government that works better and costs less. A comparative study of applications to the Ford Foundation innovations awards in the US and the IPAC awards in Canada shows extensive similarities in terms of the types of innovations, innovative process and results achieved (Borins 2000). This research also showed that in both countries 'local heroes' – middle managers and front-line staff – were the originators of approximately half the innovations – a surprisingly large role given traditional public sector constraints. Although the complexity of their federal systems often causes frustrating overlap and duplication, they also provide opportunities to innovate in what the American jurist Brandeis called 'laboratories of democracy.'

Prospects for future public service reform

In both the US and Canada, one of the main drivers of NPM – the economic pressure of government deficits – has given way to massive surpluses. As a consequence, one of the major issues in the federal election campaigns in both countries was fiscal policy – taxing and spending. Conservatives favoured large tax cuts and little increase in government spending, while liberals advocated smaller tax cuts and more spending. In Mexico, taxes were also a political issue but, as will be discussed, from a very different perspective.

In the US, government reform was not a major issue, but it was mentioned in both the Democratic and Republican platforms. Vice President Gore took credit for the reinventing government initiatives of the Clinton Administration, in particular cost savings, reductions in staffing, improvements in service and increased use of the Internet by the federal government. He pointed to surveys showing sharply increased levels of trust in government since 1993. He promised to continue reinvention and placed a strong emphasis on new applications of the Internet. His specific initiatives included putting virtually every federal government service on-line by 2003, creating an 'interactive town square' where departments would post performance results and solicit citizen feedback, establishing a web-site (G-bay) to auction government surplus equipment and providing a digital key to any citizen for secure access to government records and transactions.

The Republican position on government reform criticized, rather than praised, the Clinton administration's record, but made similar, though less specific, promises. It claimed that states with Republican governors had taken the lead in making government citizen-centred, results-oriented and market-based, and that a Bush administration would emulate them. The platform promised an expansion of e-government, for example in procurement; strict adherence to the Government Performance and Results Act, which it claimed the Democrats had ignored; and rationalization of overlapping and/or competing programmes. Stephen Goldsmith, the former Republican mayor of Indianapolis and a champion of reinvention, was a senior domestic policy adviser to Governor Bush.

With Bush eventually being declared the winner of the contested 2000 presidential election in the US, if Goldsmith is appointed to a senior domestic policy position in a Bush administration, it would be an indication that government reform will assume a high priority. Goldsmith introduced contestability for local public services as a mayor, and contestability, contracting-out or privatization initiatives would all be consistent the Republicans' pro-market orientation.

Given its chequered past, what can be predicted about the future of public administration reform in Canada? Consider both financial and ideological factors. The Liberal government's position in the 1997 and 2000 election campaigns was that it would use half of the government surplus to reduce debt and cut taxes and the other half to increase programme spending. The conservative opposition parties (Canadian Alliance and Progressive Conservatives) preferred more emphasis on tax cuts and debt reduction than on spending, whereas the social democratic opposition party (New Democrats) advocated the opposite. The Liberal Party's approach can best be interpreted as reflecting a continued belief in a strong and activist federal government, with the Programme Review of the mid-nineties reluctantly undertaken to preserve the government's power in the long run. The government can now use its surpluses to restore some programmes it cut earlier in the decade and to undertake new initiatives. From this perspective, reforms such as the increased use of IT and alternative service delivery have the virtue of reducing programme delivery costs, giving the government programme more value for money.

Canada is a land of strong regional loyalties, with the strongest of those loyalties creating the ongoing threat of dividing the country. The federal government and the separatist government in Quebec are engaged in an ongoing struggle for the loyalty of francophone Quebeckers.[3] One reason for the intensity of the struggle is that so many senior politicians and public servants are themselves francophone Quebeckers, creating a conflict of visions within one extended family. The implication of this struggle is that it encourages the activism of both governments. The Quebec government promotes the 'Quebec model', which is premised on a strong public sector playing a leading role in economic development. The federal government, in its turn, cannot be activist only in Quebec, and programmes designed to spend money in Quebec inevitably have spillovers in the rest of the country.

These larger priorities have implications for public administration. Consider, first, how service quality initiatives are presented and, second, the future of the public service. The Canadian government has given its service quality initiatives the rubric of 'citizen-centred service', in contrast to the US government, which talks about customer service (for example in its 1997 report entitled Putting Customers First). The Clinton Administration made it clear that it is trying to emulate business (Gore 1997). Business is popular in America and governments, whether Republican or Democratic, hope to increase their popularity by identifying with it. The Canadian government emphasizes that it serves citizens, not customers. The explanation given is that sometimes the public sector serves unwilling customers (taxpayers, prisoners) and that there are often stakeholders involved beyond the immediate recipient of a service. I surmise that there is another, unacknowledged, reason for the insistence on the term citizens. The Canadian government is struggling for the loyalty of its citizens, particularly francophone Quebeckers. Providing good service is seen as a way of building loyalty to the state.

The Canadian government has made a priority of rebuilding a career public service after the downsizing of the last few years. It is now recruiting extensively at the entry level, rather than recruiting from outside at middle or senior ranks. (The only area where there has been substantial recruitment from outside at the middle level is in information technology.) The government has also put an emphasis on rebuilding the policy capacity of the public service. In the years of downsizing and budget-cutting, there were few opportunities to develop new policies. Now that funding for new programmes is readily available, the public service has a role to play in implementing them. Thus the federal government is attempting to rebuild the public service along the lines of the traditional model. A traditional public service would also be consistent with the priority of fighting separatism, because career public servants, especially the twenty-five to thirty percent who claim French as their mother tongue, could be expected to be more loyal to the federalist cause than people on short-term contracts.

In contrast, both the UK and New Zealand have opened their public services to the outside to a greater extent, in particular through the recruitment of chief executives and other managers in their agencies. The US allows the President to appoint (subject to Congressional confirmation) several thousand top officials. The Clinton administration has shown the strengths of this system, with many excellent appointments, such as Robert Rubin and Lawrence Summers in economic policy-making at the Treasury, Robert Reich leading a reinvention of the Department of Labor's regulatory role, and Steve Kelman at the Office of Management and Budget leading the administration's procurement reforms.

Jocelyne Bourgon, Cabinet Secretary to the Government of Canada from 1993 to 1999 attempted to summarize the Canadian approach in terms of what she called the 'Canadian model' of public management reform (1998). Her model emphasizes a continuing strong role for government and maintains a career public service working in the traditional departmental structures. This 'Canadian model' is closer to old public administration than to NPM. Whether other countries will emulate it or whether it is a response to the unique context of the Canadian federal government remains to be seen.

Finally, mention must be made of Mexico, the third major North American nation. In seventy years of rule by the PRI (Party of Institutionalized Revolution), that country has witnessed a dysfunctional blurring of the lines between politics and administration, with the paradox that although the most senior positions are held by a technocratic elite educated at the world's most prestigious universities, the system they rule is rife with corruption. To this point, Mexico has not had much of an administrative reform programme. The most significant initiatives have been aimed at putting in place the preconditions for administrative reform, such as the establishment of a truly independent electoral commission by former President Ernesto Zedillo. President Vincente Fox has put forward an ambitious reform package that includes a war on corruption, better tax collection and the establishment of a meritocratic civil service. Fox's appointment of Francisco Gil Diaz, who earned the nickname 'Iron Taxman' as undersecretary of tax collection from 1978 to 1982, portends a priority on ending cheating and broadening the tax base. Fox himself has a background in business and, like many public managers in the US and Canada, talks about applying tools such as total quality management and performance indicators to the public sector (Lichfield 2000). Fox's reform programme will have major implications for public management, and the result may well be that the public management reform spotlight in North America now shifts to Mexico.

Conclusion

This chapter has outlined a unique form of NPM in the US and Canada. It lacks the comprehensiveness of the reform programmes of the UK and New Zealand. In neither the US nor Canada did all the relevant factors – economic pressure, commitment by political leaders and a clear ideology – align to support comprehensive change. The key factor in Canada was economic pressure and in the US – at the federal level – the high-level championship of Vice President Gore.

Despite the different sets of causal factors in the two countries, and their different political systems, their public management reform programmes display substantial similarities. These include:

- the importance of bottom-up reform, in particular the efforts of front-line staff and middle managers, especially if sanctioned from above (for example, the US federal government's reinvention laboratories), as well as reforms undertaken by subnational governments;
- the influence of ideas originating in the private sector, such as service quality, total quality management and business process re-engineering;
- the importance of initiatives to improve service quality and to set objectives and measure performance;
- the critical role being played by information technology in two countries that are at the forefront of the IT revolution; and
- rather than major structural reform of government, the use of alternative service delivery mechanisms that cross boundaries of departments and levels of government and that incorporate as partners the private and non-profit sectors.

One factor unique to Canada is the separatist threat. Its influence is apparent in a number of ways: the insistence on maintaining a high profile for the federal government, the view that enhancing service will strengthen ties of citizenship, and the preference for a traditional public service loyal to the federal government.

Notes

1 Clinton indicated in other ways that he did not consider reinvention a very exciting issue. Speaking off the record at a National Press Club Dinner some months after it had been learned that he had been inviting major contributors to the Democratic Party to stay overnight in the White House, Clinton joked that for $10,000 contributors would be able to hear Al Gore explain reinvention, while for $20,000 they would be able to escape hearing Al Gore explain reinvention.
2 I recall a conversation in the early nineties with an assistant to the finance minister in the Ontario government, then the social democratic New Democratic Party. The assistant boasted that the investment banking firms in New York always returned his phone calls. Of course they would: the Government of Ontario was one of their best customers!
3 Sometimes the struggle assumes comic dimensions, such as a quarrel between the federal and Quebec governments about whether the Canadian or Quebec flags should be more prominent on cheques issued for a joint scholarship programme (Leblanc 1999).

References

Auditor General of Canada (1996) 'Service Quality' Report, Chapter 14 (Ottawa).

Auditor General of Canada (2000) 'Service Quality' Report, Chapter 1 (Ottawa).

Borins, S. (1995) 'Summary: Government in Transition – a New Paradigm in Public Administration' in Commonwealth Secretariat, ed., *Government in Transition: The Inaugural Conference of the Commonwealth Association for Public Administration and Management* (Toronto: Commonwealth Secretariat): 3–23.

Borins, S. (2000) 'What Border? Public Management Innovation in the US and Canada' *Journal of Policy Analysis and Management* 19: 46–74.

Borins, S. and Kocovski, S. (1997) 'Public Management Innovation in the Provinces' in Bourgault, J., Demers, M., and Williams, C., eds, *Public Administration and Public Management: experiences in Canada* (Quebec: Les Publications du Quebec): 219–28.

Boston, J., Martin, J., Pallot, J., and Walsh, P. (1996) *Public Management: the New Zealand model.* (Auckland: Oxford).

Bourgon, J. (1998) *Fifth Annual Report to the Prime Minister on the Public Service of Canada* (Ottawa: Privy Council Office).

Ford, R. and Zussman, D., eds (1997) *Alternative Service Delivery: transcending boundaries* (Toronto: KPMG and the Institute of Public Administration of Canada).

Gore, A. (1993) *Creating a Government that Works Better and Costs Less: Report of the National Performance Review* (New York: Times Books).

Gore, A. (1996) *The Best Kept Secrets in Government* (Washington, DC: US Government Printing Office).

Gore, A. (1997) *Putting Customers First: Standards for Serving the American People* (Washington, DC: US Government Printing Office).

Greenspon, E. and Wilson-Smith, A. (1997) *Double Vision: the inside story of the Liberals in power* (Toronto: Seal).

Jones, L. and Thompson, F. (1999) *Public Management: institutional renewal for the twenty-first century* (Stamford, CT: JAI Press).

Kettl, D. (2000) *The Global Public Management Revolution: a report on the transformation of governance* (Washington, DC: Brookings Institution Press).

Leblanc, D. (1999) 'Flag Flap Fires up Federal Scholarship Feud in Quebec' *The Globe and Mail*, 9 July: A4.

Lichfield, G. (2000) 'Mexico Survey: Revolution Ends, Change Begins', *The Economist*, October 28: 1–15.

Organization for Economic Co-operation and Development (1995) *Governance in Transition: public management reforms in OECD countries* (Paris: OECD).

Organization for Economic Co-operation and Development (1999) *Budgeting in Canada* (Paris: OECD).

Osborne, D. and Gaebler, T. (1992) *Reinventing Government* (Reading, MA: Addison-Wesley).

Osborne, D. and Plastrik, P. (1997) *Banishing Bureaucracy* (Reading, MA: Addison-Wesley).

Pollitt, C. and Bouckaert, G. (2000) *Public Management Reform: a comparative analysis* (Oxford: Oxford University Press).

Roberts, A. (1996) 'Worrying About Misconduct: The Control Lobby and the PS 2000 Reforms' *Canadian Public Administration* 39: 489–523.

Roberts, A. (1997) 'Performance-Based Organizations: Assessing the Gore Plan' *Public Administration Review* 57: 465–78.

Thatcher, M. (1993) *The Downing Street Years* (New York: HarperCollins).

Thompson, J. (2000) 'The Reinvention Laboratories: Strategic Change by Indirection', *American Review of Public Administration* 30: 46–68.

Chapter 12

Australia, the New Public Management and the new millennium

Peter Carroll and Peter Steane

Introduction

This chapter evaluates convergence in NPM. The first section provides working definitions for the concepts of NPM and convergence. The second section assesses Australia's experience of public sector reform over the last two decades to see whether or not NPM has become the dominant paradigm. The third section examines a selection of examples of convergence in Australia, APEC (Asia–Pacific Economic Cooperation), Hong Kong and New Zealand to see whether or not processes of international convergence related to NPM are occurring. The Conclusion looks to the future, to see whether we can forecast what shape convergence might take, in light of the conclusions this chapter draws, those being that:

- NPM has become the dominant paradigm in Australia.
- There is clear evidence of what we define as *principles convergence* in Australia, New Zealand and APEC.
- There is substantial divergence in terms of sources, content, learning and structure.

NPM and convergence: characteristics and issues

This section aims to provide working definitions that can act as sets of criteria in our later assessment of NPM in Australia and the evidence for international convergence.

NPM is characterized by features that have been outlined by a number of authors (Hood 1991; Hood and Dunleavey 1994; Hood 1996; Lynn 1996). Essentially, NPM is a form of public management:

1 whose proponents affirm that private sector management models and techniques can be applied in the public sector;
2 that is associated with a commitment to plural models of the provision of public services by a mixture of business, the non-profit sector and government actors, emphasizing the importance of cost, choice and quality in the precise mix of service providers;

3   that is associated with a revised role for government in the provision of public services, characterized as 'steering not rowing';
4   that expresses a strong belief in the role of the market and quasi-market mechanisms in coordinating the supply and demand for public services and the use of contractual mechanisms for the governance of provision;
5   that attempts a separation of the political decision-making processes from the management of public services.

We use these criteria to help us determine whether or not the current shape of the public sector in Australia and, to a much more limited extent, the Asia–Pacific, can be described as illustrative of NPM. This is influenced by developments on a more global scale. For example, the OECD Report on Regulatory Reform (OECD 1997) argues that effective regulatory reform means the development of a more efficient, less intrusive public sector regulatory capacity. This report represented a significant agreement between countries regarding regulatory reform that covers all government legislation, policy and associated activity.

Convergence: a definition

Policy convergence is defined as a process by which one or more policies in different jurisdictions become increasingly similar over time (see Bennett for a useful discussion, although his classificatory scheme is not adopted in this chapter, 1991: 218–219). The processes can be separated, at least for conceptual convenience, into extra-jurisdictional and intra-jurisdictional. The former describe the processes of learning that occur as decision-makers become aware of a policy that might be worth adopting in their domestic jurisdiction. The latter describes the activities that occur within a jurisdiction as the policy in question is developed and adopted – or transferred. It is important to stress that convergence in this sense involves movement over time towards some common point in terms of policy content, not merely the identification of random similarities and differences in policy (Bennett 1991: 219). Hence, we can identify:

*   The *sources* of convergence, ranging from one to several.
*   The *learning processes* by which convergence occurs.
*   The *principles* or assumptions that underlie the policy in question.
*   The *content* of the policy that is converging.
*   The *form* or *structure* adopted for the operation of the policy in question.

Perfect convergence would exist where sources, learning, principles, content and structure were identical in two or more jurisdictions, which is an unlikely but by no means impossible occurrence. Even in the countries of the European Union (EU), for example, the common adoption of policy at the EU level, an example of principles convergence, does not mean that the content of the policies and the manner of their administration in each of the member states will be identical in all respects. *Rhetorical* convergence would characterize the situation where a government expresses a sympathy for (in our case) NPM, but does nothing of substance to achieve NPM. Other forms of convergence could be characterized according to which dimension or dimensions of convergence were most similar, being *principles* convergence, *content* convergence, where the objectives and policy instruments used are common, and *structural* convergence of form.

We would expect principles convergence to be the most common, followed by content and, finally, convergence of form. We expect principles convergence to be common, at least where the states in question are committed to similar ideological perspectives, for example, as regards their preferences for types of economic system. The member states of the OECD, for example, constitute, in their own words,

> … a club of like-minded countries. It is rich, in that OECD countries produce two thirds of the world's goods and services, but it is not an exclusive club. Essentially, membership is limited only by a country's commitment to a market economy and a pluralistic democracy.
>
> (http://www.oecd.org/about/general/index.htm)

In other words its members and, hence, most of its publications, are concerned with promoting, maintaining and enhancing the operations of market economies in democratic settings. In such situations, we would argue, there is likely to be a distinct convergence among member states as regards basic, common principles or assumptions in a wide range of policy areas.

In contrast, regarding policy content and structural form (particularly the implementation process), our argument is that they are determined very much by the situational context in the country concerned, demanding modification as the complex process of bargaining and negotiation occurs in the effort to achieve policy acceptance, legitimation and implementation. In contrast, if the underlying principles or assumptions are not adopted then mere rhetoric is involved or, at best, 'mistaken', convergence. In what follows it is clear that it is *principles* convergence that is most common.

Indisputable evidence of convergence is difficult to provide. The problem to be faced is that the question of convergence is a great deal more complex than it first seems. Convergence from where, from what 'point', or source, to what recipient country, to what extent, in what form – these are just some of the questions that have to be both asked and answered if an answer is to be provided to our basic question. NPM, after all, can be characterized as a set of ideas (closely related to liberalism), a specific policy prescription or an empirical reality (where a specific country has implemented reforms that are based on the principles of NPM). Have Australian governments, for example, based their reforms on the UK's experience, so that we may talk about a process of simple, dyadic convergence from the UK to Australia? Or, have they based their reforms on a complex set of ideas and country-specific examples derived from several sources? Or, just to confuse the matter a little further, do each of the reforms that, taken together, constitute NPM have different origins, representing what might be called complex, multi-source convergence? Are we to judge that convergence has occurred only when all aspects of a policy are taken up in another jurisdiction? If so, then convergence is a very rare beast. Or, is it sufficient if the basic principle or assumption underlying the policy becomes embedded in another jurisdiction, that is, a convergence of principles?

These questions arise from the extra-jurisdictional context that Australia operates in, and are addressed in the next section.

Characteristics of Australian public sector reform: an example of NPM?

This section considers the extent to which the five characteristics specified in our working definition of NPM are evident in the public sector reforms in Australia. A full analysis would take far more space than that available. Hence, we draw attention to a selection of key reforms, supplemented with extensive references that the reader can consult.

The first characteristic is the extent to which private sector management models and techniques have been applied to public organizations. Australia and New Zealand have introduced a myriad of policies and practices largely modelled on the business sector. Corporatization, for example, has been introduced to varying government organizations as a quite explicit attempt to mimic the virtues of the contemporary business firm in the public sector. The Queensland government has chosen corporatization rather than privatization as the major means of reform of its public enterprise sector (Stevens and Wanna 1993: 98–99). In addition, there has been a significant adoption in Australian governments of client-centred reforms in service delivery (McGuire 2000).

The second characteristic is a strong commitment to diverse and pragmatic models of service where business, public and non-profit organizations compete and cooperate is evident among Australian governments, although the extent of the commitment varies. Contracting out of activities previously undertaken by the public sector means that a new type of purchaser–provider relationship arises, where the state may retain responsibility for overall provision but not delivery (Smith 1995; Dixon et al. 1996). This development derives from concerns to introduce greater client-focused service delivery. Such interest continues in the form of service charters, which have been mandated for all federal agencies in Australia (McGuire 2000). As suggested, the impact of this specific aspect of contracting out is significant. It has meant the creation of a whole range of public private partnerships and quasi-independent agencies that have assumed considerable importance in service delivery. Partnerships (in the broad, rather imprecise meaning of the term) generate a new 'architecture' of governance where networks arising from partnerships can become a key social phenomenon in service delivery. The recent case of the Australian Commonwealth Government awarding A$700 million worth of contracts to church groups for job placement programmes in relation to Centrelink is an example of such an architecture or network of actors (Steane and Carroll 2000). In other words there is a strong and growing commitment to diverse and pragmatic models for service delivery.

In regard to the third characteristic, there is little question that there has been a substantial, if not complete, Australian acceptance of the view, embedded in NPM, that 'steering, not rowing', should be a central characteristic of the state in Australia. In terms of substantive reforms, as opposed to political rhetoric, this is most obviously the case in regard to the large-scale privatization of public enterprise that has taken place at the federal and state levels over the period 1985–2000. State 'rowing', in terms of ownership and management of public enterprise has been sharply reduced. Qantas, the Commonwealth Bank, Telstra and the bulk of federal enterprises have been wholly or partially privatized. At the state government level the privatization record is more variable, going furthest in Victoria under the successive governments of Premier Kennett and being most limited in Queensland, where both National Party and ALP (Australian Labor Party) governments have been reluctant to fully privatize their enterprises. However, considerable corporatization of enterprise and of other statutory authorities has taken place (Maddock 1994; King 1998). The growing influence of the 'steering not rowing' view also can be seen in the rapid increase in contracting out of non-core services and activities previously undertaken by governments. As indicated above, the single largest example of such contracting out has been the dismantling of the Commonwealth Employment Service (CES), with the vast bulk of its employment services being contracted out on a competitive basis to not for profit and for profit organizations. The Salvation Army, for example, has been the most successful competitor, becoming the nation's largest provider of contracted out employment services.

The fourth characteristic, a strong belief in the role of the market and quasi-market mechanisms in coordinating the supply and demand for public services, in addition to the extensive use of contracting out for the governance of provision of services, has become a characteristic of Australian governments. Commonwealth minister David Kemp, for example, in describing the intent of planned reforms to the commonwealth public service, noted:

> The maturing of our democracy is also a major force for change, pushing governments to control their expenditure and meet increasing citizen expectations. Governments now are exploring and adopting demanding tests of what services should be provided and by whom. Opening the provision of services to competition, being a purchaser rather than a provider of services and shedding non-core functions are global themes.
>
> (Kemp 1998)

It should be noted that the use of contracts for governance purposes is restricted to relationships between government and non-government bodies, for, under the Australian Constitution, is it not possible for one part of government to contract with another part for the provision of services, as different parts of the same government are not permitted to litigate with each other for non-performance of contracted obligations (Worthington 1999: 11). However, while formal, legal contracts are not a feature of intra-government relations, they are, as indicated above, an increasing feature of government and private body relationships.

Finally, the argument that NPM is characterized by a separation of the political decision-making processes from the management of public services is not obvious in the Australian context. There is certainly a growing, if not unanimous belief that the policy development and decision-making function should be more clearly separated from day to day management responsibilities. However, the public service is still regarded as a prime source of policy-related advice, a central element of its traditional role at the highest levels (Kemp 1998). What has changed is the acknowledgement that it is no longer the sole source of such advice,

Policy advice itself today is increasingly contestable. There is a growing number of analytical think tanks and lobby groups which actively voice their private interests in policy advice. The public service is no longer the sole source of advice to governments, but it does remain the government's key advisory voice in the public interest (Kemp 1998).

The most dramatic example of a deliberate attempt to institute a distinct split or divide between the policy process and management is the creation of Centrelink. In summary, the second largest commonwealth department, Social Security, was split into two parts, with responsibility for the provision of the welfare and employment-related services being delegated to a new, statutory authority, Centrelink (Worthington 1999). The CEO of the new organization is responsible not to the minister, but to the board of Centrelink, with the board being responsible to the minister. The dramatically smaller department retained the policy development and advice role.

The above is merely a brief summary of some of the more important examples of reform that lead us to believe that Australia has adopted NPM. We would argue that it is sufficient to permit the drawing of at least two broad conclusions:

1   Australian governments can be characterized as having adopted NPM, if to varying extents and in varying ways. What is important is that there is clear evidence that the principles underlying NPM have been accepted by governments of all persuasions, with increasing acceptance over time. An example of *principles* convergence.

2   That acceptance has not meant uncritical, simple adoption of NPM policies developed elsewhere, but, for the most part, an informed use of NPM, modified to meet Australian circumstances, so that convergence becomes *divergence* as policy is developed and implemented to meet local circumstances.

NPM: convergence or divergence?

Policy convergence we defined as a process by which one or more policies in different jurisdictions become increasingly similar over time. It is important to stress that convergence in this sense involves movement over time toward some common point in terms of policy content, not merely the identification of random similarities and differences in policy (Bennett 1991: 219). The public policies, for example of the EU, Thailand, Indonesia and Australia, display endless similarities and differences. Their study may be of some value, but it is not the purpose of this section. Rather, the intent of this section is to examine whether or not the adoption of NPM can be seen as an example of convergence from some common policy source, using examples from the countries of the Pacific Rim, with an emphasis upon Australia, Hong Kong and APEC.

Our basic argument falls into three parts:

1   That there are clear signs that NPM has become the preferred model for government in several countries within the area as the following examples, drawn from the region, illustrate.
2   That the extent and type of convergence varies, with it being greatest in terms of the adoption of underlying principles or values, but falling away rapidly in terms of the *structure or form* for implementation of the reforms that is adopted. In large part this divergence is a response to differing social, economic, cultural and political contexts.
3   That convergence can be single or multi-sourced. In the case of Centrelink and the Trans-Tasman Mutual Recognition Agreement it was multi-sourced, whereas in the case of the Australian adoption of mutual recognition it was single sourced.

We illustrate our view by looking at four cases of convergence: Centrelink, mutual recognition in Australia, mutual recognition in APEC and Hong Kong's cyberport. There is no pretence that these examples represent a statistically valid sample of cases. They represent the authors' current research interests in the area, but all provide useful examples of convergence at work.

Centrelink

The provision of social security in Australia provides a case study of a working partnership designed to institute a purchaser–provider split between the Department of Social Security (DSS) and what became known as Centrelink, the part of the DSS that managed the provision of employment services (Worthington 1999). The model for this relationship, according to Worthington, had its origins in a sympathetic analysis of the purchaser–provider contractual approaches in several countries, including the United Kingdom, Canada and New Zealand, as well as in the growing literature that addresses the question of purchaser–provider splits and partnerships. Convergence takes place, based not upon one source but from a number of sources.

In Australia the provider organization, Centrelink, was established as a separate statutory authority under its own legislation so that its independence from the purchaser, DSS, was assured. Nevertheless, the government maintained a close working relationship between both organizations by having them located within the same ministry and by appointing senior DSS executives to the Centrelink Board of Management. The Chief Executive is responsible to the Board of Management and through the Board to the Minister for Social Security. The strategic partnership agreement between the Department for Social Security and Centrelink can be understood as a memorandum of understanding that acknowledges shared responsibility for performance.

At a first, simple level of analysis, as indicated, this was an example of convergence, with the DSS adopting a purchaser–provider model developed in the UK and elaborated in the literature read by those responsible for developing the concept in DSS (Worthington 1999). However, further analysis soon shows that this was not a simple case of convergence, for substantial divergence occurred during the development and implementation of the concept. In particular, the relationship that was put in place did not rely upon a legal contract between the DSS and Centrelink, nor did it permit the minister in the DSS to have direct control over the operations of Centrelink. This was in marked contrast to the situation in regard to such purchaser–provider splits in, for example, the UK. In regard to the lack of a legal contract there were two reasons for divergence. First, such a legalistic frame was regarded as unnecessarily adversarial, based on the absence of trust between the partner organizations and counterproductive to longer-term relationships (Worthington 1999). Furthermore, constitutional constraints prohibited litigation between federal government agencies, so a formal contract was irrelevant. Second, the means adopted for reducing the influence of the minister, a board established by statute with its own authority, was different from the 'splits', adopted in the UK, where no such board intervened between the minister and the operating agency.

In other words the Centrelink example is that of single source, principles convergence, accompanied by a process of policy 'reinvention', that led to a divergence in terms of the content and form of the resulting policy.

Mutual recognition in Australia

Systematic and vigorous regulatory reform, combined with the liberalization of international trade and investment has been a key aspect of the introduction of NPM within and between most states in the region, including Australia. The broad aim has been a reduction in the burden of regulation faced by business, burdens it can ill afford in an increasingly competitive, global economic environment (Carroll and Painter 1995). Regulatory reform has involved a variety of mechanisms, from review to the replacement of inflexible, prescriptive regulation with more flexible instruments, such as the growing use of the mutual recognition principle. Mutual recognition is an agreed decision rule between two or more parties that has as its intent a reduction in regulatory barriers to trade and the movement of labour between jurisdictions. It specifies that the subjects of the agreement (goods, services or the movement of people), provided they have met all relevant regulatory standards in the jurisdictions partner to the agreement, will be deemed acceptable for import and use in all participating jurisdictions, even where the regulatory standards in the country of origin are different from the importing country.

The EU pioneered the use of mutual recognition as a means of breaking down inter-jurisdictional barriers to international trade, making it a centre-piece of the Single European Act (Carroll 1999). From the early 1990s Australia adopted the notion of mutual recognition in a series of mutual recognition acts. It was an act of what might be called single-source convergence, sourced from the EU. The acts were aimed at breaking down the remaining barriers to trade between the Australian states. They were followed by a Trans-Tasman Mutual Recognition Agreement between Australia and New Zealand, in what might be described as multi-sourced convergence, drawing upon both the EU's experience and Australia's more recent experience. On the face of it these are both clear examples of convergence. However, whereas the principle of mutual recognition was adopted the extent of convergence was in fact limited. As Carroll (1999) has shown the adoption of mutual recognition in Australia varied from that implemented in the EU. First, the scope of the policy goals involved was far narrower than in the EU. Second, the specific purposes in adoption of mutual recognition varied. In the EU, for example, its adoption had as one of its goals the enhancement of political integration, whereas this was not the case in Australia. Rather, in Australia it was seen primarily as a means to hasten greater economic integration, albeit with a more cooperative rather than competitive federalism in mind. Similarly, there were wide variations in the way in which the agreements in relation to mutual recognition were implemented, suggesting divergence in terms of scope, importance and implementation, to suit national circumstances (Carroll 1999, Painter 1998).

Hence, in the case of mutual recognition we have an example of single-source principles convergence (Australia), multi-source principles convergence (Trans-Tasman) and, again, substantial divergence in policy content and form.

Hong Kong's cyberport

Another example of convergence can be seen in relation to Hong Kong's planned cyberport. This is an example of a public private partnership, where the state and private sector interests enter into a close working relationship, rather than the state taking sole responsibility for the activity in question, seen as increasingly typical in the UK and the Netherlands. As with the above examples, a more detailed examination shows that although convergence does seem to have taken place, in the sense that we can identify a public private partnership, divergence also is present. In the latter case this seems to be caused by the differing nature and importance of relationships in the Chinese context.

Hong Kong's Chief Executive, Tung Chee Hwa, announced to the Legislative

Council on 14 January 1999 that the Special Administrative Region (SAR) would itself review its policies and operations to meet the needs of the community better. One outcome of this statement is Hong Kong's cyberport, planned for completion in 2004, as a public–private partnership. The cyberport is aimed at positioning Hong Kong as the internet hub of the emerging 'knowledge economy' in the Asia–Pacific region. The cyberport is essentially a 'multi-function polis' of corporate clients sharing facilities, yet with secure database centres and high-speed connectivity and a strong foot-hold in China. Contracts have been received from thirty-four companies to date, including Microsoft, Cisco, Yahoo and Oracle (Government of Hong Kong 1999). The mix of government support and infrastructure, sound legal and business processes and educated professionals has resulted in a public–private partnership where motivations and business behaviour seem to positively align. It displays at least some of the essential features of a public private partnership characteristic of NPM (Carroll and Steane 2000).

However, further analysis suggests some divergence in the areas of networks and obligations. In the case of the Hong Kong cyberport, the government seems to have displayed entrepreneurial skills in brokering the arrangement to create a partnership that is situated within a dense set of family networks. In general, in a Western country partnerships are more likely to arise from and be placed within hierarchical networks along the lines of a traditional Weberian bureaucracy. In China, familial networks generally attract obligations and modes of association affiliative in nature compared with the hierarchical network, where obligations are more objective and instrumental in nature. Such a difference in social and institutional context illustrates a divergence in context, which is not surprising. In the West, obligations to other actors in a partnership are often defined impersonally by scope and boundary, with personal relationships being incidental to the partnership, at least in its earlier stages, whereas in an Asian context, obligations within a partnership may be based upon personal, family relationships as well as those formally specified for the partnership. The division between public and private becomes problematic. On the surface it might manifest the attributes of a public–private partnership as commonly understood in a Western (Westminster or Congressional) system, but its real dynamics might well be based upon a web of personal and family relationships.

Thus, we have in this case an example of convergence from uncertain sources, most likely the UK and the USA, in the shape of the use of a public private partnership for cyberport, but in practice a likely divergence from Western norms in terms of its operations.

APEC, Australia–New Zealand relations and the use of mutual recognition

NPM is not confined to the national level. It has an increasing, international and regional importance in the Asia–Pacific region, with leaders cooperating to spread its influence in the form of principles such as mutual recognition, on a voluntary basis. This can be seen in regard to the APEC and the Trans-Tasman Mutual Recognition Agreement between Australia and New Zealand.

APEC was established in 1989 as an informal, regional grouping. It has since become a more important regional organization promoting open trade and economic cooperation. It includes all the major economies of the region with a combined gross domestic product of over US$16 trillion in 1998 and forty-two per cent of global trade. In Osaka on 19 November 1995, APEC economic leaders adopted the Osaka Action Agenda, a blueprint for implementing their commitment to free and open trade and investment, business facilitation, and economic and technical cooperation.

Trade and investment liberalization in APEC proceeds on a voluntary basis and there has been an important use of mutual recognition as a means of achieving liberalization. Under the Early Voluntary Sectoral Liberalization initiative, for example, APEC is working to free trade in several key industrial and services sectors including a telecommunications equipment, mutual recognition arrangement (APEC 1998).

After the introduction of mutual recognition legislation within Australia, it was soon adopted in regard to relations with New Zealand, in the shape of the Trans-Tasman Mutual Recognition Agreement, 1996. Tariff barriers between the two countries had already been eliminated under the earlier Closer Economic Relations agreement (CER). The Trans-Tasman Agreement has two main principles. The first is that goods should be sold between Australia and New Zealand without restrictions caused by differences in product standards or other regulatory requirements. The second is that persons registered to practise in a mutually recognized occupation should have mobility between countries without the need to undergo further testing or examination. Should disputes arise over aspects of regulation and registration, those disputes may be heard by the Administrative Appeals Tribunal in Australia and a newly created equivalent tribunal in New Zealand.

In the two later adoptions of mutual recognition the initial source of convergence was the Australian experience, reinforced by Australian representatives urging the adoption of mutual recognition in APEC forums. In the New Zealand case the source was again Australia, with New Zealand public servants and ministers having observed the introduction of mutual recognition in Australia on a first-hand basis, as members of, for example, the Council of Australia Government's (COAG) Committee on Regulatory Reform. This was the intergovernmental committee charged by COAG with proposing the mutual recognition legislation and, as with many COAG bodies, it contained New Zealand representatives. However, it was not only Australian experience and influence that persuaded key decision-makers, but their own understanding of the success of the EU's experience with the wider use of mutual recognition following the 1985, Single Europe Act. In addition, while the Trans-Tasman MRA was being negotiated, New Zealand reached a separate mutual recognition agreement with the EU regarding the recognition of standards assessment procedures for goods.

The future

In this section we indicate what may become important characteristics of the public sector in the Asia–Pacific region. Given our definition of NPM and our findings in regard to its transfer by associated processes of principles convergence and content and form divergence, then multiple futures are possible, indeed likely, depending upon the state and period in question. This is particularly so in the Asia–Pacific region where there exist a wide variety of states of differing types faced with differing problems and widely differing historical traditions. Hence, we would expect a future for the region in which within the same time period some states would enter a post-NPM situation while others would barely be entering it. If we relate our view of the future to our earlier definition of NPM (195–198), then the following is possible:

• The continuing dominance of the view that private sector management models and techniques can be applied in the public sector.

At present this is an increasingly dominant view in the region, but to greatly varying extents. If, post the 1997 Asian financial crisis, previous rates of economic growth re-appear, then we think this view will become increasingly dominant in the stronger economies. In turn, they will press their views on their weaker and poorer neighbours through regional organizations such as APEC.

• A commitment to plural models for the provision of public services by a mixture of business, the non-profit sector and government actors, emphasizing the importance of cost, choice and quality in the precise mix of service providers. Some of these could be regarded as public–private partnerships, but perhaps not in the sense used in the non-Asian OECD countries.

There will be great variation in the extent of such plural models in the region. A weak business and not for profit sector are not conducive, in the short or medium terms, to rapidly increased use of these two sectors in, for example, the provision of welfare or major infrastructure developments Given the variety of states that exist in the South East Asian and East Asian areas, it is difficult to generalize regarding the areas as a whole. States such as Singapore, Hong Kong and South Korea, for example, have strong, technologically advanced private sectors. They are more than capable of working closely with government to provide almost any service, welfare or infra-structural. Others, such as Laos and Cambodia, do not have the same resources or capacities. Hence, even if their governments wished to use their private sectors for the provision of a wide range of services, they would be limited in their ability to do so.

• Some will be steering, some will be rowing.

The government decision to steer rather than row requires, at the least, a thriving private sector (both business and not for profit) willing and able to take responsibility for development, and a government able and willing to support such development. There are some states in the region that clearly do not display either characteristic at present. Laos or Cambodia, for example, have for the most part weak, inefficient private business sectors ground down by years of war and civil unrest. In such a situation is it likely that the Laotian public sector will undertake to restrict itself to a predominantly 'steering' role in the provision of public services? We think not. By way of contrast, Australian federal governments seem committed to a 'steering, not rowing', role, confident that the business and non-profit sectors will take up the role they vacate, or, where total withdrawal is not possible or desirable, willing and able to work in a variety of public private partnerships.

- Strong beliefs in the role of the market and quasi-market mechanisms in coordinating the supply and demand for public services and the use of contractual mechanisms for the governance of provision.

Again, there is likely to be substantial variance in the prevalence and dominance of these beliefs in the region. It is likely that states will fall into one of three possible groupings. One, the 'believers', those in which the beliefs are dominant, informing all relevant policy, for example, Singapore, Australia and New Zealand. Two, the 'converts', where there is growing belief, modified by a differing historical experience, especially where that experience has indicated that non-market mechanisms can be used successfully to promote economic development, such as Japan, Korea and Taiwan. Three, the 'sceptics', where there is a belief that markets have some value, but that it is a value that should be subordinated to political and social ideals, such as China and Vietnam.

- A separation of the political decision-making processes from the management of public services.

This is likely not to be a major characteristic of any government in the region or any region, for that matter. The notion that politics can be divorced from decision-making is to fundamentally misconceive the nature of politics. At a national level, governments are subject to continuing pressures from influential groups, whether they be democratic or otherwise. While these can be resisted some of the time they cannot be resisted all of the time – 'politics will out'. It would be naive, for example, to imagine that senior managers in Centrelink would not become interested in and, to varying extents, influential upon policy, however much those in the policy-oriented core of the department attempted to resist such encroachment. Splitting policy and operations may well change the structure of power in an organization, but it does not signal the end of internal politics or future attempts by ministers to become more directly involved in major management issues.

Conclusions

As indicated in our introduction, we draw three main conclusions:

- NPM has become the dominant paradigm in Australia.
- There is clear evidence of what we define as *principles convergence* in Australia, New Zealand, APEC and Hong Kong.
- There is substantial divergence in terms of sources, content, learning and structure.

The adoption of NPM is an example of the convergence of principles and, to some extent, the assumptions and ideological base upon which those principles rest. In Australia and New Zealand it is the dominant paradigm. However, this does not mean that we have a case of total or perfect convergence, although it is far more that mere rhetoric. As our limited cases indicate, even the whole-hearted acceptance of a set of principles does not mean convergence in terms of dependence based solely upon one source of ideas (convergence of sources), nor the convergence of learning processes (Australia 'learnt' from the EU; New Zealand 'learnt' from both Australia and the EU regarding mutual recognition). Nor does it mean that the content of public policy converges, other than as regards the basic principles of the policy in question. A wide range of differing policy instruments, for example, might be used in policies that seem to address similar issues in different countries, suggesting content divergence as much as convergence. Similarly, there is little evidence to suggest that the organizational forms or structures of government are converging in governments that have adopted or are adopting NPM.

References

APEC (1998) *APEC Mutual Recognition Arrangement on Conformity Assessment of Electrical and Electronic Equipment*, APEC, http://www.apecsec.org.sg/scsc/scsc_mraeee1.html.

APEC (2000) *Activities by Groups – Standards and Conformance*, Report of Subcommittee on Standards and Conformance, APEC, http://www.apecsec.org.sg/committee/standards_upd.html.

Bennett, C. (1991) 'What is Policy Convergence and What Causes it?' *British Journal of Political Science*, 21: 215–233.

Carroll, P. (1999) 'Globalisation and Policy Convergence: The Adoption of Mutual Recognition in the European Union and Australia', *Public Management*, 1(3): 387–406.

Carroll, P. and Painter, M. (eds) (1995) *Microeconomic Reform and Federalism*, Federalism Research Centre, The Australian National University, Canberra.

Carroll, P. and Steane, P. (2000) 'Public Private Partnerships: Sectoral Perspectives'. In Osborne, S. (ed.) *Public Private Partnerships: International Perspectives on Theory and Practice*, Routledge, London.

Dixon, J., Kouzmin, A. and Korac-Kakabadse, N. (1996) 'The Commercialisation of the Australian Public Service and the Accountability of Government: A Question of Boundaries', *International Journal of Public Sector Management*, 9(5/6): 23–36.

Government of Hong Kong (Special Administrative Region) (1999) *Cyberport News*, December, http://www.info.gov.hk/itbb/english/cyberport/index_n.htm.

Hood, C. (1991) 'A Public Management for All Seasons?' *Public Administration*, 69(1): 3–19.

Hood, C. (1996) 'Beyond Progressivism: a New "Global Paradigm" in Public Management?' *International Journal of Public Administration*, 19(2): 151–178.

Hood, C. and Dunleavey, P. (1994) 'From Old Public Administration to New Public Management', *Public Money and Management* 14(3): 9–17.

Kemp, D. (1998) 'APS Reforms – Minister's Statement' Ministerial Media and Communications, at http://www.psmpc.gov.au/publications98/apsreformminister.htm.

King, S. (1998) 'Privatisation in Australia: Understanding the Incentives in Public and Private Firms', *Australian Economic Review*, 31: 313.

Lynn, L. (1996) 'The New Public Management as an International Phenomenon: A Skeptical View', *International Public Management Journal*, 1(1).

McGuire, L. (2000) 'Service Charters – Global Convergence or National Divergence? – A Comparison of Initiatives in Australia, the United Kingdom and the United States'. Paper presented at 4th International Research Symposium on Public Management (IRSPM IV), Erasmus University, The Netherlands, April.

Maddock, R. (1994) 'Privatisation: the Financial Implications', *Economic Record*, 70: 465.

OECD (1997) *The OECD Report on Regulatory Reform*, Vols I and II, OECD, Paris.

Painter, M. (1998) *Collaborative Federalism – Economic Reform in Australia in the 1990s*, Cambridge University Press, Melbourne.

Smith, C. (1995) 'Clarifying the Exchange: A Review of Purchaser/Provider Arrangements', Resource Management Improvement Branch Discussion Paper, No. 2, Department of Finance, Canberra.

Steane, P. and Carroll, P. (2000) 'Australia, the OECD, and the Post-NPM World'. In Jones, L.R., Guthrie, J. and Steane, P. (eds) *New Public Management: Learning from Experiences* (2 vols) Ablex-Jai Press, Stamford, CT.

Stevens, B. and Wanna, J. (eds) (1993) *The Goss Government*, Macmillan, Melbourne.

Worthington, R. (1999) *A Case Study of Strategic Partnering in Australia*, OECD, Paris.

Chapter 13

The New Public Management

A perspective from Africa

Kempe Ronald Hope Sr

Introduction

Since the 1980s, the NPM has been entrenched in theory and practice across the world. Many governments and several international organizations have embraced the NPM as the framework or paradigm through which governments are modernized and the public sector re-engineered to 'strengthen the connections between government and the mechanisms, both in government and civil society, that are responsible for how well government works' (Armacost 2000: v).

Indeed, the NPM offers important lessons and analyses for public management throughout the world and African countries are no exception to the process of implementation of efforts aimed at achieving the outcomes embodied in the said NPM. This chapter explores the relationship between the basic features of the NPM, as applied to public sector reform in Africa, and critically examines the impact stemming therefrom. Let us begin by first delineating the basic features of the NPM concept.

The basic features of the NPM concept

Although adequately addressed in Part I and other parts of this book, a brief outline of the basic features of the NPM concept is necessary here to locate the framework against which the objectives of this chapter are to be accomplished.

The NPM represents the culmination of a revolution in public management that emerged in the 1980s. Rather than focusing on controlling bureaucracies and delivering services, public managers are now responding to the desires of ordinary citizens and politicians to be 'the entrepreneurs of a new, leaner, and increasingly privatized government' (Denhardt and Denhardt 2000: 549). As such, the NPM is clearly linked to the notion of trust in economic rationalism through the creation of public value for public money.

The NPM concept is centred on the proposition that a distinct activity – management – can be applied to the public sector, as it has been applied in the private sector, and that it includes a number of elements (Aucoin 1990; Bale and Dale 1998):

1 the adoption of private sector management practices in the public sector;
2 an emphasis on efficiency;
3 a movement away from input controls, rules and procedures toward output measurement and performance targets;
4 a preference for private ownership, contestable provision and contracting out of public services; and
5 the devolution of management control with improved reporting and monitoring mechanisms.

The basic foundation of the NPM is the use of the economic market as a model for political and administrative relationships. The institutional aspects of the NPM are heavily influenced by the assumptions of public choice theory, principal–agent theory and transaction cost economics (Kaboolian 1998). The NPM movement is driven to maximize productive and allocative efficiencies that are hampered by public agencies which are unresponsive to the demands of citizens and led by bureaucrats with the power and incentives to expand their administrative empires. In addition, the NPM makes a rigid formal separation between policy-making and service delivery (Self 1993; Kelly 1998).

According to the Public Management Committee of the OECD (1995) and as summarized by Mathiasen (1999), the NPM is aimed at fostering a performance-oriented culture in a less centralized public sector and is characterized by:

1 a closer focus on results in terms of efficiency, effectiveness and quality of service;
2 the replacement of highly centralized, hierarchical structures by decentralized management environments where decisions on resource allocation and service delivery are made closer to the point of delivery, and which provide scope for feedback from clients and other interest groups;
3 the flexibility to explore alternatives to direct public provision and regulation that might yield more cost-effective policy outcomes;
4 a greater focus on efficiency in the services provided directly by the public sector, involving the establishment of productivity targets and the creation of competitive environments within and among public sector organizations; and
5 the strengthening of strategic capacities at the centre to guide the evolution of the state and allow it to respond to external changes and diverse interests automatically, flexibly and at least cost.

The NPM is also therefore related to the notion of re-engineering the public sector or the reinventing of government. Re-engineering is a management philosophy that seeks to revamp the process through which public organizations operate in order to increase efficiency, effectiveness, and competitive ability. It calls for changes in the structure of public organizations, their culture, management systems, and other aspects in support of the new initiative. In addition, it encompasses client-oriented, mission-driven, quality-enhanced and participatory management, using resources in new ways to heighten efficiency and effectiveness (Barzelay 1992; Osborne and Gaebler 1992; Halachmi 1995).

The NPM can also be regarded as a normative reconceptualization of public sector management consisting of several inter-related components. It emerged in response to the economic and social realities which governments everywhere have had to face during the past two decades (Borins 1995). Those realities include:

1   too large and expensive public sectors;
2   the need to utilize information technology to increase efficiency;
3   the demand by the public for quality service;
4   the general collapse of centrally planned economic systems which underscored the poor performance of government services worldwide; and
5   the quest for personal growth and job satisfaction by public sector employees (Borins 1995; Commonwealth Secretariat 1995).

Other intellectual and practical justifications for the NPM have also evolved along the lines of the New Public Service (NPS) being a mutually reinforcing and normative model of managing and service delivery in the public sector, where values such as efficiency and productivity should not be lost but should be placed in the larger context of democracy, community and the public interest and, according to Denhardt and Denhardt (2000: 553–557), be based on the following tenets:

1   Serve, rather than steer: public servants should help citizens articulate and meet their shared interests, rather than attempt to control or steer society in new directions.
2   The public interest is the aim, not the by-product: public managers should contribute to building a collective, shared notion of the public interest which should result in the creation of shared interests and shared responsibility.
3   Think strategically, act democratically: policies and programmes meeting public needs can be most effectively and responsibly achieved through collective efforts and collaborative processes.
4   Serve citizens, not customers: public servants should not merely respond to the demands of 'customers' but focus on building relationships of trust and collaboration with and among citizens.
5   Accountability isn't simple: public servants should be attentive not only to the market but also to statutory and constitutional law, community values, political norms, professional standards and citizen interests.
6   Value people, not just productivity: public organizations and the networks in which they participate are more likely to succeed in the long run if they are operated through processes of collaboration and shared leadership based on respect for all people.
7   Value citizenship and public service above entrepreneurship: the public

interest is better advanced by public servants and citizens committed to making meaningful contributions to society rather than by entrepreneurial managers acting as if public money were their own.

All of the foregoing features of the NPM are being applied around the world, in a sweeping manner, as governments use the management reform process to reshape the role of the state and its relationship with citizens. That process, as Kettl (2000: 1–3) has summarized it, has embodied six core characteristics:

1   Productivity: how can governments produce more services with less tax money?
2   Marketization: how can governments use market-style incentives to root out the pathologies of government bureaucracy?
3   Service orientation: how can governments better connect with citizens to make programmes more responsive to the needs of the citizen?
4   Decentralization: how can governments make programmes more responsive and effective by shifting programmes to lower levels of government or shifting responsibility within public agencies to give frontline managers greater incentive and ability to respond to the needs of citizens?
5   Policy: how can governments improve its capacity to devise and track policy?
6   Accountability for results: how can governments improve their ability to deliver what they promise?

These characteristics duly suggest that the NPM movement puts particular emphasis on seeking to solve problems which have to do with governance. Kettl (2000) has convincingly demonstrated that the governance issue here is derived from the implicit assumption that the government of the past century will not effectively tackle the problems of the next and the success or failure of the NPM movement will, ultimately, depend on how deeply its reforms become part of a nation's governance systems such as the political institutions and civil society. Seeking and/or maintaining good governance through the reform initiatives inspired by the NPM is the ultimate goal of this global public management revolution.

The NPM and public sector reform in Africa

Since the early 1980s, significant efforts have been made in sub-Saharan Africa towards the reform and transformation of public sector management. Those efforts have been driven primarily by the fact that state bureaucracies in Africa under-perform, are invariably too large and corrupt and lack a sense of responsibility and accountability (Hope 1997, 2001; Hope and Chikulo 1999). All societies need a capable public management structure to keep order, collect revenue and carry out programmes. The sub-Saharan Africa region, for the most part, lacks these public management endowments (Goldsmith 1999).

The specific pressures driving the NPM reforms in sub-Saharan Africa are derived from the crisis of governance that has been plaguing most of the countries in the region. Those pressures have been thoroughly discussed elsewhere (Hope 1997, 2001; Bangura 1999; Amoako 2000; Hope and Chikulo 2000) and only a brief summary will be offered below.

Pressure for NPM reforms

Perhaps the most influential pressure has been the economic/fiscal crises that the African states have had to endure since the mid-1970s. Many of the countries have now started to grow economically again. However, for the majority, poverty and economic stagnation still loom large and there is still ongoing concern about balance of payments problems, the heavy burden of debt, the size of public expenditure relative to the declining sources of public revenue and the increasing cost of delivering public services. These concerns about economic and fiscal matters have led, in turn, to NPM reforms encompassing an assault on the active role played by the state in managing the economy and in the direct provision of services.

The second pressure for NPM reforms in Africa is derived from the political forces in play in many of the countries. There still exists a malfunctioning and unstable political order across too many parts of Africa and, consequently, there remains the need for the transformation of public management to create basic systems of governance, devise institutions that are more democratic, promote and build civil society and reshape relationships with citizens (Hope 1997, 2001; Kettl 2000). In other words, moving toward modes of public management that support the rule of law, and transparent and accountable government, as well as a predictable legal framework with rules known in advance and a reliable and independent judiciary.

The next pressure is the institutional one in the sense that complex institutional mechanisms exist that make it difficult to implement various policies in a timely and effective manner. Successive African governments have complained that standard bureaucratic procedures frequently handicap their ability to respond effectively to global and national challenges. Indeed, part of the problem here has been the changing role of the public sector in Africa and the rapid acceptance by governments of their new role in driving the re-engineering process. In this context, NPM reforms have been aimed at creating management structures and institutional mechanisms within government that enhance the capacity and capability for effective policy management and successful policy implementation.

The final pressure for NPM reforms in Africa comes from the influence of international experiences. Larbi (1999) has argued that the wind of change towards market reforms and political pluralism that swept across the Western nations in the 1980s and the collapse of the Soviet Union had the sobering effect on crisis states, such as those in Africa, that public management reforms should be undertaken. Indeed, much of the structural adjustment and other measures of economic liberalization and state restructuring that have been occurring in Africa since the 1980s are the direct result of such influences.

The nature and impact of NPM reforms

This section analyses the nature and impact of selected strategies of NPM reforms as applied to the public sector in Africa. Based on the content of the previous sections of this chapter, we can summarize a point of departure here, as Bangura (1999: 5) has done, as follows: 'NPM reforms seek to reconfigure the relations between states, markets, and societies by giving prominence to market forces, managerial efficiency, and accountable government.'

Decentralization

A good summary of the concept of decentralization, including its costs and benefits, applicable to Africa can be found in Hope (2000, 2001) and Hope and Chikulo (2000). Much of the decentralization that has occurred in the last decade has been motivated by the political rationale that good governments are those closer to the people. The spread of multi-party political systems in Africa is creating demand for more local voice in decision-making. Political changes have therefore given voice to local demands and the need to bring economic and political systems closer to local communities.

Within the context of the NPM, decentralization is seen as a government tool for providing high-quality services that citizens value; for increasing managerial autonomy, particularly by reducing central administrative controls; for demanding, measuring and rewarding both organizational and individual performance; for enabling managers to acquire human and technological resources to meet performance targets; for creating a receptiveness to competition and an open-mindedness about which public purposes should be performed by public servants as opposed to the private sector (Borins 1994); for empowering citizens through their enhanced participation in decision-making and development planning and management; for improving economic and managerial efficiency or effectiveness; and for enhancing better governance (Silverman 1992).

The primary modes of decentralization in Africa that are attributed to NPM reforms are deconcentration, delegation, devolution and privatization. Deconcentration is the passing down of selected administrative functions to lower levels or subnational units within government agencies or departments. It is the least extensive form of decentralization. However, it is the most common form of decentralization employed in the agriculture services, primary education, preventive health and population subsectors (Silverman 1992). In Botswana, for example, the central government has created and supervises district councils as well as a national Rural Development Council for the coordination and implementation of, among other things, rural development activities such as drought relief measures and agricultural development.

Another popular method of deconcentration in NPM reforms is that of the breaking up of monolithic bureaucracies into agencies – the 'agencification model' of public sector reform. Leaving aside, for the purposes of this chapter, the debate on whether agencification is a pure form of deconcentration or contains elements of delegation, the 'agencification model' has emerged as a choice mode of decentralization in many African countries. In South Africa and Zambia, for example, independent revenue authorities have been created with corporate outlooks on governance to increase the efficiency and accountability of tax collection beyond the bureaucracy of their finance ministries.

Delegation is the transfer of specific authority and decision-making powers to organizations that are outside the regular bureaucratic structure and that are only indirectly controlled by a government, such as parastatals, regional development corporations and semi-autonomous agencies. Delegation is seen as a way of offering public goods and services through a more business-like organizational structure that makes use of managerial accounting techniques normally associated with private enterprise. It has been used extensively in Africa. In Kenya, for example, public corporations have been used to organize, finance and manage large-scale agricultural projects such as tea production. In Lesotho, a parastatal was created to finance and manage a huge water development project in the country's highland area. In Botswana and Ghana, autonomous hospitals with independent management boards have been established to improve efficiency in service delivery; improve responsiveness to users' needs and preferences through market-based initiatives such as user fees; and reduce the financial and managerial burden of large hospitals on the health ministries (Maganu 1990; Larbi 1998, 1999).

Devolution is the granting of decision-making powers to lower authorities or managers and allowing them to take full responsibility without reference back to the authorizing government. This includes financial power as well as the authority to design and execute development projects and programmes. Devolution is the strongest form of decentralization. Its essence is discretionary authority, and it allows for the reduction in the levels of administration through which activities have to pass, and no reference back to a central administrative machinery is required. Ghana, for example, has put into place a public financial management programme which gives managers greater control of their budgets (Larbi 1999); and Ethiopia has devolved very extensive legislative, executive, judicial and fiscal powers to the regional authorities (Koehn 1995).

Decentralization, through devolution, provides a mechanism that enables the population to participate in the process of governance, as well as a framework for allowing the community's interests to be represented in government decision-making structures (Hentic and Bernier 1999). It is therefore a key element of NPM-type reforms. The more participatory the decision-making process, the more legitimacy it acquires in the eyes of all observers both domestic and international.

Privatization is taken here to mean the transfer of operational control and responsibilities for government functions and services to the private sector –

private voluntary organizations or private enterprises. From a wider perspective, privatization encompasses a wide range of policies to encourage private sector participation in public service provision and eliminate or modify the monopoly status of public enterprises (Rondinelli and Kasarda 1993). Privatization can be a complex process, frequently involving choices between the need to improve financial and economic efficiency; political opposition and varying degrees of unpopularity; and distinguishing between sectors and services that are essentially in the public interest and those which should be hived off to the private sector (Hentic and Bernier 1999).

Privatization in Africa has taken many forms. It has included the commercialization of government services which are contracted out to an outside agency; joint ventures between government agencies/ministries and private entities; the sale of some government services or functions, such as water supply or telecommunications, to the private sector; management contracts for the private sector to manage specific government functions or services such as postal services; the leasing of government assets that are used to provide public services; or the granting of concessions to private entities to operate and finance some public services delivery. During the past two decades, privatization has progressed globally and has come to be seen as highly desirable in Africa (Hope 2001). 'The process has been prompted in many cases by economic necessity and enabled by the political changes occurring across Africa' (White and Bhatia 1998: 1). However, privatization is more of a management reform issue than a political one.

The primary reason for pursuing privatization in Africa is that state-owned enterprises or parastatals tend to be loss-making and divert scarce public funds that could be put to better use in meeting other public policy goals such as better health care and education services. In addition, public enterprises generally suffer from extensive corruption and bureaucratic management structures that get in the way of efficient service delivery. The most recent available data indicates that in sub-Saharan Africa as a whole, the total sales value of privatization transactions increased from approximately US$1 billion during the period 1988–93 to US$2.7 billion by the end of 1996 (White and Bhatia 1998; Hope and Chikulo 2000). Overall, the total number of public enterprises in Africa is estimated to have fallen by about thirty-seven per cent between 1990 and 1995 (Sarbib 1997). This figure has certainly increased significantly since then.

Africa's contemporary leaders have moved forcefully in the restructuring of their economies. Many countries, including Angola, Botswana, Ghana, Kenya, Mozambique, South Africa, Tanzania, Uganda and Zambia, for example, have all launched extensive privatization programmes. Some francophone countries, including Cameroon, Côte d'Ivoire, Gabon and Senegal, have also completed major privatization programmes involving their electricity, telecommunications, water and banking sectors (Samuel 1999). A good summary of African infrastructure privatization can be found in African Development Bank (1999).

In the telecommunications sector, several countries, including Botswana,

Ghana, South Africa, Uganda and Côte d'Ivoire, for example, have either concluded the privatization of their telecommunications enterprises or are seeking strategic investors to do so. In particular, in the area of wireless service, there has been considerably private sector activity through the bidding for cellular operators' licenses. The electricity sector's privatization has primarily been by way of management contracts followed by leases and demonopolization and build–own–operate (BOO). Countries such as Gambia, Ghana, Guinea, Mail, Rwanda and Sierra Leone have opted for management contracts; lease arrangements are used in Côte d'Ivoire; and Morocco and Tunisia have independent power projects (African Development Bank 1999).

The water and transportation sectors have also seen their share of privatization activities. In the water sector, the selected modality has been focused primarily on management contracts or leases. Some African countries, such as Cameroon, Côte d'Ivoire, Gabon and Morocco, have privatized their water sectors on the basis of competition for concessions. In the transportation sector, some contracting out of road maintenance had been in practice in Kenya for several years before being adopted in Algeria and other African countries. The Tanzania Railway Corporation divested itself of non-core operations and is under private management and Cameroon has concluded a concession agreement with a French–South African joint venture to run its railway facilities. In the Sudan and Senegal, locomotive repairs and maintenance have been contracted out. Also, in such countries as Nigeria, Mozambique, Togo and Guinea, ports and/or airports have been privatized through lease arrangements or management contracts. Some airlines, including Kenya Airways, Royal Air Maroc, Air Tunisia and South African Airways, have also been privatized through various modalities (African Development Bank 1999; Samuel 1999).

Apart from infrastructure, privatization in Africa has also proceeded in other areas. Services in particular have been contracted out in significant numbers. In Botswana, for example, the parastatals have contracted out a number of services including those related to maintenance and security. Similarly, in Zimbabwe, non-clinical health services such as cleaning, laundry, catering, security, maintenance and billing are contracted out, while some clinical services are contracted out on a limited scale (Larbi 1999). Also, in Uganda, Tanzania and Ghana, for example, non-core state activities have been, or are being, transferred to the private sector and greater corporatization of public sector activities is taking place (Therkildsen 1999; Hope and Chikulo 2000).

Despite the fact that there are some obvious costs to decentralization (Hope 2000, 2001), it has yielded significant benefits in those countries where properly implemented. In Africa, decentralization has drastically improved the reliability and delivery of services to the public including improved quality assurance. Moreover, through decentralization, and privatization in particular, the burden on government resources has eased somewhat, leading to the use of those resources in other priority areas. For example, the privatization of Kenya Airways provided the Kenyan Treasury with US$76 million from the sale of seventy-seven per cent of its shares in 1996 and, as a result of enhanced efficiency and better performing management some 400 new jobs have been created (Samuel 1999).

Moreover, highly centralized forms of government generate administrative pathologies. Centralized states tend to be unresponsive to the needs of citizens. Restructuring the delivery of public services, by decentralizing functions and resources, thus becomes a central claim of the NPM based on the growing body of evidence indicating that the decentralization of government services can be far more efficient than their supply by bureaus. Undoubtedly, service delivery systems based on centralized bureaucracy have now been discredited, and African governments have, commendably, been shifting their focus from hierarchy and control to participation and empowerment.

Decentralization in Africa has resulted in better governance, it has facilitated the development of more effective and efficient public sector management, it has increased popular participation in government, it has allowed for better mobilization and use of resources and it has encouraged market-like responsiveness to the provision and consumption of public services (Hope 2001). Its use as an instrument of NPM reforms must be expanded and deepened in Africa. Indeed, there is a growing momentum across the African continent for reform initiatives that shift resources, responsibility for service delivery and accountability for results from central governments to more decentralized levels. In some cases, such as in Ethiopia and South Africa, this has even been entrenched in federal-style constitutions.

Reform of the public bureaucracy

During the 1980s, many African countries concluded that their public or civil servants were not providing public goods and services in the most cost-effective and efficient manner. Consequently, reform of the public bureaucracy became necessary to pursue and maintain the path of economic liberalization and good governance that had been embarked upon. In this new century, African governments are also beginning to realize that the globalization wave dictates that further and deeper reforms of the public bureaucracy are required in order to successfully ride the rising tide of borderless economic activities encompassed in that globalization wave.

NPM-type reforms have been, and are being, applied to African public bureaucracies because these bureaucracies are seen as unprofessional, often lacking capacity to solve the tough new problems of their governments; too bloated in size in relationship to their outputs; suffering from dysfunctional rigidity; lacking in, and not caring about, measurement of their performance; preoccupied with their own rules and practices rather than promoting, protecting and serving the public interest; and, generally, being too corrupt and intent on maintaining their own patrimonial and territorial interests.

Although some African governments had, from time to time embarked on public service reform, for the majority, the efforts became concentrated in comprehensive strategies that were included in the economic liberalization packages of structural adjustment that were facilitated by the World Bank and IMF (Interational Monetary Fund). The basic thrust of the reform process was, and continues to be, to build a professional, meritocratic and qualified public workforce to ensure effective and efficient delivery of public services and combat bureaucratic corruption. Without such reform, the performance of the public bureaucracy and, hence, of their respective governments, will continue to be deficient. A government's performance can only be as good as the people who do its work. African governments, or any government for that matter, will perform poorly if there is a failure to recruit, retain, reward appropriately and assure the integrity of highly skilled public officials (Kettl *et al.* 1996; World Bank 2000; Hope 2001).

The key elements of the process of reform of the public bureaucracy in Africa have been centred around pay and employment measures, productivity enhancement, capacity building, training, improving accountability and transparency and making management more effective. Pay and employment reform measures in Africa have been extensively discussed and documented in Lindauer and Nunberg (1994), and Robinson (1990), Lienert and Modi (1997) and Goldsmith (1999). Owing to the concern that two major contributors to bureaucratic corruption in Africa are the erosion and the compression of salary scales of public servants, pay and grading reform has been at the forefront of pay and employment measures in the attempts to reform the public service.

Pay and grading reform generally has five objectives:

1   an increase in overall real pay levels;
2   the decompression of pay scales to improve the competitiveness of civil service pay at higher levels;
3   a new grading system based on job evaluations;
4   the introduction of performance-based pay; and
5   the improvement of pay policy-making and administration (de Merode and Thomas 1994).

The experience of pay and grading reform suggests some success in outcomes. In Ghana, Mozambique and Guinea, for example, the net pay compression ratio of the civil service improved; the ratio of the highest-paid echelon to the lowest-paid widened; and real pay improved spectacularly.

In addition, several countries, including the Gambia, Ghana, Guinea and Uganda, have made considerable progress in simplifying their grading structures. That, in turn, has acted as a magnet to attract and motivate some top professionals including those with scarce skills such as physicians and accountants. Many countries have also been able to downsize their civil services and thereby reduce the number of surplus employees on the government payroll. A number of methods have been used in this regard including enforcing mandatory retirement ages, abolishing job guarantees for high school and university graduates, ensuring attrition through hiring freezes, introducing voluntary departure schemes, making outright dismissals and eliminating 'ghost' (fictitious) employees from the payroll (Hope 2001).

Also, some countries, such as South Africa and Ghana, have moved toward competitive and open recruitment procedures with selection based on merit as an integral part of their employment reform measures. This helps to ensure that vacancies are filled on the basis of skills and competence rather than on other factors such as ethnicity and kinship. Similar merit-based systems were put in place with respect to promotions. Merit-based promotions tend to attract more individuals into the public bureaucracy who have strong preferences for making an impact on their government's task of providing public goods. Together, merit-based recruitment and promotion serve as mutually reinforcing mechanisms to build commitment towards the goal of an efficient public service. Other countries, such as Botswana, have also decentralized some human resource management functions to ministries. Permanent secretaries of these ministries are, among other things, empowered to appoint, promote and discipline their staff members.

Productivity enhancement strategies in Africa are primarily aimed at bringing about a greater customer orientation in goods and services delivery and an improvement in the quality of those goods and services delivered while at the same time creating a much more positive attitude toward work by the public servants. In Botswana, for example, the government introduced the productivity and quality improvement programme in 1993 by creating work improvement teams (WITs) within various institutions and departments of ministries. WITs are based on the Japanese framework of Quality Control Circles. Similar types of quality circles can be found in Mauritius (Hope 2001).

Other popular methods used for productivity enhancement in Africa are the introduction of performance management systems in government agencies and ministries and the use of performance contracts for individual employees and departments. Performance management systems are regarded as means of getting results from individuals, teams and the organization at large within a given framework of planned goals, objectives and standards. It allows for the setting of targets and the development of indicators against which performance can be later measured. Performance management systems have been put in place in Uganda, South Africa and Ghana and are currently being tried out in Botswana.

Performance contracts or agreements specify standards of performance or quantifiable targets which a government requires public officials or the management of public agencies or ministries to meet over a stated period of time. At the end of the stated period, performance can then be measured against these standards or targets. Performance contracts have been used in a number of African countries, including Ghana and Senegal, particularly in their public enterprises. Other countries, such as Botswana, also employ performance contracts to measure and assess the performance of permanent secretaries. By 2004, the majority of civil servants in Botswana will be subjected to performance contracts as the performance management system becomes fully implemented.

Capacity building has now taken centre stage in what is regarded as the second phase of NPM-style reforms currently being implemented in Africa.

Capacity building has come to the fore because African governments and donors have come to recognize the centrality of capacity in the development process in the region. Capacity is the combination of human resources and institutions that permits countries to achieve their development goals. Lacking capacity, a government cannot adequately perform the tasks that make an economy function. The need for capacity exists in virtually all areas of the public sector in Africa. Consequently, capacity building is important to generate the capability for those countries to develop indigenous and self-reliant development policies and strengthen the interface between government, civil society and the private sector. Apart from the region-wide Partnerships for Capacity Building (PACT) being implemented by the African Capacity Building Foundation (ACDF) based in Zimbabwe, other countries, such as Tanzania and Guinea, have their own ongoing efforts for public sector capacity building financed through Adaptable Programme Loans (APLs) from the World Bank.

Training is an integral part of efforts to build capacity in the African public sector. Many African countries now have institutes of public administration or administrative staff colleges to train their civil servants. Others, such as Botswana, have set up national productivity centres for training in productivity and quality improvement. Training provides an essential means through which African states can develop a career civil service in order to modernize and develop. As argued by Agere (1999), the strengthening of the civil service is an integral part of policy reform which can best be accomplished through the use of public sector training institutes which have a mandate to train civil servants in the management of the new responsibilities linked to good governance and economic liberalization.

An emphasis on improving accountability and transparency can be found in most public sector reform efforts in Africa. Anti-corruption measures and the development of codes of conduct for public officials are two strategies most prevalent in that regard and, in some countries, such as Uganda, they are encompassed in national integrity systems (Hope and Chikulo 1999; Hope 2001). In both cases, the intent is to bring about a stronger allegiance to the nation-state and, hence, a commitment to the national interest rather than to personal and sectional interests; and produce public servants who are vigilant, upright, honest and just. In other words, they are meant to instil an atmosphere of public accountability and ethical behaviour in public servants so that they respect not only their obligations to be honest, obey the laws and behave within the confines of bureaucratic rules and regulations, but also demonstrate the highest standards of personal integrity, honesty, fairness, justice and openness.

Making management more effective entails providing public managers with the necessary tools to deliver public services in a more efficient and cost-effective manner. This includes management structures and institutional mechanisms that improve policy development, coordination and implementation for better public sector outcomes. In addition to the need to have some control over human and financial resources, public managers in Africa are also being provided with efficiency tools such as better management information systems. Indeed, major improvements have been achieved through the use of information technology for efficient revenue collection, financial management and accounting, and interdepartmental communication systems (Kaul 1996). In countries such as South Africa, Ghana, Nigeria and Mauritius, operational and management control systems are in place (Odedra 1993). These are applications that are designed to improve operations, management control and decision-making capabilities.

Reforming the public bureaucracy in Africa through NPM-style strategies is, ultimately, intended to make public service accountable, transparent and responsive to the public in the delivery of public goods and services. The lessons of experience of public bureaucracy reform in developing countries, including Africa, suggests some mixed results with the application of strategies from the NPM menu (Manning 2000). However, this ought not to have been surprising to anyone familiar with the African scene, where there are varying levels of capacity and institutional frameworks for implementing development policy. Indeed, the application of NPM-style reforms is intended to rectify some of these deficiencies and improve public sector performance. Undoubtedly, many countries in Africa have benefited tremendously from public bureaucracy reform based on NPM-style activities (Hope 2001). In particular, public sector wage bills have declined, there is greater penetration of information technology, and the concentration of bureaucratic power at the expense of accountability and transparency has diminished considerably in most countries. Nonetheless, like the developed countries, reforming the public sector in Africa is a work in progress and better assessment indicators will be available in the next few years as the second phase of reform measures take hold.

State transformation

During the past few decades, state transformation has been rapidly occurring in both the developed and developing countries, including in Africa. That transformation revolves around the nature and division of responsibility within and beyond government, and the extent to which the delivery of public goods and services is being met (Thynne 2000). The fundamental change is related to the manner in which countries pursue growth and/or development, moving to a mode of operation where the state conducts itself more like the private sector through reforms such as those suggested by the NPM.

Since there is overwhelming evidence of a positive correlation between economic liberalization and development, the challenge for African countries has been one of unshackling their economic markets to further the process of liberalization and create the environment required for development to be sustained. This challenge takes on even greater importance in the context of globalization which refers to a world in which national economies, producers and investors increasingly behave as if the world economy is borderless and consists of a single market and production area with regional or national subsectors, rather than a set of national economies linked by trade, investment and financial flows (Hope 2001).

To that end, many African countries have been putting in place modes of administration that avoid the errors of their previous statist frameworks. Under the best of circumstances, state intervention in Africa has been found to retard economic growth, restrict economic development and often result in famine, starvation, malnutrition and general deterioration in the quality of life (Hope 2001). In other words, the state was an obstacle to development. State transformation in Africa now entails a re-dimensioning with the aim of creating what can be called 'smart government' or 'modernized government'. That is, the type of government that focuses on its strategic roles with an organizational design and managerial set up that permit it to perform its roles in an optimally effective and efficient manner.

Conclusion

The application of NPM-type reforms in Africa, despite their mixed results, has, from the point of view of this author, been mostly successful. There still exists such things as extensive bureaucratic corruption. However, Hope (2001) cites data that indicate that African economies have been recording positive rates of economic growth during the past few years, foreign investment is returning and the size and costs of running government are declining. These are all positive indicators and they did not emerge through divine intervention. They are, undoubtedly, the result of policy reforms, primarily NPM-type reforms, which have been implemented during the past two decades.

Over the next few years, and assuming no policy reversals, there will be even further gains recorded as a result of the application of the second phase of NPM-type reforms. Consequently, the conclusion here is that there is an improving performance of the state in Africa which, in no small measure, is attributable to NPM-type reforms.

References

African Development Bank (1999) *African Development Report 1999*. New York: Oxford University Press.

Agere, S. (1999) *Strengthening MDIs: The Role of Management Development Institutions in Public Service Reform*. London: Commonwealth Secretariat.

Amoako, K.Y. (2000) *Perspectives on Africa's Development*. New York: United Nations.

Armacost, M.H. (2000) 'Foreword'. In Kettl, D.F. (ed.) *The Global Public Management Revolution: A Report on the Transformation of Governance*. Washington, DC: Brookings Institution Press.

Aucoin, P. (1990) 'Administrative Reform in Public Management: Paradigms, Principles, Paradoxes, and Pendulums', *Governance* 3(2): 115–137.

Bale, M. and Dale, T. (1998) 'Public Sector Reform in New Zealand and its Relevance to Developing Countries', *The World Bank Research Observer* 13(1): 103–121.

Bangura, Y. (1999) 'New Directions in State Reform: Implications for Civil Society in Africa', Discussion Paper 113. Geneva: United Nations Research Institute for Social Development.

Barzelay, M. (1992) *Breaking Through Bureaucracy: A New Vision for Managing in Government*. Berkeley, CA: University of California Press.

Borins, S. (1994) 'Government in Transition: A New Paradigm in Public Administration', Report on the Inaugural Conference of CAPAM. Toronto: Commonwealth Association for Public Administration and Management.

Borins, S. (1995) 'The New Public Management is Here to Stay', *Canadian Public Administration* 38(1): 122–132.

Commonwealth Secretariat (1995) *From Problem to Solution: Commonwealth Strategies for Reform*. London: Commonwealth Secretariat.

de Merode, L. and Thomas, C.S. (1994) 'Implementing Civil Service Pay and Employment Reform in Africa: The Experiences of Ghana, the Gambia, and Guinea'. In Lindauer, D.L. and Nunberg, B. (eds) *Rehabilitating Government: Pay and Employment Reform in Africa*. Washington, DC: World Bank.

Denhardt, R.B. and Denhardt, J.V. (2000) 'The New Public Service: Serving Rather than Steering', *Public Administration Review* 60(6): 549–559.

Goldsmith, A.A. (1999) 'Africa's Overgrown State Reconsidered: Bureaucracy and Economic Growth', *World Politics* 51(4): 520–546.

Halachmi, A. (1995) 'Re-engineering and Public Management: Some Issues and Considerations', *International Review of Administrative Sciences* 61(3): 329–341.

Hentic, I. and Bernier, G. (1999) 'Rationalization, Decentralization and Participation in the Public Sector Management of Developing Countries', *International Review of Administrative Sciences* 65(2): 197–209.

Hope, K.R. Snr (1997) *African Political Economy: Contemporary Issues in Development*. Armonk, NY: M.E. Sharpe.

Hope, K.R. Snr (2000) 'Decentralization and Local Governance Theory and the Practice in Botswana', *Development Southern Africa* 17(4): 519–534.

Hope, K.R. Snr (2001) *Development Policy and Management in Africa*. Gaborone: Center of Specialization in Public Administration and Management, University of Botswana.

Hope, K.R. Snr and Chikulo, B.C. (eds) (1999) *Corruption and Development in Africa: Lessons from Country Case-Studies*. London: Macmillan.

Hope, K.R. Snr and Chikulo, B.C. (2000) 'Decentralization, the New Public Management, and the Changing Role of the Public Sector in Africa', *Public Management: An International Journal of Research and Theory* 2(1): 25–42.

Kaboolian, L. (1998) 'The New Public Management: Challenging the Boundaries of the Management vs. Administration Debate', *Public Administration Review* 58(3): 189–193.

Kaul, M. (1996) 'Civil Service Reforms: Learning From Commonwealth Experiences', *Public Administration and Development* 16(2): 131–150.

Kelly, R.M. (1998) 'An Inclusive Democratic Polity, Representative Bureaucracies, and the New Public Management', *Public Administration Review* 58(3): 201–208.

Kettl, D.F. (2000) *The Global Public Management Revolution: A Report on the Transformation of Governance*. Washington, DC: Brookings Institution Press.

Kettl, D.F., Ingraham, P.W., Sanders, R.P., and Horner, C. (1996) *Civil Service Reform: Building a Government That Works*. Washington, DC: Brookings Institution Press.

Koehn, P.H. (1995) 'Decentralization for Sustainable Development'. In Rasheed, S. and Luke, D.F. (eds) *Development Management in Africa: Toward Dynamism, Empowerment, and Entrepreneurship*. Boulder, CO: Westview Press.

Larbi, G.A. (1998) 'Management Decentralization in Practice: A Comparison of Public Health and Water Services in Ghana'. In Minogue, M., Polidano, C. and Hulme, D. (eds) *Beyond the New Public Management: Changing Ideas and Practices in Governance*. Cheltenham, UK: Edward Elgar.

Larbi, G.A. (1999) 'The New Public Management Approach and Crisis States', Discussion Paper 112. Geneva: United Nations Research Institute for Social Development.

Lienert, I. and Modi, J. (1997) 'A Decade of Civil Service Reform in Sub-Saharan Africa', IMF Working Paper WP/97/179. Washington, DC: International Monetary Fund.

Lindauer, D.L. and Nunberg, B. (eds) (1994) *Rehabilitating Government: Pay and Employment Reform in Africa*. Washington, DC: World Bank.

Maganu, E.T. (1990) 'Decentralization of Health Services in Botswana'. In Mills, A. Vaughan, P. Smith, D.L. and Tabibzadeh, I. (eds) *Health System Decentralization: Concepts, Issues and Country Experience*. Geneva: World Health Organization.

Manning, N. (2000) 'The New Public Management and its Legacy' at the World Bank website www1.worldbank.org/publicsector/civilservice.

Mathiasen, D.G. (1999) 'The New Public Management and Its Critics', *International Public Management Journal* 2(1): 90–111.

Odedra, M. (1993) 'IT Applications in the Commonwealth Developing Countries'. In Harindranath, G. and Liebenau, J. (eds) *Information Technology Policies and Applications in the Commonwealth Developing Countries*. London: Commonwealth Secretariat.

Organization for Economic Cooperation and Development (1995) *Governance in Transition: Public Management Reforms in OECD Countries*. Paris: OECD.

Osborne, D. and Gaebler, T. (1992) *Reinventing Government*. Reading, MA: Addison-Wesley.

Robinson, D. (1990) *Civil Service Pay in Africa*. Geneva: International Labour Organization.

Rondinelli, D.A. and Kasarda, J.D. (1993) 'Privatization of Urban Services and Infrastructure in Developing Countries'. In Kasarda, J.D. and Parnell, A.M. (eds) *Third World Cities: Problems, Policies, and Prospects*. London: Sage.

Samuel, S.B. (1999) 'A New Look at African Privatization' at the International Finance Corporation website www.ifc.org.

Sarbib, J.-L. (1997) 'Privatization in Africa: Present and Future Trends', Presentation to the African Development Bank Group 1997 Annual Meeting Symposium on Private Sector Development in Africa, Abidjan, Côte d'Ivoire.

Self, P. (1993) *Government by the Market? The Politics of Public Choice*. London: Macmillan.

Silverman, J.M. (1992) 'Public Sector Decentralization: Economic Policy and Sector Investment Programs', Technical Paper No. 188. Washington, DC: World Bank.

Therkildsen, O. (1999) 'Efficiency and Accountability: Public Sector Reform in East and Southern Africa', mimeo. Geneva: United Nations Research Institute for Social Development.

Thynne, I. (2000) 'The State and Governance: Issues and Challenges in Perspective', *International Review of Administrative Sciences* 66(2): 227–240.

White, O.C. and Bhatia, A. (1998) *Privatization in Africa*. Washington, DC: World Bank.

World Bank (2000) *Can Africa Claim the 21st Century*. Washington, DC: World Bank.

Chapter 14

New Public Management in developing countries

Willy McCourt

Introduction

In this chapter I will discuss the application of NPM in developing countries. After discussing problems of definition and setting out my working definition of NPM, I will discuss the difficulty that many of us have in defining NPM before moving on to discuss the developing country experience. In discussing that experience I will refer to some other features of public management in developing countries, especially the continuation of 'traditional' public administration and the application of what I shall call the 'Washington model' of civil service reform. After making some tentative comments on the political context in which NPM is applied, I conclude with a discussion of the prospects of applying NPM on a wider scale.

I draw in this chapter on several chapters in *The Internationalization of Public Management: Reinventing the Third World State* (McCourt and Minogue 2001). Its chapters are written by British-based scholars, several of them colleagues of mine at the Institute for Development Policy and Management (IDPM) in Manchester.

Working definition of NPM

In the face of some sceptical commentators, there is broad agreement among the contributors to this book that something called NPM does actually exist. The fact, however, that most of us have felt the need to spend time establishing a definition suggests that we need an agreed definition of NPM: we will talk past each other if we all talk about different things. A definition of NPM, I think, should be:

- Prescriptive, taking account of exhortatory, 'guru' models of public management.
- Descriptive, taking account of what has actually happened.
- Theoretical, specifying links with social sciences theory, notably public choice and agency theory in economics.
- Political, recognizing that any model of public management necessarily has a political dimension.

Pending such an agreed definition, my working definition comes from the OECD's widely quoted 1995 review of public management developments (OECD 1995). It lacks a theoretical basis and a political dimension, but it comes from an authoritative source, is based on an empirical survey and has an operational form.

The OECD model has the following elements:

1   devolving authority, providing flexibility;
2   ensuring performance, control and accountability;
3   developing competition and choice;
4   providing responsive service;
5   improving the management of human resources;
6   optimizing information technology;
7   improving the quality of regulation;
8   strengthening steering functions at the centre.

In this chapter I deal with the first, third and fourth of these, giving pride of place to the first, which is fundamental to NPM, if not synonymous with it. Human resource management, information technology and regulation (5, 6 and 7 on the list) are the subjects of separate chapters in McCourt and Minogue (2001).

NPM in developing countries

The debate about the application of NPM in developing countries is still in its early stages. NPM's advocates (Bale and Dale 1998) and detractors (Nunberg 1995; Schick 1998; Matheson 2000) alike argue mainly in a priori terms. Although I have already noted the need for an agreed definition, what is understood by NPM in the development literature can be idiosyncratic (Batley 1999). In this section I will review the empirical evidence in the light of my working definition of NPM.

A health warning

If evaluation material on industrialized country experience is sparse, material on developing countries is fragmentary and there are few analytical studies. This is not because developing country governments are reluctant to expose themselves to scrutiny. The ubiquitous donor presence has resigned senior officials, or even ministers, to making themselves available even to the itinerant researcher. In this respect they differ from their sometimes more defensive industrialized country counterparts (Broadbent and Laughlin 1997). But governments lack money and donors lack interest; until very recently, donors have been busy with issues of governance and of financial and human resource management. Nor is there much independent academic research going on. There are few of us publishing on developing country public management, and our interests are somewhat distorted by the fact that much of our research and consultancy income derives from donors. Calling for research is the great academic cop-out, but call for it I do.

I should also point out that the bulk of my examples are from former British colonies in sub-Saharan Africa and South and Southeast Asia, but there are some examples from other regions.

Devolving authority (while still pulling the strings)

Devolving authority from the centre to line ministries or semi-autonomous agencies has pride of place in the OECD's list of NPM activities, and several of the chapters in this collection refer to it. Yet there is nothing new about devolving authority as such from the standpoint of the development literature, where the debate about decentralization considerably pre-dates NPM (see, notably, Rondinelli 1981; Smith 1985; Elcock and Minogue 2001, for a useful summary of the literature). One useful outcome of that debate is the distinction between two forms of devolving authority:

- deconcentration, the top-down delegation of central administrative functions, retaining accountability to the centre;
- devolution, the transfer from centre to locality of real decision-making powers.

In these terms, devolving authority NPM-style is clearly a version of deconcentration, albeit given a distinctive twist through a characteristic stress on maximizing performance, using management devices such as performance contracts between the centre and the agency, rather than on ensuring lawfulness using legal instruments. This is of course the 'agencification' model represented by the UK's 'Next Steps' initiative. We can see a number of countries experimenting with UK-style executive agencies. They include Ghana, Jamaica, Singapore, Tanzania and Uganda (Polidano 2001). The experiments are recent, and their scale is modest. By the middle 2000, for instance, Uganda, the African apple of the aid donor's eye under its dynamic President Museveni, had merely put a toe in the water. Although the Ministry of the Public Service had identified 135 potential agency candidates, only two of them were up and running. Tanzania had gone a little further by the same point, with four agencies in place, but this was some way behind the government's initial target of having twenty-four operating by the end of 1998. It is really too early to evaluate these experiments (Clarke and Wood 2001). Similar experiments in deconcentration have been carried out by some local governments in Mexico, including Mexico City (Klingner 2000).

There are other slightly less recent instances of deconcentration. One example is the ambitious attempt by several African countries, including Ghana, to create a freestanding health service. This takes the UK's National Health Service, established in the late 1940s, as its model (Polidano 2001). An interesting second example is the independent Revenue Authority model, implemented by sub-Saharan countries like Mozambique, South Africa, Tanzania, Uganda and Zambia (and also as far away as Pakistan). These are bodies that owe their origins to the twin imperatives to increase tax and customs revenue and to reduce corruption in revenue collection. Here we do have some performance information: revenue increased dramatically in Kenya and Zambia, but remained indifferent in Uganda, whose Revenue Authority was plagued by corruption, mismanagement and poor relations with the finance ministry (Clarke and Wood 2001). As Clarke and Wood (2001) note, both Tanzania and Uganda have used legislation as the main device for ensuring the performance of their Revenue Authorities. Their constitutions tend to be similar to those of the earlier generation of parastatal bodies like the Tanzania Harbours Authority, set up by Act of Parliament in 1977.

In reality, administration in many places remains highly centralized, even if only in theory. A trivial but telling example is that government departments are often unable to discipline staff even when they have *prima facie* evidence of a criminal offence, because all formal disciplinary matters are handled by a central department into which staff files are apt to sink without trace. This is the case in Sri Lanka (McCourt forthcoming a), Swaziland (McCourt 2000) and Tanzania (McCourt and Sola 1999), to give just three examples.

Theoretical centralization in the old public administration model is in some ways a façade which officials find 'ways round'. But so, often, is devolving authority in the NPM model, with the centre still pulling the strings behind the façade – jerking them more violently, maybe, through increased demands for information induced by the centre's anxiety over its loss of power (Nunberg 1995).

Centralization can, certainly, be counter-productive to the point of absurdity. It is important to remember, in the age of the Internet, that these are countries where even simple communication between central and outlying government offices can be tricky. Only two years ago, in the author's own experience, Tanzania's Institute of Development Management had no telephone connection with the outside world, because thieves had cut down the telephone lines to steal the copper wire. (Faxes went through the office 'in town' of a 'moonlighting' lecturer who had set up a private consultancy business.)

But centralization can have a positive aspect. In 1995 the UK government's Department for International Development (DFID) responded to a request to support the development of Nepal's Public Service Commission (PSC), the body responsible for civil service recruitment. NPM doctrine suggests that 'agencification' should improve the performance of such a body, and also its responsiveness to its internal clients. In the UK itself, the corresponding body has been successively 'agencified', privatized and then sold on within the private sector to a larger company. But the government declined to take this route, being forced to yield to the weight of opinion among senior government officials who were still smarting from the effects of an earlier World Bank-sponsored public enterprise reform programme. This programme, far from unleashing entrepreneurial zeal by removing the dead hand of government, had merely swapped control by unresponsive but fairly impartial central bureaucrats for control by politicians who were neither responsive nor impartial. Moreover, such professional recruitment capacity as existed in government was concentrated in the PSC owing to economies of scale. Nepal's situation resembled that of the UK at the time of the Northcote–Trevelyan reforms or the USA at the time of the Pendleton Act, not the UK or the USA in the 1990s. Centralization along traditional public administration lines was decidedly the lesser of two evils (McCourt forthcoming b).

This reluctance to seize the proffered NPM devolution chalice is not unique to Nepal. Similar concerns have been voiced in Ghana (Larbi 1998); in Tanzania (McCourt and Sola 1999); and in Zimbabwe, where they actually led to the abandonment in 1996 of the new performance management system (Makumbe 1997). In those countries, as in Nepal, officials had greater confidence in the integrity of the central agency, despite its lack of responsiveness, than in the local agencies. In 1996 the central government official in charge of Tanzania's local government reform programme, speaking to an audience of local government officers, confided that his government's commitment to decentralization, the main ostensible plank of its World Bank-funded local government reform programme, was unlikely to materialize. The murmurs of relief that greeted this confidence still echo in the present author's ears.

Developing competition and choice (while constrained by capacity)

Private provision of public services is what enables government's role to change from 'steering to rowing', in the celebrated phrase (Osborne and Gaebler 1992). Developing country governments have participated in this role change. Alongside the wholesale privatization of state-owned enterprises (Cook and Kirkpatrick 1995), not always seen as part of NPM, contracting out of some common services such as security has occurred in Ghana (Larbi 1998), Trinidad and Tobago (Commonwealth Secretariat 1996) and Zimbabwe. In the health sector, a survey of experience in India, Mexico, Papua New Guinea, South Africa, Thailand and Zimbabwe found evidence of a variety of services being contracted out, including professional services like in- and out-patient hospital care in South Africa and Zimbabwe (Bennett and Mills 1998).

As with devolving authority, developing competition is constrained by incapacity. Bennett and Mills (1998) found considerable problems in management of contracts, with the public 'client' failing to perform even very basic functions like paying contractors on time and keeping records of contracts negotiated. Performance contracts in Bolivia appear to have contributed to improved performance, but at the expense of some abuses which because of political factors were not penalized (Mallon 1994). A study of experience in India, Pakistan and Senegal again found problems, caused in these cases by unclear performance specifications and failure to enforce contract terms. In one example, a Treasury department insisted on moving the goalposts in mid-contract (Islam 1993). It is not surprising that Bennett and Mills conclude that where government's capacity is weak, direct service provision may be a lower-risk delivery strategy.

Moreover, the public client's inability to manage contracts can be matched by the private sector's inability to operate them. Many developing countries continue to have 'dual economies'. They have sophisticated but small modern formal sectors, with multinational firms often to the fore, alongside dynamic but unsophisticated informal sectors. India, where software mogul Azim Hasham Premji is reported to be the world's second-richest person, with personal wealth of US$50 million, is an extreme example (*Toronto Star* 2000). Despite some donor-led *dirigisme* aimed at 'market strengthening', neither sector may be well placed to do the 'rowing' on behalf of government.

Finally, the vaunted public–private partnerships can work out very differently from NPM theory. Carroll and Steane (Chapter 12, this volume) discuss the potential for Chinese family networks to skew them to their advantage in Hong Kong. They also discuss the role of non-governmental organizations (NGOs), notably the Salvation Army, in providing services in Australia. NGOs and other civic organizations have also played an important role in developing countries. Angola, where NGOs have filled the vacuum left by the virtual collapse of state service provision (Christoplos 1998), is a dramatic example.

But it is important to note that NGOs are not public–private partnerships in the way that Carroll and Steane or NPM orthodoxy envisage them. Almost always, NGOs are acting as the agent of international donor agencies, who in the 1990s increasingly used NGOs to bypass governments of whose capacity and integrity they had come to despair (Hulme 2001). The argument for NGOs as an alternative to, as opposed to a partner with, government was still vigorous in the new century (Krueger and Srinivasan 2000). Moreover, even where there is a relationship between the NGO and the state, it can be a parasitical one: in Tanzania, NGOs have battened on local councils' vehicles and other resources to carry out their own rural programmes.

Providing responsive service (but responsive to whom?)

Steps to improve the quality of public services through management mechanisms such as total quality management (TQM) have been taken in a number of countries, including Brazil, Jordan and Malaysia (Sarji 1995; da Silva 1999). Quality circles have been reported in Botswana, Malaysia, Mauritius, the Philippines and Sri Lanka (Commonwealth Secretariat 1996; Eldridge and McCourt 1998; McCourt and Ramgutty-Wong 2000). Attempts to increase the participation of citizens have been very widespread, with initiatives including the setting up of Public Complaints Bureaux in Malaysia and Singapore, and the carrying out of service delivery surveys in India, Jordan, Mexico, Nicaragua and Uganda (respectively Paul and Sekhar 1997; Kattermann 1999; Klingner 2000; Meyers and Lacey 1996; Langseth 1995). Citizen's – or client's – charters, following the UK model, have been adopted in Jamaica, Malaysia, Malta and South Africa (Commonwealth Secretariat 1996; *Sunday Times* 1999). In many cases NGOs and civil society organizations have been instrumental in advocating greater public participation in service delivery (Hulme 2001).

What has the experience been? We lack an independent analysis of the recent foray into service delivery surveys, many of them carried out under World Bank auspices on the initiative of Samuel Paul, an enthusiastic World Bank official. However, there is suggestive evidence from two countries that surveys have not been owned by government and may not translate ultimately into service improvements (Kattermann 1999; see also Clarke and Wood 2001). This is not wholly surprising, given that the methodology was originally developed in a policy test tube in Washington (Langseth 1995). In Mexico, reforms that emphasized customer service were distorted by President Zedillo's insistence that the centralized, hierarchical one-party system that was the context for reform should not be disturbed (Klingner 2000). Common (1999) has pointed out that there is a discrepancy between the appearance and the reality of service reform in Malaysia. In a particularistic setting, TQM and quality circles have been partly an attempt by government, over the heads of its 'customers', to cement the unstable merit principle in place, whereas initiatives in general have been dyed as deeply with Muslim as with NPM rhetoric.

An interesting final example is the service delivery White Paper produced by the new ANC-led South Africa's first post-apartheid government (Government of South Africa 1997). Its first draft drew on British experience, and gave pride of place to Citizen's Charter-style mechanisms. 'Stakeholders' (a very South African term) in government, NGOs and trade unions heavily criticized it for its managerialist assumption that a structure for service delivery already existed which merely needed to be streamlined. In reality, the need was to create structures from scratch in non-White areas, which the previous government had ignored, and to restore the credibility of structures which citizens had boycotted during the anti-apartheid struggle.

In short, the problems that have afflicted these attempts at NPM-style service delivery are, arguably, in large measure the problems of the top-down, 'managerialist' approach that is inherent in NPM (Pollitt 1993; McCourt 2001).

Comparing the developing country and OECD experience

It is interesting to note that some of the constraints on NPM implementation are also found in industrialized countries. Where devolving authority is concerned, decentralist policies in the UK have translated in practice into an eclectic mix of decentralization and centralization (Talbot 1997). Doig (1997) has argued that transferring responsibility from a single central agency to a plethora of individual departments and agencies increases the risk of corruption. Where providing responsive service is concerned, the problem of the top-down approach is also found in the UK, where only one in three out of a 1,000 people polled had seen a copy of the Citizens' Charter, only one in ten had read it and a grand total of sixteen people were satisfied with it (O'Conghaile 1996). And it is a pity that the industrialized country experience with management innovations like TQM and quality circles is not better known. Quality circles, for example, have failed to take root in either the public or the private sector (Trosa 1995; Hill 1991 respectively).

NPM in developing countries: a summary

What can we conclude about the application of the NPM model? First, we can conclude there are significant instances of NPM implementation, despite the misgivings of those who have argued a priori that it is inappropriate. Moreover, what I have reported here almost certainly understates the extent of activity by developing country governments, given the general scarcity of documentation in the public domain. On the other hand, and even on a charitable reading, it is clear that the extent of implementation is modest and still in its infancy in many places. All of the contributors to McCourt and Minogue's (2001) agree on this, as do the findings of a large research project conducted by the University of Birmingham (Batley 1999). Thus I refute the claim that NPM is a 'global paradigm'.

Nor have even these modest experiments been straightforward. Some of the difficulties, notably those caused by a 'top-down' approach, are arguably inherent in NPM. Others are contingent, caused by problems such as the corruption and lack of capacity which pervade so many public activities in developing countries. Moreover, even where governments have tried to implement NPM, I believe that what I have reported in this chapter represents a process of refraction. This has been not just at the level of content (to invoke the taxonomy used by Carroll and Steane in Chapter 12 in this volume), but even at the level of principles, as we saw in Malaysia. What appears to happen is that a given NPM practice gets refracted through the prism of a particular country's laws, culture, political imperatives and so on. In the words of Shakespeare (1951: 7), it

> doth suffer a sea-change,
> Into something rich and strange.

This is inconvenient for researchers: homogeneity is easier to deal with. But for those who have a preference for a diverse public management in the face of homogenizing globalization, even if it is only an aesthetic one, such high-flown language may be appropriate.

What else is happening?

Why has the scale of NPM implementation been so modest? Of course we should not expect the transfer of NPM to be immediate: there is always a dissemination effect, as the slow but fairly steady spread of privatization in developing countries shows (Cook and Kirkpatrick 1995). At the time of writing, for instance, India's union government was still squaring the political opposition to privatization coming from the influential Hindu fundamentalist RSS and, more ambivalently, from the opposition Congress party. But in truth, NPM is the runt in the developing country public management litter, and has had to struggle to establish itself in the face of competition from its older brothers and sisters. Part of understanding why the scale of implementation has been so modest is to understand what else has been going on.

Continuation of the public administration model

As with the death of Mark Twain, reports of the demise of traditional public administration are somewhat premature. The simple inertia that the institutionalist school makes so much of, as Ferlie and Fitzgerald point out (Chapter 20, this volume), is one reason for this. The public administration model, 'with its emphasis on probity and due process rather than outcomes' (Ferlie and Fitzgerald 2000: 3) is to this extent appropriate to countries where corruption is a real problem (as we have seen in Nepal and Tanzania). There is evidence that where service provision is corrupt, the public will prioritize the honesty of service delivery over its quality (Borins and Warrington 1996). Such a concern, as has been argued elsewhere (McCourt forthcoming b), may be better met by a Weberian bureaucratic than by NPM-style service provision. There are also, as we shall see, specific political reasons why public administration subsists in so many places. For a variety of reasons, the public administration model 'Like a wounded snake, drags its slow length along' (Pope 1966: 74).

The 'Washington model'

The public administration model is very well known to readers. I want to talk in greater detail about some of its siblings in the public management litter. The most notable is what I have called elsewhere the 'Washington model' of civil service reform (McCourt forthcoming c). As country after country embarked on reform after Ghana's bellwether programme began in 1982, a blueprint emerged in which a reduction in the size of the civil service, typically expressed as a conditionality or 'structural benchmark' in a World Bank or IMF loan, was specified in the context of a reduction in overall government expenditure whose aim was to restore macroeconomic stability and facilitate growth (Lindauer and Nunberg 1994). Recognizing that the alleged overstaffing which reform was supposed to rectify had often been at the expense of lower wages, the blueprint included provision for the savings from job reduction to be used to raise wages for the survivors, especially senior officials. For senior officials, salary decompression was indicated, since their salaries were supposed to have fallen relative to junior officials and their private sector counterparts.

If NPM implementation has been modest, the 'Washington model' has been very big business indeed. Between 1987 and 1996 the World Bank assisted no fewer than sixty-eight developing and transitional countries with reform programmes in this area (Nunberg 1997). China, the world's most populous nation, embarked in 1998 on a reform programme designed to cut the number of its civil servants by half – in other words, by a projected four million people (Economist 1998). Actual reductions in individual countries like Ghana and Uganda are equally dramatic (McCourt 1998). So pervasive have these programmes been, especially at their high-water mark in the mid-1990s, that they became equated with civil service reform, as the Netherlands' then Minister for Development Cooperation pointed out (Pronk 1996). Even in industrialized countries the scale has been dramatic: staff retrenchment programmes were carried out between 1987 and 1992 in the public sectors of twenty-two of the twenty-seven member countries of the OECD, making it by some distance their most widespread Human Resource initiative (OECD 1994).

I wish to stress the importance of distinguishing this model from the NPM model. Certainly for the World Bank and IMF, who have been its principal sponsors, the two models are almost mutually exclusive. Governments are supposed to rectify the administrative fundamentals, in terms of the size and cost of their civil services, before they allow themselves to think about the quality of the services that they provide for their citizens. This, I think, explains the bank's scepticism about NPM, to which we have already referred. Governments, in the bank's eyes, should not try to run before they can walk.

Although this in theory gives us a two-phase model of reform, with the Washington model as Phase 1 and NPM, perhaps, as Phase 2, in reality the Washington model can represent too high a fence for governments to jump over. The record of governments that have had a go at the Washington model with the World Bank's help has been dismal, as the bank and the IMF have been honest enough to recognize (Abed *et al.* 1997; Nunberg 1997). But like a horse in a show-jumping arena, governments are not supposed to go on to Phase 2 till they have successfully negotiated Phase 1. Here is one powerful reason why the scale of NPM implementation in developing countries has been so modest.

Other public management initiatives

There are some other initiatives that have combined to crowd NPM off the agenda in many places. They include drives to reduce corruption and to strengthen merit-based staffing practices, to both of which I have already referred. I will briefly review a few other important initiatives.

The poverty agenda

Rather surprisingly, in view of their record in the 1980s and 1990s, the World Bank and the IMF have just rediscovered poverty, with the IMF adopting a poverty objective for the first time at its 1999 annual meeting (World Bank 2000). It is the result of a rare conjunction of the political planets at the turn of the century, with centre or centre-left administrations governing the powerful shareholder countries of France, Germany, the UK and the USA. The rediscovery implies a degree of government activism that is hard to square with the Bank/ IMF's previous conviction 'That no government or little government was better than big government', as one of the Bank's staffers put it (Chaudhry 1994: 199). Consequently it is not clear how big a difference this new emphasis is going to make to the practice of World Bank and IMF lending, although it is already having an impact on debt relief. To the extent that the difference is substantial, it is likely to militate against NPM adoption. NPM, with its characteristic stress on the means of government at the expense of its ends (Osborne and Gaebler 1992: xxi), has nothing to say about poverty, unless it can turn itself inside-out; not so much 'Physician, heal thyself' as 'NPM, reinvent thyself'.

Domestic imperatives

Poverty or no poverty, NPM or no NPM, normal politics continues. When Harold Macmillan was asked what was the hardest thing he had to deal with as the UK's Prime Minister, he famously replied, 'Events, dear boy, events'. 'Events' exacted their inexorable response. The World Bank was highly sceptical about one such response, a major decentralization in Sri Lanka that was current at the time of writing. This inevitably expensive programme was an attempt to address a political rather than an economic problem, namely the government's continuing war against the Liberation Tigers of Tamil Eelam (*Financial Times* 2001; McCourt forthcoming a). Most of us are aware of the catastrophic scale of the AIDS pandemic, especially in Southern Africa. Swaziland, to take one example, has estimated that it needs to recruit thirteen teachers for every ten teaching vacancies to take account of the expected mortality rate. With problems like these, many governments will be forgiven if they decide that implementing NPM at the moment would be so much fiddling while Rome burns.

Politics and NPM: why the dog did not bark in the night

The dissemination effect, inappropriateness and competition from other public management initiatives do not quite exhaust the reasons why NPM has not been implemented more widely in developing countries. There is a species of inertia for which a different explanation is needed from the institutionalist explanation that Ferlie and Fitzgerald (Chapter 20, this volume) provide, one that addresses the fact that the status quo persists because changes that have been canvassed, including NPM, are politically infeasible. As I was developing such an explanation at the time of writing, I can only outline it here.

The starting point for this explanation is the powerful evidence that something called 'political commitment' is at the root of the failure of many public policy initiatives, including in the area of public management. Professor Borins (Chapter 11, this volume), for instance, attributes the sluggish progress of NPM reform in Canada and the USA to it. A World Bank study found that political commitment strongly predicted overall outcomes in no fewer than seventy-three per cent of eighty-one World Bank operations completed between 1980 and 1988 (Johnson and Wasty 1993; see also Nunberg 1997). We know that it is inadequate analysis simply to lay the blame for this at the government's door; indeed, it would be an example of what psychologists call the 'fundamental attribution error' (Jones 1972; Nelson 1990). It follows that we need to understand the political context to understand why change is so difficult.

A basic element in the political context for most developing countries is the political settlement bequeathed by the departing colonial power at independence. Independence represented a particularly powerful 'archetype transition', to use Ferlie and Fitzgerald's phrase. It has both concrete and intangible features: one concrete feature is usually a written constitution with entrenched clauses that are almost impossible to overturn. Archetype transition in some countries has also taken the form of revolutions, wars and *coups d'état*, whose effects may be enduring. It is striking that the two governments in sub-Saharan Africa most often cited as radical reformers, Ghana's and Uganda's, came to power through a *coup d'état* and a revolution respectively. Most countries, with rare exceptions like East Timor and South Africa, are desperate to avoid any more painful archetype transitions. Much government effort is devoted to keeping the lid on the always-simmering pot.

Inevitably there are also vested interests in the status quo. Many have argued that the repeated failure, going back at least to 1977, of reform efforts in Swaziland, a country that is a veritable graveyard of reform reports, serves the interests of an oligarchy centred on the king. Swaziland's king is an absolute monarch who takes precedence over the Westminster-style elected government with which he nominally shares power. He has important commercial interests from which much of his income derives (Wamalwa 1976; Bischoff 1988).

Institutional theory, as outlined in Chapter 20 by Ferlie and Fitzgerald, directs our attention to the phenomenon of isomorphic change (DiMaggio and Powell 1983), or, in simpler language, convergence; that is, to the way in which organizations, both public and private, supposedly come to resemble each other. My provisional explanation, on the other hand, directs our attention to the phenomenon of stasis, that is the way in which political and other factors arrest convergence. My contention is that this lack of movement, like the dog that famously did not bark in the night in the Sherlock Holmes story, may be as significant as movement towards convergence.

If my provisional analysis is correct, then we public management specialists need to hone our political antennae. It also follows that making public management initiatives stick is harder than much of the public management literature fondly assumes. But the recent example of Northern Ireland (the author's home country) perhaps reminds us that positive change is possible even in the most intractable circumstances.

Conclusion: applying NPM in developing countries

In this chapter I have dealt with the application of NPM in developing countries, beginning with a brief discussion of problems of definition. In addition to focusing on the developing country experience with the NPM model, I have reviewed some other current features of public management in those countries, especially the continuation of 'traditional' public administration and the application of the Washington model of civil service reform.

We have spent a good deal of time in this chapter discussing the application of NPM. But what about its applicability? Based on my reading of both the OECD and the developing country literature, I believe that scope exists. The OECD evidence on NPM elements like the use of performance indicators, contracting out and quality management approaches is promising (McCourt 2001). The developing country evidence is less promising, but not to the point of ruling these elements out. If they can be separated from other unpromising elements such as quality circles and citizen's charters, especially where these are definitely unproductive, they will be more attractive to the developing country policymakers for whose attention NPM has to compete. Developing countries could usefully learn more about them, and public management scholars could do more to help them apply them critically. But governments will need to be alive to the process of refraction that these elements will undergo as they are implemented. In particular, if my provisional analysis of the 'political commitment' construct has any value, they will need to be aware of the political context in which initiatives will take place.

Alongside all of this run the other political imperatives and the 'events' to which governments have to respond. Here one is conscious of how different they are from the imperatives and events, some of which Chapter 20 by Ferlie and Fitzgerald reviews, that were the crucible from which NPM emerged in the first place, and of how ill-equipped NPM is to respond to them. I have argued elsewhere (McCourt 2001) that what is needed is a major effort to develop indigenous public management models better suited to developing countries, but one must be pessimistic about the likelihood of this materializing soon. In the meantime, governments must make the best of the goods on offer and NPM, as it were, is on 'special promotion'. Scholars like those who have made such thoughtful contributions to this collection have a role to play in helping governments tailor those ready-made goods to their own requirements.

Bibliography

Abed, G. *et al.* (1998) *Fiscal Reforms in Low Income Countries: Experience under IMF-supported Programs*. Occasional Paper no. 160. Washington, DC: International Monetary Fund.

Bale, M. and Dale, T. (1998) 'Public sector reform in New Zealand and its relevance to developing countries', *World Bank Research Observer*, 13, 1: 103–22.

Batley, R. (1999) 'The new public management in developing countries: implications for policy and organizational reform', *Journal of International Development*, 11: 761–5.

Bennett, A. and Mills, S. (1998) 'Government capacity to contract: health sector experience and lessons', *Public Administration and Development*, 18: 307–336.

Bischoff, P. (1988) 'Why Swaziland is different: An explanation of the kingdom's political position in Southern Africa', *Journal of Modern African Studies*, 26: 457–71.

Borins, S. (1997) 'What the new public management is achieving: a survey of Commonwealth experience'. In Jones, L., Schedler, K. and Wade, S. (eds) *Advances in International Comparative Management: International Perspectives on the New Public Management*. Greenwich, CT: JAI Press, 49–70.

Borins, S. and Warrington, E. (1996) *The New Public Administration: Global Challenges, Local Solutions: A Report on the Second Biennial Conference of CAPAM*. London: Commonwealth Secretariat.

Broadbent, J. and Laughlin, R. (1997) 'Evaluating the new public management reforms in the UK: a constitutional possibility?' *Public Administration*, 75: 487–507.

Chaudhry, S. (1994) 'Selected discussion points'. In Chaudhry, S., Reid, G. and Malik, W. (eds) *Civil Service Reform in Latin America and the Caribbean*. Washington, DC: World Bank, 199–202.

Child, J. (1972) 'Organizational structure, environment and performance: the role of strategic choice', *Sociology*, 6: 1–22.

Christoplos, I. (1998) 'Public services, complex humanitarian emergencies and the humanitarian imperative: perspectives from Angola'. In Minogue, M., Polidano, C. and Hulme, D. (eds) *Beyond the New Public Management: Changing Ideas and Practices in Governance*. Cheltenham: Edward Elgar, 260–77.

Clarke, J. and Wood, D. (2001) In McCourt, W. and Minogue, M. (eds) *The Internationalization of Public Management: Reinventing the Third World State*. Cheltenham: Edward Elgar, 70–89.

Common, R. (1999) 'Malaysia's "paradigm shift": the legitimisation of administrative change in a Southeast Asian state', paper presented at Third International Research Symposium on Public Management, Aston University, 25–26 March 1999.

Commonwealth Secretariat (1996) *Current Good Practices and New Developments in Public Service Management*. London: Commonwealth Secretariat.

Cook, P. and Kirkpatrick, C. (1995) *Privatization Policy and Performance: International Perspectives*. Hemel Hempstead: Prentice-Hall.

Da Silva, M. (1999) 'TQM in the Brazilian public sector'. In Ho, S. (ed.) *TQM and Innovation: Proceedings of the Fourth International Conference*. School of Business: Hong Kong Baptist University.

DiMaggio, P. and Powell, W. (1983) 'The iron cage revisited: Institutional isomorphism and collective rationality in organizational fields', *American Sociological Review*, 48: 147–60.

Dodoo, R. (1997) 'Performance standards and measuring performance in Ghana', *Public Administration and Development*, 17: 115–21.

Doig, A. (1997) 'The privatization of the Property Services Agency: Risk and vulnerability in contract-related fraud and corruption', *Public Policy and Administration*, 12, 3: 6–27.

Dolowitz, D. and Marsh, D. (1998) 'Policy transfer: a framework for comparative analysis'. In Minogue, M., Polidano, C. and Hulme, D. (eds) *Beyond the New Public Management: Changing Ideas and Practices in Governance*. Cheltenham: Edward Elgar, 38–58.

The Economist (1998) 'Zhu takes on the red-tape army', *The Economist*, 14 March: 45.

Elcock, H. and Minogue, M. (2001) 'Local government: Management or politics?'. In McCourt, W. and Minogue, M. (eds) *The Internationalization of Public Management: Reinventing the Third World State*. Cheltenham: Edward Elgar.

Eldridge, D. and McCourt, W. (1998) *Human Resource Management and Development*. London: School of Oriental and African Studies.

Ferlie, E. and Fitzgerald, L. (2000) 'The sustainability of the New Public Management in the UK: An institutionalist perspective', symposium paper for the annual conference of the American Academy of Management, Toronto, August 2000.

Financial Times (2000) 'Colombo defeated in move to end bloodshed', *Financial Times*, 9 August: 5.

Government of South Africa (1997) *White Paper on Transforming Public Service Delivery*. Pretoria: Department of Public Service and Administration.

Government of Uganda (1994) *Management of Change: Context, Vision, Objectives, Strategy and Plan*. Kampala: Ministry of Public Service.

Hill, S. (1991) 'Why quality circles failed but TQM might succeed', *British Journal of Industrial Relations*, 29: 541–68.

Hulme, D. (2001) 'Reinventing the Third World state: service delivery and the civic realm'. In McCourt, W. and Minogue, M. (eds) *The Internationalization of Public Management: Reinventing the Third World State*. Cheltenham: Edward Elgar, 129–52.

Islam, N. (1993) 'Public enterprise reform: managerial autonomy, accountability and performance contracts', *Public Administration and Development*, 13: 129–52.

Johnson, and Wasty, S. (1993) *Borrower Ownership of Adjustment Programs and the Political Economy of Reform*. Discussion Paper no. 199, Washington, DC: World Bank.

Jones, E. (ed.) (1972) *Attribution: Perceiving the Causes of Behavior*, Morristown, NJ: General Learning.

Jordan, G. (1997) 'The search for governmental efficiency'. In Massey, A. (ed.) *Globalization and Marketization of Government Services: Comparing Contemporary Public Sector Developments*. London: Macmillan, 105–27.

Kattermann, D. (1999) Personal communication to author.

Klingner, D. (2000) 'South of the border: Progress and problems in implementing New Public Management reforms in Mexico today', paper presented at symposium on New Public Management in Mexico, http://www.fiu.edu.

Krueger, A. and Srinivasan, T. (2000) 'The harsh consequences of forgiveness', *Financial Times*, 9 August: 11.

Langseth, P. (1995) 'Service delivery survey: a diagnostic tool'. In Langseth, P., Nogxina, S., Prinsloo, V. and Sullivan, R. (eds) *Civil Service Reform in Anglophone Africa*. Washington, DC: Economic Development Institute, 239–64.

Larbi, G. (1998) *Implementing New Public Management Reforms in Ghana: Institutional Constraints and Capacity Issues: Cases from Public Health and Water Services*. University of Birmingham, doctoral dissertation.

Lawrence, P. and Lorsch, J. (1967) *Organization and Environment*, Boston: Harvard University Press.

Lindauer, D. and Nunberg, B. (eds) (1994) *Rehabilitating Government: Pay and Employment Reform in Africa*. Washington, DC: World Bank.

McCourt, W. (1998) 'Civil service reform equals retrenchment? The experience of staff retrenchment in Ghana, Uganda and the United Kingdom'. In Minogue, M., Polidano, C. and Hulme, D. (eds) *Governance in the 21st Century*. Cheltenham: Edward Elgar, 172–87.

McCourt, W. (2001) 'Moving the public management debate forward: A contingency approach'. In McCourt, W. and Minogue, M. (eds) *The Internationalization of Public Management: Reinventing the Third World State*, Cheltenham: Edward Elgar, 220–53.

McCourt, W. (forthcoming a) 'Finding a way forward on public employment reform: A Sri Lankan case study', *Asia Pacific Journal of Human Resources*.

McCourt, W. (forthcoming b) 'The new public selection? Anti-corruption, psychometric selection and the New Public Management in Nepal', *Public Management*.

McCourt, W. (forthcoming c), 'Towards a strategic model of employment reform in developing countries: Explaining and remedying experience to date', *International Journal of Human Resource Management*.

McCourt, W. and M. Minogue (2001) (eds) *The Internationalization of Public Management: Reinventing the Third World State*. Cheltenham: Edward Elgar.

McCourt, W. and Ramgutty-Wong, A. (2000) 'Strategic Human Resource Management in the Mauritian civil service', Manchester: Institute for Development Policy and Management, unpublished manuscript.

McCourt, W. and Sola, N. (1999) 'Using training to promote civil service reform: a Tanzanian local government case study', *Public Administration and Development*, 19: 63–75.

Makumbe, J.M. (1997) 'The Zimbabwe Civil Service Reform Programme: A Critical Perspective', Role of Government in Adjusting Economies Paper No. 16. Birmingham: Development Administration Group.

Mallon, R. (1994) 'State-owned enterprise reform through performance contracts: the Bolivian experience', *World Development*, 22: 925–34.

Matheson, A. (2000) 'New Public Management: How well does it travel?', *Rethinking Approaches to Government Reforms*. Seminar Series, No.1. Oxford: Oxford Policy Institute.

Meyers, R. and Lacey, R. (1996) 'Customer satisfaction, performance and accountability in the public sector', *International Review of Administrative Sciences*, 62: 331–350.

Nelson, J. (ed.) (1990) *Economic Crisis and Policy Choice*. Princeton, NJ: Princeton University Press.

Nunberg, B. (1995) *Managing the Civil Service: Reform Lessons from Advanced Industrialized Countries*. Washington, DC: World Bank.

Nunberg, B. (1997) *Rethinking Civil Service Reform: An Agenda for Smart Government*. Washington, DC: World Bank, Poverty and Social Policy Department.

O'Conghaile, W. (1996) 'Current and future developments in service quality initiatives in Portugal, France and the United Kingdom'. In *OECD, Responsive Government: Service Quality Initiatives*. Paris: OECD, 65–70.

Organization for Economic Co-operation and Development (1994) *Public Management Developments*. Paris: OECD.

Organization for Economic Co-operation and Development (1995) *Governance in Transition: Public Management Reforms in OECD Countries*. Paris: OECD.

Osborne, D. and Gaebler, T. (1992) *Reinventing Government: How the Entrepreneurial Spirit is Transforming the Public Sector*. Reading, MA: Addison-Wesley.

Paul, S. and Sekhar, S. (1997) 'A report card on public services: a comparative analysis of five cities in India', *Regional Development Dialogue*, 18, 2: 119–35.

Polidano, C. (2001) 'Administrative reform in core civil services: Application and applicability of the new public management'. In McCourt, W. and Minogue, M. (eds) *The Internationalization of Public Management: Reinventing the Third World State*. Cheltenham: Edward Elgar, 44–69.

Pollitt, C. (1993) *Managerialism and the Public Services*. Oxford: Basil Blackwell.

Pope, A. (1966) 'An essay on criticism'. In Pope, A. *Poetical works*, Oxford: Clarendon, 62–85.

Pronk, J. (1996) 'Preface'. In De Haan, P. and van Hees, Y. (eds) *Civil Service Reform in Sub-Saharan Africa*. The Hague: Ministry of Foreign Affairs, 7.

Pugh, D. and Hickson, D. (1976) *Organizational Structure in its Context: The Aston Programme I*. London: Gower.

Rondinelli, D. (1981) 'Government decentralization in comparative perspective: Theory and practice in developing countries', *International Review of Administrative Sciences*, 47: 133–45.

Sarji, A. (1995) *The Civil Service of Malaysia: Towards Efficiency and Effectiveness*. Kuala Lumpur: Government of Malaysia.

Schick, A. (1998) 'Why most developing countries should not try New Zealand's reforms', *World Bank Research Observer*, 13, 1: 123–31.

Shakespeare, W. (1951) 'The Tempest'. In *Complete works of Shakespeare*. London: Collins, 1–26.

Smith, B. (1985) *Decentralization: The Territorial Dimension of the State*. London: Allen and Unwin.

The Sunday Times (1999) 'Quality service charters for the public service'. *The Sunday Times* (Malta), 9 May, 7.

Talbot, C. (1997) 'UK civil service personnel reforms: devolution, decentralization and delusion. *Public Policy and Administration*, 12, 4: 14–34.

Toronto Star (2000) 'Second-richest man, after you-know-who', *Toronto Star*, 6 August, B2.

Trosa, S. (1995) 'Quality in the French public service'. In Pollitt, C. and Bouckaert, G. (eds) *Quality Improvement in European Public Services*. London: Sage, 58–68.

United Nations (1995) *Performance Contracting for Public Enterprises*. New York: United Nations.

Wamalwa, W. (1976) *Report of the Commission of Enquiry (Structure, Conditions of Service and Remuneration of the Public Service of the Kingdom of Swaziland)*. Mbabane: Government of Swaziland.

World Bank (2000) *World Development Report 2000* (draft Chapter three). Washington, DC: World Bank.

Chapter 15

The politics of New Public Management

Some experience from reforms in East Asia[1]

Anthony B.L. Cheung

Introduction

NPM as global paradigm

Most of the public sector reforms taking place across the globe these days seem to be construed within the paradigm of NPM (e.g. Hood 1991) first spearheaded in OECD countries since the late 1980s. Reinvention of government, made popular by Osborne and Gaebler (1993) and former US Vice President Al Gore's (1993) programme to streamline the US federal government, is now the buzz-word of administrative reforms everywhere. In Asia, for example, the Hong Kong government launched a public sector reform programme as early as 1989 (Finance Branch 1989; Cheung 1992), with much input from international management consultants. Taiwan's government announced an administrative renovation programme in 1993 and subsequently a government reinvention programme in 1998 (Wei 2000), all formulated in the latest NPM-speak. Even in socialist China, government restructuring, transformation of government functions, downsizing and civil service reform has formed part of the administrative reform programme since the 1980s, partly to cope with the needs of a new socialist market economy and partly to seek simpler administration and higher efficiency (Jiang, X. 1997).

It is tempting for observers of various national administrative reforms to consider them as an offshoot of worldwide trends and efforts under globalization which will eventually see the advent of a global convergence in the form of NPM (e.g. Kaboolian 1998). Whether or not NPM is considered to be in the ascendancy in Asia, as in OECD countries, depends on how the global NPM is operationalized for the sake of analysis of reforms undertaken in various countries. After all, NPM is more of an academic description of public sector reforms than the term actually used by governments.

Hood's (1991) classical definition of NPM identified the following elements: leaving managers 'free to manage'; performance standards and measurement; output controls; breaking up public sector entities into 'corporatized' units; competition through term contracts and public tendering; discipline and parsimony in resource use; and adoption of private sector management style.

The OECD notion of the new paradigm of public management pointed to greater focus on results in terms of efficiency, effectiveness and quality of service; decentralized management environment; alternatives to direct public provision and regulation; efficiency improvement through productivity targets and competition; and strengthening the strategic capacity of the centre (OECD 1995). The 1996 International Conference of Administrative Sciences, in its general report prepared by Ormond (1997)[2] based on exchanges with a wide range of practitioners in OECD countries, identified two central challenges to government administration: 'capacity to respond' to the multiple needs of citizens and enterprises; and 'capacity to renew' the government so as to cope with emerging political and economic realities. To enhance the capacity to respond, governments in OECD countries have in varying degrees been driven by 'budget pressures to deliver more with less, thereby spurring public sector reform and improved economic performance; public demand for better, more targeted services, especially seen in relation to the private sector; and [the] concern to clarify the role and legitimacy of government' (Ormond 1997: 29). Efforts to improve the capacity to renew include: redefining and restating the mission of government; selecting and designing policy instruments; opening up civil service developments; educating people about government; and building strategic capacity to change public institutions (Ormond 1997: 34). These broad objectives of reform and renewal of the public sector imply a wider mission than just efficiency enhancement and a break from the classic Weberian model of bureaucratic public administration (Hughes 1994: Chapter 2).

In terms of reform rhetoric, Asian countries seem to be embarking on similar objectives to redefine the role and functions of government. Some Asian governments presented their public sector reforms as a process of government renewal to respond to globalization. For example, the Malaysian Chief Secretary Ahmad Sarji exhorted the civil service 'to be more efficient and effective in this borderless world and highly-competitive global environment' (Sarji 1996: 50). Singapore's *Public Service 21* reform initiative similarly aimed 'to make the service more responsive to the demands of a globalizing economy and a better-educated population' (Ibrahim 1995: 1). Hong Kong's civil service reform was presented as a response to the challenge of the twenty-first century (Civil Service Bureau 1999). Kim (2000: 1) observed too that 'in order to meet the challenges of globalization and the current economic crisis, administrative reform in Korea was driven by the need to create good governance by providing a strong foundation for economic recovery and sustainable growth'. While China arguably has a more domestically generated reform agenda as part of its larger economic restructuring and opening-up project, the leadership has time and again emphasized the need of 'going to the world arena' and 'drawing on advanced management experiences and methods from other countries' (Song 1997).[3] The fact that the Chinese Ministry of Personnel hosted the 1991 EROPA Conference and the 1996 International Conference of Administrative Sciences attests to the government's eagerness to get in tune with the global administrative reform trends.[4]

Global discourse, political and cultural differences

A globalization discourse of administrative reform assumes growing policy interdependence and economic and political integration so that the same management technologies and skills can be applied to national settings. Reforms are thus perceived as largely instrumental and managerial – a matter of improving government performance and management based on so-called objective and rational methods. In Asia, the urgency of reform was recently highlighted by the economic challenges posed by the 1997 Asian financial crisis. This further view sees reforms of public institutions in newly developed or developing economies as being triggered by economic crisis followed by external advice from international organizations. For example, the World Bank describes the reform story in East Asia as follows:

> Before the recent economic crisis that swept through the East Asia and Pacific Region, public institutions were largely thought to be working well, credited with many of the virtues associated with the 'Asian miracle'. ... This view has changed in the wake of the past few years' political and economic turmoil. Public sectors throughout the region have had difficulties responding to the crisis, which has exposed previous institutional weaknesses that had escaped notice during periods of economic growth.
>
> (World Bank 2000: 85)

> Throughout the region, governments have no choice but to *improve their efficiency* in resource management, improve the *effectiveness of their service delivery* and *regulation*, and augment the *progressivity of their policies* in a way that improves their *transparency and accountability*.
>
> (World Bank 2000: 86, emphasis in original)

Although it is true that increasingly the globalized 'international environment forms much of the *context* of national policy-making' (Harrop 1992: 263, emphasis added), the outcomes of national reforms are in no way homogeneous. As I have previously argued in a survey of global public sector reforms (Cheung 1997), such reforms may have covered some similar policy and instrumental tools being adopted in different national political circumstances for vastly different reasons and with different impacts. Even among OECD countries, significant diversities were observed in terms of the style, focus and locus of NPM-style reforms.

Economic imperatives are no doubt important drivers of reform in public institutions. However, such reform is still mediated by local politics and strategies of the governing elites. In Asian countries, such as China, Malaysia or the newly industrialized economies (NIEs), administrative reforms are mostly pursued within the context of managing state building and economic growth in a state-directed paradigm of governance rather than an opposed logic of state contraction as perceived in some Western welfare states. Indeed, economic development in East Asia has always been anchored on strong, interventionist but pro-market public sectors. Unger and Chan (1995), for example, observed that the governments of high-growth East Asian economies 'shared a common advantage in adopting state-corporatist solutions: every one of them already possessed well-organized bureaucracies with established traditions'. After the recent Asian financial turmoil, the predominant role of state-led institutions has not in essence been diluted in these national jurisdictions. Even coercive prescriptions for reform by international organizations such as the World Bank and the International Monetary Fund cannot override local conditions. As Polidano discovered in his survey of administrative reforms in the core civil services of developing countries:

> while many developing countries have taken up elements of the NPM agenda, they have not adopted anything close to the entire package. Moreover, they are simultaneously undertaking reforms that are unrelated or even contrary to that agenda. The NPM is only one among a number of contending strands of reform in the developing world.
>
> (Polidano, forthcoming)

In the case of coercive NPM policy diffusion in developing nations, some critics have further observed that 'few of the reforms do anything to relieve [them] from the pressures of international debt challenges' and that 'many systems remain more or less the same as before with slight modifications' (Cooper 1995: 187).

The reason for discrepancies between assumptions or expectations and outcomes is that the domestic dynamics of a country's political institutions and culture are capable of modifying transferred policies and programmes (Common 1998: 71), not to mention distorting them entirely. In terms of reform agenda-setting, although there are no doubt more interactions between global issues and trends with the national and local levels, and even though the policy agenda may now embrace a more 'global' outlook, the modes of decision-making, implementation and delivery remain national and local (Parsons 1995: 235). Similarities in market frameworks, administrative technologies and policy instruments alone cannot be taken as sufficient conditions for global convergence, for different management reforms may just be 'fundamentally alike in all unimportant aspects' (Wallace Sayre, quoted in Allison 1986). *Politics* remain an overriding factor in reform agenda-setting and implementation. The impact of globalization on national public sector reforms provides only an externally-induced context. The success of reforms however depends very much on building a domestic capacity for change, which is determined by internal factors. Public administration and management is about public governance that involves the steering of various 'societal processes in a complex network of many other co-directing actors [who] have different and sometimes conflicting objectives and interests' (Kickert 1997: 33). Diversities in domestic administrative agenda are therefore the norm rather than the exception in global public management and governance.

This chapter examines civil service and public sector reforms in three East Asian jurisdictions, namely Hong Kong, China[5] and Singapore, within the framework of domestic reform agenda-setting evolution, to highlight the salience of *politics* rather than politics-free *managerialism*, which seems to many to underpin the NPM paradigm. In these jurisdictions, the politics of governance are seen to have significantly motivated NPM-like reforms and to have determined the process and consequences of such reforms. Each of them represents a different reform trajectory. Hong Kong's civil service reform is essentially bureaucracy driven in response first to political and then also to economic difficulties. Singapore, like Hong Kong, is governed by a meritocracy, but this meritocratic elite is both political and bureaucratic. Its reform seeks to reinforce the longstanding nation-building strategy of the country since independence, rather than to reduce the capacity of the state as implied by the managerialist logic of NPM. In China, state sector reforms are part and parcel of the larger post-Mao reform project to create 'market socialism', in order to take the collectivist burden off the shoulders of the state without weakening its dirigiste powers. The historical trajectories of these jurisdictions have as much impact on the process and direction of their reforms as horizontal influences from international trends and organizations globally.

Hong Kong

Public sector reform in the 1990s: crisis of legitimacy rather than efficiency

Since the 1990s, Hong Kong has embarked on a myriad of public sector reform initiatives. These included the setting up of self-accounting trading funds, privatization, contracting out, devolution of human and financial resource management responsibilities, customer orientation, performance pledges, and most recently an enhanced productivity programme and civil service reform (Finance Branch 1989; Efficiency Unit 1995; Civil Service Bureau 1999). When explaining the emergence of these reforms, this author argued elsewhere that the Hong Kong experience did not fit into the Western NPM route driven mostly by an efficiency crisis of the state (Cheung 1996a). Hong Kong had not experienced any prolonged economic or fiscal crisis. Government overloading was not significant in view of the relatively small public sector and the low level of public expenditure in relation to the economy (historically not more than twenty per cent of GDP), until the late 1990s when economic slowdown triggered by the 1997 Asian financial crisis began to induce calls from the private sector for cuts in the civil service wage bill. On the contrary, there have been persistent demands for more public services provision and intervention over the years, despite the official embrace of a 'positive non-interventionist' philosophy (Cheung 2000a).

Until several crises of mismanagement and sleaze cases involving civil servants in the post-1997 Special Administrative Region (SAR)[6] had tarnished the previous 'infallible' legacy of the civil service, the Hong Kong government had enjoyed a high reputation for being generally efficient and effective, and there was not the same sense of an efficiency crisis as was prevalent in some OECD countries in the 1980s. Whereas factors such as government oversize, macroeconomic and fiscal problems, New Right ideology and party political orientations were cited as being responsible for the rise of NPM (Hood 1996), such factors, if relevant, hardly featured much in the Hong Kong reform scene.

Hong Kong's NPM-like public sector reforms in the 1990s were not primarily motivated by standard global claims about suppressing 'big government', improving efficiency or coping with a fiscal crisis. They were more related to macro-political changes in the territory's transition towards the 1997 changeover in sovereign control, resulting in the decline of the political authority and relative autonomy of the then British administration. It was imperative that the government be reformed in such a way as to shore up its leadership in transitional governance (Cheung 1992, 1996a). On the other hand, the expansion and growing organizational complexity of the public sector throughout the 1980s, coupled with the more turbulent and pluralist context of public policy and public services, had brought about problems of policy leadership and internal coordination. Such problems could not be properly accommodated within the existing structure adopted since the government machinery was last reconfigured during the McKinsey reform of the mid-1970s (McKinsey and Company 1973).[7]

Public sector reform in Hong Kong in the 1990s was therefore not simply induced by efficiency concerns per se, but should be understood as an indigenous bureaucratic strategy to reshape the public sector institutional configuration in face of a looming crisis of external legitimacy and internal coordination. Featuring corporatization, privatization, trading funds and contracting out, this reform helped to play down political tensions and 'managerialize' otherwise politically loaded policy and administrative issues. It in effect underlined a government-restructuring strategy to 're-manage' the changing external and internal environments, in an attempt to restore legitimacy for the public service within a context of weakening political authority prior to the transfer of sovereign power to China in 1997. A shift towards the microeconomic notion of efficiency in service provision as justified by NPM rhetoric helps to *depoliticize* performance evaluation of the public sector, hence reducing pressure for greater political accountability. There was also a need to 're-manage' the public bureaucratic institutions on the part of central agencies – such as the Finance Branch (an equivalent of the Treasury) and Policy Branches[8] (or quasi-ministries) – so as to strengthen central policy and resource coordination in an increasingly politicized environment.

'Efficiency' as a reform theme provided a ready and convenient platform for such reconfiguration of institutional relationships. Departments as an agency had always sought to enhance their operating autonomy under the supervision of their Policy Secretary, and to be free to deal with their clientele and map out their own managerial strategies. Emerging professional power in some departments and statutory authorities (such as the Hospital Authority and

Housing Authority) also demanded a more balanced power-sharing regime *vis-à-vis* their administrative officer counterparts who constitute the cadreship of the policy centre within the government. Two sets of bureau-shaping strategies, following Dunleavy's (1991: Chapters 7 and 8) typology, had set in, and public sector reform formed the arena for the two strategies to interact, to give rise to a new bureaucratic configuration. Policy Branches had their policy and resource control powers fully legitimated as policy managers, in exchange for granting managerial and micro-budgetary autonomies to departmental mandarins and managers as executive agents. The re-delineation of branch–department relationship, presented as a pure management improvement in line with NPM thinking, underscored a further continuation of the process of politicization and ministerialization of the administrative class civil servants, first started by McKinsey two decades ago (Huque *et al.* 1998: 146–149).

This new relationship was also extended to empower the policy secretaries' leadership and control over statutory authorities, non-departmental public bodies, trading funds and public corporations through framework agreements in which strategic and resource targets are specified. The 'trading fund' reform, while opening up new room for management flexibility and operational autonomy much to the benefit of departmental managers, has yet to prove the claim of improvement in producer efficiency and gain to customers. The question is still begged whether 'it is an outcome of design to prove [trading funds'] viability by selecting those services which are monopolistic and have high revenue-earning capacity as the target of reform' (Cheung 1998).

Civil service reform after 1997: political challenges more than managerial failure

Similar to public sector reform in the 1990s which was motivated by domestic political dynamics rather than a global managerial agenda, civil service reform in the post-colonial Hong Kong is driven, shaped and constrained by an internal political crisis. At the time of the transfer of sovereignty to China, the Hong Kong civil service was very much cherished as an important legacy of British rule – a symbol of professionalism and meritocracy.[9] A human resources management review undertaken by the Civil Service Branch in 1993 had already called for the devolution of personnel authorities to line departments and for moving towards a performance-oriented culture with wide-ranging reform proposals. However, the government at that time did not pick up sufficient political will to push for significant management changes, for fear of inviting resistance from civil servants and their unions, and suspicion from China about any British move to alter the status quo prior to the handover of sovereignty. Besides, while the economy was still booming and the government was accumulating huge fiscal surplus during the final years of British rule, there was a lack of sense of urgency in civil service reform.

So despite NPM ideas having assumed some global influence by the 1990s and Hong Kong already embracing a public sector reform initiative, civil service reform could not get on to the agenda for want of the necessary *'politics'* or, to view it from another angle, because of the constraints imposed by the politics of the time. The same overriding impact of *politics* was again witnessed when civil service reform was finally promulgated by the post-1997 SAR government in March 1999, albeit in a reverse fashion.

After the 1997 handover, the Asian financial crisis has transformed the scenario of reform. With Hong Kong experiencing the worst economic slowdown in thirty years, accompanied by rising unemployment, increasing company closures, worker lay-off and wage cuts, public sentiments towards civil servants have changed. Public sector employees enjoying life-long job security and higher-than-market salaries became targets of the public's efficiency scrutiny. Various setbacks and maladministration incidents quickly accumulated into a credibility crisis for the new government that, ironically, was still being run by the same bureaucracy much praised previously. Civil service failure was in a sense played up because of the public dismay with the government's performance in managing major crises and the economy. Sleaze cases served to trigger the larger tide against the civil service as a whole, fuelled by media criticisms and attacks by politicians.

On the surface, the post-1997 crisis of the civil service is simultaneously one of efficiency, efficacy and probity among civil servants. Both the global NPM trend and the domestic political and economic fluctuations have served to focus public attention increasingly on how costly it is for the civil service to deliver public services. For example, a consultancy review in early 1999 found that civil servants of the Housing Department cost over forty per cent more than private companies in providing public housing estate management and maintenance services. A series of events caused the erosion of confidence in civil service efficacy. These included: the bird flu saga in December 1997, resulting in a messy chicken slaughter action; the incompetent response by monetary authorities to international speculators' attacks on the Hong Kong dollar in the first half of 1998; and the chaos following the opening of the new international airport at Chek Lap Kok in July 1998. Meanwhile, the increasingly critical Director of Audit has published a series of value-for-money audit reports, criticizing the misuse of public funds by government departments and agencies and pointing fingers to unsatisfactory middle management and the under-performing junior civil servants. Several cases of malpractice implicating top civil servants were also exposed by the media.

It was partly to face up to the public uproar and partly to seize the window of opportunity to shake up civil service management that the Chief Executive Tung Chee-hwa announced plans to overhaul the civil service in January 1999. The subsequent Civil Service Reform consultation document (Civil Service Bureau 1999) called for responding to the challenges of the twenty-first century and a rapidly changing external environment, and identified three main directions of structural change (para. 1.6), in order to achieve:

- an open, flexible, equitable and structured civil service framework;
- an enabling and motivating environment for civil servants; and
- a proactive, accountable and responsible culture.

The rhetoric of the reform package sounds typically NPM. Indeed, the more controversial proposals related to the wider use of contract terms to replace permanent and pensionable terms of employment, the introduction of performance-related pay, and the provision of voluntary and management-initiated retirement arrangements (so as to facilitate privatization schemes and to retire directorate staff with no potential for further promotion).

Staff reacted to the reform with anxieties and misgivings. During May and June 1999 several large-scale protest marches against the reform were organized by the unions, the first time in civil service history, with junior staff accusing senior management of using them as the scapegoat for poor government performance caused by policy failure and mismanagement. The reform has become a 'political' tug of war between staff and management,[10] and politics is again at the centre of reform. What is ironical is that while the government's crisis of efficacy opened up the window of opportunity for civil service reform, the controversies triggered by reform proposals in turn fuelled anti-government actions emerging in mid-2000, causing the Chief Executive a serious crisis of legitimacy.[11] He was criticized by various stakeholders as having introduced reforms on too many fronts in addition to civil service reform (such as in education, housing and social welfare subvention policy), although he saw such reforms as indispensable in the age of globalization and new economy (Tung 2000).

Re-legitimation of bureaucratic power: managerial solutions to political problems

In examining public sector reforms a managerial discourse of reform centred on efficiency benefits would have over-emphasized issues such as the procedural and structural defects of bureaucratic hierarchies and underplayed the importance of 'efficiency' as a legitimating factor which provides a rhetorically appealing rationale for administrative changes triggered by non-managerial issues. In practice, most institutional reforms take place as a process of organizational change within a political-historical context where dynamics can only be fully captured by a political discourse of reform (Cheung 1996b: 45–46). The institutional failure of public sector hierarchies may have more to do with the failure in the 'ordering' of interaction of contending interests between state and society, between politicians and bureaucrats and between administrative bureaucrats and service managers and professionals in the changing environment of governance.

The Hong Kong case illustrates such contention of interests and the wider political repercussions, with public sector reform being a proactive strategy adopted by the mandarins to re-legitimize public bureaucratic power by resorting to NPM rhetoric and practices which advocate managerial freedom and authority. Holding onto the traditional mode of bureaucratic legitimation based on Weberian control and accountability would have constrained rather than protected the bureaucrats' power. An NPM alternative, on the other hand, would open the way to a reinvention of bureaucratic power under the new managerialist image, to better face the challenges of the political transition.

Despite belated criticisms about its high cost, Hong Kong's civil service continues to be one of the most efficient and corrupt-free civil services internationally. What the civil service is suffering are more deep-seated problems than those of efficiency and performance. Its crisis is caused by the nature of the Hong Kong public bureaucracy as a political institution entrusted with the function of permanent government, unchecked in its powers under the so-called 'executive-led' principle, now caught between autonomy and accountability in a new and more politically charged environment after the handover (Cheung 2000b). Without a fundamental constitutional reform to establish accountable governance, the civil service institution would be appraised in terms of both its political and administrative competence, thereby having to bear the full brunt of any government failures, whether managerial or political.

The full implications of civil service reform have yet to unfold over time. It is worth recalling that Hong Kong's administrative history during colonial times had repeatedly seen administrative reforms used by the governing bureaucracy to cope with political problems and challenges of various kinds to bureaucratic supremacy. A bureau-shaping strategy (Dunleavy 1991) of the administrative elite was the prime mover of past reforms that were packaged as managerial changes for better government but served mainly to respond to political challenges to colonial rule at the time (Cheung 1999). For example, the 1967 pro-communist riots and the elite mass gaps thus revealed induced the colonial administration to modernize the government under the McKinsey reform of the 1970s. The 1970s social protest movements exposing the accountability crisis of the government drove the government to provide better points of coordination of public services at the local level through the 1980 district administration scheme. More recently, the political transition in 1997 partly prompted the reconfiguration of governance through public sector reform. Political factors created the need and room for changes which had to take the form of management reform, because the same politics had also imposed constraints on institutional choice. Civil service reform after 1997 can be conceived within a similar administrative reform paradigm. Such an understanding of the political agenda of administrative reform pursued by the bureaucratic elite to strengthen its crisis-weathering capacity, is to some extent corroborated by accusations in some quarters, particularly the staff unions, that the current civil service reform is an exercise targeted at the bottom rather than the top. There is strong rank-and-file suspicion that the administrative mandarinate is sacrificing its subordinates in order to contain the damage of its political crisis.

Singapore[12]

Public sector reforms and Public Service 21: strengthening the public sector and state leadership

Since the early 1990s, the Singapore Government has been engaging in a series of reforms of the public sector. New initiatives include: budgetary and institutional reforms in the form of budgetary devolution, 'budgeting for results' (1994), creation of self-accounting 'autonomous agencies' (1997) and 'zero-based reviews'; privatization, corporatization and contracting out; personnel management reforms; client-orientedness and the appointment of 'service quality managers' in all ministries (1991) (Jones 1999).

In May 1995, a programme known as 'Public Service for the 21st Century' was launched, with an aim to nurture an attitude of service excellence and to foster an environment which induces and welcomes continuous change for greater efficiency and effectiveness (PS21 Office undated). Known as PS21 for short, the new programme has since symbolized the government's overall efforts to reorientate the culture and outlook of the civil service and public organizations. Four elements are highlighted:

- *staff well-being* – seeking to develop a sense of self-worth through responsibility and achievement in tasks among civil servants, commensurate with their potential and through competitive employment terms *vis-à-vis* the private sector;
- *ExCEL (Excellence through Continuous Enterprise and Learning)* – mainly through Work Improvement Teams and Staff Suggestions Schemes, with the target that by the year 2000 every public officer should spend not less than 100 hours of annual working time on training;
- *organizational review* – introducing management-driven strategic multi-agency change (notably corporatization and the establishment of 'autonomous agencies') as well as dealing with inter-unit procedural bottlenecks; and
- *quality service* – promoting courtesy, accessibility, responsiveness and effectiveness, or CARE, in the delivery of public service, to meet rising public expectations and to maintain competitiveness.

Since 1959, when it attained self-government, Singapore has had a long tradition of administrative reforms in search of meritocratic excellence. Quah (2000: 6) identified five main features of these reforms: meritocracy; clean government; comprehensive administrative reform; competitive pay for senior public officials; and policy diffusion. The concern for attracting 'the best and the brightest' to join public service should be seen against the background at the time of decolonization when the colonial administration was regarded as corrupt and incompetent and when Singapore was wrought with poverty and all kinds of social turmoil. The ruling People's Action Party's (PAP) belief in strong government was associated with an emphasis on rule by the brightest, which Vogel (1989: 1053) described as 'macho-meritocracy'.

Given the central position occupied by the civil service in its strategy for meritocratic elite rule, the PAP government has never been shy of paying civil servants well, and not in any way denigrating them even during economic setbacks as, for example, seen in OECD countries during the 1980s when 'big government' and the bureaucracy were blamed for inefficiency and fiscal deficits. Indeed, the 1994 White Paper on *Competitive Salaries for Competent and Honest Government* linked salaries of ministers and senior civil servants to the top earners in major private sector professions. It is clear the government would not allow the civil service to lose the best talent to the private sector.

PS21 is not a reform agenda imposed on the civil service by PAP ministers. It was initiated by the permanent secretaries as a self-improvement programme to face external uncertainties and public expectations better. According to Lim Siong Guan (1996), who was the main driving force behind the reform in 1995 as one of the permanent secretaries and is now Head of the Civil Service, the 'vibrations of change have not touched all levels of the Public Service nor are its full ramifications widely understood.' An important reason why this was so, in his view, related to the fact that 'it is basically a change about change – not a change to a specific final state but an acceptance of the need for change as a permanent state' (Lim 1996). He went on to elaborate why such a change about change is essential:

> Singapore has succeeded because of clean and effective government, free of corruption, meritocratic, efficient and responsive, fair and impartial, able to offer Singaporeans continuous improvement in their quality of life with economic progress and a safe and secure environment. ...
>
> These characteristics will continue to be important in Singapore life. They form the fundamentals of good governance. The question is whether they are adequate formulas for the future, a future of greater complexity, exploding information flows, much less predictability and shorter reaction times.
>
> ... Singaporeans must strive to be good thinkers, conceptualists and entrepreneurs, and not succeed only because we are fast learners, careful followers and diligent workers. The Public Service must move in this direction too.
>
> (Lim 1996)

While acknowledging the need to be responsive to two particular developments of the twenty-first century, namely a public that is increasingly demanding higher standards of service, and an economy that is increasingly outward oriented, Lim saw the role of the public service not only in terms of changing in step with developments in Singapore society and the international environment, but also moving ahead 'to point [to] and lead the way forward, create and facilitate programmes for national growth, and be a model for efficiency, innovation and service quality' (Lim: 1996). The content of PS21 may look much alike other public sector reform initiatives elsewhere, as Lim too admitted that 'maybe [there is] nothing much [special about it] if you read all the management books about change' (Lim 1996), but the agenda-setting context of reform in Singapore is different from some other countries. In countries such as in OECD, the failure of the state and the overgrowth of the public sector are some of the major reasons for streamlining and reform. PS21 is less about downsizing but more about changing the mindset of the Singapore state, to 'overlay the role of a facilitator and nurturer upon a Public Service whose traditional role is that of regulator and controller' (Lim 1996). Therefore the reform has not sought to reduce the role and importance of the state as such, but rather to maintain the same strong administrative state by means of refining its role so as to keep in step with the latest developments and future challenges.

PS21 as a bureaucratic agenda for excellence: a reverse logic to NPM

PS21 does put some emphasis on learning from the ideas and lessons of successful private sector corporations, such as their management approaches, their customer orientedness, their productivity standards and their drive to excel. But its fundamental concept is not simply to keep up with the private sector. Its intent is to be 'at the head of the pack in seeking continuous improvement and innovation', so much so that the public service will become a catalyst for change, a standard bearer, and a pacesetter (Lim 1996). Hence unlike some NPM rhetoric which contains an implicit denigration of public sector effectiveness, thus advocating privatization and contracting out, Singapore's reform instead seeks to maintain and further strengthen the public service as a leading institution of meritocratic excellence.

Because of such strategic goals within the broad frame of governance, PS21 has taken up objectives which are somewhat beyond, if not in sharp contrast to, a typical NPM agenda. NPM is commonly associated with the private management model, 'managerialism' (Pollitt 1993) and 'entrepreneurial' government (Osborne and Gaebler 1993). Although it has a similar emphasis on learning from successful private sector companies and indeed encompasses specific devolutionary management measures such as budgetary devolution to ministries and the setting up of 'autonomous agencies', similar to the British 'Next Steps' agency concept, PS21 is ultimately about state leadership rather than public management.

Writing in 1998, after he assumed the office of permanent secretary in the Prime Minister's Office (and thus Head of the Civil Service), Lim Siong Guan took PS21 to a higher and more visionary plane. As he put it, the aim of reform in public service is to transform it 'from reactivity to proactivity, [and] from a satisfaction with the present to a questioning of the future' (Lim 1998: 128). His emphasis for PS21 was placed on:

- potential rather than performance;

- process rather than results;
- coordinated vision rather than coordinated action;
- most for input rather than least for output; and
- leadership rather than management (Lim 1998: 128–131).

The crux of reform is promoting innovation and creativity, rewarding potential (through promotion) and facilitating change (such as through scenario-based planning), vision and commitment. To achieve these objectives, excellence in management functions is not enough. Public service requires aspiring and anticipatory leaders with a broad strategic mindset. Reform helps to ensure that the public sector is not weakened or assigned to second place *vis-à-vis* the private sector, as is often implied by NPM rhetoric elsewhere. It also extends beyond the more mundane concerns for output measurement and efficiency emphasized by a managerialist articulation of NPM. Lim summed it best when he said: 'While a Public Service can keep on going with mediocre leadership, if it aspires to be first class, it requires superior leadership' (Lim 1998: 130).

Thus, the 1994 White Paper on *Competitive Salaries for Competent and Honest Government* aimed to prevent any brain drain from the civil service to the private sector. Not only that, the civil service, through reform, geared itself up for attracting more talent into government. Measures such as the introduction of a Dual Career Scheme and the opening up of the Administrative Service to lateral recruitment from the private sector aimed to ensure 'the incorporation of some of the best of national talent into the Government' (Lim 1998: 131). At the same time, all top public sector jobs, including chairmanship, CEO and directorship positions in government-linked corporations (GLCs), as well as ambassadorships, were in principle open to assignment of Administrative Service officers (Lim 1996). As a result, the 'administrative' core of the meritocratic bureaucracy is to be further strengthened in providing state leadership and direction to the economy and the rest of society.

From PS21 to S21: governance reform for national building and reinventing the developmental state

PS21 is clearly a reform initiative to promote a capable, innovative and forward-looking public sector. Many of its measures are not dissimilar to reform initiatives launched elsewhere. However, simply regarding PS21 as indication of yet another country's conversion to the newly fashionable global faith of NPM is to miss the domestic significance of the reform and its ramifications for the PAP's governance over the changing society and economy of Singapore. The reform should be appraised within the context of Singapore's evolving system of state-directed economic and social development. Similar to the Hong Kong case, Singapore's PS21 was not introduced at times of fiscal difficulties or an overloaded government, as in the OECD experience. Rather, it marked the continuing efforts of a pro-active and pre-emptive state in steering society and enterprises (public and private) forward, to face what the state leadership perceives as the new century's challenges to the survival and prosperity of the nation and to take advantage of opportunities presented by globalization. Indeed, following PS21, which apparently gives a forward-looking horizon, the PAP government has come up with a political agenda known as S21 – Singapore 21 – in April 1999. To such an extent, PS21 is but part of the government leadership elite's renewed nation-building agenda.

Such an agenda is evident in the thinking of the second-generation political leaders, such as elder statesman Lee Kuan Yew's son Deputy Prime Minister Lee Hsien Loong. Unlike the elder Lee's first generation PAP leadership, who put economic growth first in their governance strategy, the second-generation leaders are relatively more sensitive to the changing political demands of the population. Prime Minister Goh Chok Tong, who bridges between the founding generation and second-generation leadership, has advocated a 'gentler and kinder' kind of governance by confronting the dilemma. As he put it: 'How paternalistic should we be, and how much room can we give to the people?' (*Straits Times* 18 December 1998). In order to enable the country to be a robust economy and society, the new generation PAP leaders see a strong government with 'intellectual leadership' and 'moral authority' as crucial, so that the government can set the national agenda by the force of its arguments and the success of its policies (Lee 1998: 7). Ultimately the goal of governance reform, incorporating public service reform, is about strengthening and institutionalizing such good leadership, built upon the 'combination of a vibrant civil society and strong government' (Lee 1998: 7). Such governance renewal process is at the centre of S21 which emphasized forming the 'heartware' of the twenty-first century by confronting major dilemmas facing the nation (*Straits Times* 7 March 1998).

Addressing some of the dilemmas, S21 recognized that Singaporeans want to have a bigger say in national decisions, and that there is a need for more consultation and consensus building, although these should not hamper the government's ability to act quickly and decisively. The civil service is also expected to be more receptive to ideas and suggestions. The ultimate goal is to cater to the social cohesion and identity building amidst the changing Singapore social landscape, by dealing with issues of public dissatisfaction, alienation and participation, hoping to nurture a relatively more 'active citizenry'.[13]

Public service and governance reforms in Singapore relate further to the context of the Singapore 'developmental state' striving to reinvent itself in light of changes brought about by globalization challenges. Globalization may be seen by some as helping to break down national barriers and to give added impetus to a borderless global market order, thus reducing the influence of national governments and policies. It can alternatively prompt a resilient developmental state into re-articulation of the state–economy configuration. As Low argues:

> Economic globalization can be a political basis for new kinds of state intervention or re-articulation of the state. Existing institutions and policies are challenged by perception, expectation and uncertainty of the future.

Systemic failures, greater interdependence and contagion effects as in the Asian crisis have further legitimized strategic trade, investment policies and industrial policies. These created a new rationale for state intervention, designing domestic architectures of supply in critical technologies, enabling domestic firms and MNCs to compete effectively in global markets.

(Low 2000)

Even Hong Kong, long held by some Western free market economies to be the bastion of *laissez-faire* capitalism, has increased state interventions lately because of both domestic political reasons and the impact of global economic change and the Asian crisis (Cheung 2000a).

The calls for a more creative and active citizenry are also partly in response to a more stable and affluent middle-class population's demands for participation and responsive governance, and partly to nurture the kind of creative, innovative and risk-taking society that can support and sustain a knowledge-based economy. Prime Minister Goh Chok Tong's 'kinder and gentler' governance agenda is therefore premised on domestic needs as well as global changes. However, it seems clear there is no retraction of the dominant state manager role in the economic governance of the nation, not to mention its political governance that is still under firm PAP control.

PS21, as a major administrative reform programme to strengthen institutional capacity for innovation and leadership and to alter attitudes towards change, is part and parcel of the larger state-managed project (encompassing S21) to reinvent the Singapore development corporate state, so as to maintain the same old state–economy complex under a strong government leadership that is both proactive and pre-emptive in the face of changes in the domestic and global environments. Instead of challenging and weakening that strong developmental state, globalization and the Asian financial crisis seem to have legitimized those strategic moves made by the PAP government to reinvent the structure of interventions and indeed to create a new agenda and rationale for reinvented state-directed political, administrative and economic governance.

China

Administrative reform in place of political reform: politics still taking command

In China, reforms of the government and state sectors (including state-owned enterprises) have been implemented as part of its post-Mao economic system reform-seeking to transform a previously state command economy into a socialist market economy. Three phases can be identified according to Zhang (1997).[14] In the first phase, from 1978 to 1987, old administrative units were gradually dismantled (such as the people's communes), government organizations were streamlined and some experimental changes were introduced to the cadre personnel management system (such as limited open recruitment and the elimination of the *de facto* system of life tenure system for leading cadres). In the second phase, from 1987 to 1992, administrative reforms mainly involved government organization restructuring at the central level centring around the transformation of government functions, and a more fundamental reform of the cadre personnel management system resulting in the introduction of the state civil service in government at all levels. The current phase of reforms, beginning in 1992, covers the nationwide governmental restructuring entailing the transformation of government functions, rationalization of relationships with enterprises and service and civic units, streamlining of administration, promotion of work efficiency, introduction of tax-sharing system as part of public finance and budgeting reforms and the reform of local-central government relations. In most of these reforms, the impact of politics has been very much felt whether in the design or implementation of reform measures.

The first comprehensive programme of cadre system reform[15] was officially unveiled at the thirteenth Chinese Communist Party Congress in 1987 by the then General Secretary Zhao Zhiyang in his major address to the Congress (Zhao 1987; Burns 1989). Its fate is a good illustration of the politics of reform in the China context. Zhao originally proposed a new state civil service system that would divide between two layers – an upper 'political officers' category and a subordinate 'professional officers' category. The former referred to elected officials nominated by the Communist Party and appointed by the appropriate state authorities (i.e. the national and provincial people's congresses) as stipulated by the Constitution and legal statutes. In contrast, the professional officers were to be recruited on the basis of merit and regulated according to civil service law. Similar to civil servants in liberal democracies, they would enjoy permanent tenure and be subject to performance appraisal and retirement requirements. Other pertinent features of cadre system reform included:

- the *institutionalization* of the selection, recruitment, appointment, dismissal, appraisal, punishment, rotation, training, resignation and retirement of cadres;
- the establishment of *laws and regulations* to regulate and monitor the exercise of personnel authorities and the implementation of various procedures;
- the *redefinition of the leadership role of the Party* whereby such a role would be played out over macro-personnel policies and systemic design only, rather than in day-to-day operational control and supervision functions which should rest with the government's Ministry of Personnel; and
- the *disaggregation* of the cadre system through scientific classification into different institutional and functional sectors, separating party organs and military establishments from the state sector, separating state agencies and enterprises, and delineating clearly job categories, levels and ranks with associated qualification requirements and reward stipulations (Cheung 1996c).

Zhao's 1987 proposal to differentiate between political and professional officers followed a broader reform strategy mooted at the time to separate the state and the Party. However, as events unfolded, the resistance of party elders to give up political control over the state had proved to be insurmountable. As Lam and Chan (1995) pointed out, the politics of civil service reform in China were very much shaped by the structure of power and institutional arrangements at the upper echelons of the Communist Party. Not only was reform constrained by the party leaders' concern to maintain unchallenged control over the changes and their outcome, it had also to compete for scarce leadership attention and political blessing. The less favourable political climate following the Tiananmen crackdown on the pro-democracy movement in 1989 transformed the scene of the 1990s. It resulted in toning down the political dimension of reform even though the managerial aspect has remained on the national agenda (Jiang, Z. 1992: 37–8) mainly in terms of government downsizing and restructuring and the establishment of the state civil service system. Political reform has since disappeared in official statements and reports, and political reformers have to camouflage their project with the rhetoric of management reform.

The Provisional Regulations on the State Civil Service promulgated in August 1993 marked the advent of a new modernized civil service regime which puts merit and efficiency as its foremost institutional goals, alongside political loyalty to the Communist Party (State Council 1993). However, the dichotomy between political and professional officers as originally envisaged has been replaced by the division between 'leadership' and 'non-leadership' positions (Clause 9 of the Provisional Regulations). In essence, the principle of 'party-managing cadres' has persisted, although it can be argued that given the new political landscape of the economic reform era, the actual powers of party committees have become less all-embracing than in the old 'commissar' days. Despite the emphasis on 'management by categories' (Chan 1998: 83–4), the Party still exercises political control of appointment under the *nomenklatura* principle inherited from the Soviet model.[16]

The salience of civil service reform in China lies in its pursuit of efficiency and rationality, as most provisions of the Provisional Regulations are concerned about. Such a reform attempt, put into an international perspective, could be seen as similar to the global administrative reforms of the 1980s and 1990s to 'debureaucratize' state organizations in order to enhance institutional competence (e.g. Caiden 1988). However, in another sense, civil service reform in China can be construed as a process of 'rebureaucratization' because it represents a transformation of the administrative machinery from one previously dominated by revolutionary cadres into a bureaucracy closer to the rational–meritocratic Weberian model. Indeed, the emphasis of reform is on job regulation and classification. The reform is not intended to bring about the depoliticization of the bureaucracy. Quite the opposite, civil servants are still required to be a loyal arm of the Communist Party. The new state civil service system 'with Chinese characteristics' therefore constitutes an uneasy marriage of two divergent organizational logics – the still Leninist notion of socialist cadreship and the Weberian notion of bureaucratic rationality. Politics thus continue to dominate the newly reinvented and re-managerialized institution of state functionaries.

Wage system reform: rational goal and irrational outcome

In tandem with civil service reform, the first major overhaul of the cadre wage system took place in 1985 with the introduction of the *'structural wage system'* comprising basic salary, post pay, seniority pay and bonus payments. The recognition of differentiation in functions and thus post pay was to help promote the principle of 'pay according to work'. In practice this had resulted in irrational organizational expansion through the creation of new and higher-paid positions by agencies hoping to secure for their staff a larger post pay income. The problem was, in the absence of a mechanism to enable basic salary to be adjusted in line with inflation, wages had fallen behind the rising living cost, leaving job promotions and agency upgrading as the only institutional means for cadres to access higher wages. The 1985 wage reform was supposed to facilitate the agency structuring reform of 1982 that sought to reduce the number of agencies and organs and to streamline their personnel establishment so as to rein in overall fiscal spending. In effect it had worked in the reverse direction of encouraging agencies to upgrade and expand in order to open up new positions that could attract budgetary resources from the state.

After the formal launch of the state civil service system in 1993, a new wage system known as 'post and grade wage system' was introduced comprising four elements: basic pay, post pay, grade pay and seniority pay. With more differentiation in post and grade classifications, rank-and-file civil servants at the bottom of the job ladder were now given more room for salary increase according to grade level and post pay scales than senior level staff. Cadres could also enjoy regular wage rises in post pay after passing evaluation tests, in addition to biennial general pay level adjustments for all cadres to catch up with inflation and the rising wage level of enterprise employees.[17]

Despite the state's 'efficiency' objectives to achieve greater differentiation and progressivity, wage reform as implemented have created opposite results (Cheung and Poon 2001). For example, wage differentials between the highest- and lowest-rank cadres in effect have narrowed – from 22.8:1 in 1956 to 10.2:1 in 1985, then to 6.1:1 in 1993. Because of the encouragement to local governments to pay cadres at the work unit level supplementary wages out of local extra-budgetary resources, pay egalitarianism has been revived in a disguised way. Local wage subsidies now take up a substantial part of cadres' take-home pay (up to seventy per cent in some southern localities) and tend to be distributed by local managers in an egalitarian pattern. Such unexpected consequences are an outcome of the institutional-negotiative nature of reform implementation in the China context, involving the articulation of a delicate policy balance among major stakeholders (central policymakers, local officials and managers, and rank-and-file cadres) each seeking to optimize three rationalities – economic, bureaucratic and social distributional (Cheung and Poon 2001).

Restructuring and downsizing the state sector: 'temples cannot be demolished if Buddhas cannot be put away'

The implementation of civil service reform goes hand in hand with the structural reforms of government agencies. In theory, streamlining and cutting down the size of the cadre bureaucracy can help to release the fiscal resources to pay remaining cadres more, hence helping to attract and retain talent as well as to reduce the risk of official corruption. However, downsizing is constrained by a separate institutional logic and contingent upon the economic conditions. Despite the official emphasis on the 'three determinations' (standing) principles – i.e. 'first determine the function, then determine the structure, finally determine the staff establishment' – structural streamlining has been a most difficult task because of the lack of outlet for staff to be made redundant. As a Chinese saying goes, 'if you can't put away the Buddhas, neither can you abolish the temple!' If civil service reform can bring about a lean but efficient workforce, this should also facilitate agency restructuring; but restructuring cannot proceed much further if downsizing the workforce is made difficult by organizational dynamics and unfavourable economic circumstances.

In fact, downsizing, or 'agency restructuring' in official parlance, has been an ongoing concern ever since the founding of the People's Republic in 1949. Downsizing exercises were mostly politically motivated as Chan observed:

> Downsizing overhauls in China can be perceived of as attempts in adjusting the extent of functional integration or differentiation of the state organs of the central government in relation to the remainder of the body politic. Institutionalization of the state is the tool employed to deal with the problem of political erosion of administrative authority in China.
>
> (Chan 1999: 306)

A feature of China's downsizing history is the so-called vicious cycle of 'streamlining–swelling–streamlining–swelling' resulting from the restructuring of the central government and the decentralization of functions to subnational governments, followed by new waves of recentralization based on political needs and further rounds of extension and swelling of the central bureaucracy. In the past downsizing had not worked because there was no outlet for cadres whose employment was state responsibility. What happened was that when the central ministries were cut down, their cadres simply were downloaded to the provincial and then county level, thus swelling the bottom. Then the centre became suspicious of rising localism and concerned about losing control, and delegated functions were clawed back from below together with the large number of cadres, thus swelling the top again. The cycle repeated itself throughout the decades with each round of swelling resulting in a more bloated bureaucracy because of the cadre system having to accommodate more school leavers dependent on state employment.

The current round of downsizing and government restructuring promoted by Premier Zhu Rongji since March 1998 has underlined the government's overall strategy to redefine the state and its capacity in the new era of market economy. The changes entail not just the downsizing of the state bureaucracy and restructuring of the government hierarchy in the general sense, as most fiscally stricken governments are now doing in other countries, but also a reformulation of state–economy and state–society relations – including reforms of state-owned enterprises (SOEs), the commodification and privatization of housing and healthcare, and the introduction of new contributory social security schemes to replace the previous workunit-based welfare. The leaders' attempt is to create a leaner but stronger state that is capable of steering economic development and nation-building.

However, the unchanged nature of China's highly authoritarian party state also means that there is a 'political' limit to the extent of administrative reforms. The process of administrative reforms is also contingent upon micro-politics at the local level of the workunit. The traditional system of workunit-based life-long employment and welfare had meant not just workforce immobility, but also a system of organized dependence, as Walder (1986) described it, whereby there was high fusion of workunits' and cadres' interests in both the economic and political senses. The current restructuring exercise seeks to downsize government agencies (by fifty per cent in three years according to Premier Zhu's stated target in early 1998) and to take welfare responsibilities away from the workunit, in a process of so-called 'societalization' (*shehuihua*).[18] This obviously carries the potential of threatening the entrenched interests of workunits and cadres alike, triggering incessant institutional negotiations in the formulation and actual implementation of reform measures.

Zhu's downsizing target is overly ambitious, and might just be achieved at the central government level – involving the reduction of the number of ministries, commissions and agencies by twenty-two to twenty-nine in 1998 – by downgrading and amalgamating some ministerial agencies. The structural streamlining exercise followed the principles of separating government and enterprises and of government retaining only macro-economic coordination and steering functions. However, the efficacy of such a restructuring process when extended to lower governmental levels remains to be seen. What sometimes happens is that while local governments are quite prepared to surrender functions involving expenditure responsibility (such as giving up education and healthcare services to the private sector in the name of societalization), they are keen to retain and take upon themselves regulatory functions which give them greater opportunity to impose all kinds of fees and penalties on enterprises, as a source of extra-budgetary revenue to support their bloated bureaucracy.

With civil servants staffing the central government agencies accounting for only less than ten per cent of the 5.3 million-strong state bureaucracy nationwide, any cadres displaced by downsizing at the national government level can easily be redeployed to and absorbed by subnational governments. However, as the spillover effect trickles downwards, there is a limit to how far downsizing can work, particularly if the economy is not performing sufficiently well to create the necessary re-employment opportunities in the private sector. Sometimes the official staff establishment might have been reduced according to central directives, but local authorities would try unofficial ways to accommodate the displaced cadres, such as coercing enterprises or creating quasi-government units to take them on board. The room for institutional choice in reform is thus bound by national, local and workunit politics. The actual impact of reform implementation is usually much less than the leaders' reform rhetoric claims.

Paradox of state sector reforms: central policies versus local politics and decentralization versus restrengthening central state capacity

In the post-Mao era, reforms can easily be perceived as part of a process of breaking up top-down state monopoly, marketization and privatization (Prybyla 1990). Recent initiatives in decentralization, downsizing, civil service institutional and wage reforms, SOE reforms, budgetary and fiscal devolution, and the whole range of policy reforms in housing, health care and social security, such as those recommended by the World Bank in its *China 2020 Reports* series (World Bank 1997), seem to smack of the influence of global privatization and NPM trends. However, it would be over-simplistic to interpret these reforms within a linear debureaucratization and destatization paradigm. Quite the contrary, the assertion and reimposition of state power have persistently been a central concern throughout various aspects of reform. Although the reforms by and large have sought to confine the growth and extension of the previous Leninist party-state, the power of the state was never intended to be belittled.

Under the communist logic of governance, the supremacy of the party state rule is not to be challenged. The state constitution requires adherence to the 'Four Cardinal Principles', one of which is to follow the leadership of the Chinese Communist Party. With the fundamental party state structure remaining intact, political powers are configured through the evolving patterns of distribution of state functions, resources and policy powers, and central–local interactions. Administrative and management changes are frequently pursued to articulate and deal with political conflict and differences. Political conflicts often result in intra-structural changes taking the form of reorganization of agencies and inter-governmental relations (between national, provincial and other local levels), transfer of powers and functions within the state hierarchy, and rearrangements in personnel systems and practices. Administrative reforms have always been some kind of political reshuffling in disguise. Given the feature that the whole country had been organized as a cadre hierarchy with every citizen attached to a state-owned workunit until recently, changes in organizational and personnel arrangements are bound to result in interest dislocation and political conflict, often wrapped in ideological and sometimes even revolutionary rhetoric.

The advent of economic reform has caused gradual but lasting changes to the power landscape, but it has not essentially altered the 'politicalness' of reform at both the national policy level and the organizational/workplace level. Intense politics are frequently observed in apparently rational and innocent reforms of a managerial nature. Because of the imperative to maintain Party control and the myth of state socialism which still assumes the ultimate responsibility for people's employment and welfare, reforms are very often pursued in a paradoxical manner – letting go of functions, powers, resources and responsibilities on the one hand, and trying to recoup control and direction on the other. As a result, a zigzagging process of control–decontrol and devolution–recentralization can be observed throughout various administrative reforms. Privatization and marketization go hand in hand with the assertion and restrengthening of state capacity. Unintended outcomes quite contrary to reform objectives arise from time to time, partly as a result of such paradoxical policy implementation, and partly s a result of the intense intra-bureaucratic institutional bargaining underpinning all reform exercises. In the process the real 'rules of the game' are defined and reshaped on the ground.

China has certainly become a more complex and, to some extent, disaggregated polity following the advent of economic and administrative reforms in the past two decades. The redefinition of the role of the Communist Party in government, the withdrawal of government from micro-economic management, the corporatization of SOEs, and an increasing degree of decentralization in both the state and the economy have all contributed to a significant reconfiguration of governance. As a result, 'it has become increasingly possible during the reform era to distinguish different institutional and political 'centres', or at least parts of the centre' (Goodman 2000).

Such differentiation and disaggregation are not unidirectional. As the central state decentralizes and downsizes, it is very much conscious of the political risks involved in terms of weakening state capacity and creating provincial 'feudal lords' that might accumulate enough economic and political resources to defy central policies. Administrative reforms returning incentives to the local government and enterprise levels have certainly contributed to economic development. Fiscal devolution of the 1980s, for example, has seen extra-budgetary funds generated by local economic activities becoming an increasingly important part of local governments' fiscal capacity, to help underwrite development expenditure. However, decentralization has also bred local protectionism, so that tensions continue to exist whereby the centre tries hard to strike an organizational balance between an over-controlled hierarchy and excessive localism, the same institutional dilemma that had underscored the cycle of 'decentralization–swelling–decentralization–swelling' prevalent in past administrative history.

Again using fiscal devolution as illustration, the 1980s saw the haphazard and uncoordinated manner in which the old highly centralized fiscal system was allowed to break down, whereby the central government devolved fiscal responsibilities to lower levels largely as a strategy of load-shedding, resulting in the 'contracting-out' of service responsibilities and related revenue collection powers to the localities.[19] In the process of load-shedding, and accommodating the stress thus imposed on local budgets, the central government has tolerated and even encouraged local governments to seek 'self-reliant' solutions that have resulted, over time, in the present situation where resources allocated by government (at all levels) *outside* the budget far exceed those on-budget (Wong 1998, 1999).[20] By now, putting things back to normal within the official budget is financially difficult and politically contentious.

The irony of China's present fiscal system is that while the tax burden on paper remains one of the lowest in the world and on the decline – from 15.17 per cent of GNP in 1990 to 11.01 per cent in 1997 (State Administration for Statistics 1999) – causing persistent state budget deficits and the continued weakening of the state's fiscal capacity, the real fiscal burden falling on citizens is actually on the rise and creating local resentment. The crux of the matter is that local governments have been allowed over the years to impose all kinds of fees and charges to the extent that there is a phenomena of 'fees higher than tax' and 'fees displacing tax' (Liang 1999). Sometimes, the state has to grant cheap loans to, or even to bail out, inefficient SOEs and service organizations for the sake of 'stability and solidarity' (Liang 1999: 19).[21] At the same time the state's taxation regime is becoming fragmented and under-regulated, resulting in inefficient tax collection and serious tax loss.

While decentralization has certainly facilitated China's rapid opening up and economic development, it has also resulted in widening regional disparities and social instability, because of unequal pre-existing economic infrastructural endowment and unequal opportunities for accessing foreign trade and investment. There is constant concern about a state capacity crisis looming which cuts down the state's ability and resources to curb unbalanced growth by means of resources injection to poorer areas (as lately exemplified by the call for a 'Look West' policy to attract investment in inner western provinces, directives to forge more inward trickling down of opportunities and inter-governmental fiscal transfers). As Vice Minister of Personnel Zhang Zhijian put it in 1997: 'the purpose of reform is to promote development, and to maintain political and social stability is the fundamental prerequisite for pushing forward reform and development. The reform of the administrative system is an undertaking with risks. It calls for high attention to political and social stability' (Zhang 1997: 136).

Since the 1990s, there have been repeated calls for restrengthening the central state capacity, partly to curb excessive local protectionism and partly to maintain strong national policy leadership. In a sense, government restructuring can also be seen as a means to streamline the central government hierarchy and its steering functions so that the state's capacity to monitor and direct the nation and subordinate governments can in fact be enhanced without carrying with it the burden of micro-economic and state welfare responsibilities as in the old socialist central-planning days.

Conclusion

Public sector reforms in Hong Kong and Singapore over the past one to two decades have clearly exhibited reform features, terminology and techniques which look similar to many reform initiatives implemented by OECD countries under the umbrella of a NPM paradigm. In China, reforms were originally driven by the ruling party's objectives to restructure the economy and to put in place a modern administration that is more compatible with the new market economy. More recently, resulting from greater international networking, some of the reforms have been given added impetus and flavour by the global NPM boom (e.g. in terms of government reinvention, downsizing, and privatization of state-owned enterprises) and the influence of international organizations such as the World Bank.

However, this is as much as the global reform trends achieve in terms of impact. The context of reform and its real politics remain wholly determined by domestic conditions as well as the motives and interests of internal policy actors and stakeholders. As the discussion in this chapter shows, the reform experience of the three important East Asian economies, although rooted in different social and political systems, has all pointed to the influence of both societal and intra-bureaucratic *politics*, as well as the strategic choice and political agenda of state managers (whether they be political elites or senior administrative mandarins). Such institutional and political dynamics are seen to have directed, shaped, and at the same time constrained, the process and consequences of reform. Managerial notions of efficiency, merit and downsizing are clearly visible in all the reforms, but only insofar as to support the programmes that ultimately aim at reconstituting, restrengthening and re-legitimating state power and capacity rather than diluting them as some 'privatization' and NPM literature portrayed the objectives of public sector reform of the 1980s and 1990s. This is natural since administrative reforms are ultimately state projects socially and politically embedded in national contexts. East Asian countries, in particular, are still very much state-centred jurisdictions one way or the other, which tend to conceive reforms in state capacity terms.

In Hong Kong, public sector reforms serve to redefine state–society interaction within the context of public policy and public service provision, and to re-configure institutional relationships within the public sector hierarchy. Their ultimate significance lies in the empowerment of the capacity of the administrative elite which is facing a crisis of legitimacy and political challenges to its powers of governance. Similarly in Singapore, both the PAP political leadership and the administrative elite within the civil service seek to reform the public sector to make it better positioned to lead the nation-building process within a new knowledge era, amidst a more demanding population and facing an increasingly competitive economic environment both regionally and internationally. Public sector reforms then are means towards the same end that previous modes of organizing the state bureaucracy had served.

In the case of China, administrative reforms have promoted the reinvention and rebureaucratization of the cadre system along modernized lines, the restructuring of state functions, as well as the decentralization and devolution of powers. But this is not just for the sake of load shedding or catching up with the world trends. Reforms are ultimately geared towards preparing the still politically centralized and authoritarian Communist Party state for coping better with its governance in a marketized and increasingly fragmentary environment where localism is on the rise to become both an impetus for and constraint on change. In all three jurisdictions, politics seem to matter more than management in the reform agenda and reform implementation.

Notes

1 This chapter partly draws upon information obtained in three research projects: *The Politics of China's Civil Service Reform: Issues of Transition and Implementation* (funded by the Hong Kong Research Grants Council), *Governance and Public Sector Reform in Asia* and *The Politics of Privatization of State-Owned Enterprises in China: Competing Policy Goals and Institutional Bargaining* (both funded by the City University of Hong Kong). The funding bodies' support to the author and his research collaborators in these projects is gratefully acknowledged.
2 Derry Ormond, Head of Public Management Service (PUMA) of OECD.
3 Song Defu, Minister of Personnel delivered the opening address to the Third International Conference of Administrative Sciences held in Beijing in October 1996.
4 The theme of the EROPA (Eastern Regional Organization for Public Administration) Conference held in Beijing in October 1991 was 'Administrative Reform towards Promoting Productivity in Bureaucratic Performance'. The theme of the Third International Conference of Administrative Sciences held in Beijing in October 1996 was 'New Challenges for Public Administration in the 21st Century: Efficient Civil Service and Decentralized Public Administration'.
5 For the purpose of this chapter, developments in China refer only to those taking place in the mainland and do not cover the Hong Kong Special Administrative Region, which enjoys different political, economic and social systems within the constitutional framework of 'one country two systems'.
6 Hong Kong became a special administrative region of the People's Republic of China on 1 July 1997, being granted administrative autonomy in all matters except foreign and defence matters under its Basic Law.
7 Following McKinsey's recommendations, the Government Secretariat was reorganized into high-powered 'resource branches' which oversaw manpower and financial resource allocation, and 'policy branches' which oversaw policy formulation. However, the role of policy secretaries had remained largely ambiguous until public sector reform in 1989, exercising only a coordinating function over departments instead of establishing a clear line supervision relationship. The McKinsey reform marked the first step of 'ministerialization' of administrative mandarins who headed policy branches (see detailed discussion in Cheung 1999).
8 'Branches' have been renamed 'Bureaus' by the SAR government since July 1997.
9 Departing British Governor Chris Patten cited 'Is Hong Kong's civil service still professional and meritocratic?' as the top one of his 16 benchmarks for assessing Hong Kong's success as China's SAR, in his final policy address in October 1996 (Patten 1996: para. 89).

10 For details of the reform and its evaluation, see this author's discussion in Cheung (2001).

11 On 1 July 2000, the third anniversary of the establishment of Special Administrative Region under Chinese rule, there were massive protests against Chief Executive Tung Chee-hwa's administration. Protesters came from various sectors: teachers who were against some elements of education reform, social workers who were critical of the new lump-sum subvention system for social service agencies, public doctors who opposed to restructuring proposals, civil servants who opposed civil service reform and privatizations, students who demanded for more democracy and homeowners suffering negative equity after the property slump.

12 For a more detailed discussion of public service reform in Singapore, please refer to this author's chapter 'Public Service Reform in Singapore: Reinventing Government in a Global Age.' In Cheung, A.B.L. and Scott, I. (eds) *Governance and Public Sector Reform In Asia: Paradigm Shift or Business as Usual?* Surrey: Curzon Press (2002, forthcoming).

13 In the words of the editorial of *Straits Times*, 30 April 1999, 'The challenge of an active citizenry'.

14 Zhang Zhijian, Vice Minister of Personnel and Vice Head, General Office of the Central Organization and Establishment Committee, China.

15 Strictly speaking, no 'civil service' in the sense of the term commonly used in modern government (to denote a politically neutral government workforce divorced from the politicians segment of government) existed in China after 1949 when the People's Republic of China was founded. The whole nation became part of the party state cadre system under tight party control. There is thus no civil service system as such which is to be reformed. What is taking place in China nowadays is in effect a reform of the traditional cadre system to bring in some features resembling those of a civil service system.

16 This refers to the list of posts at national and subnational government levels the appointment to which has to be recommended by the party organizational department of the level concerned, and approved by the party organizational department of the next higher level (up to the Central Organizational Department).

17 The general pay revision in July 1999 saw a dramatic overall increase of forty per cent, partly to help promote domestic consumption in line with the central government's macro-economic strategy.

18 This means that society, through either some local collective schemes or individual efforts, should increasingly take over from the state the responsibility and financial burden of welfare and social service provision such as housing, health care, education and social security.

19 The 1994 tax-sharing system represented for the first time an attempt to streamline central–local fiscal relations on a more structured and rational basis, followed by the Ministry of Finance's recent efforts to formulate 'organizational budgets' which show all budgetary, extra-budgetary and other resources and spending for each ministry. However, the central government's slowness in putting tax resources into an equalization transfer scheme has reinforced local suspicions about the centre's declared objective to build up healthy local finances (Wong 2000).

20 The local wage subsidy described earlier is one example of such self-reliant solutions.

21 A recent well-known case is that of the Guangdong International Trust and Investment Corporation (GITIC), a subsidiary of the Guangdong provincial government-owned Guangdong Enterprise. GITIC went bankrupt in 1998, owing some 120 Hong Kong and foreign creditors a total of US$2.94 billion. The creditors entered into a year-long protracted negotiation on debt restructuring with the provincial government. In the beginning, the central government stood firm and insisted that the matter be resolved at the provincial level without expecting any support from the central Treasury and that foreign creditors should bear the risks

of their own lending decisions. In the end, however, Premier Zhu Rongji conceded, as the incident began to deal a severe blow to the credibility of China's SOEs and financial institutions. A loan of 38 billion yen (US$4.56 billion) was extended to the provincial government, which would enable the creditors to get back about seventy per cent of their loans.

Bibliography

Allison, G.T. Jr (1986) 'Public and Private Management: Are They Fundamentally Alike in All Unimportant Respects?'. In Lane, F.S. (ed.) *Current Issues in Public Administration*, 3rd edition, New York: St Martin's Press, pp. 184–200.

Burns, J.P. (1989) 'Chinese Civil Service Reform: The 12th Party Congress Proposals', *The China Quarterly*, No. 120, December, pp. 738–70.

Caiden, G.E. (1988) 'The Vitality of Administrative Reform', *International Review of Administrative Sciences*, Vol. 54, No. 3, pp. 331–57.

Chan, H.S. (1998) 'The Institution of the State in China: At Odds with the Global Trend', *Korean Review of Public Administration*, Vol. 3, No. 2, pp. 69–91.

Chan, H.S. (1999) 'Downsizing the Central Government: The Case of the People's Republic of China', *M@n@gement*, Vol. 2, No. 3, pp. 305–30.

Cheung, A.B.L. (1992) 'Public Sector Reform in Hong Kong: Perspectives and Problems', *Asian Journal of Public Administration*, Vol. 14, No. 2, pp. 115–48.

Cheung, A.B.L. (1996a) 'Efficiency as the Rhetoric? Public-sector Reform in Hong Kong Explained', *International Review of Administrative Sciences*, Vol. 62, No. 1, pp. 31–47.

Cheung, A.B.L. (1996b) 'Public Sector Reform and the Re-legitimation of Public Bureaucratic Power: The Case of Hong Kong', *International Journal of Public Sector Management*, Vol. 9, No. 5/6, pp. 37–50.

Cheung, A.B.L. (1996c) 'Civil Service Reform in Shenzhen: Expectations and Problems'. In MacPherson, S. and Cheng, J.Y.S. (eds) *Economic and Social Development in South China*, Cheltenham: Edward Elgar, pp. 76–106.

Cheung, A.B.L. (1997) 'Understanding Public-sector Reforms: Global Trends and Diverse Agendas', *International Review of Administrative Sciences*, Vol. 63, No. 4, December, pp. 435–57.

Cheung, A.B.L. (1998) 'The 'Trading Fund' Reform in Hong Kong: Claims and Performance', *Public Administration and Policy*, Vol. 7, No. 2, pp. 105–23.

Cheung, A.B.L. (1999) 'Administrative Development in Hong Kong: Political Questions, Administrative Answers'. In Wong, H.K. and Chan, H.S. (eds) *Handbook of Comparative Public Administration in the Asia-Pacific Basin*, New York: Marcel Dekker, pp. 219–52.

Cheung, A.B.L. (2000a) 'New Interventionism in the Making: Interpreting State Interventions in Hong Kong after the Change of Sovereignty', *Journal of Contemporary China*, Vol. 9, No. 24.

Cheung, A.B.L. (2000b) 'Between Autonomy and Accountability: Hong Kong's Senior Civil Servants in Search of an Identity'. In Chapman, R. (ed.) *Ethics in the Public Service for the New Millennium*, Aldershot: Ashgate.

Cheung, A.B.L. (2001a) 'Civil Service Reform in Post-1997 Hong Kong: Political Challenges, Managerial Responses?', *International Journal of Public Administration*.

Cheung, A.B.L. and Poon, K.K. (2001b) 'The Paradox of China's Wage System Reforms: Balancing Stakeholders' Rationalities', *Public Administration Quarterly*.

Civil Service Bureau (Hong Kong SAR Government) (1999) *Civil Service into the 21st Century: Civil Service Reform Consultation Document*, Hong Kong: Printer Department.

Common, R. (1998) 'The New Public Management and Policy Transfer: the Role of International Organizations'. In Minogue, M., Polidano, C. and Hulme, D. (eds) *Beyond the New Public Management: Changing Ideas and Practices in Governance*, Cheltenham: Edward Elgar, pp. 59–75.

Cooper, P. (1995) 'Toward the Hybrid State: the Rise of Environmental Management in a Deregulated and Re-engineered State', *International Review of Administrative Sciences*, Vol. 61, No. 2, pp. 185–200.

Dunleavy, P. (1991) *Democracy, Bureaucracy and Public Choice – Economic Explanations in Political Science*, Harvester Wheatsheaf.

Efficiency Unit (Hong Kong Government) (1995) *Serving the Community*, Hong Kong: Government Printer.

Finance Branch (Hong Kong Government) (1989) *Public Sector Reform*, February, Hong Kong.

Goodman, S.G. (2000) 'Centre and Periphery after Twenty Years of Reform: Redefining the Chinese Polity', paper presented at an international conference on *Centre-Periphery Relations in China: Integration, Disintegration or Reshaping of an Empire?*, co-organized by the French Centre for Research on Contemporary China and the Hong Kong Institute of Asia-Pacific Studies of the Chinese University of Hong Kong, 24–25 March, Hong Kong.

Gore, A. (1993) *Creating A Government That Works Better and Costs Less: The Report of the National Performance Review*, New York: Plume.

Harrop, M. (ed.) (1992) *Power and Policy in Liberal Democracies*, Cambridge: Cambridge University Press.

Hood, C. (1991) 'A Public Management for All Seasons?', *Public Administration*, Vol. 69, No. 1, pp. 3–19.

Hood, C. (1996) 'Exploring Variations in Public Management Reform of the 1980s'. In Bekke, H. Perry, J.L. and Toonen, T.A.J. (eds) *Civil Service Systems in Comparative Perspective*, Bloomington: Indiana University Press, pp. 268–87.

Hughes, O.E. (1994) *Public Management and Administration: An Introduction*, London: St Martin's Press.

Huque, S., Lee, G. and Cheung, A.B.L. (1998) *The Civil Service in Hong Kong: Continuity and Change*, Hong Kong: Hong Kong University Press.

Ibraham, Z. (1995) 'Why the Public Service Push to Provide Quality Service', *Straits Times*, 6 May.

Jiang, Xianrong (1997) 'An Overview of the Reform of China's Administrative System and Organizations and Its Prospects', *New Challenges for Public Administration in the 21st Century: Efficient Civil Service and Decentralized Public Administration*, Proceedings of the Third International Conference of Administrative Sciences (October 1996) Brussels: International Institute of Administrative Sciences, pp. 127–32.

Jiang, Zemin (1992) *Quicken the Pace of Reform and Opening-Up and the Modernization Construction in order to Achieve Greater Success in Socialism with Chinese Characteristics*, report to the 14th National Congress of the Chinese Communist Party, Beijing: People's Press [in Chinese].

Jones, D. S. (1999) 'Public Administration in Singapore: Continuity and Reform'. In Wong, H.K. and Chan, H. S. (eds) *Handbook of Comparative Public Administration in the Asia-Pacific Basin*, New York: Marcel Dekker, pp. 1–22.

Kaboolian, L. (1998) 'The New Public Management: Challenging the Boundaries of the Management vs. Administration Debate', *Public Administration Review*, Vol. 58, No. 3, pp. 189–93.

Kickert, W. (1997) 'Public Management in the United States and Europe'. In Kickert, W. (ed.) *Public Management and Administrative Reform in Western Europe*, Cheltenham: Edward Elgar, pp. 15–38.

Kim, P. S. (2000) 'Administrative Reform in the Korean Central Government: A Case Study of the Dae Jung Kim's Administration', paper presented at the EROPA Hong Kong Conference 2000 on *Developing Asia's Public Services: Sharing Best Practice*, jointly organized by the Eastern Regional Organization on Public Administration and the Efficiency Unit, Hong Kong Government, 4–5 October, Hong Kong.

Lam, T.C. and Chan, H.S. (1995) 'The Civil Service System: Policy Formulation and Implementation'. In Lo, C.K. and Tsui, K.Y. (eds) *China Review 1995*, Hong Kong: The Chinese University Press, pp. 2.1–2.43.

Lan, Z.Y. and Rosenbloom, D.H. (1992) 'Public Administration in Transition?' (editorial), *Public Administration Review*, Vol. 52, No. 6, pp. 535–7.

Lee, Hsien Loong (1998) 'Singapore of the Future'. In Mahizhnan, A. and Lee, T. Y. (eds) *Singapore Re-engineering Success*, Singapore: Oxford University Press.

Liang, Peng (1999) *Reform of the Fiscal and Taxation System*, Guangzhou: Guangdong Economic Press [in Chinese].

Lim, Siong Guan (1996) 'The Public Service' in Yeo Lay Hwee (ed.) *Singapore: The Year in Review 1995*, Singapore: The Institute of Policy Studies.

Lim, Siong Guan (1998) 'PS21: Gearing up the Public Service for the 21st Century'. In Mahizhnan, A. and Lee, T.Y. (eds) *Singapore Re-engineering Success*, Singapore: Oxford University Press.

Low, L. (2000) 'Beyond Corporate Governance: Reinventing the Singapore Development Corporate State', May, manuscript not yet published, National University of Singapore.

McKinsey and Company (1973) *The Machinery of Government: A New Framework for Expanding Services*, Hong Kong: Government Printer.

Organization for Economic Co-operation and Development (1995) *Governance in Transition: Public Management Reforms in OECD Countries*, Paris: OECD.

Ormond, D. (1997) 'General Report', *New Challenges for Public Administration in the 21st Century: Efficient Civil Service and Decentralized Public Administration*, Proceedings of the Third International Conference of Administrative Sciences (October 1996) Brussels: International Institute of Administrative Sciences, pp. 27–42.

Osborne, D. and Gaebler, T. (1993) [1992] *Reinventing Government: How the Entrepreneurial Spirit is Transforming the Public Sector*, London: Plume.

Parsons, W. (1995) *Public Policy: An Introduction to the Theory and Practice of Policy Analysis*, Aldershot: Edward Elgar.

Patten, C. (1996) *Hong Kong: Transition*, Address by the Governor at the opening of the 1996–97 session of the Legislative Council, 2 October, Hong Kong: Government Printer.

Polidano, C. (forthcoming) 'Administrative Reform in Core Civil Services: Application and Applicability of the New Public Management'. In McCourt, W. and Minogue, M. (eds) *The Internationalization of Public Management: Reinventing the Third World State*, Cheltenham: Edward Elgar.

Pollitt, C. (1993) *Managerialism and the Public Services: Cuts or Cultural Change in the 1990s?*, 2nd edition, Oxford: Basil Blackwell.

Prybyla, J.S. (1990) 'Economic Reform of Socialism: The Dengist Course in China', *Privatizing and Marketizing Socialism* (The Annals of the American Academy of Political and Social Science), Vol. 507, London: Sage Publications, pp. 113–22.

PS21 Office (Singapore Government) (undated) *Public Service for the 21st Century*, Singapore. Also see http://www.gov.sg/ps21.

Quah, J.S.T. (2000) 'Public Administration Singapore Style: The Role of the Public Bureaucracy in a One-Party Dominant System', unpublished manuscript, National University of Singapore.

Sarji, A. (1996) *Civil Service Reforms: Towards Malaysia's Vision 2020*, Selangor, Malaysia: Pelanduk Publications.

Song Defu (1997) 'Speech by the [Chinese] Minister of Personnel', *New Challenges for Public Administration in the 21st Century: Efficient Civil Service and Decentralized Public Administration*, Proceedings of the Third International Conference of Administrative Sciences (October 1996) Brussels: International Institute of Administrative Sciences, pp. 13–15.

State Administration for Statistics, PRC (1999) *China Statistics Yearbook 1998* [in Chinese], Beijing.

State Council, PRC (1993) 'Provisional Regulations on the State Civil Service', *Gazette of the State Council of the People's Republic of China* [in Chinese], No. 18, 2 September, Beijing, pp. 837–49.

Straits Times, various dates, Singapore.

Tung, C. H. (2000) *Serving the Community, Sharing Common Goals*, Address at the Legislative Council meeting on 11 October, Hong Kong: Printing Department.

Unger, J. and Chan, A. (1995) 'China, Corporatism, and the East Asian Model', *The Australian Journal of Chinese Affairs*, pp. 29–53.

Vogel, E. Z. (1989) 'A Little Dragon Tamed'. In Sandhu, K.S. and Wheatley, P. (eds) *Management of Success: The Moulding of Modern Singapore*, Singapore: Institute of Southeast Asian Studies.

Walder, A. (1986) *Communist Neo-Traditionalism: Work and Authority in Chinese Industry*, Berkeley: University of California Press.

Wei, Chi-lin (2000) *Government Reinvention Movement* [in Chinese], Taipei: Morning Star Publishing Company.

Wong, C.P.W. (1998) 'Fiscal Dualism in China: Gradualist Reform and the Growth of Off-Budget Finance'. In Brean, D. (ed.) *Taxation in Modern China*, New York: Routledge.

Wong, C.P.W. (1999) 'Converting Fees to Taxes: Reform of Extrabudgetary Funds and Intergovernmental Fiscal Relations in China 1999 and Beyond', paper presented at the Association for Asian Studies Meeting, March, Boston.

Wong, C.P.W. (2000) 'Central-Local Relations Revisited: Impact of the 1994 Tax Sharing Reform in China', paper presented at an international conference on *Centre–Periphery Relations in China: Integration, Disintegration or Reshaping of An Empire?*, co-organized by the French Centre for Research on Contemporary China and the Hong Kong Institute of Asia-Pacific Studies of the Chinese University of Hong Kong, 24–25 March, Hong Kong.

World Bank (1997) *China 2020: Development Challenges in the New Century*, Washington, DC: The World Bank.

World Bank (2000) *Reforming Public Institutions and Strengthening Governance*, http://www1.worldbank.org/publicsector/civilservice/countryexperiences.htm, accessed 9 January 2000.

Zhang, Zhijian (1997) 'Establishment of an Administrative System Compatible with the Socialist Market Economy', *New Challenges for Public Administration in the 21st Century: Efficient Civil Service and Decentralized Public Administration*, Proceedings of the Third International Conference of Administrative Sciences (October 1996), Brussels: International Institute of Administrative Sciences, pp. 133–40.

Zhao, Zhiyang (1987) *Advance Along the Road of Socialism with Chinese Characteristics* [in Chinese], report to the 13th National Congress of the Chinese Communist Party, Hong Kong: Joint Publishing Company.

Chapter 16

The New Public Management in international perspective

An analysis of impacts and effects

Christopher Pollitt

Introduction

It is interesting that NPM reforms had been going on in several countries for between ten and fifteen years before the academic community began much direct assessment of whether the reformers' claims for improvement were credible and convincing (Pollitt 1995). There was certainly some *ab initio* reasoning about the 'logic' of NPM, but not a great deal of empirical work on the consequences of NPM-inspired reforms in practice. For many academics (*mea culpa*) intellectualizing about categories, models, ideologies and national convergences and differences evidently took precedence over the (deceptively) simple question of: Does it work? More recently, however, a more substantial volume of academic writing has begun to explore and evaluate the seeming consequences of NPM. In this chapter I will draw on this body of work – as well as on a range of official sources – in order to assess the available evidence on the results of the public management reform.

To attack such a huge subject in a single chapter necessarily requires the discussion to be pitched at a fairly high level of generalization. On the other hand, while the detail is both rich and occasionally paradoxical, on the broad scale attempted here there do seem to be some larger points which are worth making.

To approach the question of impact, some attention needs first to be devoted to three significant preliminary questions. First, what kind of evidential materials are available? Second, what kinds of reform are we talking about? Third, what do we mean by 'results'? These three preliminaries will be tackled sequentially in the next three sections. Subsequently, the main part of the chapter will deal with the central question of what we know and what we do not about the results of reform.

Characteristics of the available materials

A great deal of the available material on public management reform is either promotional ('look at what we are doing') or how-to-do-it ('a guide to...'). Governments produce White Papers, statements and booklets in which they attempt to convince legislatures, the media, the public and public servants themselves that their reforms are significant, well-intentioned and likely to produce a variety of improvements. Departments produce practical guidelines to help their staffs implement change (e.g. HM Treasury 1992). The promotional documents are intended to persuade, and, accordingly, they tend to be heavily freighted with rhetoric and rather light on self-criticism (e.g. OECD 1995; Gore 1996, 1997; Chancellor of the Duchy of Lancaster 1997; Chancellor of the Exchequer 1998; Prime Minister and the Minister for the Cabinet Office 1999). Consultants and other advisers are also either promotional or how-to-do-it – often they are selling their systems (re-engineering, TQM, benchmarking or whatever) and ultimately they are all selling their services to governments, public agencies and corporations. The how-to-do-it guides are more down-to-earth than glossy official reports and White Papers, but they too (necessarily and understandably) assume that success is possible and that, if staff follow the good advice, officially promulgated goals will be reached.

It would be unwise, therefore, to assume that, in aggregate, these types of rhetoric and documentation afford a full and balanced picture of what is happening 'on the ground' throughout the administrative systems of the countries concerned. One does not have to be either a cynic or a postmodernist to be aware of the frequency of rhetoric/practice gaps, or of the extent to which reform talk can take on a life of its own, somewhat divorced from everyday administrative practice (Brunsson 1989; Hood 1998; Pollitt 2001).

This chapter attempts very briefly to summarize the available *corpus* of evaluations of public management reforms – or at least that portion which has been identified and collected by the author. It seeks to establish how *confident* we can be in the many suggestions that have been made that a 'transformation' is taking place. We are often told that old-fashioned bureaucracies are being replaced by new arrangements which are faster, cheaper and more effective. We are told that new organizations can be created which are more willing to innovate and which are more responsive to citizens in all their various roles (taxpayers, residents, workers, patients, pensioners, service users, etc.). What are the warrants for these claims? How firm is the evidence?

What is happening in the world of public management reform? A first answer which is simple but wrong

For some years now there has been a powerful story abroad. It tells that that there is something new in the world of governance, termed 'the New Public management' (NPM), 'reinvention', 're-engineering' or given some equally dynamic title. This is generally presented as a formula for improving public administration and achieving, as the catchphrase for the US National Performance Review (NPR) has it, 'a government that works better and costs less'. In their influential book *Reinventing Government*, Osborne and Gaebler (1992) put it very strongly. Referring to what they termed 'the rise of entrepreneurial government' in the USA, they claimed that 'a similar process is under way throughout the developed world' (p. 328) and that it was 'inevitable' (p. 325).

From this perspective particular governments or public services can be seen as being 'well ahead' or 'lagging behind' along what is basically a single route to reform. In many of the 'promotional' publications the characteristics of the reformed public sector organization have been specified. Typically, these include:

- being close to its customers;
- being performance-driven (targets, standards) not rule-bound;
- displaying a commitment to continuous quality improvement (again, targets, standards);
- being structured in a 'lean' and 'flat' way – highly decentralized, with street-level staff who are 'empowered' to be flexible and innovate;
- practising tight cost control, with the help of modern, commercial-style accounting systems;
- using performance-related systems for recruiting, posting, promoting and paying staff.

Furthermore, if these are the characteristics of individual organizations within a reformed public sector, 'reinvented' governments will also display a distinctive approach to their work in a broader way. They will:

- 'Steer not row', i.e. become more concerned with strategy and less with carrying-out.
- Act in anticipatory ways – for a host of public problems prevention is better than cure.
- Seek to use market mechanisms wherever possible, either in the form of quasi-markets to introduce competition between public providers, or by contracting out or privatizing services which were previously undertaken directly by the state.
- Seek inter-organizational partnerships, both within the public sector ('joined-up government') and with the private and voluntary sectors.

So this is one, simple answer to the question: What is happening? Governments are redesigning institutions and procedures so as to conform to the new model outlined above. Everyone is doing more or less the same thing, because they have little choice. Powerful forces in the environment are obliging governments to change. Some are further ahead than others.

A second, more complicated, but more accurate answer

The community of scholars conducting comparative analyses of public management reforms is not large but, over the past decade, it has produced a number of significant studies (e.g. Pierre 1995; Trosa 1995; Flynn and Strehl 1996; Hood 1996; Olsen and Peters 1996; Kickert 1997; Lane 1997, 2000; Pollitt and Summa 1997; Peters and Savoie 1998; Premfors 1998; Pollitt and Bouckaert

2000). What these show is a world in which, although the broad aims of producing more efficient, effective and responsive public services may have been widely shared, the mixtures of strategies, priorities, styles and methods adopted by different governments have varied very widely indeed. As Flynn and Strehl said of their research 'We quickly found that there were reasons to doubt the idea of convergence' (1996: 4). Guy Peters suggests that although there is 'a set of relatively common stimuli for change ... What is different is how political systems have interpreted the ideas and responded to the demands and/or opportunities for introducing administrative change' (Peters 1997: 266). This is a position that is broadly shared in my own work, although I would add that reform *ideas* themselves have also varied considerably from country to country, and certainly the priority given to different components (e.g. privatization, contracting out) has fluctuated enormously (Pollitt and Bouckaert 2000).

It should be acknowledged, however, that some leading scholars still support the main thrust of Osborne and Gaebler's analysis. For example, it is claimed that movement towards NPM 'has been striking because of the number of nations that have taken up the reform agenda in such a short time and because of how similar their basic strategies have been' (Kettl 2000: 1). These scholarly accounts are, however, usually far more nuanced and less 'breathless' than *Reinventing Government*. Kettl, for example, acknowledges significant differences between the USA and Westminister-type systems, and concludes with the very non-Osborne and Gaeblerish statement that 'The question of convergence and divergence remains very much open' (Kettl 2000: 66).

Part of the explanation for diversity is that countries have not *started* from the same point, either in terms of the make-up of their public sectors or in terms of the way they think about the role and character of the state (Pierre 1995; Kickert 1997; Ministry of Finance 1997; Pollitt and Summa 1997; Guyomarch 1999). 'Path dependent' explanations fit public management rather well (Premfors 1998; Pierson 2000a). Furthermore, governments have not all possessed the same *capacities* to implement reforms. In some countries, such as Germany, changing the central administrative structures is politically and legally very difficult. In other countries, such as New Zealand and the UK, it has been comparatively easy (Pollitt and Bouckaert 2000). Even here, however, lesser differences can be detected (for contrasts between the USA and the 'Westminster' countries, see Kettl 2000; for differences between New Zealand and the UK, see Boston 1995).

A subsidiary weakness in the 'simple' version is that it posits a uniform past, in which 'traditional bureaucracy', like some ponderous dinosaur, ruled the earth. This is simply wrong – much of post-war 'big government', in many OECD countries, consisted of sprouting welfare state organizations that were usually *not* organized along strict bureaucratic lines. State schools, hospitals and social and community services agencies took on variety of forms, and in many of these autonomous professionals, not bureaucrats, were often the key actors (Clarke and Newman 1997).

So, not every country is taking the same route, and, in particular, the radical reforms implemented during the 1980s and early 1990s in New Zealand and the

UK are certainly *not* universally regarded as a desirable model to emulate. Indeed, in some countries leading opinion formers regard the NPM with considerable suspicion (e.g. for France, see Guyomarch 1999; for Germany, see Derlien 1998 and Konig 1996 and for Sweden see Premfors 1998). In Finland the Minister with responsibility for administrative reform, though certainly keen to pursue change in various ways, recently said that 'we seem to have a political consensus to hang onto the Nordic service production model' (Siimes 1999: 6).

The USA is an interesting case in this regard because, although it has been a fountain of rhetoric for reinvention and re-engineering, the federal executive's capacity for implementing coherent, broad-scope reforms is severely limited by the well-known fragmentation of the American political system (Peters 1995). Here is a government whose rhetoric frequently outreaches its implementation capacity – witness the history of some of President Reagan's reforms during the 1980s or, further back, the disappointing histories of, *inter alia*, PPB, MbO and ZBB (Savoie 1994; General Accounting Office 1997). By contrast one might think of, say, Denmark, which has carried through extensive public management reforms but without much publicity or public controversy, or Finland, which, without fanfares, launched and sustained a major modernization effort between 1989 and 1997 (Ministry of Finance 1997).

The point about rhetoric diverging from reality, though familiar enough in general terms, deserves some elaboration. When we are assessing the accuracy of stories of an international convergence on NPM, we need to distinguish between at least four different 'levels' of the concept. First, there is a convergence of *talk* – the emergence of NPM as a dominant paradigm, rhetorically speaking. Second, there is a convergence of *decisions* – governments deciding to implement competitive tendering for public services or executive agencies at arm's length from ministries, or whatever. Third – because decisions do not always lead to the predicted actions – we can distinguish convergence of actual *practices* (everyone is *doing* TQM or benchmarking, and in more or less the same way). Fourth, there could eventually be a convergence of *results* – most or all jurisdictions adopt NPM techniques and instruments, and most or all jurisdictions subsequently enjoy better performance (whether measured in outputs, outcomes or some more complicated mixture of criteria – see below). In a perfect world all four levels of convergence would match up. In the real world we know they do not, but we do not know how wide the divergences are, especially in terms of the gap between the first two levels and the second two. Circumstantial evidence, supported by certain reasoning about the way reform ideas are used, suggests that convergence of talk and decisions may be considerably more marked than convergence of practice – or certainly than convergence of results (Pollitt 2001).

Defining 'results'

Before one can assess evidence about impacts, one has to decide what kind of thing is going to count as a 'result'. This is by no means straightforward. For example, a result could be any one or more of the following:

1 savings (reduced budget appropriations);
2 improved processes (e.g. faster more accessible complaints procedures; quicker turn-round times for repairs or the processing of licenses; 'one stop shops' offering several services in one place);
3 improved efficiency (better input/output ratios, e.g. more students graduate per full time equivalent member of staff; the same number of drivers' licenses are issued with twenty per cent fewer staff);
4 greater effectiveness (less crime, poverty, functional illiteracy; homelessness; drug abuse; gender or ethnic inequality; more new jobs created; more contented and trusting citizens, etc.);
5 an increase in the overall capacity/flexibility/resilience of the administrative system as a whole (e.g. through the recruitment and training of more skilled, more committed public servants).

Furthermore, each of these categories contains its own conceptual puzzles, definitional problems and pitfalls in operationalization (Pollitt and Bouckaert 2000: Chapter 5). Some of these will be alluded to further as the evidence on results is examined in later sections.

There is, however, one major limitation to the above list. It takes a very literal view, and leaves little space for 'results' of a more symbolic or ideological character. Clearly, though, the implementation of NPM reforms can have a wide range of such effects. For example, the managerialization of the public sector includes processes:

> by which an occupational group claims to be the possessor of a distinctive – and valuable – sort of expertise, and uses that expertise as the basis for acquiring organizational and social power. They also indicate the ways in which topics of public and political concern become colonized – owned, even, by particular types of knowledge in ways that organize power relations.
>
> (Clarke *et al.* 2000: 8)

These aspects of NPM are as integral to its character as any effects it may have on efficiency, effectiveness and so on. However, it is beyond the scope of this chapter to deal with them as well as the five more obvious features alluded to above. Here we will stay largely *within* the NPM paradigm, critiquing it on its own terms. A number of other works step *outside* the paradigm, in order to deal with the more ideological and symbolic aspects of NPM (e.g. Pollitt 1993, 2001; Clarke and Newman 1997; Clarke *et al.* 2000;).

What evaluations have been done?

There have been surprisingly few independent, broad-scope evaluations of the public management reforms (Pollitt 1995, 1998). Those which have been conducted tend to suffer from some fairly fundamental conceptual and methodological limitations (which have sometimes been acknowledged, and on other occasions not). Australia carried out one very large study (Task Force on Management Improvement 1992) and New Zealand conducted at least two important reviews (Steering Group 1991; Schick 1996). In the US there are various evaluations in train around the NPR, but the main studies were not yet available at the time of writing. However, a series of assessments of the implementation of the Government Performance and Results Act (GPRA) has been produced by the General Accounting Office (e.g. General Accounting Office 1998). In the UK, broad scope evaluations have been noticeable by their absence, although there have been a number of more focused assessments of specific reforms (e.g. Employment Service 1994; Next Steps Team 1998, but these were both 'in-house' reviews and therefore their independence can be questioned). The Blair government appears to be more committed to the idea that evaluation should be a regular part of the reform process. A few countries have made a deliberate effort systematically to review their reform experiences, using independent evaluators (Holkeri and Summa 1996) but these initiatives have been very much the exception rather than the rule.

The most common limitations to these studies have been the following:

- An absence of reliable baseline measures, so that before-and-after comparisons become rather speculative.
- An absence of benchmarking, e.g. the productivity gains of a privatized firm may be praised without it being noticed or admitted that comparable non-privatized corporations have made similar gains over the same period (Naschold and von Otter 1996: 24–25).
- Limited or no gathering of the views of service users.
- Scarcity or absence of data on transitional costs. For example, the first major report on the New Zealand reforms contains no cost figures at all – Steering Group 1991 – and the huge Australian evaluation acknowledges the difficulty of assigning savings to the reforms – Task Force on Management Improvement 1992. Kettl (1994: 9) makes the same point about the US NPR. In a later work he broadens the comment: 'no good reliable data are available in any country regarding the savings that the reforms produced' (Kettl 2000: 51).
- Scarcity or absence of data on step-changes in transactional costs and/or on other continuing 'side effects' such as the loss of trust or a degree of value confusion (see, for example, Kirkpatrick 1999 for the UK and Jorgensen 1999 for Denmark).
- Opinion gathering being limited to, or biased towards, senior staff (a number of surveys have shown that middle- and lower-level staff are often more critical of reforms than their bosses).
- Little analysis of contextual variations which may mean that a similar type of reform will work well in one situation or locality, but not in another (Pawson and Tilley 1997).
- Limited or no attention to attribution problems. Often several reforms have proceeded simultaneously, and external conditions have also been changing. This makes it very hard confidently to attribute results to specific reforms.

As one official evaluation put it: 'it is unlikely to be possible to disentangle the effects of Agency status from other elements of E[mployment] S[ervice] performance: and ... it is unlikely to be possible to create an exact picture of what would have happened if ES and Agency status had not occurred' (Employment Service 1994: 10).

- Narrow range of criteria applied to the findings (e.g. productivity measures only, with no attention to equity, to staff morale or to externalities). In effect, most of the evaluations fail to distinguish between and/or miss out altogether many of the types of 'result' listed in the previous section of this paper.

There is little sign that these significant limitations to evaluation designs are being addressed. Recent evaluations (e.g. Schick 1997; Next Steps Team 1998) appear to be just as prone to these major limitations as those undertaken five to ten years ago.

What results have been found?

The limitations – or downright absence – of evaluations discussed in the previous section mean that many important questions cannot be answered, or can only be answered tentatively, with many qualifications and reservations. Nevertheless, some aspects are clearer than others, and various bodies of evidence lie around the world, inviting scholarly sorting and interpretation. In making a small start to that large labour, I will organize my brief comments under the same headings as were used in the section 'Defining results' (above). Thus we begin with the claims of reform to achieve economies in the operation of the public sector.

Savings

One German scholar attempted to test what he described as the 'OECD hypothesis': that bureaucratic regimes would perform less well in macro-economic terms than regimes which had modernized themselves according to the NPM prescription. He concluded that:

> Confronting our findings with the hypothesis formulated by the OECD as to the relationship between macroeconomic performance (economic growth, productivity and unemployment), on the one hand, and the regulation regime (bureaucratic governance by rule and its alternatives) on the other, the OECD hypothesis has to be strikingly refuted: all the countries with bureaucratic governance by rule exhibit with respect to almost all the dimensions a markedly better macroeconomic performance than the other countries
>
> (Naschold 1995: 39)

Naschold goes on to acknowledge that there are considerable difficulties in interpreting this apparent negative correlation. (He might have been even more cautious had be been writing two or three years later, when the economic performances of New Zealand and the UK had much improved, and the German and Japanese economies were in considerable difficulties!) Even if one confines one's attention to a narrower range of macro-economic indicators than those cited by Naschold, interpretation remains deeply problematic. For example, the OECD database shows that government outlays as a percentage of nominal GDP fell between 1985 and the late 1990s, at least in the majority of the countries discussed in this chapter. However, it would be rash indeed to attribute this shrinking proportion to management reforms. There are all sorts of interpretive pitfalls which forbid any such conclusion (Pollitt and Bouckaert 2000: Chapter 5). We do not know how far reductions have been achieved by privatization – once-only transfers to the private sector – rather than any real economizing among core public sector activities. We also have to allow for the state of the economies as a whole – a rising or falling ratio may be as much due to growth or recession in the market sector as to 'savings' in the public sphere. A further problem is that a country-by-country review shows a poor correlation between large reductions in the ratio and the depth or breadth of management reforms. Even more fundamentally, the direction of the arrow of causation is not clear. Instead of assuming that management reform leads to savings we might hypothesize that forced savings lead to management reform. This second interpretation is strongly supported by one of the few reasonably sophisticated analyses of public sector productivity yet undertaken (Murray's interpretation of the Swedish experience in 1998).

By the same token, it would be rash to conclude from the parallel OECD figures which show *rising* public debt (also as a percentage of nominal GDP) for many countries that management reforms increase state borrowing. A more prudent position would be to accept, however reluctantly, that movements in macro-economic aggregates simply will not tell us anything clear and sure about the effects of *management* reform. Optimistically, 'separating the impact of government reforms from other changes that fuelled economic growth is an extremely difficult issue to assess that, at best, will require many more years and far more data to assess' (Kettl 2000: 52).

Therefore, we should move away from macro-economic indicators and instead ask questions about the measured savings generated by particular reform efforts. Yet, as we have already noted, the most sophisticated evaluations are unable reliably to calculate or attribute savings with respect to broad programmes of reform (Steering Group 1991; Task Force on Management Improvement 1992). It is only when much more specific and local changes are examined that testable estimates of savings begin to appear. At this level it appears reasonably clear that many reforms *have* led to savings. The 'promotional' government publications referred to in the introduction are full of examples. Vice President Gore writes of buying government staplers for $4 instead of $54 (Gore 1996: 5). A range of UK executive agencies report reduced unit costs, year on year (e.g. Chancellor of the Duchy of Lancaster 1997: 117–118).

Some of these achievements are impressive. Some *would* be impressive, if they were independently validated and shown to be a fair and true picture. Many, however, are hard to assess. A 'saving' on one dimension may have been offset by increases in expenditure elsewhere, or by quality reductions, or by scope of service reductions, or by shifting costs elsewhere in the public sector (and therefore achieve no overall advantage for the state as a whole). Yet one must not carp too much: when a reform of procurement policy frees (or obliges) public servants to purchase simple requirements (staplers, office furniture, security services) from cheaper suppliers, it requires a contortion to see this as other than an improvement.

One kind of 'saving' that appears relatively easy to count is a reduction in the number of civil servants ('downsizing' in management parlance). OECD data show that some countries – not necessarily those one might expect – have been able to make large reductions in the ratio of government employment to total employment (especially the Netherlands and the UK). Other countries have experienced an increase (Finland, France). Once again, however, there is need for interpretive caution when deploying big aggregates of this kind. For example, during the 1990s Finland actually made large reductions in the numbers employed on the 'state' (central) budget. However, the OECD figures do not fully reflect this, partly because of the high unemployment which suddenly hit Finland in the early 1990s, shrinking the second variable in the ratio. A second factor was that quite a few jobs were moved off the 'state' (i.e. central government) books but onto employment registers of municipalities or other 'non-state' public bodies. Another example would be the large contribution to public sector reductions made in some countries by the downsizing of military forces and their associated civilian employees during the 1990s (for the USA, see Kettl 2000: 21). This had a very little to do with NPM and everything to do with the 'peace dividend' at the end of the Cold War.

The OECD statisticians do their best, but varying definitions of government employment plague their comparisons. Despite all these qualifications, however, it is clear that some governments have been able to make substantial reductions in the numbers of core public servants they employ. Mrs Thatcher downsized the non-industrial civil service by more than a fifth. Vice President Gore's NPR reduced the federal workforce by 240,000 as of the beginning of 1996 (Gore 1996: 5). If one examines changes in government employee compensation as a percentage of GDP there appears to be a good correlation between 'aggressive reformers' and large reductions in this ratio (see Table 16.1).

Improved processes

Again, anecdotal evidence crowds together in the promotional literature. With respect to American pensions 'Ten million workers in small businesses could benefit from the new, simplified 401(k)-type plan – no red tape, just a simple form' (Gore 1996: 47). The UK Driver and Vehicle Testing Agency repeatedly reduced the average waiting time for a driving test appointment – although at the same time the waiting time for car tests with its sister agency (the Driving Standards Agency) drifted upwards (Chancellor of the Duchy of Lancaster 1997: 63 and 64). And so on. Most of us probably also have personal experience of

Table 16.1 Changes in government employee
compensation as a percentage of
GDP, 1990–97

Country	Change (%)
UK	−34.2
New Zealand	−14.4
USA	−8.6
Sweden	−6.4
Netherlands	−6.1
Germany	+3.1
Japan	+4.3
France	+9.1

Source: OECD Analytical Databank; see also Kettl
(2000: 56).

improvements: desk staff better trained to handle difficult requests; greater
attention paid to the decor, comfort and cleanliness of waiting areas; simplified
forms. Techniques such as TQM and re-engineering generate many measured
process improvements, occasionally of spectacular proportions. There is now a
great deal of public sector knowledge about how to improve individual processes,
once the will to do so and the appropriate techniques are brought together in
the same place (Ingraham *et al.* 1998). Modernized management has some real
success stories to tell.

Once more, however, there is an argument for viewing these specific
achievements in a broader and more ambiguous context. With complex,
interdependent public services, improvements along one dimension may be
achieved at the cost of the neglect of another. For example, improving against a
target of *x* per cent of cases cleared within a given time period may tempt officials
to neglect a small percentage of really difficult and time-consuming cases (see
the UK National Audit Office study of the Benefits Agency–National Audit Office
1998). Or take the case of the local authority which invests a significant volume
of its scarce resources in automated electronic information points, with the aim
of providing local residents with a fast, clear twenty-four-hour information service
about the Council's services. For those who use the screens, these aims may be
achieved – the process of informing them has been unmistakably improved.
However, for a variety of reasons, the elderly and certain minorities for whom
English is not the first language make virtually no use of the information points,
and women generally use them far less often than men. Meanwhile, possible
moves to increase in the resources going towards informing these other groups
(e.g. through hiring more interpreters in minority languages) have been
postponed – indeed resource levels may even have been cut back – because the
kiosks are the project of the moment. In such circumstances (closely adapted
from a real case) it is clear that the information process has been improved for
young and middle-aged white men, but whether it has been improved *in general*

depends on the extent to which other aspects of the service have remained the same, or been squeezed by resource diversions to the flagship project.

Improved efficiency

For two decades, the efficiency criterion has lain at the heart of many management reform initiatives. Re-organizing so as to achieve more outputs per input or the same outputs for reduced inputs is one of the core skills of good managers. Achieving a certain percentage 'efficiency gain' became an annual routine for UK government departments and agencies, and for NHS hospitals during the 1980s and early 1990s. Furthermore, in principle at least, the measurement of efficiency is somewhat less difficult than that of either quality or effectiveness. With quality measurement there is always the awkward initial step of trying to find some consensus among users as to what, for them, constitutes 'quality'. Effectiveness measurement entails research into impacts 'out there', beyond the organization, and may be both costly and methodologically complex. Technical, 'X' efficiency, however, requires a comparison between organizational inputs and organizational outputs – both of which are usually recorded (or recordable) without too much external research or conceptual head-scratching.

A first point to make is that efficiency gains may be achieved at the cost of other, less desirable effects. Thus a UK study of the effects of contracting out local services came to the conclusion that, while efficiency may have risen in many cases, equal opportunities hiring had suffered (Escott and Whitfield 1995).

Second, there is the same 'systems' point that we noted above in respect of improved processes. An example to illustrate this comes from the re-engineering of the process for obtaining pathology test results in a large public hospital. The handling of specimens was completely redesigned, and the average time taken to deliver to the doctor's desk (or screen) was significantly reduced – all for no extra resources. This appears to be a clear efficiency gain. However, this had no effect on overall lengths of stay for patients (a proxy for the efficiency of the hospital system as a whole) because the doctors' own work patterns remained unreformed, and they simply 'absorbed' the faster turnaround times within their own routines.

Third, while many of the claims of efficiency gains are probably perfectly reasonable and accurate, it would be prudent not to take all assertions at face value (Hencke 1998). Consider the widely accepted idea that contracting out public services (whatever its other effects may have been) has regularly led to efficiency gains:

> claims that that empirical studies find 'consistently' and 'without exception' that contracting out is more efficient than municipal supply are demonstrably untrue. Even taken at face value, only around half of the studies discussed in the paper (a review of contracting out in US local

government) is associated with lower spending and higher efficiency. Furthermore, many of the studies contain specific methodological flaws that cast doubt on the evidence on the impact of service contracts ...

(Boyne 1998: 482)

Neither is this an isolated case. Talbot's research into the performance indicator systems used by UK 'Next Steps' executive agencies showed that measurements of their efficiency were both patchy and volatile. Roughly half the declared aims and objectives were not covered by indicators at all, while two-thirds of the 'key performance indicators' for a sample of ten agencies had been dropped or replaced within a six-year period (Talbot 1996, 1997). Embarrassing measures, where performance is declining or stubbornly low, may be quietly discarded and redefined indicators put in their place (as was famously the case for the headline UK official definition of unemployment during the 1980s). Equally, reorganizations themselves may disrupt time series data by altering the sphere of jurisdiction of an organization or changing data collection methods or categories. Reliable time series of well-validated efficiency measures turn out to be much rarer than one might have thought (as Pollitt *et al.* 1998 found for UK hospitals, schools and housing agencies). A recent study of five European national audit offices showed that even Supreme Audit Institutions, when they conduct performance audits, often seem to be able to construct and apply true efficiency measures in only a minority of their studies. More often they fall back on assessing the presence or absence of good management practice – a highly imperfect surrogate for efficiency (Pollitt *et al.* 1999: Chapter 6).

Of course, the frequent absence of 'gold standard' measures does not show that efficiency has fallen (or risen) but it does cast a different light on the apparent abundance of improvement claims. Many of these are probably entirely justified. Others are demonstrably suspect.

Greater effectiveness

For at least thirty years civil servants and evaluators have recognized that assessing the effectiveness of many public policies and programmes is an extremely difficult task. Occasionally some particular programme will enjoy the benefit of an available, valid and relevant indicator of outcome, but often the links between programme activities and final outcomes are tentative or obscure. There are several well-documented reasons for this complexity (Pollitt 2000). Politicians frequently mandate policy objectives which, in Wildavsky's famous phrase are 'multiple, conflicting and vague'. Thus the initial question of what outcomes are being aimed at may be hard to answer in operational terms. Then there is the problem of timescales: the final outcomes of some educational, health and environmental programmes, for example, may lie a long way down the road – longer than many politicians and citizens are willing to wait before passing judgement. A third common difficulty is that of safely attributing observed effects to the programme in question. If unemployment falls, how much of that is due to the retraining programme and how much to a general improvement in economic conditions? If the health status of a community improves is it the health promotion programme, or improved housing, or increased incomes leading to better diets, or some combination of all these things?

By itself, management reform alters none of these constraints. Indeed, the evaluation of the effectiveness of management reform itself is subject to precisely these challenges – the aims of the reform are often hard to operationalize, the timescales over which effects occur can be long drawn-out and the attribution of observed effects is frequently uncertain (Pollitt 1995).

These difficulties are widely acknowledged by the more thoughtful practitioners and politicians. In New Zealand – a country rightly famed for the thoroughness of its management reforms and the sophistication of its systems – the minister with responsibility for the civil service opened a 1997 conference of senior public managers with the following words:

> Quite properly, a great deal of effort was invested in the first few years in mastering the new technology – in making sure that outputs were properly specified, correctly priced, and so on. But within two or three years there was a sense that we might be becoming, instead of input-fixated, output-fixated ...
>
> My own impression is that we still have plenty to do, to make the system work effectively ... A first step towards this should be, I suggest, a conscious effort by senior Public Service managers to lift their eyes from individual outputs and to spend longer thinking about the Government's strategic result areas – about outcomes in other words'
>
> (East 1997)

Similarly, the UK Labour government, after fifteen years of intense and unremitting management reforms declared in 1999 that henceforth the need was to focus on outcomes rather just on inputs, functions or value-for-money (Prime Minister and Minister for the Cabinet Office 1999: 15–18). Significantly, when one examines how the Department of Health (to take one example) responded to this call, one finds a departmental report in which, of a total of thirty-six targets, only five are cast in terms of outcomes, and all these five set 2010 – at least two elections away – as the date by which their outcomes are to be achieved (Department of Health 2000: Chapter 2).

We should not be surprised, therefore, when we discover that cases where there is unmistakable evidence of management reform producing more effective government action are rare. The connections between management reform and the effective delivery of long term policy goals are often both distant and complicated by factors that lie beyond the control of public managers.

More capacious/flexible/resilient administrative systems

Systems improvements are not to be judged on the basis of the success or failure of a single project, programme or policy, but rather in a more holistic way. For example, the transformation of a rigid, inward-looking, slow-moving bureaucratic hierarchy into a 'flat', responsive, multi-disciplinary agency could be said to have increased that system's *capacity* to cope with new developments in its environment. As in this example, systems changes are broad-scope and will frequently involve both major structural changes and an engineered shift in the dominant organizational culture.

Reformers have made many claims for systems transformations. For example, Vice President Gore writes that in the US federal government 'Many bosses are changing the way they do their jobs – encouraging innovation and customer service instead of just making workers toe the line' (Gore 1996: 16). Towards the end of Mr Major's Conservative administration the UK Cabinet Minister for the Public Service wrote that:

> In my current and my previous Ministerial posts I have been struck by the way in which the Next Steps programme has transformed the civil service ... This *Review* contains many examples of improvements in the quality of service provided to the public ... It also demonstrates very clearly the Government's commitment to openness, managerial accountability and better-focused, better-managed systems.
>
> (Chancellor of the Duchy of Lancaster 1997: v and viii)

Such claims may well be justified, but at the same time they may be largely rhetoric. Distinguishing between the beef and the blather is often difficult. One problem is that there is no real agreement on an operational definition of a transformation. Another is that the currency of systems claims is hard to cash into specific measurements or indicators. Thus claims of 'better accountability' or cultural change or greater responsiveness are relatively easy to illustrate with a sound-bite anecdote but very hard to capture in a general measure. Who has measured cultural change? Who has reliable statistics on changes in 'accountability'? In what units may one count shifts in the 'responsiveness' or 'capacity' of a system of public administration? On those (still quite rare) occasions when systematic research has been carried out on such matters, the findings have by no means all pointed towards positive 'transformations', though they have certainly registered that change is underway (Task Force on Management Improvement 1992; Talbot 1994; Rouban 1995). And if a representative sample of citizens is asked questions, the picture is no more clear cut. After a period of intensive reform, including the implementation of the Citizen's Charter, and the roll-out of the Next Steps programme to embrace three quarters of the entire civil service, a UK white paper commented as follows:

> Research with the People's Panel ... shows that more people agree than disagree that our public service providers are friendly, hard-working and keen to help. But, although the number of people who are satisfied is increasing, many services still fall short of expectations. Two out of five

people think services have got no better in the last five years, and over one in three thinks they have become worse.

(Prime Minister and Minister for the Cabinet Office 1999: 23)

From a strict scientific perspective, therefore, the jury is still out on 'systems transformations' – and it may be out for some time.

Conclusions

What general conclusions can be reached concerning the 'results' of NPM? First, it is hard to see them clearly: there are a lot of conceptual problems about quite what it is we are looking for, and also some methodological and interpretive puzzles about what the available data can be said to show. Second, in so far as we *can* get a good look, there definitely is a story to tell. Management reform has not all been windy rhetoric, by any means. Downsizing has been accomplished in a number of countries (although in some cases the figures count transfers to other parts of the state sector as reductions). In many specific and local instances measured efficiency has increased. The influence of published targets in prompting improvement on specific dimensions has been demonstrated time and time again (even if such measurement can also prompt perversions – Pollitt 2000). In many cases, also, specific services have certainly become more user-sympathetic and flexible. These results can be declared with pride. At the same time it should be conceded that their full cost – 'side-effects' and all – is frequently obscure. Other features of services, which are not measured or publicised, may have taken a turn for the worse. Other groups – of staff or citizens – may have suffered degenerating conditions as a consequence of the drive to improve the more salient aspects of a particular service. It is only rarely that the full balance sheet is visible.

Two other things can be said. Some of the larger claims heard from time to time for NPM must be judged either false (so far at least) or unproven. Large savings in aggregate public expenditure have seldom accrued from management reforms *per se*. A government's legitimacy is not likely to be heavily influenced by such reforms either – the chief determinants of public attitudes towards their governments seem to lie elsewhere. The correlation between the implementation of NPM reforms and macro-economic performance is hardly striking, with Germany, Japan and the USA being three of the most successful economies (by most criteria) over the last twenty-five years and yet none of these being among the group which has implemented the most radical reforms (indeed, Germany and Japan have been among the *least* active in this respect). Furthermore, the achievement of more *effective* (as distinct from more efficient) government is hard to demonstrate. Even in that minority of cases where, arguably, improved effectiveness *can* be demonstrated, there is usually considerable ambiguity over to what it should be attributed. The splendid coat of many colours envisaged by some reformers – slim, fast, effective, decentralised, open, trusted government – still lies more in the realms of hope and imagination than in demonstrated and warranted reality.

Finally, we should remember that the jurisdiction of the NPM paradigm is limited. Its heartlands have never really extended beyond Australasia, North America and the UK. Although some methods and techniques may have been selectively borrowed by other countries – especially the Dutch and the Nordics – these countries have never unconditionally accepted the managerialist perspective. Managers have never risen quite as high or politicians fallen quite so low in public esteem as in the USA and the UK. As one senior Dutch civil servant said recently to a visiting New Zealander, 'When will you Anglo-Saxons learn that pulling grass up by the roots doesn't make it grow any faster?'.

Acknowledgements

This chapter represents an extensive re-working of a paper originally presented at the International Summit on Public Management Reform, Winnipeg, Canada, June 1999. I am grateful in various ways to the organizers of that event. A less developed version was later published in *Public Management* (vol. 2, issue 2, pp. 181–199). Finally, I am indebted to Rune Premfors of SCORE, University of Stockholm, for his perceptive comments.

References

Boston, J. (1995) 'Lessons from the Antipodes'. In O'Toole, B. and Jordan, G. (eds) *Next Steps: improving management on government?* Aldershot, Dartmouth, pp. 161–177.

Boyne, G. (1998) 'Bureaucratic theory meets reality: public choice and service contracting in US local government', *Public Administration Review*, 58: 6, pp. 474–484.

Brunsson, N. (1989) *The Organisation Of Hypocrisy: talk, decisions and actions in organisations*, Chichester, John Wiley.

Chancellor of the Duchy of Lancaster (1997) *Next Steps: agencies in government: review, 1996*, Cm 3579, London, The Stationery Office.

Chancellor of the Exchequer (1998) *Modern Public Services for Britain: investing in reform*, Cm 4011, London, The Stationery Office.

Clarke, J. and Newman, J. (1997) *The Managerial State*, London, Sage.

Clarke, J., Gewirtz, S. and McLaughlin, E. (eds) (2000) *New Managerialism, New Welfare?*, London, Sage.

Department of Health (2000) *Departmental Report: the government's expenditure plans, 2000–2001*, Cm 4603, London, The Stationery Office.

Derlien, H-U (1998) *From Administrative Reform to Administrative Modernization*, Bamberg, Verwaltungswissenschaftliche Beitrage.

East, P. (1997) Opening Address to the Public Service senior Managers' Conference, Wellington, NZ, 9 October.

Employment Service (1994) *Employment Service: an evaluation of the effects of agency status 1990–1993*, London, Employment Department Group.

Escott, K. and Whitfield, D. (1995) *The Gender Impact of CCT in Local Government*, Manchester, Equal Opportunities Commission.

Flynn, N. and Strehl, F. (eds) (1996) *Public Sector Management in Europe*, London, Prentice Hall/Harvester Wheatsheaf.

General Accounting Office (1997) *Performance Budgeting: past initiatives offer insights for GPRA implementation*, GAO/AIMD-97–46, Washington, DC, GAO, 27 March.

General Accounting Office (1998) *The Results Act: observations on the Department of State's Fiscal Year 1999 Annual Performance Plan*, GAO/NSIAD-98–210R, Washington DC, GAO.

Gore, A. (1996) *The Best-kept Secrets in Government: a report to President Bill Clinton*, Washington, DC, US Government Printing Office, National Performance Review.

Gore, A. (1997) *Businesslike Government: lessons learned from America's best companies*, Washington, DC, National Performance Review.

Guyomarch, A. (1999) '"Public service", "public management" and the "modernization" of French public administration', *Public Administration*, 77: 1, pp. 171–193

Hencke, D. (1998) 'Jobcentres fiddled the figures', *The Guardian*, 8 January, p. 2.

HM Treasury (1992) *Executive Agencies: a guide to setting targets and measuring performance*, London, HMSO.

Holkeri, K. and Summa, H. (1996) *Contemporary Developments in Performance Management: evaluation of public management reforms in Finland: from ad hoc studies to a programmatic approach*, paper presented to PUMA/OECD, 4–5 November, Paris.

Hood, C. (1996) 'Exploring variations in public management reform of the 1980s'. In Bekke, H., Perry, J. and Toonen, T. (eds) *Civil Service Systems in Comparative Perspective*, Bloomington, Indiana University Press, pp. 268–317.

Hood, C. (1998) *The Art of the State: culture, rhetoric and public management*, Oxford, Oxford University Press.

Ingraham, P., Thompson, J.R. and Sanders, P. (eds) (1998) *Transforming Government: lessons from the re-invention laboratories*, San Francisco, Jossey-Bass.

Jorgensen, T. (1999) 'The public sector in an in-between time: searching for new public values'. *Public Administration*, 77: 3, pp. 565–584.

Kettl, D. (1994) *Re-inventing Government? Appraising the National Performance Review*, Washington DC, Brookings Institution Press.

Kettl, D. (2000) *The Global Public Management Revolution: a report on the transformation of governance*, Washington, DC, Brookings Institution Press.

Kickert, W. (ed.) (1997) *Public Management and Administrative Reform in Western Europe*, Cheltenham, Edward Elgar.

Kirkpatrick, I. (1999) 'The worst of both worlds? Public services without markets or bureaucracy'. *Public Money and Management* 19: 41, pp. 9–14.

Konig, K. (1996) *On the Critique of New Public Management*, Speyer, Speyer Forschungsberichte, p. 155.

Lane, J-E. (ed.) (1997) *Public Sector Reform: rationale, trends, problems*, London, Sage.

Ministry of Finance (1997) *Public Management Reforms: five country studies*, Helsinki, Ministry of Finance.

Murray, R. (1998) *Productivity as a Tool for Evaluation of Public Management Reform*, paper presented to the European Evaluation Society Conference, Rome, 29–31 October.

Naschold, F. (1995) *The Modernization of the Public Sector in Europe*, Helsinki, Ministry of Labour.

Naschold, F. and von Otter, C. (1996) *Public Sector Transformation: rethinking markets and hierarchies in government*, Amsterdam, John Benjamins Publishing Company.

National Audit Office (1998) Benefits Agency: performance measurement, HC9S2, London, The Stationery Office.

Next Steps Team (1998) *Towards Best Practice: an evaluation of the first two years of the Public Sector benchmarking project, 1996–98*, London, Efficiency and Effectiveness Group, The Cabinet Office.

OECD (1995) *Governance in Transition: public management reforms in OECD countries*, Paris, PUMA/OECD.

Olsen, J. and Peters, B. (eds) (1996) *Lessons from Experience: experiential learning in administrative reforms in eight democracies*, Oslo, Scandinavian University Press.

Osborne, D. and Gaebler, T. (1992) *Reinventing Government: how the entrepreneurial spirit is transforming the public sector*, Reading, MA, Addison-Wesley.

Pawson, R. and Tilley, N. (1997) *Realistic Evaluation*, London, Sage.

Peters, G. (1995) 'Bureaucracy in a divided regime: the United States'. In Pierre, J. (ed.) *Bureaucracy and the Modern State: an introduction to comparative public administration*, Aldershot, Edward Elgar, pp. 18–38.

Peters, G. (1997) 'A North American perspective on administrative modernisation in Europe'. In Kickert, W. (ed.) *Public Management and Administrative Reform in Western Europe*, Cheltenham, Edward Elgar. pp. 255–270.

Peters, G. and Savoie, D. (eds) (1998) *Taking Stock: assessing public sector reforms*, Montreal, Canadian Centre for Management Development/McGill-Queen's University Press.

Pierre, J. (ed.) (1995) *Bureaucracy in the Modern State: an introduction to comparative public administration*, Aldershot, Edward Elgar.

Pierson, P. (2000) 'Increasing returns, path dependence, and the study of politics', *American Political Science Review* 94: 2, pp. 251–267.

Pollitt, C. (1993) *Managerialism and the Public Services*, Oxford, Blackwell.

Pollitt, C. (1995) 'Justification by works or by faith? Evaluating the New Public Management', *Evaluation*, 1: 2, pp. 133–154.

Pollitt, C. (1998) 'Evaluation and the New Public Management: an international perspective', *Evaluation Journal of Australasia*, 9: 1/2, pp. 7–15.

Pollitt, C. (2000) 'How do we know how good public services are?'. In Peters, G. and Savoie, D. (eds) *Revitalising the Public Service*, Montreal and Kingston, Canadian Centre for Management Development and McGill/Queens University Press.

Pollitt, C. (2001) 'Clarifying convergence: striking similarities and durable differences in management reform', *Public Management Review*, 3: 4, pp. 1–22..

Pollitt, C. and Bouckaert, G. (2000) *Public Management Reform: a comparative analysis*, Oxford, Oxford University Press.

Pollitt, C. and Summa, H. (1997) 'Trajectories of reform: management change in four countries', *Public Money and Management*, 17: 1, pp. 7–18.

Pollitt, C., Birchall, J. and Putman, K. (1998) *Decentralising Public Service Management*, Basingstoke, Macmillan.

Pollitt, C., Girre, X., Lonsdale, J., Mul, R., Summa, H. and Waerness, M. (1999) *Performance or Compliance? Performance audit and public management in five countries*, Oxford, Oxford University Press.

Premfors, R. (1998) 'Reshaping the democratic state: Swedish experiences in a comparative perspective', *Public Administration*, 76: 1, pp. 141–159.

Prime Minister and Minister for the Cabinet Office (1999) *Modernising Government*, Cm 4310, London, The Stationery Office.

Rouban, L. (1995) 'The civil service culture and administrative reform'. In Peters, B. and Savoie, D. (eds) *Governance in a Changing Environment*, Montreal and Kingston, Canadian Centre for Management Development and McGill-Queen's University Press, pp. 23–54.

Savoie, D. (1994) *Thatcher, Reagan, Mulroney: in search of a new bureaucracy*, Toronto, University of Toronto Press.

Schick, A. (1996) *The Spirit of Reform: managing the New Zealand state sector in a time of change*, Wellington, NZ, State Services Commission.

Siimes, S-A. (1999) 'Personnel management also in the forefront', *Public Management in Finland*, pp. 4–7.

Steering Group (1991) *Review of State Sector Reforms*, Auckland, State Services Commission.

Talbot, C. (1994) *Re-inventing Public Management: a survey of public sector managers' reactions to change*, Corby, UK, Institute of Management.

Talbot, C. (1996) *Ministers and Agencies: responsibility and performance*, London, CIPFA.

Talbot, C. (1997) *Public Performance: towards a public service excellence model*, Discussion Paper No.1, Llantilio Crosseny, UK, Public Futures.

Task Force on Management Improvement (1992) *The Australian Public Service Reformed: an evaluation of a decade of management reform*, Canberra, Management Advisory Board, AGPS.

Trosa, S. (1995) *Moderniser l'administration: comment font les autres?* Paris, Les Editions d'Organisation.

Part IV

Researching the New Public Management

Chapter 17

The New Public Management
An action research approach

Chris Huxham

The aim of this chapter is to provide some insight into ways in which action research can contribute to the development of theory about *the implementation of* the NPM ideals. There are many forms of action research, so it is important to begin by saying what is meant by the term here. For readers who have encountered action research before, I emphasize that I am *not* concerned here with varieties of action research that are forms of self-development or organizational development such as those propounded by Eldon and Chisholm (1993), Reason and Bradbury (2000), Stringer (1996) and Whyte (1991). The promotion of ideological positions about participation and empowerment that is intrinsic to many of the latter approaches is also not pertinent to this chapter.

The focus here is on a variety of action research that has been explicated in some detail by Eden and Huxham (1996). It is a methodology for carrying out research into management and organizations. While some such forms of action research stress explicit setting and testing of hypotheses (Alderfer 1993), the Eden and Huxham approach is firmly set within the phenomenological paradigm. As, for example, with ethnographic research, this form of action research derives theoretical insights from naturally occurring data rather than through interviews or questionnaires (Marshall and Rossman 1989). Its distinctive feature as a research methodology is its *requirement* that the researcher actually *intervenes* in the organizations studied, working with organizational members on matters of genuine concern to them. In these circumstances, *rich* data can be collected about what people do and say – and what theories are used and are usable – when they are faced with a genuine need to take action. The data are 'timely' in the sense that they are collected at the point of happening, rather than through *post hoc* recollection and rationalization. Such data have the potential to provide both new and unexpected insights so theory development processes are inductive – leading to 'emergent theory' – in order to encourage this.

Action research can complement other approaches to understanding NPM. It is particularly appropriate for investigating issues in the *implementation* of policy because it can lead to deep conceptualizations about what can happen in practice and the reasons for this. It is well placed in its potential for developing theory that will be of relevance to practice because each intervention provides an opportunity for the researcher to revisit theory in order to design the intervention, and to develop it further as a result (Diesing 1972).

Ensuring research rigour when intervention settings form the research sites involves paying serious attention to '... systematic method and orderliness ... in reflecting about, and holding onto, the research data' (Eden and Huxham 1996: 534). This implies that the researcher must be clear about the nature of the intervention, the ways in which data are collected and the processes through which the resulting theory is developed. This chapter explores some aspects of what rigorous action research involves, and the types of theoretical insight that can be derived from it, by navigating our way around a case study of its use.

The case that forms the basis of the chapter concerns a research project about leadership in partnership settings. In selecting this exemplar, I am taking for granted that the promotion of partnerships of public, private and non-profit organizations as a system of governance is a key policy thrust of NPM and that understanding the nature of effective leadership in such settings would be seen by some policy makers, at least, as important (see other chapters in this book). I will discuss the research context in which the project was set, the intervention settings in which data were collected, the theory development process and (in brief summary) the theory that resulted. I will bring in commentary about action research on the way.

'Leadership in partnership' may be taken as typical of the kinds of policy issues that are implicit in NPM. The particularity of this topic has little relevance to the methodological issues in using action research to understand how policies become enacted in practice. However, since we shall be journeying only through a single project, we shall be highlighting a particular instance of action research. Even in the context of our own research into collaborative partnerships we derive emergent theory using many other variations of analysis procedure (see, for example, Vangen and Huxham 1998b; Eden and Huxham 2000; Huxham and Vangen 2000a). A case study in which we have used a very different action research approach to developing practice-oriented theory to support collaborative practice is described in Huxham and Vangen (1998).

How action research is carried out is contingent upon the research aims, the intervention contexts and the researcher's intervention style and analytical preferences. The methodology, as well as the theoretical output, is almost always emergent because the researcher cannot know in advance what intervention opportunities will arise, or what past interventions may suddenly seem relevant for re-review. In addition, the researcher cannot know in advance exactly what analysis process will be used, because the development of emergent theory requires the researcher to 'play' with and 'massage' the data, sometimes in many different ways over prolonged periods of time in order to 'reframe [the data] into something new' (Thomas 1993: 43). Nevertheless, by looking in some detail at one project I aim to highlight possibilities and issues that are relevant to other situations.

CASE STUDY: RESEARCHING LEADERSHIP IN PARTNERSHIP

Background and methodological considerations

The 'leadership project' has been carried out jointly with my colleague, Siv Vangen. It is ongoing as I write this chapter, but the aspects of it described here were completed nine months ago. The theory derived at that stage is explicated in detail in Huxham and Vangen (2000b). The project forms an element of a programme of research that has so far spanned more than ten years, which aims to develop practice-oriented theory about convening, designing, managing, participating in and facilitating collaboration between organizations (Huxham and Vangen 2000c). The object is to create theory that will be of value to practitioners (Vangen 1998; Vangen and Huxham 1998a; Huxham and Vangen 2001) as well as meeting the criteria for rigorous research (Eden and Huxham 1996). The concepts of *collaborative advantage* and *collaborative inertia* have emerged from the research and subsequently driven the agenda. Collaborative advantage signifies the generic benefit to be expected from partnership; a synergy from working together leading to outcomes that the organizations could not achieve on their own. Collaborative inertia signifies the outcome that our research shows to be common in practice; the rate of output from partnership appears slow, and even successful outcomes are achieved only after much pain or hard grind. Much of our research has focused on understanding the reasons why collaborative inertia is so often the practical outcome and whether and how it is possible to improve upon this.

Our work on leadership was unusual for us in that it did not arise out of our own research agenda generated by our previous understanding of partnership but was stimulated by colleagues in the policy analysis field whose perspective led them to argue for its importance in informing policy makers. We were doubtful about whether leadership was a subject that could or should contribute to a practice-oriented theory because data from our previous action research interventions indicated that there had been little spontaneous use of the terms 'lead', 'leader' or 'leadership' by practitioners involved and none had highlighted 'leadership' as an area of concern. Nevertheless, if policy-makers were interested in the concept, it was clearly worth investigating further.

The imposed nature of this topic landed us with a dilemma that can often arise in action research: it was unclear how we would recognize the subject we were studying. Action research of this sort demands that the theory is derived emergently from the data (Eden and Huxham 1996). So far as is practical, the aim is to suppress pre-understanding (Gummesson 1991) in order to promote the emergence of new and creative insights. This means that, so far as is reasonable, predefined conceptualizations should not be used to guide data collection. However, since our previous research indicated that practitioners would rarely refer explicitly to leadership, deciding how we would recognize it during an intervention became a major methodological issue. It would clearly not have been feasible to collect data in a way that would be totally consistent with the 'emergent' philosophy. We needed some guidance on how to differentiate data on leadership from the mass of potentially collectable data. However, in the spirit of the action research philosophy, we felt it to be important that the methodology should open up – rather than close down – possible theoretical perspectives, so this 'winnowing' process (Wolcott 1990) could not be guided by a single predefined framework.

Although action research emphasizes an open attitude to data collection and theory building, there is clearly a tension to address when researching an area where there is extensive pre-existing theory. On the one hand, too much reliance on predefined theory can act to blinker the researcher, inhibiting their ability to think or see beyond the theory. On the other hand, predefined theory can be an eye opener, directing attention to aspects of a situation that might otherwise be missed. It is therefore important to create an appropriate balance between using such theory and suppressing it.

In this case, we were clear from the start that our theoretical understanding of the demands of collaborative environments captured in our previous research would be central in directing our attention to aspects of the situations that appeared to lead the partnership forward. However, in order to increase the chances that we would not miss other possibilities, we tried to broaden our perspective through conversations with other researchers from a range of backgrounds about what leadership in partnership might mean. We also made a, *deliberately cursory*, review of an assortment of apparently relevant literature with the aim of using the variety among the theoretical perspectives as triggers for data collection. This included the mainstream theories of leadership (Fiedler 1967; Stogdill 1974; Burns 1978; Graef 1983; Bass 1990; Brymen 1996) emphasizing leadership traits, styles and so on; research on leadership in collaborative settings emphasizing leadership tasks, skills and behaviours (Bryson and Crosby 1992; Chrislip and Larson 1994; Feyerherm 1994; Purdue and Razzaque 1999); and references to leadership in research on collaboration in both public and private sector settings, emphasizing, for example, the distinction between formal and informal leaders (Øvretveit 1993), different types of leader such as administrators (Axinn and Axinn 1997) or the CEO of a joint venture (Cauley de la Sierra 1995) and whether the leadership function is carried out by one or many of the member organizations (Lynch 1993).

The methodology that we eventually used was the result of much discussion between ourselves and with other researchers. In order to maintain the desired open theoretical perspective, we decided that we would record *anything* that we observed or heard during action research interventions that *might* be argued to have something to do with 'leadership'. At the data collection stage it would not be essential that the argument could be sustained; it was important only to ensure that possibilities were recorded.

Data sources and data gathering

In contrast to those forms of action research that are concerned with individual and self-development, this kind of action research is not restricted to a single intervention setting. It can be helpful to locate theory generation in multiple settings, since this both broadens the possibilities for data collection and makes it easier to draw out the generic significance of the output. In the leadership project, the broad approach to data recording described in the last section was applied in various intervention settings. These will be described later in this section following some general observations about data gathering interventions.

The question of what constitutes an 'action intervention' is a matter of some philosophical interest in action research. It is of significance because the particular strength of emergent theory derived from action research, as opposed to, for example, ethnography or in-depth interviews, is argued to be its grounding not only in the data (Glaser and Strauss 1967) but also in action (Eden and Huxham 1996). What matters, it is argued, is what people say and do at the point of action. An extreme view might be that only interventions that involve practitioners who have particular concerns about which they must make decisions and take action should be regarded as legitimate bases for action research. Situations are, however, often not clear-cut in this respect and my own view is that there is a wide range of degrees of action orientation in interventions and that all may be regarded as legitimate bases for action research providing the researcher is conscious of this when working with the data generated and interprets the data in this light.

Action research does not specify the amount of time that minimally or maximally must be spent with practitioners in order for an intervention to generate legitimate research data. Data from both short- and long-term interventions have value. However, while data from long-term interventions may be used in isolation to generate theory, data from short-term ones must necessarily be used in combination with other data as a contribution to theory building. Each intervention adds *new* slants or insights to the developing theory.

However, a characteristic of using action research in the context of NPM settings is that, if carried out over prolonged periods, the intervention settings often interrelate. We have rarely actively sought out interventions, and have instead, generally, reacted to opportunities, often in the form of requests from practitioners. Consequently, we have found ourselves enmeshed in a web of collaborative settings and are often surprised to discover 'small-world' links between one and another. For example, as will be seen in the leadership project settings, individual practitioners often reappear in new settings, bringing with them their history from the previous ones.

This means that data collected in previous settings may provide an important context for interpretation of later events or comments. It often also means that data collected in later settings can provide confirmations about, or new insights into, the interpretation of data collected on earlier occasions. For example, the role an individual or organization plays in a later partnership, may help to explain their role in an earlier one, or *vice versa*. While this kind of data may arise out of the formal aspects of the intervention, chance comments made by people reflecting with hindsight on their earlier involvements with us are also often very enlightening. In action research, important data often come when least expected, so the researcher has to be continually alert to ensure that they get recorded and integrated into the theory development process. This mode of operation thus has some characteristics of longitudinal research (Pettigrew 1990), even though individual research settings may be short term. Over several years, the theoretical insights generated gradually become refined and enriched, and confidence in their robustness and their range of applicability increases.

The means of actually collecting the data within these many settings is usually a matter of choice. In some respects, the ideal situation is when an intervention tool can double as a means of recording data. For example, computer-stored maps that capture the varied views and perspectives of the practitioners involved can be used as a facilitation tool in strategic thinking workshops (Eden and Ackermann 1998). These provide a rich data source, already captured in a form that is amenable to analysis. However, only certain types of data can be captured in this way, and many research aims demand at least some additional data recording. There are many options available to the action researcher, ranging from overt methods such as video recording or supplementary interviews through to discreet note-taking. The choice of data collection design clearly has implications for the interpretation of the results; this has been discussed in detail elsewhere (Huxham and Vangen 1998).

The interventions that have informed the research programme have been extremely varied in all of the above respects, with some being much closer to the action than others, some lasting a long period and others being but a brief interaction. A wide range of data collection methods has been used. The interventions used as the data sources in the leadership project were a microcosm of these and so provide examples of the range of possibilities.

Health and related partnerships

Four interrelated partnerships were central to the data collection in the project. The longest intervention was with a city-based health promotion partnership that was recognized by the World Health Organization. Two large public agencies and twelve other bodies, including universities and the local Council for Voluntary Organizations made up the official membership as listed in its constitution document. Our introduction into this partnership was through one of our policy analysis colleagues who had connections with it through previous work. Unusually for us, the legitimacy for entry was founded on the basis of the funding for the research. At that time, an acting partnership manager, who was normally the representative on the partnership from one of the key member organizations, was covering the maternity leave of the appointed manager. He appeared to see potential value in linking up with us as experts in partnership practice, and in the investigation of leadership.

The main chunk of data that was used from this partnership was derived in connection with a project being championed by the acting manager to develop and run a series of workshops for representatives from the partnership's formal working groups and community projects on the theme of developing a joint approach to (or at least mutual learning about) converting the research results produced by the working groups and projects into usable output. Our intervention thus consisted of several planning meetings with the acting manager (and, later, the appointed manager) and the partnership administrator, the one such workshop actually held and some follow up meetings. One of us actually chaired the workshop and we both acted as facilitators during the small-groups session that formed an important element of it. The data used in subsequent analysis included notes made during and after the meetings and the workshop. In these, the typical notes that any consultant or facilitator would make as part of the design process were supplemented by our own commentary and we sometimes noted direct quotations from the practitioners. Other forms of data used were the formal partnership documentation such as a development plan, the flip chart notes created by participants at the workshop and the follow-up report produced by the partnership administrator.

There were subsequent discussions about other possible lines of work in which we might be involved and notes of these were also made. One of the authors was invited to become a member of one of the management committees of the partnership and so the committee paperwork as well as notes made during the meetings and phone calls and other interactions in connection with the partnership business were also available as data, but most of this occurred after the analysis referred to in this chapter took place.

It is not possible here to relay the full variety of types of insight into leadership that were gained from these data, but issues to do with the way the structure of, and externally imposed constraints on, the partnership affected what was actually achieved by those aiming to lead were very evident. The effect of discontinuities, such as that caused in this case by maternity leave, on the outcomes of leadership endeavours was also highlighted as were the roles played by different types of positional leader in the partnership. Many leadership activities were also apparent, including struggles to control the agenda and the mobilization of the resource of the partner organizations.

The health promotion partnership was itself one of the partners in the second partnership from which we collected data. This was concerned with creating synergy through learning from initiatives in three UK cities on the subject of integrating health, regeneration and environmental sustainability activities. We were invited to attend an early meeting between two of the partners as part of our introduction to the health promotion partnership and were asked to contribute suggestions about how the partnership might progress. At this meeting we were able to make almost complete verbatim notes of the discussion. Unfortunately, owing to availability constraints, we were unable to attend other meetings to which we were invited, but issues concerning the partnership were repeatedly put on the agenda by the manager of the health promotion partnership as small items for discussion at the end of our planning meetings about the workshop series. She was keeping us updated in the hope of later involving us more centrally, and, at the same time, using us as sounding boards regarding the issues that were currently engaging her attention. We kept notes of the issues she raised. Another key figure in the partnership was one of our policy analysis colleagues, who represented one of the partner organizations, so we also received occasional updates from him.

Our intervention in this partnership was therefore not large, but we were able to get both detailed data from a (potentially) critical start-up meeting and a sense – albeit, largely one-sided – of the way in which it developed over time. Among the insights we gained from this data were examples of the kinds of approaches that people use to lead the partnership in directions they think are helpful.

Our third data collection setting arose out of our connections with the first two. This collaborative community project was a funded formal project of the health promotion partnership and we visited it as an exemplar of an initiative that might be of interest to the three-cities project. In itself, this was a very brief, and not very action-oriented one-off interaction between ourselves, some of the three-cities participants and some of the key staff of the project. The staff talked with us for a couple of hours about their experiences in the project and we made detailed notes as they did so. This meeting, however, led to our fourth source of data. These same individuals were community representatives on a community regeneration partnership and one of us interviewed them and other representatives as a contribution to a related research project being carried out by our policy analysis colleagues into the role of community leaders on urban partnerships. A report was written summarizing the main findings and this formed the basis of a focus group meeting organized by us. The data from this work were derived from unstructured in-depth interviews and detailed notes taken at the focus group session. It was not intended to be action research, but the data provided useful insights that complemented those derived from other settings. In particular, it led to insights about ways that people try to use the power of their position to provide effective leadership. It also highlighted the leadership task of creating processes through which members could contribute effectively to the partnership's activities.

Other partnerships

Data from work with a number of other partnerships was used to support and enrich that from the four above. Two, in particular, were thoroughly reviewed for insights on leadership. The first of these was an EC-funded partnership of three environmental organizations. It had originally been constituted with four partnerships, but one had withdrawn when it found an alternative means of addressing its own aims. The collaborative aim was to provide joint support in the areas of finance and IT for the collaborating organizations and to stage a networking conference and some multicultural training. One of us was contacted by a representative from one of the organizations who was a member of the partnership's management group. He had previously been at a seminar in which we had led a small group workshop. The role taken with this group was essentially that of sounding board to the management group. After one year of their project, they were keen to review their collaborative processes. The intervention involved phone calls and a meeting with the initiating representative and then attendance at three full meetings of the group. At the first of these, the future processes of the partnership was the only agenda item. At later ones, it formed a part of the agenda. It was eventually agreed that the intervention had triggered enough rethinking for the partnership to progress without a continued presence at group meetings and the role changed to that of sounding board to the convenor of the group as she devised an evaluation process for the work of the partnership.

Data collection in this case was predominantly by notes taken during the meetings. Many aspects of leadership were highlighted by this partnership. For example, it emphasized the role played by communication processes in affecting what is actually achieved by those attempting to lead. It also highlighted particular issues that arise when the members are themselves involved in cooperative and collaborative arrangements. The leadership activity of enthusing member organizations becomes particularly challenging under these circumstances.

The second partnership was a rural regeneration partnership. We were contacted by the partnership manager and asked to work with her to design and run a one-day workshop for the partnership. The partnership had a history of some difficulty in the relationships between members, but after three years had managed to make progress. However, it had reached a milestone, with funding running out and new government initiatives encroaching on its role, and needed to assess whether it should put energy into sustaining its future. Our work with this partnership involved many telephone calls and a meeting with the manager before and after the workshop, facilitation of the workshop and production of a report for participants. As in other cases, our principle data collection was in the form of notes made during and after the many interactions, including the workshop. Partnership documents, flip charts from the workshop and the report supplemented these. The partnership manager, in this case, was particularly eloquent and insightful in the commentary she provided as briefing for us while we were designing the workshop. We therefore were able to gain a very large number of perspectives on leadership. Among these were the dominant role that a formally designated lead organization can play and the barriers that partnership structures can place in the way of members taking active leadership roles.

Approximately eighteen months after this workshop, one of us was asked by one of the participants to contribute to a similar event for a small town community regeneration partnership within the area covered by the rural partnership. This provided additional data, some of which retrospectively triangulated with that from the earlier events.

Other interventions that influenced our thinking through providing pieces of data that had relevance to leadership were many and various. On one occasion, for example, we invited the director of a community organization to be a speaker at a seminar that we were running. We had previously worked with her over a number of years as facilitators of a collaborative working group concerned with child poverty that she convened. During her presentation, she revealed transformations in the working group – now a partnership of only two organizations – since we had last worked with them. This same story had been recounted to one of us over a lunch with another member of the original group some months earlier. The new data both confirmed the previous account and presented it from a different perspective. This provided additional insight into ways that those seeking to lead can deal with members who are perceived to be non-contributing.

We were also involved in a number of ways in work with civil servants concerned with designing, implementing and supporting the UK government's Modernising Government policy and (among other things) this led us to focus on the effect that government imposed structures may have on those trying to take a lead at local level. It also led us to concentrate on what is needed to develop the ability of public sector managers to operate in a world where partnership is a taken for granted.

A final example is a long standing supervisory relationship with an enterprise agency employee who is carrying out a PhD using her organization's role in promoting a regional partnership as the basis for her research. This highlighted issues concerned with agencies taking a self-appointed lead-organization role.

From intervention to conceptualization

Finding a way to turn the data collected into theoretical conceptualization is probably the most challenging aspect of action research and, as was mentioned earlier, there can be no predefined methodology for doing this. Writing in the context of critical ethnography, Thomas richly captures the essence of the challenge:

> Interpretation of data is the defamiliarization process in which we revise what we have seen and translate it into something new, distancing ourselves from the taken-for-granted aspect of what we see.... We take the collection of observations, anecdotes, impressions, documents and other symbolic representations that seem depressingly mundane and common and reframe them into something new.
>
> (1993: 43)

In the leadership project, analysing the data captured involved us in extensive discussions concerned with sense-making, data massaging and finding representations and linkages. Clearly, there are benefits in having more than one researcher involved in an action research project since this allows this process of 'playing' with the data to be more creative, more rigorous and more fun.

With hindsight, we were able to identify several stages that the analysis had passed through. The specifics of these have been described in detail in Huxham and Vangen (2000b). Here, we provide an overview of the stages in order to give an indication of one approach to theory building.

Firstly, we each independently reviewed the recorded data from the health promotion partnerships, identifying any items for which it was now felt that a sustainable argument could be made for relevance to leadership. As before, this process was partially informed by – but not limited by – the range of perspectives on what leadership could mean that was discussed earlier. Some data items, such as:

- How can members be mobilised to contribute actively to the collaboration? or
- Jane's creation of a health framework as a basis (in the first instance) for getting partners to get started,

were direct quotations or descriptions of what happened during an intervention. Others, such as:

- design/use documents/frameworks as effective leadership tools; or
- what processes can be designed that will help representatives to bring in the resources of their organization?

were interpretations or generalizations drawn from the specific examples.

The second stage then involved lengthy negotiations between ourselves about whether and how each data item should be included in the analysis. These debates – which were essential to ensuring 'theoretical sensitivity' (Glaser 1992; Strauss and Corbin 1998) – involved clarification of:

1   the meaning of the item;
2   the wording of the description of the original comments, actions or events and the reasons why these could be interpreted as relevant to leadership; and
3   the linkages between each new data item and those previously accepted.

Gradually clusters of data and interpretations began to emerge. We also added in concepts deriving from the literature. On this occasion we used the mapping software, Decision Explorer, which is designed to assist with the analysis of qualitative data, to store and organize the data clusters (Banxia 1996; Eden and Ackermann 1998). Decision Explorer is a convenient tool because it allows large volumes of data to be handled flexibly. However, any means of recording data in a way that it can be 'played with' can be used. On other occasions, for example, we have used Post-it notes to record data items.

As we built each data cluster, one of the interpretation concepts was chosen through further discussion and negotiation, as its designated label. These labels are similar to the axial codes of grounded theory (Strauss and Corbin 1998). Both the cluster boundaries and the labels sometimes changed as further data were considered.

The third stage of the analysis – which was similar in purpose, though not in form, to the 'selective coding' of grounded theory – involved reviewing the clusters and the linkages between them, with a view to creating a conceptual *framework*. As with stages 1 and 2, we first carried out individual reviews that were then discussed and debated. At this stage some clusters were excluded on the grounds that they did not contain enough data. Others, which had been subdivided because they contained too much data to handle in one cluster, were considered jointly from the point of view of the framework. One cluster was reluctantly excluded on the grounds that space constraints in the article we were writing precluded its inclusion at this stage. Five clusters eventually formed the basis of the framework. These were labelled 'leadership processes', 'leadership structures', 'the leader', 'leadership tasks' and 'shaping the partnership's agenda'.

The fourth stage involved reviewing data collected in the other interventions mentioned earlier, taking the emerging framework as an additional – and important – guide to interpreting its relevance to leadership. This helped to put additional flesh on the framework and provided a loose test of its robustness in the light of other partnerships than those around which it had been created. The process did not preclude the possibility of new clusters emerging. That none did at this stage, confirmed the solidification of the clusters (Marshall and Rossman 1989).

Finally, in order to build the clusters into a coherent framework – stage 5 – we drafted and redrafted the theoretical arguments, circulating these for comment, presenting the arguments in academic conferences and using them with practitioners in further action research interventions. The cluster concerned with 'shaping the partnership's agenda' eventually became the backdrop for the whole framework. The clusters on 'leadership processes', 'leadership structures' and 'the leader' were drawn together and conceptualized as 'leadership media'. We eventually decided that the label, 'leadership activities' would better represent the issues captured in the final cluster than its original label of 'leadership tasks'.

The theoretical arguments that were eventually presented in the leadership article (Huxham and Vangen 2000b) were thus subjected to wide-ranging scrutiny and refined accordingly. Nevertheless, we view them as an interim statement in a developing story.

The emerging conceptual framework

Readers who are interested in the theoretical outcomes of the leadership project, should refer to that article (Huxham and Vangen 2000b). However, it seems worth summarising here the main thrusts of the conceptualization in order to give an indication of the *type of* theory that can emerge from action research.

At the start of the project, we had no expectations for the kind of output that we would produce. Nevertheless, the perspective on leadership that emerged from the above processes surprised us.

We had deliberately sought data that would bring as many perspectives as possible onto the notion of 'leadership' in collaborative settings. However, in retrospect it is clear that our focus on the development of practice-orientated theory led us to concentrate on a conception of leadership as being connected with 'making things happen' in the partnership. We found ourselves focusing on influences upon the outcomes of partnership activity (Berger 1997). In formal terms, we defined this perspective as being concerned with *the mechanisms that lead a partnership's policy and activity agenda in one direction rather than another.*

Our data, however, demonstrated clearly that much of what does happen in partnerships is influenced by factors other than just the participants in the system. We were thus led to a conceptualization of collaborative leadership that viewed it as being not only enacted by participants who may be identified as leaders, but also by the structures and communication processes embedded within the partnership. We therefore identified three leadership 'media', structures, processes and participants.

The data also demonstrated that the three media are often, to a large extent, outside of the immediate conscious control of the members of the partnership. Structures and processes are often imposed upon a partnership by, for example, funders or legalities. Alternatively, they also often emerge from the activities of the partnership with members unconscious of the structural and processual changes that are implicit in their actions. Similarly, the most influential participants in partnerships are not always the members of the partner organizations. For example, in many cases, partnership managers, whose role is to support the partnership and who are not usually employed by any of the member organizations, spend much more time driving partnership activities forward than do the members themselves.

We grouped the three leadership media under the heading of *contextual leadership*, arguing that they affect the outcomes of individual leadership initiatives. Our data showed individuals – both members and other participants – becoming involved in 'informal leadership' activities (Hosking 1988) that are intended to take the partnership forward. Three categories of activity were explored as exemplars in the original paper, but our current work is focusing on further data scanning to uncover and elaborate on more of these (Vangen and Huxham 2000).

The three exemplars were *managing power and controlling the agenda, representing and mobilizing member organizations* and *enthusing and empowering those who can deliver partnership aims*. In each case, the issues underlying, and different perspectives on, the activity were explored and examples of ways that individuals had tried to address the leadership challenges were identified. However, the important general conclusion that we drew from the data was that while their activities clearly affect the outcomes of the partnership, those aiming to 'lead' are frequently thwarted by dilemmas and difficulties so that the outcomes are not as they intend. Wherever the data showed 'leaders' achieving the outcomes they wished for, they also showed them devoting very significant personal attention to championing the cause. This highlighted the paradox that the single-mindedness of 'leaders' appears to be central to collaborative success.

At the most general level, the practical implication that we drew from this conceptualization is that leading any one of the 'leadership activities' through to completion requires a very large amount of resource in the form of energy, commitment, skill and continual nurturing on the part of the 'leader'. Leading across the full range of activities and processual concerns that need to be addressed to drive forward a partnership holistically is thus highly resource consuming.

This general conclusion was consistent with conclusions from other aspects of our research programme on partnership. However, this conceptualization highlighted a new range of generic activities that participants in partnerships find themselves grappling with, and clarified further the nature of the practical constraints that limit the potential to conclude them successfully. When we reviewed, with hindsight, our initial concern that leadership might not be a subject that should contribute to a practice-oriented theory of partnership, we concluded that researching partnerships from the viewpoint of leadership had been instrumental in adding an important dimension to theory. We have still to resolve our view about whether or not the terminology, 'leader' and 'leadership', is helpful in using the insights with practitioners.

Concluding comments

The aim of this chapter was to use the leadership in partnership project as a case study to demonstrate how action research can generate theory that can highlight the practical issues facing individuals who have to implement policy drives on the ground. In describing the case, we have aimed to:

1   highlight the kinds of considerations that influence the recording of data;
2   raise some issues about the nature of action research intervention settings and their implications for theory building;
3   provide some examples of such settings;
4   provide an example of a method for deriving emergent theory from the data collected; and
5   provide an example of the kind of theory that can be generated.

Action research does not replace other forms of NPM research, but complements it, providing new insights that can contribute to a holistic overall picture. Obviously the data collected in action research is serendipitous to the extent that it can only be collected where interventions take place; what is possible is generally bounded by the needs of the intervention rather than needs of research so other forms of theory development will always be needed to tackle aspects of the wider picture that are not researchable in this way.

The strength of this kind of action research, however, is that data collection necessarily leads to generation of descriptive theory about the practical reality of the situations studied. Because the researcher is immersed in the intervention situations, it often happens that data is collected that the participants themselves are unaware of or have not objectified. For this reason, therefore, the insights produced have the chance of being closer to real experiences than to policy rhetoric or to espoused, *post hoc* explanations (Argyris and Schon 1974) which practitioners might give in an interview. In the leadership in partnership project, for example, it is unlikely that any of those involved would have been able to conceptualize the affect that imposed structures were having upon them, or consciously articulate their involvement in any of the three leadership activities explored. Neither would they have recognized in advance the extent to which their endeavours to move the partnership forward were being thwarted by factors inherent in the situation. Descriptive theory of this sort does not prescribe for practice, but can provide practitioners with a means to make sense of their situations and a platform from which to make considered choices about action. It has clear potential for informing policy decisions.

Acknowledgements

The research project on leadership in partnership that forms the case study for this chapter was carried out jointly with Siv Vangen and would not have been the same without her. I would like to express my thanks to her for allowing me to use our joint material in this way. I also wish to thank Murray Stewart and Robin Hambleton, whose collaboration with us triggered this research, and Colin Eden, who long ago set me thinking about action research. This research project was partially supported by Economic and Social Research Council grant number L130251031.

References

Alderfer, C. 1993. Emerging developments in action research. *Journal of Applied Behavioural Science* 29 (Special issue), 389–492.

Argyris, C. and Schon, D. 1974. *Theories in Practice*. San Francisco: Jossey Bass.

Axinn, G. and Axinn, N. 1997. *Collaboration in International Rural Development*. London: Sage.

Banxia. 1996. *Decision Explorer User Guide*. Glasgow: Banxia Software.

Bass, B. 1990. *Bass and Stogdill's Handbook of Leadership: theory, research and managerial applications*. New York: The Free Press.

Berger, A. 1997. Public leaders and multi-sectoral collaborations: assessing the influence of leaders on partnership outcomes. Paper presented at the Academy of Management Annual Meeting, Boston.

Brymen, A. 1996. Leadership in organizations. In Clegg, S., Hardy, C. and Nord, W. (eds) *Handbook of Organization Studies*: London: Sage, pp. 276–292.

Bryson, J. and Crosby, B.C. 1992. *Leadership for the Common Good: tackling public problems in a shared-power world*. San Francisco: Jossey-Bass.

Burns, J. 1978. *Leadership*. New York: Harper and Row.

Cauley de la Sierra, M. 1995. *Managing Global Alliances. Key steps for successful collaboration*. Wokingham: Addison-Wesley Publishing Company.

Chrislip, D. and Larson, C. 1994. *Collaborative Leadership: how citizens and civic leaders can make a difference*. San Francisco: Jossey-Bass.

Deising, P. 1972. *Patterns of Discovery in the Social Sciences*. London: Routledge and Kegan Paul

Eden, C. and Ackermann, F. 1998. *Making Strategy: the journey of strategic management*. London: Sage.

Eden, C. and Huxham, C. 1996. Action research for the study of organizations. In Clegg, S., Hardy, C. and Nord, W. (eds) *Handbook of Organization Studies*: London: Sage. 526–542.

Eden, C. and Huxham, C. 2001. The negotiation of purpose in multi-organizational collaborative groups. *Journal of Management Studies*. 38 (3): 351–369.

Elden, M. and Chisholm, R. (eds) 1993. Action research special issue. *Human Relations*, 46 (2): 121–298.

Feyerherm, A. 1994. Leadership in collaboration: A longitudinal study of two inter-organizational rule-making groups. *Leadership Quarterly*, 5 (3/4): 253–270.

Fiedler, F. 1967. *A Theory of Leadership Effectiveness*. New York: McGraw-Hill.

Glaser, B. 1992. *Basics of Grounded Theory Analysis*. Mill Valley, CA: Sociology Press.

Glaser, B. and Strauss, A. 1967. *The Discovery of Grounded Theory*. New York: Aldine de Gruyter.

Graef, C. 1983. The situational leadership theory: a critical view. *Academy of Management Review*, 8 (2): 285–291.

Gummesson, E. 1991. *Qualitative methods in management research*. Newbury Park, CA: Sage.

Hosking, D. 1988. Organizing, leadership and skilful process. *Journal of Management Studies*, 25 (2): 147–166.

Huxham, C. 1996a. Advantage or inertia: Making collaboration work. In Paton, R., Clark, G., Jones, G., Lewis, J. and Quintas P. (eds) *The New Management Reader*. London: Routledge, pp. 238–254.

Huxham C. and Vangen S. 1998. Action research for understanding collaboration practice: emerging research design choices. Paper presented at the 24th International Congress of Applied Psychology, San Francisco.

Huxham, C. and Vangen, S. 2000a. Ambiguity, complexity and dynamics in the membership of collaboration. *Human Relations*, 53 (6): 771–806.

Huxham, C. and Vangen, S. 2000b. leadership in the shaping and implementation of collaboration agendas: how things happen in a (not quite) joined up World. *Academy of Management Journal* (Special forum on managing in the new millennium), 43 (6): 1159–1175.

Huxham, C. and Vangen, S. 2000c. What makes partnerships work? In Osborne S. (ed.) *Managing Public Private Partnerships for Public Services*. London: Routledge.

Huxham, C. and Vangen, S. 2001. What makes practitioners tick: Understanding collaboration practice and practising collaboration understanding. In Genefke, J. and McDonald, F. (eds) *Effective Collaboration: managing the obstacles to success*. Basingstoke: Palgrave, pp. 1–16.

Lynch, R. 1993. *Business Alliances Guide: the hidden competitive weapon*. New York: Wiley.

Marshall, C. and Rossman, G. 1989. *Designing Qualitative Research*. London: Sage.

Murrell, K. 1997. Relational models of leadership for the next century not-for-profit organization manager. *Organization Development Journal*, 15 (3): 35–42.

Øvretveit, J. 1993. *Co-ordinating Community Care: multidisciplinary teams and care management*. Buckingham: Open University Press.

Peters, M. and Robinson, V. 1984. The origins and status of action research, *The Journal of Applied Behavioural Science*, 20, 113–124.

Pettigrew, A. 1990. Longitudinal field research on change theory and practice. *Organization Science*, 1: 267–292.

Purdue, D. and Razzaque, K. 1999. Connections and expectations: Partnerships, community leaders and the problem of succession. Paper presented at the 6th International Conference on Multi-Organizational Partnerships, Tilburg.

Stogdill, R. 1974. *Handbook of Leadership: a survey of theory and research*. New York: Free Press.

Strauss, A. and Corbin, J. 1998. *Basics of Qualitative Research: techniques and procedures for developing grounded theory*.

Stringer, E. 1996. *Action Research: a handbook for practitioners*. Thousand Oaks, CA: Sage.

Thomas, J. 1993. *Doing Critical Ethnography*. Newbury Park, CA: Sage

Vangen, S. 1998. Transferring insight on collaboration into practice. PhD Thesis, University of Strathclyde.

Vangen, S. and Huxham, C. 1998a. Creating a tip: issues in the design of a process for transferring theoretical insight about inter-organisational collaboration into practice. *International Journal of Public–Private Partnerships*, 1 (1): 19–42.

Vangen, S. and Huxham, C. 1998b. The role of trust in the achievement of collaborative advantage. Paper presented at the 14th EGOS Colloquium, Maastricht.

Vangen, S. and Huxham, C. 2000. Enacting leadership for collaborative advantage. Paper presented at the Annual Conference of he British Academy of Management at Edinburgh, September.

Wolcott, H. 1990. *Writing up Qualitative Research*. Newbury Park, CA: Sage.

Whyte, W. (ed.) 1991 *Participatory Action Research*. London: Sage

Chapter 18

Organizational research and the New Public Management

The turn to qualitative methods

Ewan Ferlie and Annabelle Mark

Introduction

This chapter considers issues of research methods in the study of the NPM as seen from the discipline of organizational studies. Organizational studies is only one of a number of social science disciplines which have an interest in this field (economics; political science and sociology all represent important other strands) but it does have a distinctive contribution to make in the study of the NPM.

This is because an important theme within the NPM has been macro-level change to the form and functioning of public agencies. These changes have moved the characteristic public sector organization away *from* the old public administration template (the vertically integrated bureaucracy with accountability to Parliament but often also with dominant professional groups) *towards* more managerialized and marketized forms, more strongly influenced by private sector modes of organization. The contemporary public sector is organized in very different ways from twenty years ago.

For example, there are a number of significant shifts in organizational form. We have seen the privatization of the old Morrisonian public corporation in the field of economic policy. There has been a transition to new forms of private firms with strong shareholder rights, moderated by new regulatory regimes. Within the field of social policy (where privatization has proceeded at a much more moderate pace), there has been the introduction of the purchaser/provider split based on contracting rather than hierarchy; the creation of novel purchasing agencies which are both small and strategic; the development of new provider organizations with at least some devolved powers for example 'Next Steps' Agencies and NHS Trusts. We have also seen the downsizing and delayering of traditionally large scale public sector organizations exemplified by Regional Health Authorities and some central Whitehall departments, with the outsourcing and market testing of peripheral functions.

There have been important changes to organizational systems within the public sector, as well as structures. At the most general level, increasing political and public distrust of the behaviour of public sector providers has resulted in a shift from tacit systems of self-regulation to explicit systems of external regulation. Concern has been fuelled by a number of high profile scandals (Redfern 2001) which suggest that traditional patterns of professional self-regulation are inadequate. We see the creation of a number of new regulatory and audit-based organizations which intend to shape the behaviour of public sector professionals so as to ensure uniform and high levels of service quality (such as the Audit Commission, the National Institute for Clinical Excellence and the Commission for Health Improvement), although there may also be highly dysfunctional and resource intensive outcomes in terms of an ever-escalating audit burden (Power 1997). The move from hierarchically based to contract-based forms of coordination is also significant. There has also been development of a strong performance management function and developing of enhanced IT capacity, which has permitted greater use of benchmarking and the use of comparative Performance Indicators.

There have also been top-down attempts to shift the organizational culture of the public sector away from an administrative and towards a more 'managed' and 'entrepreneurial' orientation, and there may be some tension between these two organizing principles. Top managerial roles have been empowered and there have been important shifts in Human Resource Management strategy to more individualized job contracts. The power of the public sector trade unions has declined. Effort levels have been increased within a strategy of work intensification so that an individual's experience of a public sector job may be quite different from that of twenty years ago.

Neither have these change efforts been confined to the period of Conservative governments (1979–97). More recently, the 'modernization' agenda pursued by the post-1997 Labour government involves further organizational change which still seeks to move away from the public sector of the 1970s. Policy rhetoric stresses the development of high-quality and easy to access services, implying the development of further control systems. It is unclear how much change has really happened at front-line level, and the obstacles to 'delivery' have been famously underestimated.

Has the pendulum begun to swing back? Recent problems associated with semi-privatized organizations have led to public disquiet, for example with the complex contracting regime evident within the railway system. There have recently been suggestions for reintegration and a return to hierarchy so as to ensure adequate control and a safety-based culture. Will Railtrack be the first privatized utility to be taken back into public ownership?

The progressive transfer of private sector ideas into the public domain has also been criticized by some management academics: Drucker (1995) has attacked the adoption of private sector based management theory by the public sector as quite inappropriate given its distinctive purpose. Wilson (1989) argues that public sector agencies remain radically distinct from private firms. Given these policy and intellectual limits to the New Right wave of the 1980s, public *organizations* may remain an important analytic focus. Du Gay (2000) criticizes the whole concept of entrepreneurial government and reaffirms the ethical and due process advantages of the bureaucratic form. These then are highly contestable areas with a variety of perspectives and positions.

It is necessary in this chapter to characterize organizational studies as an academic discipline. Then we review the spread of research approaches within the discipline as a whole and highlight the increasingly important role played by qualitative forms of research (such as case studies). Examples of such research, particularly drawn from the health care sector where the authors have a particular interest, are included. We conclude by outlining a possible NPM organizational research agenda.

What is 'organizational studies'?

Organizational studies is a social science which has developed from its original base within sociology (here we draw on Ferlie 2001). Compared with psychology or sociology, however, it typically operates at a higher level of aggregation than these other disciplines' focus on the individual or team, locating itself usually at the organizational or system-wide level. An organization may be defined as a particular setting (such as an outpatients clinic), a large producing unit (such as a hospital) or an organizational field (the population of all hospitals within a health care system). The discipline thus operates at a relatively high level of analysis, between the meso- and macro-level. However, it is less 'macro' than other disciplines, such as policy analysis or political science, which often concentrate on system-wide institutions rather than local settings. An important concept for this level of analysis is *context* (Crompton and Jones 1988), as it is the context of such organizations which may determine how they really function.

Second, organizational studies is often field based and hence contains an empirical component (while trying to avoid the danger of empiricism). It is often concerned to gather primary empirical data from local organizational settings rather than engage in other forms of argumentation, such as normative or purely theoretical arguments.

Third, it has a theoretical as well as an empirical orientation. It is particularly interested in how people behave within formally constituted organizations. It sees such behaviour as socially embedded, through such forces as norms, culture, discourse, power relations and the role of institutions, rather than, say, the role of incentives, prices or market structure which is the domain of economics, or the impact of legal governance regimes and the distribution of property rights which are the concern of socio-legal studies. Patterns of organizational continuity and change represent another important area, and the 'management of change' is a policy-orientated version of this theme.

Organizational studies is a social science with its own internal dynamics and vigorous debates. It reflects the mega-trends observable within social science as a whole, with the emergence of feminist, neo-Marxist and postmodernist subgroups of researchers alongside more orthodox groupings. A comprehensive recent overview (Clegg *et al.* 1996) suggests that there is not one organization theory but many. For example, American organizational studies tend to be positivistic (number crunching) and functionalist (designed to improve managerial performance); European organizational studies tends to the critical (anti-managerialist or neo-Marxist) and British organizational research (as in other fields) occupies an intermediary position between the two. Particular professional associations and journals reflect these various positions, although some attempts to mix these different approaches have also been made (Cooper and Jackson 1997).

Some organizational research is explicitly value committed rather than endeavouring to be value neutral, proclaiming the emancipatory role of research especially for lower-level participants within organizations. An example would be exploring – and exposing – the use of power within organizational decision-making. Value neutrality has been traditionally prized by the proponents of the natural scientific method, and this position was adopted within some early and positivistic organizational research. However, the presumption of 'objective organizations' has been heavily criticized within more cognitive perspectives which suggest that organizational settings contain an important element of social construction. Weick (1995) has revealed how the 'sense-making' process within organizations creates an ongoing interpretation of reality through retrospective sense-making of situations in which individuals find themselves: this sense-making in turn shapes both organizational structure and behaviour. There is an emergent post-modern discourse within organizational studies (Cooper and Burrell 1988; Hatch 1997) which allows for multiple simultaneous interpretations, and ultimately refutes the idea of validity at all. While this approach may seem untenable, a greater understanding of the orientating role of underlying values is also now more evident in the work of major authors such as Kurt Lewin and Edgar Schein (Cooke 1999), suggesting that the search for value neutrality within organizational analysis may be a chimera. Research may instead involve the interpretation of multiple meanings, as post-structural methods suggest (Hassard and Pym 1993), rather than a search for the one authoritative voice (Petersen *et al.* 1999).

Organizational research: the turn to qualitative methods

A basic distinction often drawn is between quantitative and qualitative research paradigms. The term 'paradigm' implies that they are incommensurable (Burrell and Morgan 1979): that mixing them is like trying to mix oil and water. Others argue for a mixed methodology and seek to engage with both perspectives (Mark and Dopson 1999) on the grounds that they are complementary rather than contradictory. Clegg *et al.* (1996) suggest that the main shift within organizational studies has been from a functionalist paradigm (based on the assumptions of 'normal science') to an interpretive paradigm which accords particular importance to meaning and more recently to discourse (Manning 1992). The present discussion uses the categories first developed by Stablein (1996) to structure the discussion; in the UK context, Bryman (1988, 1992) provides a helpful overview.

Quantitative organizational research

Despite the observations of Clegg *et al.*, the tradition of quantitative organizational research lives on, especially in America and also within near market applied research which often uses survey methods. Donaldson (1996) defends the paradigm of organizational research as 'normal science' where positivistic methods are appropriate. Comparative survey methods can plot organizations along various dimensions, using a quantitative scale or series of ordered categories. These data are coded up and analysed using correlation statistics or modelling techniques (such as multiple regression). There are concerns to ensure the generalizability of findings so that replication studies are seen as an important strength.

Quantitative methods have produced classic works within organizational research, such as the 1960s Aston Group study of the organizational structure of firms (Pugh 1997). The Aston Group developed instruments to measure the underlying dimension of organizations (in fact firms), such as the degree of centralization or formalization with attention to the reliability of these instruments. They used modelling techniques such as multiple regression to predict organizational structure from their questionnaire data and knowledge of firms in their sample. Other authors have applied this contingency theoretic approach (there is no one best way but optimal design is contingent upon factors such as the organizational size) in predicting the rate of innovation in health and welfare agencies from a knowledge of other variables (Aiken and Hage 1971). These approaches could in principle be adapted to the study of NPM organizations, for example plotting large groups on a set of underlying organizational dimensions (e.g. centralization, formalization) and even using modelling techniques. Organizational economists might wish to use econometric modelling techniques to model the cost and production functions evident within NPM style agencies, and to compare these with private sector models or historic models derived from old-style public administrative agencies.

Questionnaires and survey methods

Stablein (1996) suggests that the questionnaire is probably the single most popular method (one study he cited suggests that thirty-sex per cent of authors primarily use this method) within organizational research. Questionnaires can be structured in nature (using formal scales such as Likert scales) or looser, relying on verbatim text, where discourse analysis may come into play. However, they are frequently used for the collection of 'countable' data. Stablein found that the questions of reliability and validity were not addressed sufficiently in much of the organizational literature (the bio-medical literature is stronger in this respect). The postal survey is certainly often used to gather basic descriptive information about populations of health care organizations, either cross-sectionally or preferably on a longitudinal basis. It is good at capturing formally available information on organizational structure; weaker on accessing more informal information which resides in other areas. Such methods could be used to gather data on stakeholders' (users, staff) perceptions and experience of NPM organizations, perhaps using Likert scales, including across significant populations (which qualitative methods would find difficult). National surveys of patients' experience – and views of service quality – represent a good example of this approach.

Experimental and quasi-experimental methods

Stablein (1996) suggests that there is greater use of experimental and quasi-experimental methods within organizational research than one might think. One study he reviews suggests about thirty per cent of articles reviewed used experimental procedures either in the field or laboratory (this method tends to be used by organizational psychologists within laboratory-based experiments). The Randomized Control Trial model, with its presumption of double-blind randomization, is rarely used, but quasi-experimentation (following the classic text of Campbell and Stanley 1966) may be more feasible. Within quasi-experimental design, it may in principle be possible to compare two matched sets of public sector organizations, one of which receives an intervention [say, TQM or BPR (business process re-engineering)] and the other which does not, and to assess differential outcomes over time. Oakley (2000) argues for greater use of quasi-experimental methods in areas such as health services research, quoting the experience of social experimentation in the American Great Society programmes of the 1960s as a role model. A contrary position is adopted in the model of 'realistic evaluation' (Pawson and Tilley 1997), which is better able to cope with the 'noise' generated by real world public agencies.

In practice – and despite research commissioner pressure to adopt them – the difficulty of matching and the inability to contain extraneous factors make quasi-experimental designs difficult to implement. An example of inappropriate research steering can be seen in the national evaluation of management training for hospital consultants (Mark 1993), where the incentives to adopt such research strategies were as much politically as methodologically led. Such designs often prove increasingly inappropriate as the research process develops: they promise much more than they can deliver (Pawson and Tilley 1997). Even within the American evaluation tradition, there are less 'scientistic' and more politically sensitive approaches available (Browne and Wildavsky 1983).

Qualitative researchers would strongly contest the utility of the quasi-experimental paradigm within an organizational context, particularly when the intervention or technology being introduced and evaluated is highly diffuse in nature. It is in practice impossible to compare like with like, so that apples are in the end being compared with oranges. For example, a study of the introduction of TQM projects within the NHS found a high degree of local customization so that the intervention ended up being highly locally disparate (Joss and Kogan 1995). The same circumstances have complicated the evaluation of new technologies such as NHS Direct (ScHARR 1998), where sites could not be seen as a homogeneous intervention group.

Secondary data

Such data include routinely generated sources such as employment figures, annual reports and production figures. Often such data are generated by non-researchers for managerial purposes, and Stablein (1996) rightly suggests that such data are of poor quality from a research point of view. They may be helpfully used in applied managerial evaluations, such as those carried out by inspectoral or regulatory bodies. They may also have a secondary use within research, especially where they are used in a complementary way over and above primary data, for example in the Bowns and McNulty (1999) study of the implementation of a BPR programme within a hospital, which included data routinely generated by the NHS information system as well as primary data collection from the researchers themselves. In the 1990s, there has been an explosive growth in applied managerial evaluations which are being asked for by the policy system, although their methodological base is often poor (Ovretveit 1998). The time and cost constraints often encountered in such evaluations may produce a research style which has been summarized as 'poverty in pragmatism' (Mark and Dopson 1999).

Qualitative organizational research

Looking back over a generation of organizational studies, Clegg and Hardy (1996) argue that the key trend within the discipline has been the erosion of the functionalist paradigm, typically based on quantitative data collection. Instead, a plethora of alternative approaches has emerged, based on interpretive, sense-making, phenomenological, neo-Marxist or postmodernist approaches. They conclude:

> despite some defensive ploys by the establishment to weed them out, these new, different and alternative arenas, modes and perspectives of research are expanding, multiplying and overlapping.
>
> (Clegg and Hardy 1996: 2)

Qualitative research has a long history within social science, going back at least to the Chicago School of urban sociology. It assumes (Denzin and Lincoln 1994) a prime interest in processes and meanings rather than measurement. Such researchers investigate how social experience is constructed and given meaning within particular social contexts, drawing on an anthropological research tradition which can also be applied to public sector settings (Good 1994). Organizational research continues to be strongly influenced by these qualitative traditions.

Ethno data

Stablein (1996) refers to *ethno data* as a major method within organizational research, where ethno researchers discover and communicate an organizational reality as it is experienced by inhabitants of that reality (Hammersley and Atkinson 1995). In place of using ready-made constructs, the ethno researcher's task is to discover constructs in data, often through the use of emergent or 'grounded' theory (where themes or constructs emerge from the data through increasingly sophisticated analysis). The quality of such data is judged by the *fidelity* with which they represent these organizational worlds. There may be various such worlds, associated with different occupational groups or subcultures (Turner 1971).

Methods include non-participant and participant observation, which can produce ethnographies or 'thick descriptions' of organizational life where the researcher is immersed in the organizational setting, almost as a lived experience. Observation at meetings and analysis of documentary material are also important methods. Where interviews do occur, they may be relatively unstructured and led by the respondent rather than the researcher. Measuring a particular dimension is less important than portraying the *gestalt*, or the shape of the organization as a whole. Organizational culture is accessed through long immersion in the field, rather than through the administration of a structured questionnaire. Such methods could clearly be used fruitfully to explore processes of organizational change within NPM organizations, particularly as experienced by lower order or powerless participants: what was the experience of organizational change like for them? They would be particularly helpful in moving beyond a definition of organizational reality as espoused by top management, and accessing the perspectives of many other stakeholders that there are within public service organizations.

Case studies

Case studies represent another staple method of qualitative organizational research (Stablein 1996), associated with the work of major research institutes such as the Tavistock Institute. Much early organizational research was based on case study methods and there has been a rediscovery of this tradition over the last twenty years. Methods typically include observation, semi-structured interviews and analysis of archival material. The objective may be to portray the organization as a whole, or to trace how particular strategic decisions have been taken or implemented within an issue tracing design (strategic decisions, crisis management, top management succession). Organizations may be followed up through time in a longitudinal perspective, which enables the researcher to take account of the impact of history on the present. The handling of time and the creation of periods is then an important task, where the skills of a historian may be useful, because, as Yin (1994) suggests, it is the interpretive ability of the historian, which contrast with the mere fact-gathering inherent in just chronicling events, which distinguishes this approach.

Cases may be *analytic descriptions*, where empirical material is both presented and then analysed against wider models or theories. The case study should surface, develop or test theory. Such *explanatory* case studies can be presented in the view of the authors as exemplars of high quality work within organizational research. Researchers may take and operationalize existing social science theories, testing them for their validity within particular organizational settings. For example, Harrison *et al.*'s (1992) exploration of the impact of general management in the NHS used the social science concepts of *culture* and *power* as organising devices. Inductive methods can also be used, whereby concepts emerge through carefully selected comparative case study data, as in Pettigrew *et al.*'s (1992) analysis of the differential capacity of District Health Authorities to progress strategic service change. This raises the question of methods which are needed to enable pattern recognition within multiple cases where methodological advice is available (Langley 1999).

Text as data

'Texts' created by organizations are analysed by postmodernist and post-structuralist scholars (Stablien 1996). Such scholars deny the existence of any reality other than the text itself as representative of a specific perspective at that time point. It is encapsulated in Derrida's (1976) notion of *différance*, which demonstrates how this approach 'privileges' the written word while inhabiting speech only as a possibility. As presented by the original author, the text constitutes a reality which can then be deconstructed through textual analysis into multiple meanings. Not every text provides data for deconstruction but rather those which are influential (so called foundational texts).

The linguistic analysis of texts (such as annual reports or plans) of public agencies may provide clues to persuasion devices and the emergence of new ideological positions or discourses. Such analysis might include analysis of how key words (such as 'enterprise' or 'modernization') appears, how they are used within phrases and how they seek to persuade readers (that is, the analysis of political texts as persuasive devices). Discourse analysis is of increasing interest to some health care researchers (Brown 2000) and to health professionals who are revisiting the narratives of their own worlds to find out what they suggest (Greenhalgh and Hurwitz 1999).

Action research

Action research is an important method in its own right as it implies a different relationship between research and practice (and between researcher and researched) than is common within conventional quantitative or qualitative research. Here it can simply be noted that much action research has taken place in public sector settings such as primary care or local government (Reason 1988). This research style is often seen as sensitive to the concerns of practitioners and as able to promote local change more effectively than conventional modes of research. It is favoured by some research commissioners because of its utility to the field, its shorter time scales and its desire to contribute to real world change. Critics question its ability to generate a coherent knowledge base as opposed to a series of highly localized projects. At its worst it produces highly applied research which does not cumulate or add to a wider body of knowledge. However, Huxham's approach (1992; Chapter 17, this volume) to action research is more thematic in nature and includes careful attention to concept building: her substantive area is inter-organizational collaboration between public service agencies (surely relevant to the 'joined-up government' theme).

Focus groups

Focus groups are another important qualitative technique favoured within applied research and market research, where the objective is to uncover the 'real' views of consumers and users. Small groups of target consumers (such as 'Worcester Woman' in the case of the focus groups conducted for the Labour Party) are brought together for a group discussion of core themes, facilitated by an experienced researcher within relaxed surroundings. The presence of group dynamics and dialogue may produce more considered and richer material than would be generated in individual interviews. They are also relatively quick and cheap to set up and so offer a form of more rapid appraisal than conventional academic research. Focus group techniques have been used in order to uncover the views of users of public services (as in the recent NHS Plan).

How should we study the New Public Management?

So how should we study the NPM? As this review suggests, a wide range of methods (both quantitative and qualitative) can be employed within organizational research, as within any social science. The dominant research tradition may vary according to geography and the prevailing intellectual culture, with the USA, UK and Europe all showing different patterns. Nevertheless, the meta-level growth of qualitative research methods within organizational studies poses some interesting issues. The propositions below have emerged from the current review:

There has been a high level turn to qualitative forms of organizational research over the last thirty years within the UK

As Clegg et al. (1996) argue, there has been a shift to a number of different forms of qualitative organizational research over the last thirty years, with the decline of the old functionalist paradigm based on the 'normal science' of measurement and replication. This shift is marked in Europe and to a lesser extent in the UK, although still contained in the case of American research which retains a strong positivistic base.

Within the qualitative camp, there are also internal research traditions and disputes. Giddens(1984) for example has suggested that 'the uncovering of generalizations is not the be all and end all of social theory'. However, more conservative researchers work within the comparative case study method, where concerns about replication and generalizability are taken seriously. In this tradition, ensuring that findings have a strong empirical base is also seen as important, with stress on internal validity of the accounts offered. We also see the emergence of critical forms of qualitative research, such as neo-Marxism, postmodernism and feminism, which can be seen as lying within a 'contra science' position and which are further from the presumptions of quantitative research.

A turn to qualitative methods has repercussions for the study of the NPM

It would be strange if these methodological trends were not also apparent in the study of major current empirical phenomena such as the New Public Management. This high-level shift might imply the production of more comparative cases so as to build generalizations and theory inductively. It would also imply the presence of research groups studying the rise of the NPM through an array of critical perspectives, of a neo-Marxist, postmodernist or feminist basis. Key questions might include: Is the power of capital leading to a restructuring of the State? What are the alternative narratives or discourses that are in play? What are the power shifts and ideological representations which are associated with the NPM? Is the NPM a 'male' movement which is seeking to engage in a labour intensification process and producing 'macho' organizational cultures?

A dilemma for organizational researchers

So the turn to qualitative methods may well lead to a shift in the central methodological tendency within the analysis of current public sector organizations. But what do we do next? Some researchers will seek to operate within a postmodernist stance which finds the concept of empirical investigation in itself highly problematic. They may however find it difficult to communicate interest in their work beyond these restricted niche markets, remaining content to operate within the academic domain.

At the more conservative end of the spectrum, some qualitative researchers will be keen to maintain the tradition of field-based research and to produce work which is in dialogue with the worlds of policy and practice. Note the use of the word dialogue, which implies the presence of two speakers engaged in an equal conversation. But such policy-orientated researchers may in turn find that they face the danger of 'poverty in pragmatism' (Mark and Dopson 1999) and will be driven into very near market and applied evaluations. We argue that the main danger to academic quality in this field does not come from the over-dominance of high-quality quantitative studies. In practice, there are very few such studies and more might be welcome (for example, in the area of performance assessment and cost and production function modelling).

A key weakness in this field is the over reliance on highly applied forms of evaluation which do not engage with substantive social science. This is the 'technician' mode of NPM research, often funded through governmental agencies and designed to 'fix' an immediate policy problem. High-quality organizational analysis should relate to wider bodies of theory rather than be entirely pragmatic or empiricist in its orientation: we should make our problems rather than take them from the world of policy.

The challenge for such researchers (such as ourselves) is to show that we are capable of making such connections and breaking out from the 'technician' mode of NPM research. The received view is that British social science is biased to basic research and has insufficient applied capacity. Our view is that this particular field has rather suffered from the opposite deformation: a surfeit of applied evaluations and a lack of broad thinking. Some (Kriger and Malan 1993) are now arguing for greater venturesomeness within managerial research which entails greater attention to creative hypothesis generation and broad analytic discussion. There is here an important question of research tone as well as method. A turn to challenge, creativity and a sense of critical distance is needed in the study of NPM organizations, as in other fields of management research (Ferlie and McNulty 1997).

References

Aiken, M. and Hage, J. (1971) 'The Organic Organisation and Innovation', *Sociology* 5: 63–81.

Bowns, I., McNulty, T. *et al.* (1999) *Reengineering LRI: An Independent Evaluation of Implementation and Impact*, University of Sheffield: ScHARR.

Brown, A.D. (2000) 'Making Sense of Inquiry Sensemaking', *Journal of Management Studies* 37(1): 45–75.

Browne, A. and Wildavsky, A. (1983) 'What Should Evaluation Mean to Implementation?'. In Pressman, J. and Wildavsky, A. (eds) *Implementation*, 3rd edition, London: University of California Press.

Bryman, A. (1988) *Doing Research in Organisations*, London: Routledge.

Bryman, A. (1992) *Research Methods and Organisational Studies*, London: Routledge.

Burrell, G. and Morgan, G. (1979) *Sociological Paradigms and Organisational Analysis,* London: Heinemann.

Campbell, D.T. and Stanley, J.C. (1966) *Experimental and Quasi Experimental Designs for Research*, Chicago: Rand McNally.

Clegg, S. and Hardy, C. (1996) 'Organizations, Organization and Organizing'. In Clegg, S. *et al.*, (eds) *Handbook of Organisational Studies*, London: Sage, pp. 1–28.

Clegg, S., Hardy, C. and Nord, W. (1996) *Handbook of Organisational Studies*, London: Sage.

Cooke, B. (1999) 'The Writing Left Out of Management Theory: the historiography of the management of change', *Organisation* 6(1): 81–105.

Cooper, R. and Burrell, G. (1988) 'Modernism, Postmodernism and Organizational Analysis: an Introduction', *Organization Studies* 9(1): 91–112.

Cooper, C.L. and Jackson, S.E. (1997) *Creating Tomorrow's Organisations,* Chichester: John Wiley.

Crompton, R. and Jones, G. (1988) 'Researching White Collar Organisations: why sociologists should not stop doing case studies'. In Bryman, A. (ed.) *Doing Research in Organisations'*, London: Routledge, pp. 68–81.

Denzin, N. and Lincoln, Y. (1994) *Handbook of Qualitative Research*, London: Sage.

Derrida, J. (1976) *Of Grammatology*, Baltimore: Johns Hopkins University Press.

Donaldson, L. (1996) 'The Normal Science of Structural Contingency Theory'. In Clegg, S. *et al.*, *Handbook of Organisational Studies*, London: Sage, pp. 57–76.

Drucker, P. (1995) 'Really Reinventing Government'. In *Managing in a Time of Great Change*, New York: Truman Talley Books/Dutton, pp. 285–301.

Du Gay, P. (2000) *In Defence of Bureaucracy*, London: Sage.

Ferlie, E. (2001) 'Organisational Studies'. In Fulop, N., Allen, P. Clarke, A. and Black, N. (eds) *Studying the Organisation and Delivery of Health Services*, London: Routledge.

Ferlie, E. and McNulty, T. (1997) 'Going to Market: changing patterns in the organisation and management of process research', *Scandanavian Journal of Management* 13(4): 367–387.

Giddens, A. (1984) *The Constitution of Society*, Stanford, CA: Stanford University Press.

Good, B. (1994) *Medicine, Rationality and Experience – An Anthropological Perspective*, Cambridge: Cambridge University Press.

Greenhalgh, T. and Hurwitz, B. (1999) 'Narrative Based Medicine – why study narrative', *British Medical Journal* 318: 48–50.

Hammersley, M. and Atkinson, P. (1995) *Ethnography – Principles in Practice*, London: Routledge.

Harrison, S., Hunter, D., Marnoch, G. and Pollitt, C. (1992) *Just Managing: Power and Culture in the NHS*, London: Macmillan.

Hassard, J. and Pym, D. (1993) *The Theory and Philosophy of Organisations*, London: Routledge.

Hatch, M.J. (1997) *Organization Theory – Modern, Symbolic and Postmodern Perspectives*, Oxford: Oxford University Press.

Huxham, C. (1992) *Collaborative Advantage*, London: Sage.

Joss, R. and Kogan, M. (1995) *Advancing Quality*, Buckingham: Open University Press.

Kriger, M. and Malan, L.-C. (1993) 'Shifting Paradigms: the valuing of personal knowledge, wisdom, and other invisible processes in organisations', *Journal of Management Inquiry* 2(4): 391–398.

Langley, A. (1999) 'Strategies for Theorising From Process Data', *Academy of Management Review* 24(4): 691–710.

Manning, P. (1992) *Organisational Communication*, New York: Aldine de Gruyter.

Mark, A. (1993) 'Researching the Doctor Manager – choosing valid methodologies', *Journal of Management in Medicine* 7(4): 53–60.

Mark, A. and Dopson, S. (1999) *Organisational Behaviour in Health Care – The Research Agenda*, Basingstoke: Macmillan.

Oakley, A. (2000) *Experiments in Knowing*, Cambridge: Polity Press.

Øvretveit, J. (1997) *Evaluating Health Interventions*, Buckingham: Open University Press.

Pawson, R. and Tilley, N. (1997) *Realistic Evaluation*, Thousand Oaks, CA: Sage.

Petersen, A., Barns, I., Dudley, J. and Harris, P. (1999) *Postructuralism, Citizenship and Social Policy*, London: Routledge.

Pettigrew, A., Ferlie, E. and McKee, L. (1992) *Shaping Strategic Change*, London: Sage.

Power, M. (1997) *The Audit Society*, Oxford: Oxford University Press.

Pugh. D. (1997) 'Does Context Determine Form?'. In Pugh, D. (ed.) *Organisation Theory – Selected Readings*, London: Penguin.

Reason, P. (1988) *Human Enquiry in Action*, London: Sage.

Redfern, M. (2001) *The Report of the Royal Liverpool Children's Inquiry*, London: The Stationery Office.

ScHARR (1998) *Evaluation of NHS Direct First Wave Sites – Interim Report to the Department of Health*, University of Sheffield: ScHARR.

Schein, E. (1985) *Organisational Culture and Leadership*, San Francisco: Jossey Bass.

Stablein, R. (1996) 'Data in Organisational Studies'. In Clegg, S. *et al.* (eds) *Handbook of Organisational Studies*, London: Sage, pp. 509–523.

Turner, B. (1971) *Exploring the Industrial Subculture*, London: Macmillan.

Weick, K.E. (1995) *Sensemaking in Organisations*, Thousand Oaks, CA: Sage.

Wilson, J.Q (1989) *Bureaucracy*, New York: Basic Books.

Yin, R.A (1994) *Case Study Research Design and Method*, 2nd edition, Thousand Oaks, CA: Sage.

Chapter 19

Researching the New Public Management

The role of quantitative methods

George Boyne

Most of the empirical work by public management researchers is based on qualitative methods. Academic effort has concentrated on case studies of, or commentaries on, government policies or management practices. By contrast, quantitative research has been rare. What are the reasons for the scarcity of quantitative studies, and for the lack of statistical tests of hypotheses concerning public management processes and outcomes? What is the potential contribution of quantitative methods to the development of this field, and what are the problems of realizing this potential? The aim of this chapter is to address these questions.

The limited presence of quantitative work in public management research is reviewed in the first part of the chapter. The focus here is on the UK, and in particular on publications in the leading journals since 1980. Some potential reasons for the absence of quantitative work are then identified. These are partly technical (an apparent lack of relevant research training), and partly associated with the dominant paradigmatic assumptions in the academic community. In the second part of the chapter, the potential benefits of quantitative research on public management issues are outlined, and criteria for evaluating the quality of statistical studies are identified. In the third part, some suggestions are made for improving the quality of this form of research, and for improving its practical relevance.

Quantitative methods in public management research

The extent of the use of quantitative methods can be identified through an analysis of the contents of the leading academic journals in the public management field. Although this procedure is straightforward in principle, it involves three complex issues in practice. First, what is 'public management' as an area of academic inquiry? Secondly, which journals should be included in the assessment? And thirdly, which techniques count as 'quantitative methods' for this purpose?

Public management has emerged as an area of academic inquiry in the last two decades. Its development has run roughly parallel to that of NPM as a set of government policies and management practices (Gray and Jenkins 1995; Hughes

1998). To some extent the research focus is similar to the more traditional academic field of public administration: the finance, structures, processes and performance of public and quasi-public organizations. However, whereas traditional public administration draws principally upon theoretical perspectives from political science, public management is a more eclectic mix of economics, management, social policy, organizational behaviour and politics. Furthermore, the researchers in this new area are largely drawn not from politics departments but from business and management schools (Boyne 1996).

The novel and multidisciplinary nature of public management research creates two problems for the analysis in this chapter. These are the absence, until recently, of a single core journal in the field, and the consequent difficulty of identifying longitudinal data on the use of quantitative methods. Until the publication of the journal *Public Management* (now *Public Management Review*) in 1999, the public management academic community in the UK had no research-based journal of its own. Journals with a longer history, such as *Public Money and Management* and the *International Journal of Public Sector Management*, tend either to have a stronger practical than academic focus (as indicated by the publication of many papers by practitioners), or to have a thin theoretical and methodological base. As the aim here is to track the use of quantitative methods in *academic research* on public management, it is necessary to look to journals that do not have the term 'public management' in the title, but nevertheless publish papers that reflect the main characteristics of the field (i.e. a multidisciplinary focus on management in the public sector).

The two UK journals that best meet this criterion are *Public Administration* and *Policy and Politics*. Although the former journal continues to be dominated by political scientists, it does contain a variety of papers from other disciplines, and since the mid-1990s has contained a section labelled 'Public management'. The latter journal, despite the presence of politics in the title, has always drawn upon a wide range of disciplines, from sociology to accounting, and published many papers on the management of public organizations (e.g. Carter 1989; Hoggett 1991). Both journals explicitly encourage the submission of papers with a strong theoretical orientation, and are widely regarded as leading outlets for research articles. Indeed it could be argued that *Public Management Review* itself sits somewhere between these two journals, in terms of both academic focus and quality. The contents of *Public Administration* and *Policy and Politics* will therefore be analysed in order to track the use of quantitative methods in public management research.

Having identified both the nature of public management and the journals where its research outputs are most likely to be found, it remains to determine the research procedures that qualify as 'quantitative methods'. This term means more than the presentation, or rudimentary analysis, of some numbers. In order to count as using quantitative methods, a research article must go beyond the provision of figures in a table (e.g. raw data, averages, percentages). It is the use of the data and the sophistication of the techniques that are crucial.

The application of quantitative methods to a research problem involves an attempt to test a hypothesis, that is to establish the empirical relationship between measures of two or more theoretical constructs. Furthermore, such an attempt should evaluate whether the relationship between the measures is stronger than would be likely to occur at random. This in turn implies a test of the statistical significance of any empirical relationship that is identified. This is a more sophisticated research technique than simply checking whether one variable is related to another: the extra step is to establish whether the link is stronger than would be likely to occur by chance. Thus, for the purposes of this chapter, the term quantitative methods refers to *statistical tests of hypothetical relationships between variables*. In general, such tests are likely to be theoretically driven and therefore reflect a deductive method of research. However, some tests may be exploratory and seek to develop propositions or theories inductively from the data and statistical results.

The extent to which this quantitative style of research is employed in the public management field can now be established. Table 19.1 shows the results of an analysis of the contents of *Public Administration* and *Policy and Politics* from 1980 to 1999. The data are divided into five-year blocks in order to establish whether the use of quantitative methods has grown or declined over time. Two columns of information are shown for each journal: the number of quantitative articles, and this number as a percentage of all articles published (excluding short notes and comments). The results clearly show that the use of quantitative methods is very limited: on average, over the whole period, under five per cent of all the papers published in the two journals used this style of research. Indeed there is very little arithmetic, let alone statistics, in the papers published in these journals: the only numbers in most articles are the page numbers.

Many of the quantitative papers focus on variations in policy or performance across subnational governments, or on budgeting in central or local government (e.g. Greenwood 1983; Hoggart 1983; Boyne 1986, 1990; Barnett et al. 1990; Boyne et al. 2000). This may partly reflect the wide availability of secondary data on these topics (e.g. in publications by the Audit Commission and the Chartered Institute of Public Finance). Other quantitative papers include comparisons of public and private organizations (Dunsire et al. 1988; Domberger and Hensher 1993; Boyne et al. 1999). The statistical methods in the quantitative papers typically include correlation and multiple regression analysis.

Table 19.1 The use of quantitative methods in public management research

	Public administration Articles using quantitative methods		Policy and politics Articles using quantitative methods	
	Number	%	Number	%
1980–84	3	3.2	10	9.3
1985–89	4	4.1	5	4.4
1990–94	6	4.4	5	4.5
1995–99	3	1.7	8	6.2
1980–99	16	3.2	28	6.1

There is little sign of an increase in the use of quantitative methods over time: the 'high point' of this approach in *Public Administration* was 4.4 per cent in the early 1990s. Thereafter the presence of papers in this category collapsed to 1.7 per cent, which coincides with, and seems to be partly caused by, the 'Europeanization' of the journal. European contributors to *Public Administration* appear to be especially unlikely to seek statistical answers to research questions. Although quantitative methods are more prevalent in *Policy and Politics*, the 'market share' of this approach has declined over time, from an initial plateau of 9.3 per cent in the early 1980s. The early presence of quantitative papers (e.g. Davies and Ferlie 1981, 1982) is partly attributable to work by members of the Personal Social Services Research Unit at the University of Kent, the home of the journal in the 1970s. Much of this research was led by Bleddyn Davies, a pioneer of the statistical modelling of public management processes and outcomes. Indeed some of his early work on causal modelling and path analysis (e.g. Davies *et al.* 1971, 1972) is more sophisticated than most of the recent statistical research on public organizations. As the Kent connection weakened when the journal was rehoused in the School of Advanced Urban Studies at the University of Bristol, so the percentage of quantitative papers declined.

What are the reasons for the shortage of quantitative research? Answers to this question must be, to some extent, speculative. No formal survey or interview evidence exists on the reasons for the methodological preferences of public management researchers. Nevertheless, it is possible to draw upon informal evidence from conversations with members of the scholarly community over many years, and from the debates at the ESRC (Economic and Social Research Council) seminar series from which this present book originated. There may appear to be an irony here: a chapter in which the virtues of quantitative methods are extolled is itself drawing upon a crude interpretivist methodology. Yet this serves to illustrate that quantitative techniques are not helpful until some initial ideas and contextual information have been developed.

A technical reason for the dearth of quantitative research in public management may simply be the absence of the relevant skills. Many of the mature academics in the field 'served their apprenticeship' through a traditional PhD that involved intensive and solitary study of a specific topic, without any formal research training. It is only in the last decade or so that the ESRC has encouraged a 'foundation year' of research methods for PhD students. This is intended to ensure that all candidates are exposed to a variety of quantitative and qualitative methods. It is possible, therefore, that the next generation of researchers will have greater quantitative skills than their predecessors. This should in turn help to alleviate the 'quantophobia' that appears to be widespread in the public management community. A fear of numbers implies that many of the articles in the leading management journals (e.g. *Academy of Management Journal, Administrative Science Quarterly, Strategic Management Journal*) are inaccessible to a majority of public management researchers. In this case, the findings of such articles (to the extent that they are read at all) must be taken 'on trust'. Scholars who lack quantitative skills cannot independently evaluate the appropriateness of the empirical procedures that have been followed, or the authors' interpretation of their own results. This is not a healthy situation for a research community, the members of which should be able to constructively criticize each other's work.

Technical obstacles to quantitative research are not, by any means, a complete explanation of the neglect of this style of inquiry. The dominant research culture in the public management field seems to be unsympathetic to statistical methods on principle. Quantitative research is often falsely equated with a positivistic belief in the existence of 'facts'. For example, according to Cresswell (1994: 4), quantitative researchers believe 'that something can be measured objectively by using a questionnaire or an instrument'. Similarly, Brower *et al.* (2000) claim that 'quantitative research assumes reality can be depicted objectively as abstractions that correspond to real life' (p. 365) and that 'quantitative researchers pursue – and insist that they generate – value-free, unbiased data' (p. 366). Nothing in the process of measurement or statistical testing requires such beliefs. Indeed, most quantitative researchers are keenly aware that the measures which are tested in statistical models have been chosen from a large number of potential measures. Although the notion that the measures are 'objective' is plainly false, this does not imply that they are all wildly inaccurate or meaningless. Many different measures can serve as proxies for a theoretical concept, depending on how that concept is defined.

In addition, quantitative researchers recognize that there is no one 'correct' interpretation of statistical results: the data never speak for themselves, but must be given a voice by their creators. This is not, however, to take the extreme postmodernist position that there is no such thing as social or political reality, which implies that nothing can be measured or modelled (Brower *et al.* 2000). This perspective should properly be viewed as an assumption that can be subjected to empirical analysis. For example, how different are individual perceptions of the 'same event'? Are there multiple realities, or simply randomly fluctuating versions of the same reality? The idea that human activities and organizational behaviour are inherently indeterminate, and therefore beyond statistical investigation, is not so much postmodern as pre-scientific.

Quantitative research: potential benefits and evaluative criteria

Quantitative research can be used in a variety of ways and in many different circumstances. However, it is most likely to make a positive difference to knowledge on public management if the five characteristics which are listed below are present. These characteristics not only encapsulate the benefits of quantitative research, but can also serve as a checklist for the evaluation of a statistical study. The five items in the checklist refer not to any particular statistical procedure or technique, but to quantitative research in general. Furthermore the evaluative criteria are conceptual rather than technical, so little knowledge of statistics is required in order to apply them to the contents of quantitative studies.

A clear theoretical context

There is no shortage of theoretical perspectives on public management, largely because of the multidisciplinary character of the field. Quantitative research can contribute directly to theoretical debates by providing empirical evidence on the validity of alternative perspectives. The merits of competing theoretical views can be compared directly within the same statistical model. For example, many studies of decisions in the private sector have evaluated the relative validity of 'structure' and 'agency' models by testing measures of the external environment and managerial values (see Hansen and Wernerfelt 1989; Capon *et al.* 1990). If quantitative research frequently (or, far less likely, consistently) shows that one set of variables is more important than the other, then the associated theoretical perspective is strengthened or undermined. The 'incommensurability thesis' that competing theories cannot be evaluated on the basis of empirical evidence is 'philosophical bunkum' (Pawson 1989: 116).

Explicit hypotheses

A good quantitative study is more than a search for empirical relationships between variables: it seeks to establish whether a hypothetical link, predicted by theory, exists in practice. This implies that there is some prior expectation about the *direction* of the relationship between measures of theoretical constructs: for example, that staff morale is positively associated with organizational performance.

Statistical tests in the absence of explicit hypotheses may be little more than 'data-dredging'. The problem here is not that dredging is unlikely to uncover any statistically significant relationships between the variables that are analysed. Quite the opposite – around one in twelve statistical tests are likely to produce a 'significant' result (at the 0.05 level), purely by chance (Mock and Weisberg 1992). There may then be a temptation to construct a story to explain such a result, and perhaps to modify or challenge theoretical positions on this basis. This procedure may generate new theoretical insights, but a more logical approach is to suspend judgement until the 'new' hypothetical relationship has been tested on a different data set.

Accurate measures of concepts

Although no 'objectively' correct measures of concepts exist, it is still important that empirical variables correspond closely with theoretical constructs. The operationalization of a concept is likely to be most straightforward when it has one clearly defined dimension, and when there is wide academic consensus on its meaning. Such circumstances, however, rarely exist in the social sciences. The best that can usually be achieved is for a researcher to define a concept in a way that is justifiable in a particular research context, and to choose a measure that is consistent with this interpretation. It is then up to other members of the research community to challenge the analysis and results if they disagree with the definition or the operationalization. In this way, the very process of measurement can contribute to theoretical clarity: the task of selecting a measure, or of choosing between alternative measures, should lead researchers to think through or reappraise the meaning of a concept.

Tests of statistical significance

The use of significance tests as an evaluative criterion is controversial (see Morrison and Henkel 1970). These tests have conventionally been used to make inferences from a 'sample' about the characteristics of the 'population' from which the sample is drawn. There is some debate about the relevance of significance tests when a whole population is being analysed, such as all the councils in a particular group of local authorities. However, tests of significance are relevant even when a notional population of organizations is being analysed. It can be argued that this population represents a sample from a 'hypothetical universe' (Hagood 1970) which contains multiple samples of the same organizations at various points in time. In addition, the statistical relationships that are discovered can be regarded as a sample of all the possible combinations of the variables that *might* have occurred in a particular group of public sector organizations.

There is another important point in favour of the use of tests of significance. Whenever the relationship between variables is tested, a coefficient of some magnitude will be produced by the statistical procedure. The likelihood of estimating a coefficient of exactly zero is vanishingly small. In this context, as Winch and Campbell (1970: 206) state, 'it is very important to have a formal and non-subjective way of deciding whether a given set of data shows haphazard or systematic variation'. The alternative to formal significance tests, they argue, is to trust the 'intuitive judgement of the investigator' (Winch and Campbell 1970: 206). In addition, a coefficient which appears large in absolute terms may also have a large 'standard' error which implies that the estimate is unreliable. Therefore, some criterion is required in order to judge whether a statistical relationship is sufficiently strong to warrant confidence in the validity of a hypothesis. Tests of statistical significance provide such a criterion.

Controls for other explanatory variables

Empirical research frequently focuses on the relationship between two variables. For example, the aim may be to establish whether organizational performance (the 'dependent' variable) is influenced positively by leadership style (the 'independent' or 'explanatory' variable). However, a bivariate test of this proposition is simplistic: leadership is only one of numerous influences on performance. Indeed, no aspect of public sector management is determined by only one explanatory variable. It is therefore essential that the effect of a variable of particular theoretical interest is tested when 'controlling for' or 'holding constant' other explanatory variables. This can be accomplished through the use of multivariate statistical models. Statistical procedures such as multiple regression allow the net impact of one variable upon another to be examined when 'all other things are equal' (or at least when all the other measures of concepts included in the multivariate model are treated as if they were invariant).

This is, perhaps, the greatest benefit offered by quantitative research: the potential to tease out the effects of different variables, to disentangle the complex strands of organizational behaviour and to illuminate the separate importance (or unimportance) of each one. Qualitative research, by contrast, seems to offer no equally rigorous solution to this problem. Case study methods cannot estimate the net effect of an explanatory variable while controlling for the influence of others, except through the subjective impressions of the researcher. For example, Downs (1976: 1–2) argues that case studies of legislative behaviour:

> have traditionally been concerned with the behaviour of 'actors' in what often amounts to a narrowly defined closed system ... Unfortunately, the larger societal forces that constrain and motivate the behaviour of legislators (by determining the nature and definition of problems and the resources available to deal with them) are frequently difficult or impossible to detect when doing a single case study.

Such problems are compounded in actual case studies by the failure to state initial hypotheses and criteria of relevant evidence. Even advocates of case studies concede that 'most qualitative research does not test hypotheses' (Brower et al. 2000: 386). It has been argued that the method of 'storytelling' in case studies 'lacks rigor, lacks a definite logical structure, ... is all too easy to verify and virtually impossible to falsify. It is, or can be, persuasive precisely because it never runs the risk of being wrong' (Blaug 1980: 127, emphasis added). Fox-hunters were famously described by Oscar Wilde as the 'unspeakable in pursuit of the uneatable'. In a parallel fashion, Blaug's argument implies that many case-study researchers can be described as the 'innumerate in pursuit of the untestable'.

Quantitative research, universalism and contingency

Almost all of the statistical models in public management research have been based on 'universalistic' hypotheses. These include the arguments that if leaders have particular characteristics then the result is particular policies (e.g. that control of councils by Labour politicians is always associated with higher spending – see Boyne 1996), and that specific organizational structures have fixed implications for performance (e.g. that larger size leads to economies of scale and higher efficiency – see Boyne 1996c). According to such universalistic arguments, one variable is related to another in a uniform, definite and predictable way, regardless of the context or configuration of other variables. A practical implication is that there is 'one best way' to organize the delivery of public services.

A belief in universal laws of organizational behaviour is inconsistent with an important body of research on organizational behaviour and strategic management. This is contingency theory which, in contrast to universalism, suggests that there are no uniform relationships between variables such as organizational processes and performance (Schoonhoven 1981; Tosi and Slocum 1984; Venkatraman and Camillus 1984). Instead, the success or failure of a strategy depends on the circumstances, on the 'fit' or 'congruence' between an organization and its environment. For example, large size may be an asset in some contexts, but a liability in others.

Early work on contingency theory focused on the relationship between organizational structures and performance. Burns and Stalker (1961) distinguished between organic structures (decentralized, horizontal communication, task interdependence) and mechanistic structures (centralized, vertical communication, task specialization). They argued that neither structure is universally superior to the other, but that the appropriate structure is contingent on the external conditions faced by an organization. In an unstable environment (e.g. dynamic patterns of demand and resources), an organic structure is likely to be superior because it facilitates responsiveness to new circumstances. By contrast a mechanistic structure is better suited to a stable environment, partly because rules and procedures can be used to deal with recurring problems.

If, for the purposes of exposition, it is assumed that organizational environments can be dichotomized into 'stable' and 'unstable' groups, then the relationship between structure and performance can be illustrated as in Figures 19.1–19.3. First, Figure 19.1 shows a negative relationship between performance and the 'organicness' of organizational structures in a stable environment. Second, Figure 19.2 shows a positive relationship between organicness and performance in an unstable environment. These two equations represent the contingency view of the structure–performance relationship, which can also be modelled statistically as follows (see Wright 1976):

$$P_i = a - b\,\mathrm{SOSE}_i + b_2\,\mathrm{SOUE}_i + e_i \tag{19.1}$$

where P_i is the performance of an organization; SOSE is the extent of structural organicness in a stable environment; SOUE is the extent of structural organicness in an unstable environment; e_i is an individual organization; a is a constant; b and b_2 are coefficients that estimate the impact of SOSE and SOUE respectively on P; e is an error term.

If this contingency model is correct, then a universalistic model that fails to take account of differences in the environment will reveal a relationship between structure and performance as shown in Figure 19.3. In other words, structure appears to be unrelated to performance. The universalistic model can be expressed statistically as follows:

$$P_i = a + b_3\,\mathrm{OS}_i + e_i \tag{19.2}$$

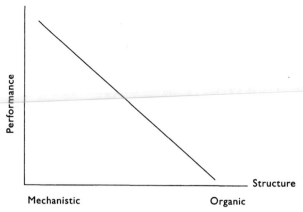

Figure 19.1 Relationship between organizational structure and performance in a stable environment

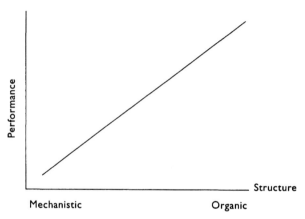

Figure 19.2 Relationship between organizational structure and performance in an unstable environment

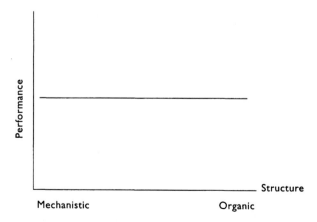

Figure 19.3 Relationship between organizational structure and performance, all environments

where OS is the extent of structural organicness (regardless of environmental context); b_3 is a coefficient that estimates the impact of OS on P (all other terms defined as in Equation 19.1).

A test of this statistical model would produce an insignificant coefficient b_3, because OS is an artificial average SOUE (positively related to performance) and SOSE (negatively related to performance). Thus a failure to take account of contingency effects in quantitative research can produce very misleading statistical results.

The importance of including contingency effects in quantitative research can be illustrated in relation to two major contemporary policy issues. The first is the resurgence of strategic planning in the public sector (Stokes-Berry and Wechsler 1995; Joyce 1999). A universalistic assumption that 'planning works' lies behind the emphasis on this method of policy formulation. For example, the statutory framework for Best Value in UK local government contains a series of prescribed elements that closely correspond with a traditional model of rational planning (see Leach 1982, for a discussion of these elements). Central government's assumption is that if local authorities follow this model then continuous improvements in performance will ensue (Boyne 1999).

However this view of the benefits of planning ignores the potential role of environmental and organizational contingencies, and can therefore be regarded as theoretically and practically naive. For example, environmental stability may moderate the relationship between planning and performance, although whether planning is more beneficial in a stable or unstable context remains unresolved (Boyne 2000). Similarly, planning may work better in organizations that have decentralized structures for policy formulation (in order to facilitate participation and commitment to the plan). In short, contingency theory suggests that planning is unlikely to work equally well in all circumstances. Indeed, in the 'wrong' environmental and organizations conditions, planning may lead to poorer performance. Any test of planning must, therefore, take variability in the context of its effects into account.

Another strategic issue that is salient for public sector organizations is whether to deliver services through a hierarchy or a market. The dominant theoretical perspective on this question is Williamson's (1975) economic analysis of transaction costs. Although his framework is not usually interpreted as a contingency model, it clearly is. Williamson (1975: 8) argues that the relative advantages of markets and hierarchies 'vary with the characteristics of the human decision-makers who are involved with the transaction on the one hand, and the objective properties of the market on the other'. For example, a market arrangement is more efficient when asset specificity and the scope for opportunistic behaviour are low, when the number of suppliers is large, and when future service requirements are known. These variables represent a set of contingencies that influence the link between a governance structure (market or hierarchy) and performance.

This contingency model can be contrasted with the crude universalistic model that underpinned government policies in the UK for much of the 1980s and

1990s. The latter model implied that markets are consistently superior to bureaucracy (as expressed, for example, in policies on compulsory competitive tendering in local government). This view is reflected in Figure 19.4, which shows a simple and direct positive relationship between markets and organizational performance, and a similarly straightforward negative relationship between bureaucracy and performance.

By contrast the contingency model, shown in Figure 19.5, is more complex, but also more theoretically sophisticated and empirically plausible. In this model it is impossible to predict whether the impact of a market or hierarchy is, a priori, positive or negative. Rather, the ultimate effect of either arrangement hinges on a set of mediating variables. Such contingency effects can easily be accommodated in a statistical model, through a set of interaction terms that capture the joint effect of a governance structure and each of the factors in Williamson's (1975) framework. Yet, quantitative studies of competitive tendering in the UK and contracting out in the USA have largely ignored such contingencies (see Boyne 1998a,b). They have therefore effectively tested universalistic hypotheses on the relative merits of markets and hierarchies.

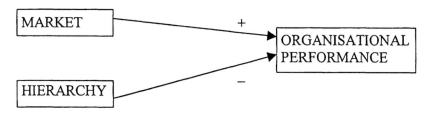

Figure 19.4 Universalistic model of the relationship between markets, hierarchies and performance

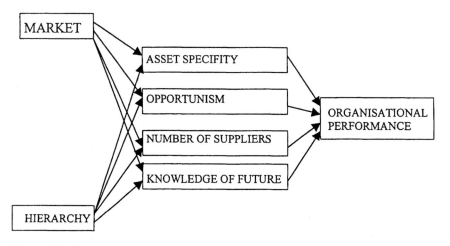

Figure 19.5 Contingency model of the relationship between markets, hierarchies and performance

In sum, theoretical arguments on organizational environments, structures and processes suggest that these variables do not simply have separate effects on performance. In other words, each one does not have a universalitic relationship with organizational outcomes. Rather, there is a variety of interactions between them, so that the impact of one is contingent on the others. Moreover, it would be possible to extend these contingency effects to include a host of other organizational variables, such as culture, human resource management and leadership. Indeed, the 'publicness' of an organization can be seen as a fundamental contingency that shapes the appropriateness of different forms of management (Boyne 2001).

The inclusion of contingency effects in statistical models would not only help quantitative research to reflect public management theory more accurately, but would also have two other benefits. First, it would build a bridge between quantitative and qualitative research by allowing statisticians to develop and test more detailed models of public organizations. Such models could incorporate, through a variety of interaction terms, some of the messy complexity of organizational life that is emphasized by case study researchers. Second, evidence on contingency effects could lead to quantitative research that is more relevant to the needs of policy-makers and managers. This evidence could answer not the universalist question, What works?, but the contingent question, What works under what circumstances?. Pawson and Tilley (1997) argue that the latter question can be answered by 'realistic evaluation' which identifies the variables that are favourable (or unfavourable) to policy success. They do not use the terminology or cite the literature, but their realistic evaluation model is simply a contingency model under another name.

Although contingency models offer substantial opportunities for improving quantitative research, it is important to note potential theoretical and practical problems that may arise. A theoretical problem is that so many contingencies may be taken into account that every organization appears to be unique, and so the capacity for theoretical generalisation is lost. As Dubin (1978: 5) argues, theory construction is an attempt to 'find order in the booming bustling confusion that is the realm of experience'. The quantity of contingency variables must therefore be limited to a theoretically constructive number. A practical problem that may arise is the use of many interaction terms in statistical models. As the number of contingency effects that are tested grows, so does the number of variables that are multiplied together in an interaction term. This places a tremendous burden on the accuracy of the operationalization of the theoretical concepts. Errors in measurement are compounded as more and more variables are added to an interaction term, and eventually all that is left is 'noise'. In this case, a statistical test of a complex interaction term with a string of variables would produce an insignificant result, even if the hypothesis on contingency effects is valid. Thus for practical reasons it is important to strike a balance between theoretical richness and statistical economy when testing contingency models.

Conclusion

Quantitative research has so far been a very minor contributor to the development of knowledge on public management and the NPM. Few empirical studies have used statistical methods to test hypotheses on the relationship between public management variables. Nor has there been much quantitative evaluation of the effects of public management reforms. The argument in this chapter has been that the public management research community is thereby missing a substantial opportunity to contribute to the development of theory and practice.

This is not to advocate that all qualitative researchers should seek to transform themselves into statisticians. A range of methods is required in order to investigate public management phenomena. Nevertheless, a better balance is needed between quantitative and qualitative approaches. Nor is it to argue that new theoretical perspectives and conceptual arguments should not be developed. Yet, much work remains to be done in establishing the empirical validity of the theories and hypotheses that are already available. Indeed, it can be argued that, as a multidisciplinary field, public management has too much rather than too little theory. A shift from further conceptual work to empirical tests of existing propositions may therefore produce net benefits, not only to the academic community but also to policy makers and managers.

References

Barnett, R., R. Levaggi and P. Smith (1990) 'The Impact of Party Politics on Patterns of Service Provision in English Local Authorities', *Policy and Politics* 18, 217–29.

Blaug, M. (1980) *The Methodology of Economics,* Cambridge, Cambridge University Press.

Boyne, G.A. (1986) 'Socio-economic Conditions, Central Policies and Local Authority Staffing Levels', *Public Administration* 64, 69–82.

Boyne, G.A. (1990) 'Central Grants and Local Policy Variation', *Public Administration* 68, 679–94.

Boyne, G.A. (1996a) 'The Intellectual Crisis in British Public Administration: Is Public Management the Problem or the Solution?', *Public Administration* 74, 679–94.

Boyne, G.A. (1996b) 'Assessing Party Effects on Local Policies : Twenty Five Years of Progress or Eternal Recurrence?', *Political Studies* 44, 232–52.

Boyne, G.A. (1996c) 'Scale, Performance and the New Public Management: An Empirical Analysis of Local Authority Services', *Journal of Management Studies* 33, 809–26.

Boyne, G.A. (1998a) 'Competitive Tendering in Local Government: A Review of Theory and Evidence', *Public Administration* 76, 695–712.

Boyne, G.A. (1998b) 'Bureaucratic Theory Meets Reality: Public Choice and Contracting Out in US Local Government', *Public Administration Review* 58, 474–84.

Boyne, G.A. (1999) 'Processes, Performance and Best Value in Local Government', *Local Government Studies*.

Boyne, G.A. (2000) 'Planning, Performance and Public Services', *Public Administration*.

Boyne, G.A. (2001) 'Public and Private Management : What's The Difference?', *Journal of Management Studies*.

Boyne, G., M. Poole and C. Jenkins (1999) 'Human Resource Management in The Public and Private Sectors: An Empirical Comparison', *Public Administration* 77, 407–20

Boyne, G., R. Ashworth and M. Powell (2000) 'Testing The Limits of Incrementalism: An Empirical Analysis', *Public Administration* 78, 51–73.

Brower, R., M. Abolafai, and J. Carr (2000) 'On Improving Qualitative Methods in Public Administration Research', *Administration and Society* 32, 363–97.

Burns, T. and G. Stalker (1961) *The Management of Innovation,* London, Tavistock.

Capon, N., J. Farley and S. Hoenig (1990) 'Determinants of Financial Performance: A Meta-Analysis', *Management Science* 36, 1143–59.

Carter, N. (1989) 'Performance Indicators: Back-Seat Driving or Hands-Off Control?', *Policy and Politics,* 17, 131–8.

Cresswell, J. (1994) *Research Design: Qualitative and Quantitative Approaches,* London, Sage.

Davies, B. and E. Ferlie (1982) 'Efficiency Promoting Innovation in Social Care: Social Service Departments and the Elderly', *Policy and Politics* 10, 181–203.

Davies, B. and E. Ferlie (1984) 'Patterns of Efficiency Improving Innovation: Social Care and the Elderly', *Policy and Politics* 12, 281–95.

Davies, B., A. Barton, I. McMillan and A. Williamson (1971) *Variations In Services For the Aged,* London, G. Bell and Sons.

Davies, B., A. Barton and I, McMillan (1972) *Variations In Children's Services Among British Urban Authorities,* London, G. Bell and Sons.

Domberger, S. and D. Hensher (1993) 'On The Performance of Competitively Tendered Public Sector Cleaning Contracts', *Public Administration* 71, 441–454.

Downs, G. (1976) *Bureaucracy, Innovation and Public Policy,* Lexington, MA, D.C. Heath

Dubin, R. (1978) *Theory Building,* New York, The Free Press.

Dunsire, A., K. Hartley, D. Parker and B. Dimitriou (1988) 'Organisational Status and Performance: A Conceptual Framework For Testing Public Choice Theories', *Public Administration* 66, 363–88.

Gray, A. and B. Jenkins (1995) 'From Public Administration to Public Management: Reassessing a Revolution?', *Public Administration* 73, 75–99.

Greenwood, R. (1983) 'Changing Patterns of Budgeting in English Local Government', *Public Administration* 61, 149–68.

Hagood, M. (1970) 'The Notion of a Hypothetical Universe'. In Morrison, D. and Henkel, R. (eds) *The Significance Test Controversy,* London, Butterworths.

Hansen, G. and B. Wernerfelt (1989) 'Determinants of Firm Performance: The Relative Importance of Economic and Organizational Factors', *Strategic Management Journal* 10, 399–411.

Hoggart, K. (1983) 'Changes in Education Outputs in English Local Authorities', *Public Administration* 61, 169–78.

Hoggett, P. (1991) 'A New Management in the Public Sector', *Policy and Politics* 19, 143–56.

Hughes, O. (1998) *Public Management and Administration,* London, Macmillan.

Joyce, P. (1999) *Strategic Management for the Public Services,* Buckingham, Open University Press.

Leach, S. (1982) 'In Defence of The Rational Model'. In Leach, S. and Stewart, J. (eds) *Approaches in Public Policy,* London, Allen and Unwin.

Mock, C. and H. Weisberg (1992) 'Political Innumeracy: Encounters with Coincidence, Improbability and Chance', *American Journal of Political Science* 36, 1023–46.

Morrison, D. and R. Henkel (1970) *The Significance Test Controversy,* London, Butterworths.

Pawson, R. (1989) *A Measure for Measures,* London, Routledge.

Pawson, R. and N. Tilley (1977) *Realistic Evaluation,* London, Sage.

Schoonhoven, C. 1981 'Problems with Contingency Theory: Testing Assumptions Hidden Within The Language of Contingency Theory', *Administrative Science Quarterly,* 26, 349–77.

Stokes-Berry, F. and B. Wechsler (1995) 'State Agencies Experience with Strategic Planning: Findings from a National Survey', *Public Administration Review* 55, 159–68.

Tosi, H. and J. Slocum (1984) 'Contingency Theory: Some Suggested Directions', *Journal of Management* 10, 9–26.

Venkatraman, N. and J. Camillus (1984) 'Exploring the Concept of "Fit" in Strategic Management', *Academy of Management Review* 9, 513–25.

Williamson, O. (1975) *Markets and Hierarchies: Analysis and Antritrust Implications* New York: The Free Press.

Winch, R. and D. Campbell (1970) 'Proof? No. Evidence? Yes. The Significance of Tests of Significance'. In Morrison, D. and Henkel, M. (eds) *The Significance Test Controversy,* London, Butterworths.

Wright C. (1976) 'Linear Models For Evaluating Conditional Relationships' *American Journal of Political Science* 20, 349–73.

Part V

Conclusions

Chapter 20

The sustainability of the New Public Management in the UK

Ewan Ferlie and Louise Fitzgerald

Introduction

In this concluding chapter, we consider the likely long-term sustainability of the NPM paradigm within the UK public services. Is it a paradigm whose time is now over or is it likely to continue as a dominant mode of organization? Many of the change programmes within UK public services in the 1980s and 1990s fell under the NPM umbrella (Hood 1991) as they included a simultaneous growth of managerialization and marketization. Early NPM-led restructuring within the UK took place under the radical right governments of the 1979–97 period. However, there was a change of political control from the Conservatives to 'New Labour' in 1997. At the time of writing (November 2001), we are at the start of the second term of the New Labour government, so now is an appropriate moment to take stock.

What impact did the 1997 change of political control have on the fate of the NPM movement? Some have already reached early conclusions about public sector management under the New Labour government. It is suggested that there may be less to New Labour than meets the eye. There are elements both of continuity and redirection, but many previous agendas (such as bringing in more private finance) have been carried forward and even accelerated. Within the health care field, Ham (1999) argues that a pragmatic new regime is attempting to use a wide variety of policy instruments but that the conflict between local devolution and central control is an unresolved tension. He speculates that a major crisis may well lead to a strong pull back to the centre. Hunter (1999: 27–28) argues that: 'what appeals to the government about the NPM, and why it is likely to survive, albeit with only marginal adjustments, is the conviction that it represents a style of management that is much closer to the government's emphasis on, and desire to encourage, social entrepreneurship than would be suggested by a return to old style paternalism which was the hallmark of public administration through the 1960s and 1970s.'

However, management research should not simply take problems from the worlds of policy and politics, but should also make them within the realm of theory. Its distinctive contribution over and above the nearby worlds of policy analysts, management gurus or 'think tanks' is to emplace short-term presenting problems within a broader theoretical literature. This is not a trivial task, as such theoretical frameworks require careful operationalization to model empirical phenomena. There may be forces outside the conventional explanation of change within the organization of public services as a pure function of switches in political control which also need to be considered. Kickert (2000) notes that the perception of public management reform as a function of changes in ideology is a particularly British stance, although his view contradicts the received idea that British social science is empiricist and non critical.

An institutionalist perspective on the reconstruction of organizational fields

This chapter seeks to provide a *theorized* assessment of the impact within the UK of the New Labour government on the overall pattern of organization and management of the public sector. It will take the example of health care as a sector where the authors have particular interests, but the analysis has implications for other public services. The paper will operationalize concepts deriving from institutionalist theory (organizational archetypes, archetype change, deinstitutionalization, and organizational transformation) (Hinings and Greenwood 1988; Greenwood and Hinings 1993; Ferlie *et al.* 1996). It will argue that the NPM movement constitutes a novel archetype within the organization and management of the public services. It can be seen as a successor archetype to the old Public Administration archetype dominant within the UK public sector for 100 years, with its emphasis on probity and due process rather than outcomes. The public sector field thus underwent a major transition from one configuration to another.

The institutionalist perspective (Di Maggio and Powell 1983; Zucker 1983, 1987) apparent within organizational theory assumes that organizations tend towards similar designs and activities across a whole field. Inertia is more pervasive than any counter-tendency to entropy. The work activities undertaken within such an established organizational regime are stable, repetitive and enduring and highly change resistant. They are institutionalized within rule like structures which are taken for granted by actors within those organizations. Alternative ways of working are difficult to conceive, let alone to adopt. Pressures for continued isomorphism come from external agents such as the State, the professions and knowledge carriers such as management consultants. These forces are especially strong within the public sector which combines a dependence on State finance and governance, powerful colleges of professional groups and a tendency to use management consultants to import new forms of practice.

Given these constraints, how does radical change ever occur within public sector organizations? Hinings and Greenwood (1988) argue that organizations tend towards coherent deep patterns or 'archetypes' which consist of three distinct but inter-related components: the formal structure; systems of decision-making and underlying interpretive schemas (which include core values, beliefs and ideology). For there to be a successful transition, simultaneous and reinforcing change is needed along all three of these dimensions. In particular, change in the ideological sphere is crucial and reflects itself in the more superficial spheres of structures and systems. Such archetypical transition ('a successful reorientation') is rare and difficult, but it is nevertheless possible on occasion to overcome high inertia levels.

Within the UK public sector, we have already suggested that there has been a successful transition from a public administration archetype to a now embedded NPM archetype. The question to consider is whether the NPM archetype will reproduce itself within the new set of political conditions, or whether there are powerful sources of deinstitutionalization (Oliver 1992) apparent.

The institutionalization of the New Public Management archetype

Despite the views of many early sceptics, the evolution of the NPM archetype within the UK health care sector (which we take as our empirical exemplar) can be seen as an example of a largely successful archetype change (Greenwood and Hinings 1993), based on the twin guiding principles of managers and markets. This transition took almost twenty years. Initially limited changes (starting with the introduction of general management as advocated as early as Griffiths 1983) accelerated into the much more synoptic restructuring of the quasi-market experiment (1990–97). While there has been some reining back of market forces in such sectors as primary care since 1997, in others flows of private finance have continued to expand (such as the recourse to private capital). There has been a progressive growth of novel audit (Power 1997), performance management and appraisal mechanisms within health care. There has been an elaboration of managerial roles, including clinical professionals moving into part time management roles as well as the introduction of general management. There has been a reduction in trade union power, and now an increasing questioning of the autonomy of medical professionals so that the managerial block can be seen as a clear gainer in terms of the distribution of power within health care organizations.

The NPM archetype is in a mature state within the UK health care sector so that many initially controversial changes have been embedded and once novel ways of working have now acquired taken for granted status. We have seen the rise of the managerial state within the public sector (Clarke and Newman 1997) more generally. Kitchener's (1998, 1999) case studies work on organizational change specifically within acute sector hospitals argued that a transition to a new Quasi-market Archetype was well advanced as early as the mid-1990s, although within a 'hybrid' regime which retained a strong clinical presence rather than a purely managerially based regime.

The rise of the UK NPM archetype: four drivers

Such an archetype transition has been driven by four fundamental forces, of which the conventionally cited changes in the political economy represents only one (to respond to Kickert's 2000 critique) but an important one. The growth of the middle class and the taxpayers' revolt against the large public sectors characteristic of social democratic states acted as a powerful driver within the political domain for public sector downsizing, a performance orientation and more 'business like' techniques. Social democratic parties largely converged on the template established by the New Right, with a fear of traditional 'tax and spend' positions. The reduction of social costs has been a key political priority and enables a reduction in taxation levels to politically acceptable levels. These political and ideological changes can be seen as an important driver within the context of the UK in the 1980s with the development of a new Thatcherite political economy of the public sector.

There are other factors to consider. Second, we also see the decline of deference towards traditional forms of authority, including public sector professionals such as doctors and teachers. There is growing customer mindedness displayed by increasingly affluent and educated consumers within public services as in their private consumption. Such consumers have far more experience of service industries (hotels; restaurants) than their parents, and expect choice, access and service. The 'money rich but time poor' (such as urban professionals) will exit to the private sector if public services are unable to provide ready access (for example, if there is rationing by waiting list).

Third, and within the division of elite labour, there has been a dramatic and sustained rise of management functions, knowledge and authority (that is, a managerialization process), comparable only to the rise of the legal and medical professions in the mid-nineteenth century. Key generic management concepts (e.g. quality improvement; governance) have been newly adopted within policy (Cm 4818 2000). Managerial control and language could replace the professionalized control and language historically dominant within health care. This managerialization process seems to have been especially prominent in the UK, with a growth of management power. This compares, for instance, with the German model of the *Rechtstaat* (Pollitt and Bouckaert 2000) where judicial and administrative forms of authority are far more important than managerial forms.

Fourth, and within the sphere of technology, new forms of performance management (Hoggett 1996) have been made possible by more powerful IT and information systems (IS). We see the creation of the increasingly sophisticated comparative databases used for external audit, performance review and benchmarking. Performance management has also been strengthened by changes in the HRM function, with moves away from 'jobs for life' and national wage bargaining to greater use of short term contracts, performance related pay and individualised job contracts.

Of these four drivers, only the first is related to the conventional sphere of the political economy (and that weakly so, as many social democratic parties have moved to the right in order to recapture their voters and accept much of the NPM agenda). Therefore our initial proposition is:

Proposition 1: a political transition from a neo-liberal to a 'reformed' social democratic regime will not by itself produce the sustained and coherent energy needed to deinstitutionalize an established NPM archetype.

Archetype deinstutionalization and transition

There is a theoretical debate about how archetype deinstitutionalization and transition occurs. Taking an evolutionary position, Oliver (1992) suggests that a tendency to entropy may occur so that an archetype may gradually fray but without a transition to a coherent new archetype. Deinstitutionalization may occur as a result of specific changes within the organization or in the organization's environment that portend certain shifts. Changes to government regulation may deinstitutionalize past practices, given the strength of the coercive forces at the command of government. These forces are if anything even stronger within public sector organizations. Mounting performance pressures, a growth in the criticality and representation of organizational members who conflict with the status quo, and an increase in the range of legitimated funding streams (and in particular a decline in dependence on monopoly state finance) could all reduce the usual isomorphic pressures.

By contrast, Greenwood and Hinings (1988) suggest that the logic of the archetype thesis is that organizations are pulled towards coherence or one dominant logic of organizing so that the gradual 'fraying' proposed by Oliver (1992) is unlikely. They recognize that some attempts at archetype change will fail (so-called 'discontinued excursions') or achieve only partial success (so-called 'unresolved excursions'). In some cases, however, there is a transition from one archetype to another (so-called 'successful reorientations'), although this is difficult to achieve and requires a number of facilitating forces to be present.

What might be the implication of their argument for possible movement towards a post-NPM archetype? Within reorienting organizations, they found evidence for the influential role of strategic and elite-level commitment to particular interpretive schemes as determinants of the push to transformation. A high level of experience and capacity was also needed which enabled organizations in transition to harness the changes in interpretive schemes to structures and systems. In addition, substantial effort was put into breaking up inertia in the early stages of the change process, particularly within the sphere of systems (rather than merely structure) to generate continuing momentum. It was considerably easier to achieve reorientation in the smaller organizations studied than very large organizations.

A change of political control: will it lead to a further archetype transition?

Change of political control

Within institutionalist perspectives, the organization and management of the public sector is seen as strongly shaped by the combined forces of the legislature, government and the professions. There has historically been within the UK a strong alliance between the State and the elite professions which were accorded substantial influence and self-regulatory capacity so that these forces were mutually reinforcing rather than antagonistic.

A radical and sustained change in the political regime might in theory (Oliver 1992) open up a further archetype transition, especially within the public sector where government has such strong influence. The move to the NPM archetype in the 1980s and 1990s was associated with a strong 'reformative' commitment (Greenwood and Hinings 1993) from the new Conservative regime, although combined with reinforcing drivers from other spheres. We need first of all to question whether there is evidence of further fundamental change occurring now in these other drivers. At first glance, it appears unlikely that informatization, managerialization and the decline of deference have been reversed as long-term social processes since 1997; indeed, they continue to reproduce themselves technologically and socially within the new period. The calls for public services to be 'user based' and for a reduction in the power of public sector professionals are as strong as ever. IS continue to be used to produce more sophisticated forms of performance management and benchmarking.

The ideological domain is however an important one in archetype change, and indeed can be seen as even more fundamental than changes to formal structures and systems. The experience of the 1980s suggests that archetype transition within the public services is more likely where there is a strong and coherent reformative ideology present which legitimates the claims of a radical break with failed old ways, particularly when this ideology is espoused by leading power centres.

Some of the difficulties of operationalizing the institutionalist perspective to large-scale empirical phenomena are increasingly apparent. Previous archetype definitions have operated in much more contained organizational contexts (Hinings and Greenwood 1988). Structure, systems and ideology represent the three basic dimensions of an organizational archetype. But how might the impact of the arrival of New Labour on these dimensions be assessed empirically? It is still too early to make a final assessment as changes in practice and especially ruling values may take place over a long time span. But there are perhaps three separate and sequential levels of analysis which can be usefully separated out. The first relates to *declared expressions of political ideology and rhetoric* specifically as they relate to or impact on the organization and management of the public sector. The second relates to *formal policy decisions* which have been taken and which reshape structure and systems. The third relates to *changing managerial practices and beliefs within service settings* and this is the most difficult (but also important) area of assessment. In this chapter, the first two levels of analysis are considered but later work needs to move on to the critical third tier of analysis.

Weak reformative ideology

Has the arrival of the New Labour regime been associated with the emergence of a strong and coherent alternative value system which might plausibly challenge the institutionalized NPM belief system? Political parties often seek to mobilize support, provide collective rationales and ensure coherence across actions through the promotion of distinctive political ideologies, which blend normative and empirical arguments. Is it possible within the realm of theory to spot an emergent new archetype of some coherence?

Many of the old criticisms from the Left of the NPM archetype related to its overemphasis on efficiency and lack of attention to questions of democratic accountability and legitimation (Weir and Hall 1994; Stewart *et al.* 1995). Some UK writers are developing citizen-centred models of local governance (Martin and Boaz 2000). International comparisons suggest that there are alternative models of public sector organization available which emphasize democratization to a far greater extent. For example, the networks-based model apparent in the Netherlands (Kickert *et al.* 1997, Rhodes 1997) stresses the central role of self-organizing networks which emerge from civil society rather than as act as a top-down implementation tool for the central State. This concern for democratic renewal as a key motor of public service reform is also evident in some Scandinavian countries with large and historically unresponsive public sectors and within South America, as the transition from military to democratic regimes has important implications for the machinery of government.

So is such a Democratic State archetype coherently present in New Labour ideology, policy and practice? An initial observation is that New Labour has evolved as an 'ideology light' movement. It seeks to be inclusive, to put together broad coalitions and place a high premium on the possession of technical expertise as well as political ideology (hence its interest in technically based approaches such as Evidence-based Policy). It appears to lack the strong set of mobilizing ideas associated with the NPM movement of the 1980s, notably the fundamental work on public choice theory, transactions costs and principal agent theory provided by the New Right. However, it is possible to distinguish two high level works of political ideology which provide evidence about the extent to which an alternative democratic state model has emerged.

Giddens: 'The Third Way'

The most elaborated expression of 'The Third Way' ideology often seen as underpinning the New Labour government has been provided in Giddens (1997) *The Third Way: The Renewal of Social Democracy*. The full title indicates that Giddens is trying to achieve the ideological renewal of social democracy, rather than its repudiation. Within a very broad work of synthesis, Giddens briefly touches on the specific question of the organization and management of the public sector in Chapter 3 ('The State and Civil Society') and Chapter 4 ('The Social Investment State'). A number of the New Right's criticisms of the old public sector are accepted and there is certainly no desire to return to the public sector of the 1970s. However, an analysis of the text suggests two very different models so that one can perhaps distinguish between Giddens 1 and Giddens 2.

Giddens 1 argues that democracy needs to be broadened and deepened, with government acting in partnership with agencies in civil society so as to combat civic decline. The retention of high levels of autonomy and self organization will be important if these agencies are not to be swamped by distorting State power. Established traditions of participative planning and community development can be complemented by experiments in direct democracy (such as citizens' juries). The Democratic State should be based on the principles of subsidiarity, transparency and probity. The fostering of active civil society is an important task for the State, with support for the 'bottom-up' politics of community renewal. This implies a greater role for service provision by non-profit organizations; more localized distribution channels; and the public sector should work to develop the capacities of local communities. While there is no sustained discussion of the professions, they might be seen as autonomous, self-regulating, knowledgeable and publicly orientated groups that can contribute to civic renewal, independently of government. The model of the Democratic State represents the beginnings of alternative to the NPM template, stressing very different values of democracy, participation and localization.

There is however a different second model (Giddens 1997: 74–75), which centres round administrative efficiency as a way of rebuilding public sector legitimacy. Giddens 2 argues that the restructuring of government should be based on the principle of 'getting more from less', understood not so much as radical downsizing as a way of delivering improved value. Government should not have recourse to the construction of quasi-markets at every opportunity, but the use of generic management tools (such as target controls; effective auditing; flexible decision structures and increased employee participation) could improve performance. Elsewhere he suggests that private–public partnerships models would give the private sector a larger role in activities which governments once provided for, while ensuring that the public interest remains paramount. These ideas are of course much more NPM orthodox so that there is a tension between the two models contained within the discussion and no unambiguous shift towards democratisation, at least where this threatens received ideas of value for money (as in local government).

Leadbetter: 'Living on Thin Air'

Primarily interested and involved in economic (rather than social) policy-making, Leadbetter (2000) argues that the need to build a knowledge based economy will require the reform and 'modernization' (a key New Labour word) of many UK institutions. Manufacturing and routine service industries will give way to post-material, intangible or 'thin air' industries based on knowledge and creativity. Leadbetter argues that the central idea of the knowledge-based economy provides a more exciting vision than provided by the ideology of The Third Way, which in practice led to a continuation of pro-market policies, slightly rebalanced by attempts to strengthen social institutions.

The public sector is seen within this analysis as an important part of the knowledge-based economy as there are many areas where markets fail and where there is a need for the provision of public goods. There is here an explicit repudiation of the New Right's claim that public sector services are necessarily poor-quality services. Some of the public sector 'brands' (such as the NHS and

BBC) have higher reputations than most UK private sector firms and are a vital part of the new economy. The public sector also provides a strong set of socially inclusive institutions, such as the NHS, to which all citizens have access. The central idea of the knowledge based economy leads to a preference for the redirection of social spending from social security into social investment (in areas such as education and training) in order to create social capital, as seen within the realm of practical politics within welfare reform programmes.

Public sector organizations are here seen as highly change resistant and as poor at innovation. They could be revitalized by a new breed of managers such as 'turnaround headmasters' in failing schools who seek to secure more value from the public assets that they are stewards of: 'the public sector does not need more restructuring or rationalisation; it needs reviving and renewing'. There is a need for a more entrepreneurial and creative orientation which could develop a greater range of innovative public services. Leadbetter recognizes that the empowering of public sector innovators and 'social entrepreneurs' is difficult as traditional vertically organized accountability mechanisms stress the virtues of predictability and standardization.

Leadbetter's key principles of public sector renewal include a policy 'to invest systematically in the creation of new services and the dissemination of new ideas, especially those which combine different departments' (p. 244). There is an interesting strand of thinking which emphasizes the building of connections between traditionally free standing public sector organizations. His analysis does not only stress managerial efficiency but also the question of political renewal: public sector organizations are political and rightly so. However, this theme of political renewal remains of secondary importance and the centre of his analysis focuses on a 'knowledge-based management' perspective which includes concerns for innovation, creativity, human capital and social entrepreneurship

Both these texts do suggest a growth of concern with a renewal of democracy within the public services as well as NPM-style ideas of efficiency, transparency and top-down accountability. But democratization is partial rather than a dominant theme and coexists along with competing themes. These texts are themselves unusual in their concern for ideology within the New Labour movement which is more often highly pragmatic and inclusive in orientation. Its ideological base can therefore be seen as far more fragile and incoherent than that underpinning the NPM movement of the 1980s. If Greenwood and Hinings's (1993) view that the underlying ideological dimension is the most important one in archetype change, this ideological weakness and·incoherence is an important limitation.

Proposition 2: New Labour's ideological base is too weak and ambiguous to act as a force which could effectively deinstitutionalize the NPM archetype in favour of a Democratic State archetype.

Strategy and policy in relation to public sector organization and management

At the second level of analysis, we move from expressions of political ideology to formally declared policies in relation to the organization and management of the public services. There are two different central departments which take an interest in this domain: the Treasury (concerned with public expenditure) and the Cabinet Office (concerned with the machinery of government).

Cm 4011 (1998) *Modern Public Services for Britain* represents the outcome of the early Treasury-led Comprehensive Spending Review. The dominant management style apparent in the text reflects a strong orientation to performance management and vertical reporting and can be seen as essentially NPM orthodox. Each spending department (for example, the Department of Health) has to sign up to a public service agreement in return for resources. For example (p. 17), 'delivery' was to be assured by such measures as close monitoring of each department's targets; reviews to protect tight timescales and maintain pressure on departments to secure service improvements. Within the NHS, for example, a central performance target of three per cent a year for value-for-money improvements was set. Performance is to be tightly monitored centrally to ensure that the periphery 'delivers.'

A secondary theme apparent in the text was 'joined up government', ensuring that different agencies would work together to tackle complex issues. Six of the reviews were carried out on a cross-departmental basis, for example, the cross-departmental review of illegal drugs which brought together the criminal justice system, the health and education agencies. Joint budgets were introduced in a small number of areas such as asylum support. Democratic renewal within the public services was not however a major theme of this text.

By contrast, the Cabinet Office's text (Cm 4310 1999, *Modernising Government*) places more emphasis on institution building, and less on purely financial criteria such as value for money. It also contains some important and critical reflections on the NPM. This text argues that the 1980s and 1990s had been characterized by an excessive concern for management efficiency and that too little attention had been accorded to the development of an effective policy process. Laterally, many complex policy areas required work across conventional boundaries, either between different central departments or between central and local government. Vertically, the split between the small strategic core and the large operational periphery characteristic of the Next Steps agency model had led to a lack of involvement from front line staff. 'Joined up government' was here identified as a key objective of a reformed policy-making process, along with an outcome orientation (more NPM orthodox), a shift towards evidence-based policy-making and a learning organization and a more futuristic and outward-looking orientation. While there was concern to ensure that public services are responsive to the needs to citizens, democratization was not elaborated as a theme.

A major facilitator of the success of the NPM in the 1980s was that public sector reform was not contained as a technical issue for the Cabinet Office but engaged the attention of the Prime Minister. Public sector reform was seen as a truly strategic issue politically. It appears that the reform of the machinery of government has remained much lower down the corporate agenda during the first Labour government, with no fewer than three ministers filling the Cabinet Office post within four years. Given this relatively weak political leadership, one presumption is that power has drifted to the Treasury with its highly NPM orthodox approach.

> *Proposition 3: the dominant policy towards the organization and management of the public sector is NPM orthodox and offers no account of radical democratisation*

Future empirical work is needed within specific public services to examine changes to managerial practices, accountability regimes and beliefs after 1997 in order to move the analysis down to the third and deepest level.

The example of health care: the dominance of performance management

In this section, we consider changes to organization and management of the health care sector as an emblematic case study. At the ideological level, the NHS is seen as a core part of the continuing public sector and indeed as a public sector 'brand' by leading New Labour theorists (Leadbetter 2000). However, the key concern within this analysis is to quicken the pace of knowledge generation and diffusion of good practice across the whole NHS. Knowledge management here represents the mobilising concern rather than a strengthening of bottom-up forms of accountability as would be expected within the Democratic State model.

Within health care, Cm 4814 (2000) represents a key text which sets out the long-term strategy to 'modernize' the NHS. This is a centrally produced document which sets out a global strategy for the whole of the NHS. The vision is one of easy to access and consistently high-quality services, with considerable amounts of new public money being made available to manage the change. This focus on quality rather than finance clearly marks a break from the approach of the 1980s. There were also interesting experiments proposed in 'process redesign', looking at optimizing the whole patient experience across the whole experience of treatment and care. However, there was no desire to democratize health care provision, with the government proposing to abolish Community Health Councils which had traditionally acted as patients' watchdogs. They proposed to introduce a new patient advocacy service instead, but critics argued that there was no evidence that this would be more effective.

By contrast, performance management regimes are progressively being strengthened, reflecting central distrust of traditional systems of professional self-regulation and a growing awareness of the obstacles to the management of change within complex public services. The response has been to set tough targets centrally to which the localities are expected to move. In addition, there is a desire to reduce local variation. National service frameworks for particular service areas are being brought in, to which clinicians are expected to adhere. There is a central expectation of consistent standards across the NHS, with a reduction in local variation. Clear targets for reform are being set to keep pace, with a performance management line in place to monitor progress. Performance assessment is to be operationalized through a new 'traffic lights' system, with 'red' organizations being targeted for tight monitoring. On the basis of analysing this key text, we conclude that the proclaimed strategy within the health care sector remains largely NPM orthodox, albeit with more emphasis on management than markets.

Concluding discussion

We have argued that the organization and management of UK public services has undergone an archetype shift from a previously dominant public administration archetype to a novel NPM archetype. This shift is a 'successful reorientation' (Hinings and Greenwood 1988) and is far more deeply rooted than the usual managerial fad or fashion (Abrahamson 1991). The implication is that sustained energy, an alternative ideology and coherent attempts at redirection will be needed *either* to move back to the old public administration template *or* to move on to a novel template that goes beyond the NPM. The chapter develops an assessment framework which could in time enable us to assess impact of the change of political regime in 1997 on the organization and management of UK public services. The proclaimed intention not to move back to the public administrative model of the 1970s is noted. The most likely alternative archetype surfaced was that of the Democratic State, which would be consistent with many of the criticisms made of the NPM model by left of centre writers in the 1980s and early 1990s.

A scrutiny of two important statements of New Labour ideology suggested that there were some signs of a move to a Democratic State archetype, but they were not likely to be of the coherence, power or scale to generate a further organizational transformation. Three key policy statements produced by the new government also showed little concern for the democratization of public services. If any alternative archetype is emerging within these texts, it appears to be that of the laterally based organization ('joined-up government'; process redesign). However, such process based principles of organization also conflict with the strong vertical lines and functions built up as a result of the NPM (McNulty and Ferlie 2002). The Democratic State archetype may be seen as no more than an 'aborted excursion' (Hinings and Greenwood 1988) and the effect of the dominant logic argument is that practice will reconverge on the NPM archetype. We propose that the UK NPM is in theory a sustainable model for the organization and management of public health care which is likely to survive the shift of political control in 1997. Alternative agendas may well emerge but they will not become dominant and will not be able to challenge the hegemony or underlying logic of a NPM template which has successfully reproduced itself. Empirical work is needed to test our assertions, both within health care and within other public services.

References

Abrahamson, E. (1991) 'Managerial Fads and Fashions', *Academy of Management Review*, 16(3), 586–612.

Clarke, J. and Newman, J. (1997) *The Managerial State*, London: Sage.

Cm 4011 (1998) *Modern Public Services for Britain: Investing in Reform*, London: HMSO.

Cm 4310 (1999) *Modernising Government*, London: HMSO.

Cm 4818 (2000) *The NHS Plan*, London: HMSO.

Di Maggio, P. and Powell, W.W. (1983) 'The Iron Cage Revisited: Institutional Isomorphism and Collective Rationality in Organisational Fields', *American Sociological Review*, 48, 147–160.

Ferlie, E., Ashburner, L., FitzGerald, L. and Pettigrew, A. (1996) *The New Public Management in Action*, Oxford: Oxford University Press.

Giddens, A. (1997) *The Third Way: The Renewal of Social Democracy*, Cambridge: Polity Press.

Greenwood, R. and Hinings, C.R. (1993) 'Understanding Strategic Change: The Contribution of Archetypes', *Academy of Management Journal*, 36(5), 1052–1081.

Griffiths, R. (1983) *NHS Management Enquiry*, London: Department of Health.

Ham, C. (1999) 'The Third Way in Health Care Reform – Does the Emperor Have Any Clothes?', *Journal of Health Services Research and Policy*, 4(3), 168–173.

Hinings, C.R. and Greenwood, R. (1988) *The Dynamics of Strategic Change*, Oxford: Basil Blackwell.

Hoggett, P. (1996) 'New Modes of Control in the Public Service', *Public Administration*, 74(1), 9–32.

Hood, C. (1991) 'A New Public Management for All Seasons?', *Public Administration*, 69(1), 3–19.

Hunter, D. (1999) *Managing For Health: Implementing The New Health Policy*, London: IPPR.

Kickert, W. (2000) 'Discussion of the paper of Sandra Dawson and Charlotte Dargie', *Public Management*, 1(4), 483–488.

Kickert, W., Klijn, E.-H. and Koppenjan, J. (1997) *Managing Complex Networks*, London: Sage.

Kitchener, M. (1998) 'Quasi Market Transformation: An Institutionalist Approach to Change in UK Hospitals', *Public Administration*, 76, 73–96.

Kitchener, M. (1999) ' "All Fur Coats and No Knickers": Contemporary Organizational Change in UK Hospitals'. In Brock, D., Powell, M. and Hinings, C.R. (eds) *Restructuring The Professional Organisation*, London: Routledge.

Leadbetter, C. (2000) *Living on Thin Air*, London: Penguin.

McNulty, T. and Ferlie, E. (2002) *Process Transformation? A Case of Reengineering in Health Care*, Oxford: Oxford University Press (in press).

Martin, S. and Boaz, A. (2000) 'Public Participation and Citizen Centred Local Government', *Public Money and Management*, 20(2), 47–54.

Oliver, C. (1992) 'The Antecedents of Deinstitutionalisation', *Organisational Studies*, 13, 563–588.

Pollitt, C. and Bouckaert, G. (2000) *Public Management Reform – A Comparative Analysis*, Oxford: Oxford University Press.

Power, M. (1997) *The Audit Society: Rituals of Verification*, Oxford: Oxford University Press.

Rhodes, R.A.W. (1997) 'Foreword'. In Kickert, W., Klijn, H.-E. and Koppenjan, J. (eds) *Managing Complex Networks*, London: Sage.

Stewart, J., Greer, A. and Hoggett, P. (1995) *The Quango State: An Alternative Approach*, Commission for Local Democracy Research Report, 10, London: Commission for Local Democracy.

Weir, S. and Hall, W. (1994) *Ego Trip*, Democratic Audit, 2: University of Essex: Human Rights Centre

Zucker, L. (1983) 'Organisations as Institutions'. In Bacharach, S.B. (ed.) *Research into the Sociology of Organisations*, Greenwich, CT: JAI Press.

Zucker, L. (1987) 'Institutional Theories of Organisation', *Annual Review of Sociology*, 13, 443–464.

Index